GOOD JOBS, BAD JOBS, NO JOBS

Labor Markets and Informal Work in Egypt, El Salvador, India, Russia, and South Africa

◆

Tony Avirgan, L. Josh Bivens & Sarah Gammage, eds.

Global Policy Network

ECONOMIC POLICY INSTITUTE

ECONOMIC POLICY INSTITUTE
1660 L Street, NW, Suite 1200
Washington, D.C. 20036

http://www.epinet.org

ISBN: 1-932066-17-9

About the Global Policy Network

The Global Policy Network (GPN) consists of labor-oriented think tanks and researchers around the world. GPN's work reflects a concern with the economic, social, and political conditions of working people in both developing and developed nations. The network's purpose is to exchange information and research among its member organizations, facilitate coordinated analysis of common issues, and provide information to others on the state of working people in the global economy. Through these activities, GPN enhances the capacity among NGOs, trade unions, and other grassroots groups in less-developed nations for independent economic analysis from the point of view of workers – the vast majority of their people.

The GPN was formed out of concern for how globalization can bring great benefits to global income and economic development. The organizations involved with GPN are committed to building a fair, prosperous, and sustainable economy for all of the world's people to share. Five think tanks comprise the Steering Committee that governs the network.

DIEESE	Inter Trade Union Department of Statistics and Socio-Economic Studies (São Paulo, Brazil)
EPI	Economic Policy Institute (Washington, D.C., USA)
FAFO	Institute for Applied Science (Oslo, Norway)
NALEDI	National Labour and Economic Development Institute (Johannesburg, South Africa)
KLSI	Korean Labor Studies Institute (Seoul, Korea)

The Steering Committee selected EPI to serve as Secretariat of the GPN, coordinating the initial organization and on-going activities of the network. EPI's efforts on behalf of GPN contributed to the creation of a new network that now works with more than 50 participants, most of which are existing or emerging think tanks. More than half are based in developing countries.

About EPI

The Economic Policy Institute was founded in 1986 to widen the debate about policies to achieve healthy economic growth, prosperity, and opportunity.

In the United States today, inequality in wealth, wages, and income remains historically high. Expanding global competition, changes in the nature of work, and rapid technological advances are altering economic reality. Yet many of our policies, attitudes, and institutions are based on assumptions that no longer reflect real world conditions.

With the support of leaders from labor, business, and the foundation world, the Institute has sponsored research and public discussion of a wide variety of topics: trade and fiscal policies; trends in wages, incomes, and prices; education; the causes of the productivity slowdown; labor market problems; rural and urban policies; inflation; state-level economic development strategies; comparative international economic performance; and studies of the overall health of the U.S. manufacturing sector and of specific key industries.

The Institute works with a growing network of innovative economists and other social science researchers in universities and research centers in the U.S. and abroad who are willing to go beyond the conventional wisdom in considering strategies for public policy.

Founding scholars of the Institute include Jeff Faux, distinguished fellow and former president of EPI; Lester Thurow, Sloan School of Management, MIT; Ray Marshall, former U.S. secretary of labor, professor at the LBJ School of Public Affairs, University of Texas; Barry Bluestone, Northeastern University; Robert Reich, former U.S. secretary of labor; and Robert Kuttner, author, editor of *The American Prospect,* and columnist for *Business Week* and the Washington Post Writers Group.

For additional information about the Institute, contact EPI at 1660 L Street NW, Suite 1200, Washington, DC 20036, (202) 775-8810, or visit www.epinet.org.

Table of contents

Acknowledgments

We gratefully acknowledge the participation and dedication of GPN partner institutions in each country: FUNDE in El Salvador; the University of Cairo in Egypt; SARDI in India; IISP in Russia; and NALEDI in South Africa.

The Economic Policy Institute's Publications Department edited and produced the book with much dedication and hard work under tight deadlines. Research assistance and editing in the project development and publication phases was provided by Gabriela Prudencio, David Ratner, Sujan Vasavada, John Schmitt, Rob Scott, and M.K. Tally.

This volume's editors, and all members of the Global Policy Network, are grateful to the Ford Foundation, particularly John Colburne, Helen Neuborne and Yahonnes Cleary for financing and supporting the workforce development research and the publication of this book.

Origins of the GPN
workforce development study

There is an increasing interest in how the process of globalization affects the economic, civic, and educational conditions of disadvantaged communities around the world. Concerns have arisen about globalization and its attendant impact on labor markets and employment standards, and there are questions about the appropriate roles of regulatory organizations. There has been particular interest in understanding the broader forces and processes that are prompting a shift in the terms and conditions of employment and contributing to changes in formal and informal employment. These changes to the labor market are particularly troublesome because they appear to undermine the earning power of less-skilled workers and erode the power of workers generally.

In late 2002, the Global Policy Network (GPN) was contacted by the Assets program of the Ford Foundation, which wanted to explore the feasibility of a multi-country study examining these various issues. Both Ford and GPN wanted countries that represented diversity in geographical location, size, and stage of development. A process of consultation resulted in the selection of Egypt, El Salvador, India, Russia, and South Africa.

Two researchers from each of the five countries meet with labor market and gender experts in early 2003. Participants in the three-day meeting collectively created a research template and methodology for the study of workforce development in the selected countries. The research was conducted primarily during the second half of 2003 and the first half of 2004.

During the second half of 2004, there was a series of "dissemination meetings" held in the capital of each of the participating countries. Representatives of government, trade unions, academic institutions, and non-governmental organizations met to review the data and discuss the policy implications of the research. Following the meetings, the studies were further modified and then prepared for publication by the research and publications departments at the Economic Policy Institute.

The result of these efforts is the five studies presented in this volume. Each chapter examines the labor market in a particular country, with a specific emphasis on the informal economy. A second phase of the workforce development project, planned for 2005, will look at other factors that destroy or create good jobs. These areas of study will include, but not be limited to, trade, privatization, labor market liberalization, and child labor.

The continuing workforce development research will be periodically updated at the Global Policy Network's Web site, www.GPN.org.

Will better workers lead to better jobs in the developing world?

By L. Josh Bivens and Sarah Gammage[1]

Nobody doubts the significance of informal employment in the developing world. When workers cannot find opportunities in traditional wage employment, the need for subsistence demands they find work somewhere else. Much of what accounts for "informal" employment is familiar even to the most casual observers: street vendors and shoeshine workers in the large cities of the developing world, for example. Other informal employment situations are a less visible feature of an economy's landscape, like home-based garment assembly and manufacturing or industrial waste recycling.

There are a number of reasons to be concerned about the existence and persistence of informal employment in the developing world. Such employment is often characterized by poor working conditions, both in terms of remuneration and the existence and/or enforcement of basic labor standards. Further, informal employment can leave too many workers frozen out of the networks they need to access to insert themselves higher up in the global value chains that their labor so often serves. Carr, Chen, and Tate (2000) demonstrate how home-based production can leave workers with insufficient information and bargaining power to claim the economic rents that globalization makes increasingly available to employers and contractors, concentrating them instead in the hands of local middlemen and transnational corporations.

Improving the economic position of informal workers is thus a powerful potential lever for raising living standards and reducing poverty in the developing world. Understanding the extent, characteristics, and dynamics of informal employment is a crucial first step in this process. To this end, the five country studies that make up this volume make an important contribution, both in benchmarking how informal employ-

1

ment should be measured and in identifying the opportunities within each country for useful policy changes.

While each of these studies attests to the importance of informal employment to each nation's economy, there is striking heterogeneity in the form and dynamics of these employment arrangements across countries. Nevertheless, one of the overarching themes to emerge from these studies is the importance of detailed, country-specific analyses, both of the reality of informal employment and the optimal policy responses. In short, although this volume does offer an analysis of informal work in five countries and an introduction to theories of informal work situations, it is not meant as a solution to the ongoing academic debates regarding a general theory of informal employment (although it is not wholly silent on this issue, either).

That said, a few common findings emerge from these studies. First, informal employment is not caused solely by a lack of good workers; rather, it is largely driven by a lack of good jobs. While expanded education is a pressing need in the developing world, the lack of qualified workers does not lie behind the persistence and/or expansion of the informal economy that has characterized many of these countries' labor markets. Second, the most simplistic theory motivating the existence of informal employment, the *"lack of growth"* hypothesis, does not seem to find much compelling support from these studies. In many countries, it appears that the informal sector is growing more rapidly than the formal sector. Much like education, faster economic growth is a badly needed tonic for the developing world, but it is not the sole impetus for more formal employment, and provides only a necessary, and not a sufficient, basis for the expansions of opportunities for informal workers.

Background

The causes of informality

There are a range of theories offered to account for the existence and persistence of informal employment. Chen, Sebstad, and O'Connell (1999) identify four overarching (or macro) theories of informality. The first, mentioned above, is the *lack of growth* hypothesis. This theory assumes that growth in gross domestic product (GDP) will automatically lead to a growing share of formal employment (World Bank 1995). A failure to see a large rise in the formal sector's share of employment thus becomes only a symptom of the larger malady—slow economic growth. It should be noted that, depending on the strictness of the definition of informality, this theory borders on tautology. Swaminathan (1991, p. 1) points to some distinctive features of activity in the informal sector:

> What these activities appear to have in common is a mode of organization different from the unit of production most familiar in economic theory, the firm or corporation. These activities are also likely to be unregulated by the state and *excluded from standard economic accounts of national income.* (italics added)

Although many informal activities are captured in the national accounts as economic transactions, some will not be measured or registered. This is particularly true for household enterprises. Where informal production and exchange go unmeasured, their contribution to economic growth also goes uncounted. Hence, by definition, an expanding formal sector will lead to higher (measured) GDP.

A second theory as to the causes of informality is the *jobless growth* theory (UNDP 1993). This theory can be thought of as the first derivative of the lack of growth theory: increased formalization requires not just *positive* economic growth, but economic growth *well in excess of the underlying rate of productivity growth*, to absorb workers into the formal economy.

In a different vein, a third theory points to a more benign driver of informality: growth in the small-enterprise sector (sometimes referred to as the *growth from below* theory). This theory posits that small enterprises, often by dint of greater flexibility and freedom from regulation, have managed to expand more rapidly than larger scale enterprises.

Lastly, the *structural change* (or *period of adjustment*) theory asserts that informality is essentially a layover between formal employment in different sectors. As economies change over time (by decreasing the agricultural share and increasing the industrial share, for example), the adjustment period between the expanding sector absorbing workers and the declining sector shedding them asserts itself as a period of informality.

A number of other authors have identified a range of region-specific theories regarding informality. Portes (1989), for example, has argued that rising informality in Latin America is a remnant of the import-substitution policies pursued from the 1950s through the 1970s, which caused a shift to more decentralized production that characterized these economies after the debt crisis and adoption of neo-liberal policies in the 1980s.

These theories and their variants inform the findings of the five country studies in this volume, as well as the discussions relating to the role of policy in influencing informalization.

Informalization: A taxonomy
These divergent theories can be used to construct a taxonomy of contexts and processes within which to place different episodes of informalization. The experiences of different countries could theoretically fit into any one of these categories; these are not meant to be macro theories about (in)formalization, but frameworks for understanding how (in)formalization is proceeding in a specific country. Further, none of these classifications are mutually exclusive explanations for a particular country's experiences with informalization.

Dualist: Informal employment is a feature of precapitalist societies that can exist side-by-side with capitalist production for extended periods of time. As economies modernize, informal employment will atrophy and eventually fade away.

Structuralist: Informal employment is the outcome of a capitalist process that conspires to keep labor costs low. Key policy issues relate to increasing the bargaining power of informal workers through enforcement of labor standards, unionization, labor market regulation, and expansionary macroeconomic policies.

Legalist: Informal employment is not necessarily a symptom of degraded quality of employment, but is a consequence of entrepreneurs striving to escape burdensome regulation and/or official corruption associated with the formal sector.[2] The accompanying policy response addresses the product market: promoting more transparent and enforceable property rights (land titling, for example) and reforming the tax and transfer system.

The case studies

This volume consists of five country studies that attempt to provide a solid foundation for understanding the extent, causes, and consequences of informalization, with the explicit goal of providing information and recommendations to policy makers. Each of the studies' authors was asked to do the following:

- Identify and document changes over time in the nature of work in informal and formal employment;

- Explore the skills and worker characteristics of individuals employed in informal and formal jobs, where possible differentiating workers by gender, age, race, urban or rural location, and job tenure;

- Develop a consistent measure of skills differences and the potential mismatch between the formal and informal employment; and

- Document observed changes over time in the terms and conditions of employment, paying particular attention to benefits such as pensions, health care, vacations, and training.

In addition to providing a platform from which to examine workforce development policies, the research highlights and analyzes the broader processes prompting changes in the terms and conditions of employment or contributing to changes in formal and informal employment. In particular, we wish to explore processes (including government policies) that may contribute to the degradation of work and stimulate an expansion of the informal sector and informal employment.

Methodology

This study was undertaken with the goal of analyzing formal and informal labor markets and exploring whether policies can be developed that: 1) improve the terms and conditions of informal employment which manifest as degraded pay, poor working conditions, or limited prospects for advance; 2) raise worker productivity; and 3) improve the terms and conditions of employment in all sectors. Explicit attention is paid to *active labor market policies* and their relevance for particular groups that may be disproportionately vulnerable to or confined to informal employment, such as youth, women, and displaced rural workers.

Active labor market policies (ALMPs) are policies aimed at reducing labor market rigidities or failures, as well as at preventing the degradation of the situation of various targeted groups such as the less educated, youth, and minority groups. ALMPs can generally be subdivided into three categories: training, direct job creation or subsidies, and improved job matching.

For example, programs such as Project QUEST in San Antonio, New Mexico exemplify active labor market policies that focus on training and job matching in developed country contexts (Rademacher et al. 2001). Project QUEST provides training for numerous occupations within multiple industries and intervenes to reduce the cost of employee recruitment and turnover. Similar programs such as those initiated under the auspices of the Garment Industry Development Corporation in New York provide training services for workers as well as technical and marketing assistance to businesses to increase worker retention and reduce the loss of jobs (Conway and Loker 1999). These programs have been successful in retraining displaced workers and securing matches with employers. But to what extent do such programs offer relevant or useful guidelines for labor markets where informal employment exceeds formal employment and where worker skills might be limited by a poorly functioning and degraded education system? Similarly, what might be the role for other labor market intermediaries such as unions in creating and sustaining good jobs?[3] The studies in this volume attempt to review the context in which ALMPs will operate and explore how they may need to be refined to address the existence of dual or highly segmented formal and informal labor markets in developing countries.

Among the contributions of the studies in this volume is a serious attempt to empirically measure the expanded definitions of informal employment identified by the International Labour Organization (ILO). In the past, many studies examining this issue have restricted their attention to the informal *sector*. A notable approach in this volume is the examination of not only informal sector employment but also informal jobs within the formal sector, including in the public sector.

The five studies collected here explore a variety of different definitions of informality, departing sharply from the conventional definition of the informal sector, which is usually limited to workers engaged in production in small or unregulated enterprises with fewer than five to 10 employees.[4]

In recent years, a group of informed activists and researchers, including members of the Women in Informal Employment: Globalizing and Organizing (WIEGO) network, have worked with the ILO to broaden the concept and definition of the "informal sector" to incorporate certain types of informal employment that were not included in the earlier concept and definition (including the official international statistical definition). They seek to incorporate into this new definition the whole of informality—including both commercial and employment relations—manifest in industrialized, transition, and developing economies and reflecting the complex dynamics of contracting in labor markets today, particularly the employment arrangements of the working poor.

These observers have supported the development of a new definition, concept, and terminology that extends the focus from *enterprises* that are not legally regulated to *employment relationships* that are not legally regulated or protected. In brief, their new definition of the "informal economy" focuses on the nature of employment in addition to the characteristics of enterprises. Under this new definition, the informal economy is seen as comprised of all forms of "informal employment"—that is, employment without formal contracts (i.e., covered by labor legislation), worker benefits, or social protection—both inside and outside informal enterprises, including:

- *Self-employment in informal enterprises:* workers in small unregistered or unincorporated enterprises, including employers, own-account operators, and unpaid family workers.

- *Wage employment in informal jobs:* workers without formal contracts, worker benefits or social protection for formal or informal firms, for households, or those employees with no fixed employer, such as employees of informal enterprises; other informal wage workers (for example, casual or day laborers); domestic workers; industrial outworkers, notably home workers; unregistered or undeclared workers; and temporary or part-time workers.

These definitions of informal employment allow us to explore the nature of work and the terms and conditions of employment for those workers lacking contracts and benefits working in either formal or informal enterprises. The expanded definition of the informal economy encompasses all those workers in wage-employment in informal jobs as well as the self-employed, including unpaid family workers, own-account workers, and employers in informal enterprises.[5] **Table 1** outlines the different categories of informal work arrangements.

Such expanded definitions of informality create a better framework for examining the changing nature of employment in economies where privatization, deregulation, and outsourcing have prompted growth in more tenuous and contingent employment. Furthermore, we are able to chart the numerous relationships and channels by which production and distribution processes are linked within and between the formal and informal economy.

The research template for the five studies included in this volume was designed to provide a structured approach to exploring the nature of formality and informality and the terms and conditions of employment for workers in formal and informal employment.

Traditional analyses of the formal and informal sector may contribute unduly to the belief that there is a discrete partition that separates informal from formal sector work. These five case studies underscore that formality and informality are characteristics on a continuum of employment and production. There are no clean joints along which the formal and informal sector naturally separate.

To determine how the traditional definition of informal and formal sectors can obscure important subtleties, we examine whether workers in the informal sector do in fact receive some of the benefits that are generally attributed to formal employment.

Principal findings

The key findings from the five country reports (Egypt, El Salvador, India, South Africa, and Russia) attest to the importance of informal employment and the size of the informal economy in each country. While the estimated size of informal employment varies, it is clear that a significant number of all jobs are informal (as shown in **Table 2**).

In Egypt, informal employment was estimated to be 6.5 million, approximately 40% of total employment. In El Salvador, the estimated 1.7 million informal workers represent 69.1% of total employment. In South Africa, 2.7 million workers in the informal economy account for 22.5% of total employment. In Russia, the informal economy was estimated to be populated by 9.5 million workers, or approximately 14.4% of total employment. In India, the 360 million workers in the informal sector represent over 90% of total employment.

TABLE 1   Categories of informal work arrangements

Category of informal work	Definition
Informal sector	Own-account workers, unremunerated family workers, domestic servants and individuals working in production units of between 1 and 10 employees.
Informal employment	Informal wage workers and unpaid family workers who may work in the formal or informal sector. These workers are defined as informal if they lack a contract, specific health and pension benefits, and social security coverage.
Informal enterprises	Defined by the nature of regulation in each context: the availability of a license, and the payment of licenses, taxes and fees.
Informal economy	Includes both private informal workers and the informal self-employed as well as employers in informal enterprises.

TABLE 2   Informal employment as a percentage of total employment in five countries

	Year	Informal employment (in millions)	Percentage of total employment
Egypt	1998	6.5	40.1%
El Salvador	2002	1.7	69.1
India	1999	360.2	92.1
South Africa[1]	2003	2.3	22.5
Russia[2]	2002	9.5	14.4

[1] Excludes domestic workers. Including domestic workers, these figures rise to 3.2 million workers, or 28% of total employment.
[2] These numbers show employment specifically in the informal sector.

Source: Authors' analysis of chapters 1 through 5.

A small percentage of workers in the informal labor market reported that informal employment was not their primary source of income. The largest such group was found in Russia, where approximately 22% of those working in informal employment held other primary or secondary jobs.

Sectoral distribution of informality

All five case studies find that, while informal employment is frequently concentrated in services, there are jobs that lack contracts and benefits throughout the economy. As shown in **Table 3**, informal employment in Egypt is visible in all sectors, with the greatest concentration of informal workers in manufacturing (29%), construction (24%), trade (19%), services (16%), and transport (11%). It is interesting to note that, while the largest numbers of informal workers are clustered in manufacturing, informal employment represents only 48% of all jobs in this sector in Egypt. In construction, however, 82% of all workers are informally employed.

There are distinct sectoral patterns in El Salvador and Russia, where the majority of informal employment is concentrated in retail and petty trade, hotels and restaurants, construction, domestic service, and light manufacturing.

In El Salvador, 33% of all informal employment is found in trade, hotels, and restaurants; 26% in agriculture, livestock, and fishing; 14% in manufacturing; and 6% each in domestic service and construction.

In Russia, 67% of those employed in the informal economy worked in non-agricultural activities. The Russian data reveal that the greatest concentration of informal workers is found in trade, hotels, and restaurants (43%), with another 30% in agriculture, forestry and fishing, 12% in transport, construction, and communications, and 10% in industry.

Own-account work

Many of those in the informal sector cluster are essentially small shop-owners or other self-proprietors, whose labor is referred to as own-account work—typically in small and microenterprises. In El Salvador, according to data from 2002, 43% of all those working in any capacity in the informal economy were own-account workers, while only 6% of individuals in formal employment were own-account workers.

In Russia, two-thirds of individuals working in the informal sector were self-employed in small enterprises, 78% of which report having fewer than five employees.[6]

Education

It is clear from all five studies that individuals with the least amount of formal education are more likely to find work in informal employment.

TABLE 3 Distribution of formal and informal employment in Egypt, 1998

	Male			Female			Total		
	Distribution of informal workers	Distribution of formal workers	Share of all workers in the formal sector	Distribution of informal workers	Distribution of formal workers	Share of all workers in the formal sector	Distribution of informal workers	Distribution of formal workers	Share of all workers in the formal sector
Mining	0.5%	0.5%	62.3%	0.0%	0.0%	0.0%	0.4%	0.4%	62.3%
Mfg.	20.3	28.5	52.6	6.1	30.5	49.5	16.6	28.7	52.3
Electricity	2.8	0.0	100.0	1.0	0.0	100.0	2.3	0.0	100.0
Construction	3.4	25.8	17.2	0.9	2.5	64.0	2.8	23.5	18.3
Trade	4.6	18.2	28.3	2.1	24.6	29.8	4.0	18.8	28.5
Transport	7.3	12.1	48.5	2.7	0.5	96.4	6.1	10.9	51.4
Finance	2.9	1.6	73.8	4.1	5.0	80.0	3.2	1.9	75.7
Services	58.2	13.4	87.1	83.1	37.0	91.6	64.6	15.7	88.6
Total	100.0	100.0		100.0	100.0		100.0	100.0	65.4

Source: El Mahdi and Amer for chapter 1 (Egypt).

TABLE 4   Workers by highest level of education and sector in South Africa, 2003

Highest level of education	Formal workers	Informal workers
None	4.1%	12.3%
Grade 0-3	2.8	7.4
Grade 4-6	8.7	16.8
Grade 7-9	17.4	29.1
Grade 10-12	43.4	29.3
Diploma	12.8	2.4
Degree	8.9	1.2
Total*	98.1	98.5

* Totals do not add to 100 because of rounding errors and a small portion of the sample whose education levels were not reported.

Source: Adapted from research by Braude in chapter 5 (South Africa).

In South Africa, in particular, the education levels of workers in the formal and informal economy differ dramatically, as shown in **Table 4**. Approximately 16% of workers in the formal economy have completed less than a sixth-grade education while 37% of workers in the informal economy have less than a sixth-grade education. By contrast, nearly 22% of formal economy workers hold a diploma or higher degree, whereas fewer than 4% of informal economy workers have the equivalent level of education. Braude estimates that 95% of all informal economy workers have less than secondary school qualifications, i.e., have not completed through grade 12 (see chapter 5 on South Africa).

A similar picture emerges from the other countries. In 1998 only 6% of all formal workers in Egypt were illiterate, while 30% of all informal workers could not read.

In El Salvador in 2002, 21% of all informal workers had not attended school and had no formal education. Approximately 22% had between one and three years of formal education and a further 25% had between four and six years of education. In total, almost 16% of informal workers had less than a secondary school education. By contrast, in formal employment only 2% of workers lacked any formal education, while 59% had completed secondary school or hold a higher qualification. The Salvadoran household survey also defines workers by their skill level according to their occupation. According to the estimates reported in chapter 2, 40% of all workers in the informal economy are unskilled, while only 15% of workers in the formal economy were classified as unskilled. In 2002, 29% of all those in formal employment were defined as professional, scientific, or technical workers—a group which generally has higher levels of educational attainment—while only 3% of all those in informal employment classified as such.

Crucially, however, these studies all agree that while individuals with more formal education are less likely to find themselves working in the informal economy, the acquisition of formal education, even to levels exceeding the average, does not guarantee formal employment. For example, 5% of all wage workers in the informal economy had a university or post-graduate degree in Egypt. In Russia in 2002, almost half those informally employed had at least a high school education. Although only 19% of all workers in the informal economy are categorized as "skilled workers" in the Russian Longitudinal Monitoring Survey, between 10% and 11% of all workers in the informal economy hold a higher degree.

Experience

A number of the case studies compiled here explore the effect of experience on informal work arrangements. Experience was defined as the number of *potential* years in the labor market: i.e., the difference between the current age of the individual and the estimated age of labor market entrance, taking into account the number of years, on average, spent in school. While this is likely to be an imperfect measure of actual experience, it does provide some information about the potential experience that each individual may have in the labor market and affords a basis from which to assess the returns on experience. Further, any measurement error is likely to be attributed equally to workers in the informal and formal economy, allowing for a comparison of these two groups.

In Egypt, El-Mahdi and Amer (chapter 1) find that average levels of experience are higher for both men and women in the formal economy as compared with the informal economy. In 1988, workers in the formal economy had an average of 18.1 years of potential experience, while workers in the informal economy had approximately 14.1 years of potential experience. By 1998, the average level of potential experience

TABLE 5 Average years of potential experience in formal and informal employment in Egypt, 1988 and 1998

Experience in years	1988		1998	
	Formal	Informal	Formal	Informal
Males	20.5	15.9	22	15.1
Females	11.2	9.3	15.2	6.2
Total	18.1	14.1	20.3	14.3
Sample size	2,392	1,187	2,933	1,403

Source: El Mahdi and Amer in chapter 1 (Egypt).

for formal-sector employees was 20.3 years as compared with 14.3 potential years of experience in the informal economy (see **Table 5**).

The Russian chapter also explores measures of skill composition and their relationship to job tenure in the formal and informal economy (see **Table 6**). Comparing conventional definitions of the informal *sector* with the expanded definition of informal *employment*, Sinyavskaya and Popova (2004) find that both tenure and experience are greater for workers in formal employment and the formal sector when compared to their informal counterparts. Workers in formal employment report an average length of 10.3 years in their current job, while workers in informal employment report an average of 1.6 years.

Hours of work
All five country studies found that workers in the informal sector work longer hours than those in formal employment. In Egypt in 1998, the average number of hours worked in the informal economy was 51.6 per week, compared to 44.6 hours per week on average worked in the formal economy (see **Table 7**). Although workers in both the formal and informal economy have seen their average work hours rise, growth in the informal sector has been 3.7 times greater.

Wages, incomes, and poverty
The wages and incomes associated with informal employment are much lower than for workers in the formal economy. In El Salvador, 62% of all workers in the informal sector earn less than the monthly minimum wage. Lara calculates the poverty rates of workers in both the informal

TABLE 6 Length of service and seniority in Russia, 2002[1]

	Employment		Sector[2]		
	Formal	Informal	Formal	Informal	Total
Average length of service in current job (in years)	10.3	1.6	10.5	2.6	9.5
Average seniority (in years)	21	14	21.1	15.2	20.4

[1] Author's analyis of Russian Longitudinal Monitoring Survey (RLMS) for 2002.
[2] The informal sector includes informal own-account enterprises, enterprises that are defined to be informal and unregistered, and workers in production units with fewer than five employees.

Source: Sinyavskaya and Popova, chapter 4 (Russia).

TABLE 7 Average hours of work per week in formal and informal employment in Egypt, 1988 and 1998

Average hours of work per week	1988		1998	
	Formal	Informal	Formal	Informal
Males	45.6	48.7	46.4	51.8
Females	38	45.2	39.4	50.1
Total	43.7	48.2	44.6	51.6
Sample size	2,389	1,187	2,935	1,400

Source: El Mahdi and Amer, chapter 1 (Egypt).

and formal economy in El Salvador and finds that, whereas only 13.3% of all workers in the formal economy are considered poor, 43% of workers in the informal economy are poor.

The Egypt study measures relative pay for workers in the formal and informal economy, and finds that informal workers earn approximately 84% of what formal economy workers earn. This sectoral gap is much greater for women; women working in the informal economy earn 53% of what their counterparts earn in the formal economy. Further, real wages for both men and women fell in formal and informal work over the period under study, with formal sector wages falling by twice as much as those in the informal sector. Despite this slower rate of decline, wages in informal employment remain significantly less than those in the formal sector.

In South Africa, wages and incomes are also highly unequal between the informal and formal economy. Braude reports that more than half of his sample of informal economy workers earned less than 500 Rand per month in 2003, while less than 1% of all formal economy workers earned less than this amount.[7] Approximately 75% of workers in the informal economy earned less than 1,000 Rand per month, while only a little more than 15% of formal economy workers wages fell in this range.

These inequalities become even starker when we consider the racial distribution of wages and incomes. The United Nations Development Project's (UNDP) Human Development Report for South Africa shows that in 1995 the average white household earned four times as much as its average African counterpart. By 2000, the average white household was earning six times the average income of the typical African household (UNDP 2000).

Wages and incomes in South Africa's informal economy are consistently lower than those in the formal economy. In chapter 5, Braude observes: "...the incomes [in the informal economy] are at best equal to the lowest minimum wage in the formal sector...Jobs created in the informal sector are not the result of the expansion of economic opportunity, but the expansion of survivalist strategies." For Braude, the growth in informal employment and informal production reflects subsistence strategies developed as a means of survival in an economy where the availability of good jobs is rationed.

Labor market segmentation by gender and race
In general, informal and formal employment exhibit significant labor market segmentation by both gender and race. Women typically earn less than men in both the formal and informal sector. In India, for example, men in informal employment earn 49% and women earn 43% of the average wage in the formal sector.

In Egypt women earned an average of 70% of male wages in formal employment and 82% of male wages in informal employment in 1988 (see **Table 8**). By 1998, women's average wages as a percentage of men's had risen to 86% in the formal economy but declined in the informal

TABLE 8 Female earnings as a percentage of male earnings by education level in Egypt (real wages in 1988 and 1998)

Level of education	1988		1998	
	Formal	Informal	Formal	Informal
Illiterate	71%	69%	61%	58%
Read and write	68	52	64	40
Below intermediate	68	50	85	38
Intermediate	61	111	80	43
Above intermediate	77	42	77	54
University	62	92	83	80
Post-graduate	55	22	54	NA*
Total	70	82	86	53

* NA = Not available.

Source: El-Mahdi and Amer, chapter 1 (Egypt).

economy to 53%. These changes took place as real wages fell dramatically in both sectors.

A similar pattern can be observed in South Africa, and further, informal employment is concentrated mostly in select racial classifications. Just over 60% of all workers in the formal economy are male, compared to 55% in the informal economy. A large majority of workers in the informal economy (85%) are black, Coloured, or Indian.

Further, women in the South African economy tend to be clustered in informal employment in trade and services. In all industries in the informal sector, with the exception of mining and quarrying, female earnings fell well below the male earnings for black workers (see **Table 9**). It should, of course, be noted that comparing average wages in each sector does not allow us to compare equivalent job categories or control for hours worked.

The case studies reveal that in three of the five countries informal employment was growing faster than formal employment over the period under study. This does not preclude that there may be periods when these tendencies reverse, or that in some countries informal employment may be pro-cyclical while in others it is counter-cyclical. Clearly these conclusions are highly sensitive to the periods under review and the definitions of informality applied. Yet these findings highlight that there may be significant growth from below where small scale enter-

TABLE 9   Female earnings as a percentage of male earnings for black workers in South Africa, September 2002

	Formal unionized	Formal nonunionized	Informal
Agriculture etc.	72%	90%	87%
Mining & quarrying	85	61	100
Manufacturing	76	70	46
Electricity etc.	65	100	NA[1]
Construction	97	65	44
Wholesale & retail	83	82	54
Transport etc.	100	129	41
Financial etc.	111	113	67
Community etc.	113	77	74
Private households[2]	67	53	100

[1] NA = Not available.
[2] Includes African, Indian/Asian, and Coloured.

Source: Braude (2004).

prises in the informal economy appear to be growing faster and absorbing more workers than enterprises in the formal economy.

Degradation of employment

The documented differences in wages, education, skill level, and job tenure between informal and formal employment in all five countries were largely expected. Notwithstanding, there are a number of alarming tendencies. In all five countries there are substantial numbers of workers with greater than average levels of education working in informal employment. Given this, it seems hard to argue that these workers are in the informal economy because they have inadequate education and/or low levels of productivity. The existence of substantial numbers of educated workers in the informal economies of each of the five countries studied provides compelling evidence that there are just not enough good jobs in these economies.

Additionally, in all five countries there appears to be a tendency toward the degradation of employment and the erosion of the terms and conditions of formal employment that persists across sectors—including those generally thought to be centers of formal employment, such as manufacturing, construction, and public employment. In several cases, more jobs in these sectors currently lack benefits, pensions, and con-tracts—the hallmarks of quality, formal-sector employment—than they did in the early 1980s.

Informal employment relationships are generally not covered by leg-islated labor protections or trade union representation. Indeed, the work relationship between the employer and employee in small-business sec-tors is rarely governed even by any sort of written contract. In Egypt, 85% of workers in Greater Cairo were found to be working without a contract, while only 74% of workers in Greater Cairo were covered by Social Security contributions.

Growing informalization thus carries with it the very real threat that large (and disproportionately vulnerable) groups of workers will find themselves shut out of pension benefits and other social insurance guar-antees that are tied to formal-sector employment. Further, the relative isolation of several forms of informal employment (home-based pro-duction, for example) leaves these workers out of networks that could provide them the information and bargaining power to claim a greater share of economic output.

One conclusion that is forcefully supported by this group of studies is that the informal sector is not in general decline throughout the devel-oping world. In short, the simple version of the structural change theory seems to provide little insight in regards to contemporary developments in informalization.

The size of the informal sector has declined or remained the same in only two of the five countries studied: South Africa and El Salvador. In South Africa, formal employment growth exceeded informal employ-ment growth over the period 1999 to 2003, and in El Salvador there has been a small decline in the growth of informal jobs over the period 1991 to 2002. This informal job decline in El Salvador, however, could in large part be driven by enormous rates of emigration from the Salva-doran economy, particularly from rural areas.

In Egypt, certainly, and perhaps in Russia, the informal sector is grow-ing at a more rapid rate than the formal sector. But Braude (chapter 5) correctly points out that assessing the true rate of growth (or decline) in informal employment is fraught with difficulties. While the South Afri-can surveys show a very slight increase in informal employment's share of total employment, it is impossible to rule out the possibility that this

FIGURE 1   GDP growth rates, 1990-2002

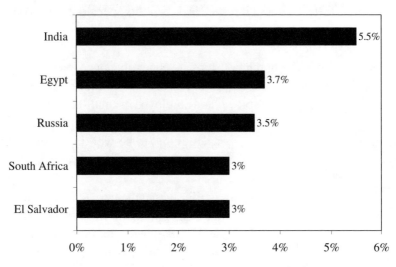

Sources: World Bank (2003).

growth is not a direct function of better techniques used to measure the informal economy in recent years. In short, the apparent growth in the informal sector could be due to actual growth, more accurate methods of empirical measurement, or some combination of both.

That said, it seems clear from the research provided in this volume that all five countries have problems generating robust growth of formal and "modern" employment, and that sitting back and waiting is not an appropriate policy response for promoting quality employment opportunities. These studies point to several possible avenues for the concerned policy maker, although no one response stands out as a cure for all ills.

Implications for policy

Strong and weak forms of "lack of growth" theory
All five countries in this sample have sustained positive economic growth over the past decade (see **Figure 1**). Between 1990 and 2004, officially measured GDP growth was in excess of 3% for all five countries.

While these growth rates may seem good by developed country standards, they still remain well below what is needed to absorb the rapidly

TABLE 10   Annualized growth rates in five countries, 1995-2000

	Population -1	Real GDP -2	Productivity -3	Absorption (4) = (1) + (3)	Slack (5) = (4) - (2)
Egypt	1.9	3	2.2	4.1	1.1
El Salvador	2.1	1.2	0.2	2.2	1.1
India	1.8	4.6	4.2	6	1.4
Russia	-0.4	2.2	1.8	1.4	-0.8
South Africa	1.8	0.9	0.6	2.4	1.6

Source: Authors' analysis of Penn World Table.

growing potential labor force in each country. **Table 10** charts rates of growth of the labor force and productivity along with GDP in each country over a relevant sample period. These data highlight the fact that it is not just positive GDP growth that is needed to generate employment and reduce labor slack, but rather *GDP growth in excess of productivity and labor force growth.*

While it is clear that positive economic growth will not lead automatically to a decline in informality or informalization, our analysis reveals that there may be insufficient aggregate demand in each of these economies relative to productivity and population growth to absorb a growing labor force. Growth is not a panacea, but closing the output gap in these economies would contribute mightily to sustaining better quality of employment, and there still seems to be substantial macroeconomic slack in these economies.

Active labor market policies
To date, ALMPs have not been used extensively in these economies, with some small exceptions. In El Salvador some targeted training programs have been developed for particular sectors—most notably youth (between the ages of 18 and 25) and the urban unemployed. The Salvadoran Institute for Professional Development (INSAFORP)[8] provides training and accreditation in business development, computing, secretarial skills, and other skills including auto mechanics, electrical work and maintenance, soldering, construction, and plastics. Thus far, no in-depth analysis of the labor market outcomes as a result of receiving this training has been undertaken. Furthermore, no data appear to be avail-

able that track the recruitment, retention, and long-term employment of trainees.

In Egypt in 2000 a National Training Fund was developed as part of a broader initiative launched under the National Employment Program. In addition, the Productive Families Scheme (PFS) was developed to provide resources to the self-employed in small family-run and owned businesses. The PFS provides access to resources, raw materials, and training for locally produced goods and crafts. There are approximately 3,474 training centers in operation with a staff of 5,700 trainers (El Mahdi and Amer 2004). The Egyptian Ministry of Social Affairs also manages a vocational skills training program that targets youth who have dropped out of secondary and primary school.

In South Africa a Skills Development Act was introduced in 1998, which developed mechanisms to address skills mismatch. A series of training programs and workplace-based learning and financial incentives were introduced to stimulate on-the-job training. A central component of the Skills Development Act addressed the introduction of new forms of skills acquisition through "learnerships and skills programs" administered through the National Skills Development Strategy, which provides a framework to coordinate workforce development. The Skills Development Levies Act of 1999 instituted a program to collect levies for skills training under the Sector Education and Training Authorities (SETAs).[9] The SETAs were charged with promoting and organizing training on a sectoral basis and not within industries. The SETA training programs allow individuals who are not formally employed within a particular industry to gain access to training and skills development, and the programs are sufficiently flexible to include small businesses and provide opportunities to the unemployed.

Russia also offers a series of employment intermediation services to facilitate hiring and reduce the time spent in unemployment. These programs are run through state employment services that provide assistance with recruitment and the job search.

Job training and human capital development

Of the three prongs of ALMPs (training, direct job creation/subsidy, and job matching aids), the first seems to be most indirect in attacking the problems of informalization. All nations, especially those in the developing world, would be well served by increasing the quality of basic, universal education available to its citizens. However, ALMPs that are devoted to job training are largely focused on the supply-side, which seems inefficient in the range of economies (Russia and Egypt, especially) where well-educated workers exist in large numbers in informal employment or in those economies where insufficient demand limits the supply of good jobs (particularly El Salvador and India).

Further, given that measurements of the informal economy are still in their infancy, it seems premature to assert that the low productivity of informal workers (even those without formal education credentials) constitutes the chief impediment preventing them from moving into formal-sector jobs.

Finally, arguing against the "first-best efficiency" of directed human capital spending are the recent findings on the pronounced procyclical patterns of formal-sector growth in Latin America.[10] Given that productivity and skill levels are likely constant over the business cycle, the finding of significant increases in formal-sector work during booms and formal-sector declines during economic slowdowns points to the dominance of labor demand in determining the allocation of workers into formal or informal employment.

Labor standards (the structuralist response)

It seems likely that resources could be more profitably invested in other dimensions of ALMPs, either by providing employment subsidies to firms in order to encourage them to formalize employment relations with their employees and/or in providing information and building social networks that will improve the information of job seekers and employers. Carr, Chen, and Tate (2000) provide an example of shea butter workers in Burkina Faso and India that are forced into home-based production. This isolation leaves them without the information or means to take advantage of emerging market opportunities and leaves them on the short side of transactions with more organized (corporate) buyers. Carr, Chen, and Tate (2000) point to a need to support individual producers in forming purchasing associations to boost their price-bargaining powers vis-à-vis other players in the market. While perhaps not apparent on its face, this recommendation seems, in a sense, to constitute a classic ALMP intervention in terms of matching workers (the home-based workers) with those institutions (purchasers, in this instance, instead of firms) who will most value their inputs. The study points to similar intermediation interventions that have taken place in Burkino Faso and India as models for improving the price and bargaining power of workers and producers in the global value chain.

Galli and Kucera (2004) point to a strong association between improved labor standards and the formalization of employment relations in Latin America. In a sense, the matching problem identified in Carr, Chen, and Tate (2000) seems to be aided through the labor market institutions associated with effective labor market protections (our own interpretation, not necessarily that of the authors). This finding also argues in favor of a deeper analysis of the role of unions in guaranteeing worker rights, overseeing enforcement and organizing, or extending benefits to, workers in the informal economy.

The range of estimates for unionization rates within the informal economy throughout the world reveal very low rates of union penetration, falling between 3% and 5%. Unions can also potentially offer job-matching and intermediation services extending membership to include informal workers (AFL-CIO 2002). This role for intermediation services, which matches workers to good jobs, argues strongly against the idea of promoting flexibility through deregulation in the labor market as a primary goal of policy makers, a policy recommendation advocated by the World Bank (1995). Galli and Kucera (2004) rightly point out that different labor standards will have different economic effects, and policy makers need to be clear on which are most appropriate for spurring formal-sector employment.

More transparent and enforceable property rights (the legalist response)

The Russia and India reports suggest another policy angle. Among the problems associated with the isolation of workers involved in informal employment is lack of access to credit markets and the resources spent inefficiently in trying to secure private property arrangements.

Both of these problems would be greatly improved through the acquisition of legally recognized title-to-assets. Field et al. (2003) examine recent experiments with the provision of legal titles to occupied dwellings in Peru. Those receiving the titles were more likely to find more remunerative work and felt less constrained to protect the right to their dwellings. Thus, the granting of titles contributed to a much improved environment for making productive employment matches.

As a subset of legalist programs and policies, measures to provide safety nets, and access to pensions and health benefits that address all workers, can significantly improve the nature of work and fall-back options available in the informal economy. Attempts to generalize access to such benefits and provide pensions and health care resources to informal workers will greatly improve the well-being of these workers.

Programs and policies that address property rights and rights to assets also have the potential to address some of the gender inequities and gender-specific vulnerabilities documented in the case studies. Where women are disproportionately concentrated in the informal economy, they have fewer rights to productive assets, earn lower wages, and are less likely to be able to accumulate savings, secure credit, or obtain pensions. These measures can be targeted to compensate for particular deficits for vulnerable workers in certain contexts.

Other interventions:
Beyond the legalist and structuralist measures

Although these studies did not directly estimate the number of informal workers in home-based and small production units, it is clear that a substantial portion of the informal economy comprises own-account workers, home-based workers,[11] the self-employed, or those in small informal enterprises. A host of policies can be enacted to support these enterprises and activities that may contribute to increasing output and consequently improving the terms and conditions of work. For example, ensuring that piped and potable water is available to these enterprises, connecting workplaces and homes to sewage, and engaging in slum upgrading can greatly improve the work environment. In some cases, investing in basic infrastructure may be more easily deployed than seeking legalist or structuralist remedies—largely because of opposition to the latter from powerful sectors and economic interests.

A mix of policy and programs?

In the classification system laid out in the introductory portion of this summary, the emphasis on improved adoption and enforcement of labor standards will prove most effective where it is determined that much of the persistence and growth of informalization is driven by structural factors. In these areas, workers have experienced declines in the quality of employment though degraded bargaining positions vis-à-vis firms as the result of the erosion of other institutions that have improved fallback options in the era of globalization.

The emphasis on formalization of property rights and social networks will be most effective when much of the persistence and growth of informalization is thought to be the results of legalist pressure—i.e., burdensome and ineffective institutions that stifle entrepreneurial drive for forcing residents to waste valuable resources asserting control of their own property and assets.

It seems likely that a blend of the approaches laid out in this introduction could prove useful for each of the countries studied. In fact, the legalist and structuralist remedies could even prove complementary at times.

Conclusion

Fostering decent work should be a fundamental objective of those concerned with improving living standards throughout the developing world. But before reasonable prescriptions can be made, the causes of the lack of quality work need to be diagnosed.

The five country studies gathered here offer a solid foundation for such a diagnosis. They all provide empirical measures of the more up-to-date and sophisticated definitions of the informal economy and track the evolution of informal work over the recent past.

Each study lays out the development of informalization against the appropriate macroeconomic context—a key contribution. Given the crucial importance of rapid macroeconomic expansion in providing the necessary condition for growth in decent employment, policy maneuvers that will influence the macroeconomy (e.g., trade and investment liberalization) need to be judged on this dimension as well as others such as microeconomic efficiency.

A few findings stand out from this set of studies. First, none of the five countries have had unambiguous success in generating sustained expansions of formal employment, even as all have posted positive GDP growth. Second, while the structure of formal employment reveals strong sectoral patterns (being most pronounced, for example, in the manufacturing and public sector), there is a significant presence of informal employment across all sectors. In short, no job, no matter what sector it is in, is immune to informality or informalization. Third, informality is disproportionately the lot of those with inferior education credentials, yet non-trivial numbers of workers with significant education credentials work in the informal economy in each sector, strongly signaling the insufficiency of good jobs, not just good workers.

Beyond this, the overarching message of these collected studies is that informality and informalization in each country follows its own trajectory and requires policies tailored to meet their specific experiences based on country-specific institutions, history, and even geography.

Endnotes

1.   We are very grateful to the contributors of this volume and to Ravi Naidoo for comments on this chapter. All analysis, interpretations, and errors in this chapter are the responsibility of the authors only.

2.   The legalist approach is best represented in de Soto (1989).

3.   See, for example, AFL-CIO (2002).

4.   The expanded definition of informality draws heavily on work by the ILO and in particular Jacques Charmes, Marty Chen, and Joann Vanek. See ILO (2002).

5.   Informal employment is the overall category that refers to both employment in the informal sector and in informal jobs.

6.   This reflects the definition of the informal sector applied by the Russian team that categorized all units of fewer than five employees as being in the informal sector, in addition to own-account workers and unpaid family members.

7.   8 Rand = US$1 in 2003.

8.   For more information consult http://www.insaforp.org.sv/.

9.   The Skills Development Levies Act mandated a contribution by employers of 0.5% of monthly payroll for the year commencing April 1, 2000. The levy was increased to 1% of payroll in April 1, 2001. Every employer registered for PAYE or that has an annual payroll in excess of R250 million must pay the levy. The levies contribute to on-the-job training and workforce development initiatives, which are overseen by inspectors under the SETA.

10.   On this, see Marquez and Pages (1998).

11.   The term "home-based workers" refers to two types of workers who carry out remunerative work within their homes—independent own-account producers and dependent subcontract workers. Carr, Chen, and Tate (2000) estimate that over 50% of all enterprises in six sub-Saharan African countries are home based.

Bibliography

AFL-CIO. 2002. *Helping Low-Wage Workers Succeed Through Innovative Union Partnerships: Lessons Learned From High Road Strategies in Philadelphia, Las Vegas, Milwaukee, and Seattle*. Working for America Institute, the American Federation of Labor-Congress of Industrial Organizations. Washington, D.C.: AFL-CIO.

Braude, W. 2004. "South Africa Country Analysis," in a report to the Global Policy Network, National Labor and Economic Development Institute, Johannesburg, South Africa.

Carr, M., M. Chen, and J. Tate. 1999. Globalization and home-based workers. *Feminist Economics*. Vol. 6, No. 3, pp. 123-42.

Chen M., J. Sebstad, and L. O'Connell. 1999. Counting the invisible workforce: The case of home-based workers. *World Development*. Vol. 27, No. 3, pp. 603-10.

Conway, M., and S. Loker. 1999. "The garment industry development corporation: A case study of a sectoral employment development approach." Economic Opportunities Program, The Aspen Institute. Washington D.C.: Aspen Institute.

de Soto, H. 1989. *The Other Path: The Invisible Revolution in the Third World*. New York: Harper and Row.

Galli R., and D. Kucera. 2004. Labor standards and informal employment in Latin America. *World Development*. Vol. 32, No. 5, pp. 809-28.

Lara, E. 2004. "El Empleo Formal y No Formal en El Salvador, Un Estudio sobre El Desarrollo de la Fuerza Laboral." Report to the Global Policy Network, Fundación Nacional para el Desarrollo, San Salvador.

Field, E. 2003 "Property rights and household time allocation in urban squatter communities: Evidence from Peru." Harvard University Working Paper: < http://www.people.fas.harvard.edu/~efield/Fieldperutime.pdf >

International Labour Organization. 2002. "Women and men in the informal economy: A statistical picture." Employment Sector, International Labour Office Geneva: ILO.

Marquez, G., and C. Pages. 1998. "Ties that bind: Employment protections and labor market outcomes in Latin America." Inter-American Development Bank, Working Paper No. 373.

Penn World Tables. 2004. Center for International Comparisons. University of Pennsylvania.

Portes, A. 1989. Latin American urbanization in the years of the crisis. *Latin American Research Review*. Vol. 24, No. 3, pp. 7-44.

Rademacher, I., M. Bear, and M. Conway. 2001. "Project Quest: A case study of sectoral employment development approach." Economic Opportunities Program, The Aspen Institute. Washington, D.C.: The Aspen Institute.

United Nations Development Program. 2000. *Human Development Report, South Africa*. Johannesburg: UNDP.

World Bank. 1995. *World Development Report 1995: Workers in an Integrating World*. Washington, D.C.: World Bank.

World Bank. 2003. *World Development Indicators*. Washington, D.C.: World Bank.

CHAPTER 1

Egypt: growing informality, 1990-2003

by Alia El-Mahdi and Mona Amer

Introduction

The last decade has been a period of major economic change in Egypt, starting with the launch of a structural adjustment program in 1991. This policy has had significant implications for the performance and the structure of formal labor market institutions, but little is known of its repercussions within the informal economy, i.e., household enterprises and workers employed without a work contract, social security coverage, or any degree of permanency.[1] This chapter analyzes the characteristics of Egypt's informal economy and its role in labor absorption during this period of economic reform and market liberalization. It deals with the informal economy as a whole by looking at both informal workers and informal economic units.

The chapter is divided into five sections. The first presents an overview of macroeconomic performance in Egypt since the 1980s, with particular attention to the economic reforms implemented since the beginning of the 1990s. The second part describes the structure of the labor market and the repercussions of economic reforms. The third section discusses the criteria used in defining informal workers and informal economic units. The fourth section compares the characteristics of informal and formal workers according to a large set of determinants (age, gender, real wages, work conditions, etc.) and over time. The final section presents the ongoing active labor market policies.

The analysis relies on four sources of data. The first is the population censuses of 1976, 1986, and 1996. The second source is the regular and national representative rounds of Labor Force Sample Surveys (LFSS). Since the regular rounds do not include questions on certain pertinent issues, we rely for a third source of data on two special rounds of the LFSS, the Labor Force Sample Survey of 1988 (LFSS 88) and the Egyptian Labor Market Survey of 1998 (ELMS 98). Both surveys were designed similarly and allow for comparison. Finally, for more in-depth analysis than is provided by the national surveys, we incorporate results from the Greater Cairo Survey of 1998. Whenever possible, we compare the results according to the different kinds of data available.

Macroeconomic performance

From the 1950s to the 1980s, Egypt developed as a state-dominated economy. The state owned and controlled most of the major industries and financial institutions, directed the economy using planning techniques, and protected domestic industries through a wall of quotas and tariff barriers.

Prices on industrial inputs, utilities, transportation, housing, consumer goods, and land rent were tightly controlled, and the government gained a degree of social peace, though at the expense of massive food, fuel, and service subsidies. Economic inefficiencies plagued the system, leading to rapidly rising inflation and recurrent balance-of-payments crises in the late 1980s. The oil price collapse of 1986 exacerbated the fiscal and balance-of-payments pressures.

Specifically during the 1980s:

- Egypt suffered from chronic budget deficits, averaging around 18% of gross domestic product. The deficits were the result of extensive food and fuel subsidies, heavy defense and investment spending, a weak tax system, and high debt service payments. The oil price collapse made this policy unsustainable. The government covered the gap in the short term through higher Suez Canal fees and modest reductions in defense spending and consumer subsidies.

- the country experienced high inflation; it averaged 17-21% in the 1987-90 period.

- Egypt maintained a complex system of multiple exchange rates.

- the Egyptian production sector became dominated by state-owned enterprises that operated in nearly all sectors of the economy. The public sector and government accounted for 40% of aggregate employment, about half of total GDP, and two-thirds of nonagricultural GDP.

- non-market pricing, used often to serve social purposes, became the norm.

- the Egyptian financial system was highly regulated, with the central bank placing limits on interest rates; allocating credit, particularly through four large state-owned banks; and employing multiple exchange rates. Domestic banks were poorly capitalized and weakly supervised (U.S. Department of the State 1994).

The economic reform and structural adjustment programs
Egypt's suffering economic performance provided the background that led to negotiations with the International Monetary Fund, formally concluded in May 1987 in the form of the Standby Agreement. The main objectives of the agreement were (1) preparing for sustained economic growth, (2) reducing the rate of inflation, and (3) stabilizing the current account deficit. Various measures covering exchange rate, monetary, and fiscal policy were stipulated to achieve theses objectives (Abdel-Khalek 2001, 25). However, the agreement was cancelled after only three months because of the failure of the Egyptian government to meet the IMF's requirements. According to the fund's officials, the Egyptian government adopted a lukewarm attitude and failed to meet performance criteria (IMF 1991).

The deterioration of the economic situation at the end of the 1980s and the large donations and debt relief programs linked to Egypt's role in the Gulf War set the stage in early 1991 for the launch of an ambitious stabilization effort, the Economic Reform and Structural Adjustment Program (ERSAP), with the IMF and World Bank. Its basic goal was to generate sufficient growth rates that would help buoy employment opportunities for the growing population, which would in turn help to reduce income disparity and alleviate poverty.

The key elements of this program included:

- reducing the size of the public sector through privatization;

- ending controls over investment and eliminating most tariffs on imports;

- selling manufactured products at market prices;

- raising energy and transport prices to realistic levels;

- reducing consumer subsidies and targeting them toward the poorest group;

- deregulating private investment and encouraging private-sector activity in all sectors, including financial services (Ash 1993; Youssef 1996; Roads 1997).

The new agreements with the World Bank and IMF required that the Egyptian government introduce several measures immediately, including: (1) the removal of ceilings on interest rates, (2) liberalization of the exchange rate, (3) the introduction of a new sales tax (Middle East Executive Report 1992), and (4) the reduction of the government's role in economic activities and investment.

Implementation of the ERSAP

Egypt's efforts to achieve stabilization in the early 1990s proved successful. Central to the success of the reform program were three elements: (1) a massive fiscal adjustment, (2) the liberalization and unification of the exchange rate—including the adoption of an exchange rate anchor—and (3) a supportive monetary policy, comprising quantified targets in the context of successive financial programs.

The combination of these elements brought about a significant reduction in inflation and a fundamental improvement in the external position. Between fiscal years 1990/91 and 1995/96, the budget deficit declined from 20.2% to 1.3% of GDP, inflation rates declined from over 14.5% to 7.3%, and foreign debt service fell from 25.8% of current account receipts to less than 11%; as a percentage of GDP, foreign debt fell from 107% to 45.9% (MOFT 2003). Trade reforms were significant: the government eliminated import bans on most commodities in 1993 and reduced the maximum tariff rate from 100% to 80% (with a few exceptions). Yet despite these liberalizations, the remaining high average tariff rate of about 30% and non-tariff barriers to importation continue to inhibit import growth.

The government liberalized and unified the exchange rate system and effectively pegged the Egyptian pound to the U.S. dollar. The exchange rate stabilized at about LE 3.31 per dollar in mid-1991, and had depreciated only slightly to LE 3.39 as of 1996 (CBE *Annual Economic Review*), assisted by generous Gulf War aid, exceptional debt relief, and strong inflows from remittances, tourism, and Suez receipts.

Before implementation of the ERSAP, the public sector comprised 339 financial and non-financial enterprises, including 314 state-owned enterprises ranging from heavy machinery companies to hotels and banks and occupying a great portion of production and employment in the national economy. Most of these enterprises held huge liabilities originating from inefficient management. With the implementation of the ERSAP, the government launched a privatization program that by the end of 1997 had wholly or partially privatized 84 enterprises accounting for LE 8.1 billion in revenue (Ministry of Public Enterprises).

At the start of the economic reform program, a little over one million workers were employed in the 314 state-owned enterprises, constituting 6% of Egypt's total labor force of 15.5 million. This number had fallen to just under half a million at the start of 2001, due to labor restructuring policies implemented by the government (responsible for a drop of 167,000 workers), natural retirement (148,000), and the transition of state enterprises to the private sector (200,000). It is therefore possible to deduce that privatization in Egypt has influenced 2-3% of Egypt's total labor force through either policies of labor restructuring or divestiture. Any direct impact that privatization has had on the labor force has to be treated within the context of this relatively small volume (PCSU 2002a).

Since 1990 the government has carried through with an early retirement program as a key restructuring component of its privatization program. During the period January 1, 1990 through December 31, 2001, approximately 195,000 workers in over 200 state-owned enterprises were retired through largely voluntary labor force restructuring programs. Nearly 38,000 additional workers accepted early retirement during 2002. The cost of labor force restructuring over this period totaled LE 4,549 million; annual savings through wage reduction resulting from this restructuring totaled LE 1,130 million. The current portfolio of state-owned enterprises set for privatization has a workforce of over 453,000 (PCSU 2002b).

Meanwhile, the budget deficit has fallen continuously and is expected to reach balance soon. At the same time, customs tariffs were lowered, exchange rates revised, and various deregulation and liberalization measures followed.

The aftermath of ERSAP

Starting in 1997, however, the Egyptian economy began to suffer, due in large part to three shocks: the Luxor massacre of November 1997, which negatively affected tourism; the Asian economic crisis of June 1997, which encouraged imports from East Asia countries; and the sharp decline in the oil prices. As a result of these shocks, the Egyptian economy has experienced a decrease in the level of saving, a decline in foreign investment, a shift from a balance of payments surplus to a deficit, a disturbance in the income distribution, and an increase in the public debt and the budget deficit (El-Said 2003).

To cope with this situation, the Central Bank of Egypt (CBE) allowed for a slow depreciation of the Egyptian pound during 2000, and on January 29, 2001 the government introduced a "managed peg" exchange rate system that allowed the exchange rate to depreciate. This move toward a more flexible exchange rate system, while paving the way for a more independent and market-responsive monetary policy, will necessitate a new mode of coordination between fiscal and monetary policies in the current period as well as in the period ahead (El Refaie 2001). (In August 2001, the CBE established a "crawling band" exchange rate system.)

Despite these efforts, toward the end of 2002 Egypt was still experiencing an overvalued real exchange rate, a budget deficit of about 6%, a vulnerable current account situation, a critically low level of international reserves, a less-than-healthy banking system, segmented consumption markets, and a protracted economic slowdown (Hassan 2003).

In addressing this situation, the government concluded that fiscal policy had been overly exploited and that it was time to utilize monetary policy. However, it was impossible to have an active monetary policy while adopting an almost fixed exchange rate regime and an open capital market. Therefore, on January 29, 2003 Egypt announced that the pound would float. As a consequence, the formal exchange rate of the pound to the U.S. dollar depreciated from $1=LE 4.62 to $1=LE 6.18 (September 2003). The informal exchange rate reached $1=LE 7.

Labor market trends

The structure and performance of the Egyptian labor market has been strongly affected by the economic reforms launched in the early 1990s. This section lays out out the main characteristics and changes that occurred during that decade. This analysis of the Egyptian labor market reveals important disparities along gender lines as well as the inability of labor demand to absorb growing cohorts of young people.

Evolution of labor force participation

The Egyptian working-age population (15- to 64-year-olds) grew from 30.0 million in 1990 to 41.4 million in 2001, according to the regular rounds of Labor Force Sample Surveys (LFSS). Among those age 15-64 in 1990, 15.7 million were in the labor force, with males making up the vast majority (11.3 million). The total labor force reached 19.3 million in 2001, 15.2 million males and 4.1 million females.

Male labor force participation declined from 75% in 1990 to 73% in 2001. This trend can be explained by two factors. First, improvements in access to education led to a decrease in the participation of youth under age 20. Second, and more importantly, those over 60 have tended to retire earlier.

Because the LFSS regular rounds fail to capture female subsistence activities, the analysis of the evolution of female labor force participation is based on the two special rounds—LFSS 1988 and the Egyptian Labor Market Survey (ELMS) of 1998. These two datasets show an overall increase in female participation rates[2] from 42% in 1988 to 46% in 1998. They also illustrate that, despite this overall increase, young females (less than 19 years old) have experienced a decline in their participation. This drop is explained by the increase in school enrollment, especially in post-secondary school where participation rates are high, particularly in rural areas. On the other hand, over the period 1988-98 participation rates of women age 20-75 increased in both urban and rural areas. Thus, women seem to enter the labor force later but also to withdraw later, and they remain active for a longer period. The increase in female labor force participation is also partly due to later marriage and to a higher participation in the labor force after marriage (Assaad 2002).

TABLE 1   Distribution of employment by major labor market segments and gender, 1988 and 1998

Employment sector	Male 1988	Male 1998	Female 1988	Female 1998	Total 1988	Total 1998
Government	20.8%	26.8%	15.7%	19.2%	19.0%	23.9%
State-owned enterprises	11.4	7.4	3.5	1.6	8.6	5.2
Subtotal public sector	*32.1*	*34.3*	*19.1*	*20.9*	*27.6*	*29.1*
Private agriculture wage work	8.7	7.7	3.0	1.1	6.7	5.2
Private agriculture non-wage work	22.4	13.5	60.4	66.7	35.7	33.9
Subtotal private agriculture	*31.1*	*21.2*	*63.4*	*67.8*	*42.4*	*39.0*
Private non-agriculture wage work	21.8	28.6	6.1	5.1	16.3	19.7
Private non-agriculture non-wage work	14.9	15.9	11.4	6.2	13.7	12.2
Subtotal private non-agriculture	*36.7*	*44.5*	*17.5*	*11.3*	*30*	*31.8*
Total	**100%**	**100%**	**100%**	**100%**	**100%**	**100%**

Source: LFSS 88 and ELMS 98; Ragui Assaad (2002).

Sectoral shifts in GDP composition and employment

Table 1 shows that the public sector remains a major employer, representing 27.6% of total employment in 1988 and 29.1% in 1998. However, this overall stability masks disparities within the group, as the share of those employed directly by the government increased while the share employed by state-owned enterprises sharply declined. The increasing share in government employment—from 19.0% to 23.9% over the 10-year period—is striking in that it happened after the launch of the ERSAP, which sought to reduce the role of the public sector. The explanation lies in the increasing demand for education and health services. At the same time, the declining share of employment in state-owned enterprises is a natural consequence of the vast privatization program implemented under ERSAP.

Even though it is declining, the agriculture sector is another important employer, accounting for over a third (39.0%) of total employment in 1998. The agriculture sector employs mainly non-wage workers, and the overwhelming majority of these are women: the share of females working in subsistence activities increased from 60.4% of all female workers in 1988 to 66.7% in 1998. At the same time, the share of male

TABLE 2 Distribution of employment by economic activity and gender, 1990 and 2001

Economic activity	Male		Female		Total	
	1990	2001	1990	2001	1990	2001
Agriculture	34.8%	27.8%	57.0%	31.9%	40.5%	28.5%
Manufacturing, mining, and utilities	17.1	14.6	9.9	9.2	15.2	13.5
Construction	7.8	9.2	1.0	0.8	6.1	7.7
Trade, hotels, and restaurants	10.0	15.1	5.4	8.6	8.8	14.0
Transport, storage, and communications	6.9	7.5	1.5	2	5.5	6.5
Finance and insurance	1.7	3.1	1.3	2.7	1.6	3.1
Public and personal services	21.2	22.6	23.6	44.8	21.8	26.7
Unclassified	0.4	0.0	0.4	0.0	0.4	0.0
Total	**100%**	**100%**	**100%**	**100%**	**100%**	**100%**

Source: Authors' calculations based on LFSS 1990 and 2001 (CAPMAS).

employment in agriculture greatly decreased over the period, particularly among non-wage workers (from 22.4% to 13.5%). This divergent trend across gender can be explained by the fact that the access to alternative employment for unskilled women is limited to subsistence activities, while unskilled men can find work abroad or in informal work outside of agriculture.

The comparison of the distribution of employment with the composition of GDP by economic activity is instructive in that it reveals big discrepancies. **Table 2** suggests that the economic activities that contribute the most to GDP are not the biggest employers. Indeed, while the trade and manufacturing sectors represented 23% and 20% of GDP respectively in 2000-01 (not shown in table), they employed only 14.0% and 13.5% of workers in 2001. Conversely, the agriculture and services sectors were the biggest employers, with shares of 28.5% and 26.7% respectively of total employment, while their contributions to GDP were relatively small (17% and 19%).

Average real wages over time

Table 3 presents the evolution of real wages by economic activity from 1977 to 2001.[3] The real wage indexes remain stable over the period, but

TABLE 3   Change in real wages by economic activity, 1977-2001

Economic activity	1977-82		1985-95		1996-2001	
	Overall change	Change per year	Overall change	Change per year	Overall change	Change per year
Agriculture	-10.9%	-2.3%	-49.5%	-6.6%	-7.4%	-1.5%
Mining	16.9	3.2	-31.6	-3.7	65.2	10.6
Manufacturing	32.2	5.7	-13.2	-1.4	23.9	4.4
Utilities	-	-	-22.8	-2.6	58.4	9.6
Construction	15.7	3	-40.9	-5.1	33.2	5.9
Trade, hotels, and restaurants	12.7	2.4	-37.8	-4.6	32.4	5.8
Transport, storage, and communications	14.1	2.7	-38.3	-4.7	44.2	7.6
Finance and insurance	27.4	5	-28.7	-3.3	33.2	5.9
Services	3.3	0.6	-32.1	-3.8	6.7	1.3
Total	**22.7%**	**4.2%**	**-28.2%**	**-3.3%**	**31.2%**	**5.6%**

Source: Authors' calculations based on data from CAPMAS, Establishment, Wages, and Hours of Work Surveys (1977, 1978, 1982, 1985, 1986, 1988-2001) and the IMF consumer price index from 1977 to 2001 (index = 100 in 1991).

this overall stability masks changes over time, and it illustrates a clear cyclical pattern. Indeed, it is possible to break down the 24-year timeframe into three periods according to the direction of variation in real wages.

- **1977-82:** a period characterized by an increase of real wages in almost all sectors corresponding with high GDP growth rates.

- **1985-95:** a period that witnessed a big erosion of real wages in all sectors corresponding with a period of slowdown in economic growth. Real wages dropped by 28.2% over the 10-year period, equivalent to a decline of 3.3% per year.

- **1996-2001:** a period of rising real wages in all sectors that compensated for the previous drop. This reversal can be explained by the fact that the Egyptian economy experienced high growth rates (over 5% per year) and low levels of inflation during the end of the 1990s.

FIGURE A   Real wages by economic activity, 1977-2001 (1991=100)

Source: Authors' calculations based on data from CAPMAS, Establishment, Wages, and Hours of Work Surveys (1977, 1978, 1982, 1985, 1986, 1988-2001) and the IMF consumer price index from 1977 to 2001 (index = 100 in 1991).

Thus, it seems that real wage trends have generally followed economic growth cycles (see **Figure A**). The trend is similar when real wages are disaggregated by gender.

Unemployment and underemployment

Unemployment is one of the most important and recurrent dilemmas that the Egyptian labor market faces. It reflects the difficulties faced by educated youth in entering the labor market and the inability of labor demand to absorb growing cohorts of new entrants.

The number of unemployed increased from 1.3 million in 1990 to 1.8 million in 2001, according to regular LFSS rounds. The unemployment rate steadily increased during the 1990-95 period from 8% to 11%. It then dropped to 8% between 1995 and 1997 and rose back to 9% in 2001. However, the drop that occurred from 1995 to 1997 was probably due to a change in the unemployment definition.[4] The LFSS 88 and

ELMS 98 data show an increase from 5.4% to 7.9% during the same period.[5]

The burden of unemployment falls largely upon new, young, and educated entrants to the labor market. Indeed, 88% of the unemployed are age 15-24, and 92% are entering the labor market for the first time. This pattern indicates that unemployment is mainly a problem of finding a place for educated youth and reveals a mismatch between the educated labor supply and demand for labor. Moreover, in 2001 almost 70% of the unemployed had graduated with an intermediate education level, and the unemployment rate reaches its peak at the intermediate level and then decreases with higher levels of learning.

Females are the most at risk for unemployment. While the unemployment rate among males was less than 6%, it was close to 23% among females in 2001. Barriers to entry and the concentration of women in a few activities can explain this overrepresentation of females in unemployment.

With the issuance of law 14 in 1964 (and its amendment by law 85 in 1973), the state became responsible for hiring all university graduates within two years of their graduation and all secondary school graduates within three years of graduation to positions in government offices (local or central) or in state-owned enterprises. The government terminated the requirement for the state-owned enterprises in 1978 in order to reduce the pressure of excess workers on these companies. Regardless, the government remained the main employer in the non-agricultural sector until the beginning of the millennium.

The ERSAP introduced some changes to this labor market practice. One of its main fiscal policy targets was to reduce the wage bill in order to help cut the budget deficit. This policy meant a decline in employment and real wage growth rates in the public sector. Employment in the public sector grew just 3% during the 1988-98 period, compared to 8% during 1976-86 period. New graduates had to seek more work opportunities in the private sector.

Even if the absorption of large cohorts of young and educated new entrants is one of the major problems that the Egyptian labor market faces, formal unemployment rates provide an incomplete representation of labor market mismatches. Another issue is underemployment. Because unemployment compensation is non-existent, a substantial number of individuals must seek marginal casual or temporary jobs and accept low wages. When this occurs, a substantial part of the labor force becomes underutilized.

Although underemployment is certainly widespread in the Egyptian labor market, it is difficult to measure. No data are available to explicate this complex phenomenon. Fergany (1998), using the LFSS 88, proposed an indirect estimation of invisible underemployment by relating it to the percentage of employed wanting to change their main job. He found that these dissatisfied job holders made up 9% of the employed in 1988; the group consisted primarily of urban males with intermediate and higher education. The reasons behind their desire for change mirrored the issues likely to face the underemployed: they wanted a more secure job, a less timing-consuming job, higher income, and a better correspondence between their qualifications and their work. This finding is all the more interesting since these workers thought that the better job positions they wanted were not available.

External migration

External migration played a significant role in regulating the excess of domestic labor supply from the mid-1970s to the beginning of the 1990s. During this period, Arab countries—especially in the Gulf region—experienced increasing oil revenues and were in need of skilled workers to implement ambitious development programs. The demand for Egyptian labor increased, and extensive flows of Egyptian workers moved to Gulf countries, in particular Iraq, Saudi Arabia, Kuwait, and Libya.

The CAPMAS estimates that one million Egyptians were working abroad in 1980. This number more than doubled in 1986, reaching 2.25 million. By the early 1990s the number of Egyptians working abroad still exceeded 2.2 million, with males representing the vast majority. Egyptian migrants in Arab Gulf countries (except in Iraq, which hosted important flows of unskilled Egyptian labor) tended to be highly skilled, educated professionals such as doctors, engineers, and teachers.

External migration played an important role in the Egyptian economy by reducing the pressure of labor supply on the domestic labor market and by providing foreign currency. Indeed, migrant remittances represent a major source of foreign currency, estimated at 3-4% of GDP. According to the International Organization for Migration (2003), "Egypt ranked fifth within the top ten developing countries remittances' receivers in 2001."

By the beginning of the nineties, several factors put an end to high rates of Egyptian migration. These included the decrease in oil prices, the 1991 Gulf War, Arab Gulf country policies of favoring national labor to foreign, and the entry of South Asians into the Gulf labor market.

Consequently, migration is no longer substantial enough to absorb a substantial share of the surplus of domestic labor supply. In the meantime, demographic pressure on the labor market is expected to increase in the near future.

Legislation in the labor market and the rule of law

In this section we present the main components of labor market regulations. While it is by no means an exhaustive review, it draws attention to the fact that the labor market regulation system is marked by large discrepancies between the private and public sectors.

After several years of tough negotiations, a new labor law (law 12 of 2003) went into effect in July 2003. It covers the private and public sectors but not administrative institutions. Among its main goals are to give more flexibility to labor market regulations, assure workers' rights in striking, and implement a fund for unemployment compensation.

The new labor law confers more flexibility on the labor market by allowing an employer in the private sector to renew a temporary contract without transforming it automatically into a permanent employment status, which had been required in prior law. This change is intended to make employers less reticent in hiring workers because they will not feel committed for an undetermined period. Also, employers gain more means to terminate a contract, and layoffs can be justified by difficult economic conditions. In return, workers who have been dismissed have a right to appeal. Workers in the public sector keep their privilege of lifetime job security, as their contracts cannot be terminated.

Egypt's social security system leads to big disparities between public and private sectors. While workers in the public sector are covered entirely by social insurance, a substantial fraction of their counterparts in the private sector lack this privilege. Because social insurance is mainly based on (high) contributions by employers, and because the inspection system is weak, employers try to escape their duties: it is estimated that 30% of private employers fail to assume their contributions. Together with the lifetime employment guarantee of employment and significant non-wage benefits, social insurance explains why workers prefer government jobs. The new law does, however, stipulate the creation of a fund to compensate workers who have been dismissed due to a partial or total closure of their establishment (El Khawaga 2003).

Regarding wage determination rules, the new law calls for the creation of a national council for wages and the setting of minimum annual increments. However, enforcement will be problematic. In the government sector, wage setting remains centralized and based mainly on seniority.

Syndicate (union) membership in Egypt accounts for just 25% of the total workforce, or 4.5 million workers. An important and sensitive issue is the right to strike. The new law recognizes the right of workers to strike, but with conditions restricting it.

Although the new labor law is a step in the right direction, additional reforms are needed with regard to taxes, the social security system, and small and micro enterprises.

Defining and measuring the informal economy

In discussing the informal sector as a whole, it is important to define the elements of informal employment and informal enterprises.

Informal employment

Informal employment usually refers to informal wage workers and non-paid family workers who are working either in the formal or informal sectors. The difference between formal and informal workers is usually associated with the availability of a work contract, with social security coverage, or with a degree of permanency in work. Accordingly, a worker could be working on an informal basis in a formal company or even in the government if he/she is not covered by social insurance or bound by a contract. At the same time, he or she could be working on a formal basis in a small informal enterprise if either of those conditions were met.

In terms of this analysis, two criteria are considered essential for formal employment: the availability of a contract and coverage under social security.

The informal enterprise

The definition of the informal enterprise is more complex. Charmes (1998) tried to capture the most widely accepted definition, which is based on the international definition of the informal sector adopted as a resolution of the 15th International Conference of Labor Statistics 1993, as follows:

> For statistical purposes, the informal sector is regarded as a group of production units which form a part, within the System of National Accounts (SNA), of the household sector as unincorporated enterprises owned by households.
>
> Household enterprises (or unincorporated enterprises owned by households) are distinguished from corporations and quasi-corporations on the basis of their legal status and the type of accounts they hold: accordingly, household enterprises are not constituted as separate legal entities independently of the household or of household members that own them, and no complete set of accounts are available which could permit a clear distinction between the production activities of the enterprises and the other activities of their owners.
>
> The informal sector is defined, irrespective of the kind of workplace, the extent of fixed capital assets, the duration of the activity of the enterprise and its operation as a main or secondary activity, as comprising:
>
> (1) informal self-owned enterprises which may employ family workers, and employees on an occasional basis: for operational purposes and depending on national circumstances, this segment comprises either all self-owned enterprises, or only those which are not registered under specific forms of national legislation (factories or commercial acts, tax or social security laws, professional groups, regulatory or similar acts, laws or regulations established by national legislative bodies).
>
> (2) enterprises of informal employers which may employ one or more employees on a continuous basis and which comply with one or both of the following criteria:
>
> • size of the establishment below a specified level of employment (defined on the basis of minimum size requirements embodied in relevant national legislation or other empirical or statistical practices: the choice of the upper size limit tak-

ing account of the coverage of statistical enquiries in order to avoid an overlap),

- non-registration of the enterprise or its employees (Charmes 1998).

In studying the informal sector researchers have chosen several definitions, which are usually based on either the number of workers (e.g., less than 5 or 10 workers), the size of capital, a combination of the two previous variables, or certain legal rules and regulations such as the availability of a license, registration, and social security coverage. These variations in the choice of the defining criteria have led to the preparation of a number of studies and results that are not possible to compare with each other, especially when looking at the role of the informal sector over time.

In the last Egyptian Labor Market Survey (ELMS 98), the distinction between the formal and informal enterprises depended on the degree of compliance of the enterprise with certain rules that imply formality, namely:

- the availability of a license,

- the commercial or industrial register (in case they are required), and

- the keeping of regular accounts.

If these conditions were satisfied the enterprise would be considered formal in nature, while the partial compliance or the disregard of these conditions would indicate an informal enterprise (El Mahdi 2002).

The informal economy
The informal economy in the wider sense includes both private informal workers and the informal self-employed and employers. Research studying the informal sector tends to exclude all agricultural activities.

Formal and informal employment: key characteristics over time

There is no lack of estimates of informal-sector employment, yet the methodology used to account for the size of informal employment varies. **Table 4** shows several estimates of informal employment over sev-

TABLE 4   Estimates of size of informal employment over various years

Sources	Year	Estimate (millions)	Methodology	Data sources
EL-Ehwany	1976	2.4	all w	EC
EL-Ehwany	1980	2.4	all w	EC
EL-Ehwany	1986	2.9	all w	EC
EL-Ehwany	1996	4.8	all w	EC
El Mahdi	1988	4.7	Inf. ww+	LFSS
El Mahdi	1998	6.5	Inf. ww+	ELMS
El Mahdi	1996	5.1	Self-E	EC+PC
El Mahdi	1998	5.5	Self-E	ELMS

Note: EC = establishment census, PC = population census, LFSS = Labor Force Sample Survey, ELMS = Egyptian Labor Market Survey. Self-E = self-employed, NPFW = non-paid family workers, W = workers.

Source: El Mahdi, compiled from various sources.

eral years. They differ depending on the source of data—establishment census, population census, or special rounds of the labor force sample surveys (1988, 1998)—and the different methods used in calculating informal status.

The bases of measuring informality in these studies include:

- the informality of workers and enterprises as discussed in the next section;

- a counting of all workers outside establishments and workers in establishments with less than five workers;

- a counting of the self-employed, non-paid family workers, and wage workers and employers in establishments employing less than 10 workers;

- a counting of the self-employed, non-paid family workers, and non-registered workers and employers.

The main point of emphasis here is that informality, despite differences in estimates, is a pervasive phenomenon, and it seems to have grown over time. The informal sector has become a refuge for new job seekers, especially during the end of the 1990s, when the public employment growth rate declined steadily.

Table 5 summarizes the change in the size of the informal sector between the two sample survey years (1988 and 1998).

Based on these definitions, employment in the informal private sector was close to 6.5 million in 1998, or more than one-third of the total employment in that year (16.2 million). This number reflects the degree of infiltration of informal activities into the economic structure of the Egyptian economy. It also reveals the existence of a non-conducive investment climate, at least for the small investor.

In the broad sense, the following trends can be observed in the informal sector:

- The number of private formal wage workers has grown at a higher rate than that for private informal workers during the 10 years studied here (1988-98). However, the base size of the latter is much bigger than the former. Therefore, the absolute number of informal wage workers is more than four times larger than the number of formal private wage workers.

- The pace of growth among informal economic units has slowed, but it is still faster than for formal private units.

- The informal sector (in the wider sense) has witnessed a rate of growth of 3.84% annually, which is faster than growth in the formal private sector of 2.9% annually.

- The informal sector in absolute terms is close to 5.3 times larger than the formal private sector.

However, another segment has not been accounted for until now, which is that of informal workers in the public sector and the government. More than 140,000 workers in 1998 were hired informally in the public sector. If this segment is added, the size of the workforce consisting of informal-sector workers, the self-employed, and employers would total 6.65 million persons in 1998, or 41% of total employment.

The perceived decline in the number of informal workers in the government ranks between 1988 and 1998 could be explained by the fact

TABLE 5   Size of the informal economy in Egypt, 1988-98 (millions of workers)

Type of sector	Total 1998	Males 1998	Females 1998	Total 1988	Males 1988	Females 1988	% change in 1998 over 1988
Non-agricultural wage workers	9.8	7.8	1.998	6.74	5.378	1.365	45.5%
Private non-agricultural wage workers	4.0	3.625	0.411	2.79	2.435	0.357	43.3
Private informal non-agricultural wage workers	3.26	2.961	0.302	2.272	2.019	0.253	43.6
Non-paid family workers	0.45	—	—	—	—	—	—
Private formal non-agricultural wage workers	0.773	0.664	0.108	0.52	0.416	0.103	48.6
Small economic units*	3.3	2.7	0.613	2.934	2.432	0.502	12.5
Informal economic units*	2.776	2.231	0.545	2.432	2.031	0.401	14.4
Formal economic units*	0.546	0.477	0.069	0.502	0.401	0.101	8.7
Informal private sector**	6.486	5.192	0.847	4.695	4.05	0.654	38.1
Formal private sector***	1.319	1.141	0.177	1.022	0.817	0.204	29.0

* Economic units are taken as a proxy to represent number of employers.
** Equals private informal non-agricultural workers + non-paid family workers + informal economic units.
*** Equals private formal non-agricultural workers + formal economic units.

Source: ELMS 98 data files.

that the government recognized that informal workers tend to request becoming permanent, formal workers. This situation posed a burden on the budget, and therefore fewer workers were hired on an informal basis during the 1990s.

Ratio of informal employment to total employment over time

Informal employment (wage workers). All private enterprises find it more convenient and less costly to hire workers on an informal basis, since the firms need not sign up the workers in the social security system and can easily lay them off. This arrangement can be attractive to workers, too; in fact, some public service workers work informally in a second job in private enterprise and prefer not to be bound by a contract.

The importance of the informal workforce can be understood only in the wider context of all wage workers. **Table 6** shows the relative magnitude of wage workers in the total labor force (1976, 1986, and 1996); **Table A1** in the Appendix shows the size of the formal and informal workforce (1988 and 1998).

Not indicated in this table is that in 1996 workers in the agricultural sector accounted for 31.0% of total employment, the public sector accounted for 32.6%, and the private non-agricultural sector accounted for 36.4%.

Table 6 shows that wage workers represented the largest group in the labor force, among both males and females, for the two decades studies here (63.4% in 1996). Women are more likely than men to be wage workers, in part because their likelihood of becoming self-employed or being an employer is more limited than for men for social and economic reasons.

Among men, the share who were self-employed declined between 1986 and 1996 while the share who were employers rose. Although it is too early to give an accurate explanation of this trend, other data sources seem to indicate that the average size of micro and small enterprises—which represent the bulk of private enterprises—is increasing both in terms of number of workers and value of capital.[6] This trend is in itself a reflection of the new globalization constraints that prohibit micro and small firms from market entry.

Among women, the share who are employers rose very slightly between 1976 and 1996, from 1.43% to 1.44%. Also, the share who are

TABLE 6 Employment status of labor force (age 6 and above) by gender (percent)

Employment status	Male			Female			Total		
	1976	1986	1996	1976	1986	1996	1976	1986	1996
Self-employed	19.81%	26.78%	21.24%	5.17%	4.09%	4.18%	18.5%	24.13%	18.63%
Employers	8.46	3.93	7.29	1.43	0.65	1.44	7.83	3.55	6.93
Wage workers	60.51	56.37	61.94	57.99	67.76	71.64	60.28	57.7	63.42
Non-paid family workers	5.64	2.51	2.65	5.7	3.37	2.35	5.65	2.61	2.6
Unemployed	0.35	3.07	0.48	0.58	0.8	0.18	0.37	2.81	0.42
New unemployed	5.23	7.34	6.4	29.13	23.33	20.21	7.37	9.21	8.0
Total	100.0	100.0	100.0	100.0	100.0	100.0	100.0	100.0	100.0
Number (thousands)	9,997	11,817	14,551	985	1,561	2,624	10,982	13,378	17,175

Source: CAPMAS, Population Census 1976, 1986, 1996, Cairo.

non-paid family workers declined, a trend that could be explained by rising educational attainment among women. The percentage of female unemployment is more than three times higher than that of males, a result of declining job opportunities in the government and public-sector companies, which are the most important job providers for females.[7]

Since wage workers represent by far the largest segment of the labor force, this analysis will concentrate on their characteristics and their changes over time. It will also focus on wage workers in informal non-agricultural activities, where the job in question is their main job. In other words, some of these workers may have other, secondary jobs, but these are not the focus here. We will rely mainly on the special rounds of labor force sample surveys—the LFSS 88 and ELMS 98—and compare the data in the two years to shed light on the changes taking place.

In addition, since some issues, such as the work environment in small enterprises, have been covered in detail in other surveys, such as the Greater Cairo Sample Survey of 1998,[8] we will take information from these sources when necessary.

Results of special labor market sample surveys, 1988 and 1998. Data from the 1998 survey show the number of non-agricultural wage workers (NAWW) to be nearly 9.8 million, out of total employment of 16.2 million (see Appendix Table A1). Among these NAWW, 4.0 million, or 41%, worked in the private sector, while the rest worked in the public sector. In the 1988 survey, 2.8 million, also 41%, worked in the private sector.

Based on the definition discussed earlier, informal employment was estimated at 3.4 million workers in 1998, representing 34.0% of total non-agricultural employment and 81.0% of total private non-agricultural employment. The last figure indicates a slight decrease compared to 1988, when the informal NAWW represented 81.3% of total private NAWW. However, the absolute number of informal workers grew from 2.6 million in 1988 to 3.4 million in 1998.

Nine percent of informal workers are employed in large enterprises. Larger companies tend to resort to hiring workers on an informal basis to avoid social security taxes and contracts. This arrangement puts companies in a better position to fire workers, without interference by the Labor Office. Another 4% of informal wage workers are employed in the public sector in either government administration or in state-owned enterprises.

Table A1 in the appendix distinguishes wage workers by their formal or informal status. The upper part of Table A1 includes all economic sectors for analysis purposes. In the lower part of the table wage workers in government and state-owned enterprises are excluded, i.e., the data cover the private sector only. The differences between the numbers in the two parts represent the informal workers hired by the public sector in the two years 1988 and 1998.

The upper part of the table illustrates several points:

- The informality share among wage workers decreased from 38.6% in 1988 to 34.6% in 1998.

- Informal status in 1998 was more clearly evident among the male workforce. Informal workers represented 39% of the total male workforce but just 17% of the total female workforce.

- Despite the importance of public-sector employment, informal wage workers still represent more than one-third of total non-agricultural employment.

The lower part of the table, which excludes public-sector employment, illustrates the following:

- The private sector provided employment to 4 million wage workers in 1998.

- Informal status among private-sector wage workers did not change much between 1988 and 1998, remaining at about 81%.

- Informal status in the private sector is higher among male wage workers (81.7% of male wage workers) than female wage workers (73.6% of female wage workers). A possible explanation for this discrepancy could be that women in Egypt tend to prefer more secure jobs even if paid lower wages, while males prefer higher wages and accept more risk or more mobility.

- The majority of private-sector enterprises prefer to hire male workers (89.9% of total private employment) and also tend to hire them on an informal basis.

TABLE 7   Distribution of wage workers by formality status, gender, and age group, 1998

Age group	Male F col%	Male IF col%	Male %F of total row	Female F col%	Female IF col%	Female %F of total row	Total F col%	Total IF col%	Total % F of total row
6-11	0.0%	0.1%	0.0%	0.0%	1.7%	0.0%	0.0%	0.2%	0.0%
12-14	0.0	2.7	0.0	0.0	6.1	0.0	0.0	3.1	0.0
15-19	0.6	19.2	4.8	1.1	21.1	19.8	0.7	19.4	6.7
20-29	17.3	37.7	41.6	21.1	44.8	69.6	18.2	38.4	47.2
30-39	29.8	22.4	67.5	40.2	18.1	91.6	32.5	21.9	73.7
40-49	30.7	10.8	81.6	25.5	2.8	97.8	29.3	10	84.7
50-59	19.9	4.8	86.5	11.3	4.9	91.9	17.7	4.8	87.4
60-64	1.6	1.1	69	0.8	0.6	86.5	1.4	1.1	71.1
65 and over	0.1	1.2	15.9	0.0	0.0	0.0	0.1	1.1	15.9
Total	100.0	100.0		100.0	100.0		100.0	100.0	65.4

Source: CAPMAS, Population Census 1976-1986-1996, Cairo.

Age and gender of formal and informal wage workers

The age structure of wage workers reveals some of the important features of the informal workforce. As can be seen in Table A1 in the appendix and **Table 7**, informal workers have certain distinct characteristics:

• There were 3.4 million informal wage workers in 1998. Female informal NAWW represented 10% of the total informal NAWW.

• Children (those 14 and younger) represent 3.3% of the informal workforce. Among female informal NAWW, 7.8% are children; the share among men is 2.8%. The formal workforce shows no child labor.

• The highest concentration of informal workers is in the 20-29 age bracket, and the shares in subsequent age brackets gradually decline. This phenomenon could be explained by the fact that, after the accumulation of some savings and experience, male workers may tend to work independently or shift to formal employment as they move into their thirties. Female workers may retire early due to marriage, or in a few cases start their own businesses.

• Above age 65, informal workers are almost all men.

The economic activities of formal and informal wage workers

The distribution of workers among type of economic activity is a manifestation of the weight of the various economic activities in Egyptian value-added and the degree of labor intensity and concentration in each area.

Table 8 illustrates several important features of wage workers' distribution by economic activity:

- Informal male workers are more evenly distributed among the different activities than are formal male workers, who are primarily concentrated in services and manufacturing. The high concentration in those two sectors is due to the inclusion of public-sector employment and the existence of large-scale industrial complexes that hire workers on a formal basis.

- Informal female workers are distributed among three main economic sectors—manufacturing, trade, and services—while formal workers are mainly situated in services, which is controlled by the government.

- The gray columns indicate the extent of formal work status in each economic activity. Electricity, services, and finance are the most formalized economic activities, while construction and trade are the least formalized.

Education and skills of wage workers

Government efforts to provide education to all children, especially in the compulsory years of schooling, resulted in a rise in literacy and in the percentage of students graduating from high schools and universities.

These changes had an impact on the qualifications of new entrants to the labor market. However, the gradual improvement in the educational quality of the workforce coincided with a lessening of the government's role as a jobs provider. Consequently, high school and university graduates turned to the private sector, which has employed the majority of wage workers on an informal basis.

Tables 9 and **10** shows the distribution of wage workers according to formal status, gender, and educational attainment in 1998 and 1988, respectively, but do not separate formal public-sector employment from formal private-sector employment. The majority of formal employment occurs in the public sector.

TABLE 8   Distribution of wage workers according to economic activity, 1998

Activity	Male			Female			Total		
	F col%	IF col%	%F of total row	F col%	IF col%	%F of total row	F col%	IF col%	%F of total row
Mining	0.5	0.5	62.3	0	0	0	0.4	0.4	62.3
Manufacturing	20.3	28.5	52.6	6.1	30.5	49.5	16.6	28.7	52.3
Electricity	2.8	0	100	1	0	100	2.3	0	100
Construction	3.4	25.8	17.2	0.9	2.5	64	2.8	23.5	18.3
Trade	4.6	18.2	28.3	2.1	24.6	29.8	4	18.8	28.5
Transport	7.3	12.1	48.5	2.7	0.5	96.4	6.1	10.9	51.4
Finance	2.9	1.6	73.8	4.1	5	80	3.2	1.9	75.7
Services	58.2	13.4	87.1	83.1	37	91.6	64.6	15.7	88.6
Total	100	100		100	100		100	100	65.4

Source: ELMS 98 data files, estimated by the authors.

The data in the tables help to answer the question, does education matter?

- In 1998, only 26.7% of illiterates found formal jobs, and they accounted for 5.8% of the formal workforce (Table 9). They made up nearly a third (30.1%) of the informal workforce.

- The numbers are almost exactly reversed for those with university degrees or more: 27% of the formal workforce has this educational qualification, compared to 5.2% of the informal workforce.

- Within the formal workforce females are better educated than males, i.e., a smaller percentage of females are illiterates and a higher percentage are university graduates, but this distinction is not so clear in the informal workforce, where 31.2% of female workers are illiterates, compared to 30.0% of males. This phenomenon could be explained by the fact that employment opportunities were available for female high school and university graduates, especially in the government and public sector, at least until the beginning of the 1990s. This would also imply that education was a necessary condition for hiring females in a formal way, while it was less important in the case of male applicants.

TABLE 9   Distribution of workers by formality status and educational attainment, 1998 (percent)

| | Male | | | Female | | | Total | | |
	F	Inf.	%F/total row	F	Inf.	%F/total row	F	Inf.	%F/total row
Education									
Illiterate	7.1	30.0	27.0	2.0	31.2	23.9	5.8	30.1	26.7
Read and write	11.4	14.2	55.6	0.7	5.8	35.7	8.6	13.4	55.0
Less than intermediate	16.7	26.9	49.2	4.0	12.5	60.9	13.4	25.5	49.9
Intermediate	28.7	21.8	67.3	38.5	31.6	85.6	31.3	22.8	72.2
Greater than intermediate	9.9	2.5	86.2	18.5	6.8	93.0	12.1	2.9	88.8
University	24.2	4.4	89.5	35.0	12.1	93.4	27.0	5.2	90.8
Postgraduate	2.0	0.2	93.4	1.4	0.0	0.0	1.9	0.2	94.6
Total	100	100		100	100		100	100	65.5
Sample size	*2,085*	*1,247*		*85*	*149*		*2,936*	*1,396*	

Source: El Mahdi 2002.

- However, the formal market provided work for a significantly higher percentage of females with intermediate education at the end of the 1990s than at the end of the 1980s. One possible explanation for this high percentage of female graduates who are hired to work on an informal basis is the difficulty of accessing the formal market at a time when they needed work. The public sector was no longer providing jobs to the majority of educated women, and so they had to seek work in the informal sector.

- A comparison of the ELMS 98 data (Table 9) with LFSS 88 data (Table 10) suggests a trend of educational improvement.[9] The educational levels of workers (males and females) have improved between the two years. The change is accentuated especially in the case of informal workers, where illiterates constituted (33.6%) of workers in 1988 but just 30.1% in 1998; also, informal illiterate female workers in 1988 were 37.6% of the total informal female workforce, compared to 31.2% in 1998. One could conclude that Egypt's educational-upgrading policies were clearly reflected in the characteristics of workers.

An analysis of average years of experience[10] (**Table 11**) by formal and informal status shows that, as expected, informal workers are less

TABLE 10 Distribution of workers by formality status and educational attainment, 1988 (percent)

Education	Male			Female			Total		
	F	Inf.	%F/total row	F	Inf.	%F/total row	F	Inf.	%F/total row
Illiterate	15.4	33.1	39.1	3.9	37.6	24.8	12.6	33.6	37.4
Read and write	18.1	19.1	56.6	1.5	5.5	46.5	14.0	17.4	56.3
Less than intermediate	12.6	25.5	40.4	4.7	15.1	49.6	10.6	24.2	41.3
Intermediate	23.3	16.0	66.7	46.4	24.6	85.7	29.1	17.1	73.2
Greater than intermediate	6.5	2.1	80.8	13.7	4.7	90.2	8.3	2.4	84.4
University	20.5	3.8	88	26.7	12.1	87.5	22.1	4.9	87.9
Postgraduate	3.5	0.4	93.1	3.1	0.4	0.0	3.4	0.4	93.9
Total	100	100		100	100		100	100	61.6
Sample size	*1,778*	*1,316*		*616*	*187*		*2,394*	*1,503*	

Source: El Mahdi 2002.

experienced than their formal counterparts. On average, informal workers had spent 14 years in the labor market in 1988 and 1998 compared to 18 and 20 years, respectively, for formal workers. Males have much more experience than females, regardless of year or formality status. This result confirms the fact that less-experienced workers are more vulnerable when facing the labor market.[11]

Table 12 shows, only for males, the distribution of level of skill (or status in the job) whenever a manual skill is required, by formal and informal status. Figures for females are not presented here because the number of observations for females is too small to yield reliable results. However, the paucity of data demonstrates that women working either formally or informally are involved in jobs that do not require a special manual skill.

The data in Table 12 reveal a clear distinction between formal and informal male workers in terms of skill requirements. Among those occupying a job that requires a special skill, informal workers are much more likely to be less skilled than their formal counterparts. Formal workers are largely craftsmen (83.3% in 1988 and 81.0% in 1998), while informal workers are less likely to be so (50.7% in 1988 and 61.2% in 1998). A much smaller percentage of formal workers (2.3% in 1988 and 2.2% in 1998) than informal workers (21.4% in 1988 and 12.6% in 1998) are apprentices. However, the trend shows a substantial improvement in

TABLE 11   Average years of experience by formality status and gender, 1988 and 1998

Experience (in years)	1988		1998	
	Formal	Informal	Formal	Informal
Males	20.5	15.9	22.0	15.1
Females	11.2	9.3	15.2	6.2
Total	18.1	14.1	20.3	14.3
Sample size	*2,392*	*1,187*	*2,933*	*1,403*

Source: Authors' calculations based on Egyptian Labor Market Survey 1998.

TABLE 12   Level of skill required and formality status for males, 1998 (percent)

Level of skill required	1988		1998	
	Formal	Informal	Formal	Informal
Apprenticeship	2.3	21.4	2.2	12.6
Assistant	14.4	27.9	16.8	26.3
Craftsmen	83.3	50.7	81.0	61.2
Total	100.0	100.0	100.0	100.0
Sample size	*296*	*502*	*262*	*617*

Source: Authors' calculations based on Egyptian Labor Market Survey 1998.

the status of informal workers in that between 1988 and 1998 they were more likely to be craftsmen and less likely to be apprentices. Thus, the gap between formal and informal workers tends to narrow from 1988 to 1998.

Work conditions: wages, social benefits, and rights at work
Comparisons in this section are derived not only from LFSS 88 and ELMS 98 but also from the Greater Cairo Sample Survey of 1998, due to the detailed data obtainable from that study.[12] However, it should be noted that enterprises in Greater Cairo are more prone than those in the

TABLE 13   Average real wages by formality status and gender, 1988 and 1998 (in Egyptian pounds)

Experience in years	1988		1998	
	Formal	Informal	Formal	Informal
Males	1,401.0	746.7	316.8	274.1
Females	979.5	608.7	273.3	145.3
Total	1,295.8	727.4	305.5	257.8
Sample size	*2,388*	*1,184*	*2,924*	*999*

Source: Authors' calculations based on LFSS 88 and ELMS 98.

rest of the country to be subject to inspection by government authorities to ensure compliance with regulations. This relatively tighter control in the study area has implications on the degree of formality, which tends to be higher in the Cairo area than in the remaining regions of the country.

Work conditions are a combination of multiple factors. We examine those areas such as wages and social security coverage that are ascertainable from the data.

Real wages. The evolution of real wages presented here (**Table 13**) refers to real wages for the last three months worked among regular workers.[13] The most striking result is the impressive drop in real wages from 1988 to 1998. Both males and females in formal or informal employment experienced a huge decline over the 10-year period. Real wages of formal workers in 1998 were just a quarter of their level of 1988, as they dropped from LE 1295.8 to only LE 305.5. Real wages in informal employment declined less sharply; in 1998 they were a third of their 1988 level.

Females are paid less than males in both formal and informal employment. Similarly, informal workers are paid less than formal workers. In 1988 formal workers earned, on average, LE 1295.8 versus only LE 727.4 for informal workers. The gap was smaller in 1998, as formal real wages declined more rapidly than informal real wages, especially among males. However, informal women were paid only about half what their formal counterparts received in 1998; in 1988 they earned two-thirds the wages of formal women workers.

Table 14A incorporates educational attainment into the evolution of real wages. As expected, the more workers are educated the more they earn either in formal or informal employment. Real wages in informal employment are in general lower than in formal employment, and this is true at almost all levels of education for both sexes and both years 1988 and 1998. However, in 1998 among males, wages in informal work were higher than in formal work for low levels of education, i.e., among illiterates or those who could just read and write. For those with higher levels of education but less than university level, real wages are close among formal and informal male workers.

Table 14B shows the evolution of gender wage ratios[14] according to formal-informal status and education from 1988 to 1998. The overall gender wage ratio in the formal sector rose from 0.70 to 0.86. This overall increase in the wage ratios benefited mostly educated women, as illiterates or those who could just read and write saw their situation deteriorate. In the informal sector the gender wage ratio fell greatly, from 0.82 to only 0.53, over the period 1988 to 1998. The results in the informal sector by education are not reliable because the sample size for females is very small.

Availability of a contract. The work relationship between the employer and the employee in small businesses in Greater Cairo is generally not governed by a contract: only 15% of workers were covered (**Table 15**). This result concurs with results from previous studies, where workers in informal and sometimes in formal enterprises did not enjoy the rights provided by a contract. However, the unavailability of a contract is not necessarily due to the malicious intentions of employers; it could also be due to their ignorance of regulations or to the fact that they are unaccustomed to writing down agreements. Therefore, a worker could have been employed for over 10 years but still not have a contract.

Within the group of those who had a contract, 63.5% worked in formal enterprises, and 59.3% were males (not shown in table). These shares confirm the fact that abiding by the rules is more likely among formal enterprises.

Permanency in work. The suggestion that lack of a contract may not adversely affect job tenure is born out by the data in **Tables 16** and **17** regarding permanency in work.

TABLE 14A Average real wages by formality status, education level, and gender, 1988 and 1998 (in Egyptian pounds)

Education	Males				Females			
	1988		1998		1988		1998	
	Formal	Informal	Formal	Informal	Formal	Informal	Formal	Informal
Illiterate	854.7	616.0	199.5	240.8	609.8	424.1	122.1	139.2
Read and write	10,78.3	795.9	243.1	301.1	732.3	410.0	155.5	119.5
Less than intermediate	11,36.5	688.9	272.9	275.7	772.9	344.2	233.0	104.3
Intermediate	1,392.0	797.7	275.2	273.4	844.4	882.0	220.0	116.8
Greater than intermediate	1,213.9	1,072.4	310.7	306.1	940.6	453.7	240.7	166.6
University	2,037.6	1,273.6	437.1	333.8	1,262.9	1,166.4	360.8	266.0
Postgraduate	3,083.2	3,737.1	687.7	319.3	1,684.3	814.3	374.5	—
Total	1,401.0	748.3	316.8	274.1	980	612.2	273.3	145.9
Sample size	1,776	1,017	2,072	863	612	161	851	131

Source: Authors' calculations based on LFSS 88 and ELMS 98.

TABLE 14B   Gender wage ratios by formality status and educational attainment, 1988 and 1998

	Formal			Informal		
Education	1988	1998	Change 1988/1998 (percent)	1988	1998	Change 1988/1998 (percent)
Illiterate	0.71	0.61	-14.2%	0.69	0.58	-16.0%
Read and write	0.68	0.64	-5.8	0.52	0.40	-23.0
Less than intermediate	0.68	0.85	25.5	0.5	0.38	-24.3
Intermediate	0.61	0.80	31.8	1.11	0.43	-61.4
Greater than intermediate	0.77	0.77	0.0	0.42	0.54	28.6
University	0.62	0.83	33.2	0.92	0.80	-13.0
Postgraduate	0.55	0.54	-0.3	0.22	—	—
Total	0.70	0.86	23.3	0.82	0.53	-34.9

Source: Authors' calculations based on LFSS 88 and ELMS 98.

TABLE 15   Prevalence of contracts

Status	Count	Valid Percent
Working with contract	63	15
Working without contract	360	85
Total	423	100

Source: Greater Cairo Survey data files.

The data show that most workers enjoy a relatively long-term and stable relationship with their employers, despite the lack of a contract. The majority of workers (68.6%) were hired to work on a permanent basis, and two-thirds (66.7%) had been working for one year or more. On the other hand, 31.4% of labor is either seasonal or temporary, and 20.3% of workers have been in their jobs for less than three months. Possible explanations for this phenomenon are that the informal market is a dynamic pool, characterized by the continuous movement of workers in and out of it and within its different ranks, and that the young age structure of workers strengthens the rate of movement.

TABLE 16 Workers' permanency in work, 1998

Status	Count	Percent
Permanent	289	68.6%
Seasonal	67	15.8
Temporary	67	15.6
Total	443	100.0

Source: Greater Cairo Survey data files.

TABLE 17 Work duration, all workers, 1998

Time categories	Count	Percent
Less than 3 months	84	20.3%
3 months -	16	4.1
6 months -	37	9.0
12 months -	41	10.1
24 months -	52	12.5
36 months -	182	44.1
Total	442	100.0

Source: Greater Cairo Survey data files.

Hours of work. Although work conditions are harder and less secure for informal workers, these workers spend longer hours on the job. This is true for both males and females. **Table 18** shows that, on average, informal workers spent 48.2 hours per week in work compared to 43.7 hours for their formal counterparts in 1988. The figures for 1998 reveal the same pattern, though the average number of working hours per week had increased for both formal and informal workers and for both sexes. Females spend less time at work than males, but the difference is smaller in informal work and narrowed from 1988 to 1998. Informal females workers worked 3.5 fewer hours than males in 1988 but just 1.7 fewer hours in 1998.

Social security coverage. One of the main determinants of workers being hired on a formal basis is their social security coverage. As **Table 19** shows, social security covers only one-quarter of the workers in Greater Cairo. It is clear that subscribing to a social security scheme is still not a widespread

TABLE 18   Average hours of work per week by formality status and gender, 1988 and 1998

Experience in years	1988		1998	
	Formal	Informal	Formal	Informal
Males	45.6	48.7	46.4	51.8
Females	38.0	45.2	39.4	50.1
Total	43.7	48.2	44.6	51.6
Sample size	*2,389*	*1,187*	*2,935*	*1,400*

Source: Greater Cairo Survey data files.

practice, and this small coverage means—among other things— that, although the majority of workers are permanent in their jobs, they are not secure about their future. In the case of retirement, illness, injury, or death, there is no compensation either to them or their families.

However, it is worth noting that 70.5% of workers who are covered by social security work in formal enterprises, and 76.3% of them are males. Like the data on contracts, these shares confirm the fact that abiding by the rules is more likely among formal enterprises.

Other issues of protection. Protection of persons working in small enterprises is not confined to social security coverage, contracts, and wages but extends to other aspects of safety. **Table 20** summarizes some of these additional coverages for the Greater Cairo area. Only 15.8% of entrepreneurs have medical coverage (the question was not asked about their workers). As to different industrial security precautions such as fire extinguishers, proper airing, and special safety measures for manufacturing/mining and other industrial activities, these are relatively limited.

Informal enterprises

As the previous discussion of the informal enterprise made clear, "informality" in business ownership or operation can be defined along several lines. There are official procedures to be complied with in business; among them are a license, commercial/industrial registration, and the payment of taxes according to regular accounts. If an entrepreneur complies with all procedures, he or she is assumed to have a formal enter-

TABLE 19 Workers' coverage by social security

Covered	Count	Percent
Yes	111	26.4%
No	312	73.6
Total	423	100.0

Source: Greater Cairo Survey data files.

TABLE 20 Availability of different safety precautions in Greater Cairo small enterprise sample

Precautionary item	Count	Percent
Medical coverage	91	15.8%
Availability of first aid kit	128	36.6
Industrial security	151	43.0
Industrial precautions	145	41.4

Note: Medical coverage is estimated for the community of entrepreneurs only (577 persons). The three last items are measured for the enterprises working inside establishments.

Source: Greater Cairo Survey data files.

prise. However, some informal enterprises comply with one or two legal procedures and some comply with none. In other words, there are degrees of informality.

The universe of firms identified in **Table 21** is sole proprietorships, partnerships, and limited liability companies to the main rules and regulations. Of these, 18.2% complied with all three main rules, meaning that 81.8% of small enterprises could be considered informal.

Table 22 compares the number of small economic units by male and female ownership and by formal/informal status between 1988 and 1998.

It shows that:

• The number of informal enterprises (2.8 million economic units) in 1998 was five times greater than the number of formal enterprises (about 550,000); informal enterprises represented 83.6% of the total number of small enterprises.

TABLE 21   Economic activity by number of legal procedures, 1998

Economic activity	Number of legal procedures				
	0	1	2	3	Total
Food, beverage, tobacco	13.0	8.7	43.5	34.8	100
Textiles	60.9	6.3	25.0	7.8	100
Wood and furniture	21.8	10.9	61.8	5.5	100
Paper products	0.0	0.0	33.3	66.7	100
Mineral non-metal	0.0	50.0	50.0	0.0	100
Chemicals	0.0	28.6	28.6	42.9	100
Basic metals	0.0	0.0	100.0	0.0	100
Metal and machinery	15.6	18.8	40.6	25.0	100
Other manufacturing	0.0	0.0	50.0	50.0	100
Total manufacturing	31.2	11.1	41.8	15.9	100
Electric, gas, water	100.0	0.0	0.0	0.0	100
General construction	0.0	0.0	100.0	0.0	100
Retail construction	16.9	5.1	71.2	6.8	100
Total construction	16.7	5.0	71.7	6.7	100
Wholesale trade	10.0	5.0	45.0	40.0	100
Retail trade	19.9	5.8	56.4	17.9	100
Hotels and restaurants	21.3	12.8	53.2	12.8	100
Total trade	19.7	6.3	55.8	18.2	100
Transportation	4.6	23.0	33.3	39.1	100
Communication	0.0	0.0	0.0	100.0	100
Total communication	4.5	22.7	33.0	39.8	100
Real estate and business services	10.8	37.8	21.6	29.7	100
Social services	25.0	21.2	34.6	19.2	100
Entertainment and cultural services	33.3	0.0	33.3	33.3	100
Personal services	22.1	19.8	50.0	8.1	100
Total services	23.4	19.9	44.0	12.8	100
Total	22.0	11.1	48.7	18.2	100

Source: Authors' calculations based on ELMS 98 data files.

- The total number of small enterprises grew by 13.2% between 1988 and 1998.

- Formal units increased between the two years by 8.7%, while informal units grew by 14.1%. These enterprises vary in size and therefore in their ability to employ workers.[15]

TABLE 22 Number of small economic units according to formality status and gender of owner, 1988 and 1998

Year	Formal			Informal			Total		
	Male	Female	Total	Male	Female	Total	Male	Female	Total
1988	400,985	101,340	502,325	2,031,219	401,303	2,432,522	2,432,204	502,643	2,934,847
1998	477,459	68,986	546,445	2,231,121	544,910	2,776,031	2,708,580	613,896	3,322,476
% change	19.1%	-32.0%	8.7%	9.8%	35.8%	14.1%	11.3%	22.1%	13.2%

Source: Authors' calculations based on ELMS 98 data files.

- Female owners of small formal enterprises had a rough time during the 1990s; their numbers dropped by 32.0%. Most new female entrants were informal entrepreneurs. Working informally thus offered a better and less costly survival mechanism.

- While the number of formal female entrepreneurs was falling, the number of informal female entrepreneurs jumped by 35.8%.

Formal male-owned units rose by 19.1%, compared to a 9.8% growth rate for male-owned informal units. This phenomenon should be considered from two aspects. First, the base of informal enterprises is still much larger than that of the formal ones; second, there is evidence indicating that small enterprises started operating at relatively larger sizes in the 1990s than during the 1980s, possibly growing too large to be included in the survey of small enterprises.

These results indicate a trend of increased informality in the Egyptian labor market, especially for the female labor force, which presumably has found it more difficult to access the private sector except through informal arrangements. This phenomenon coincides with the privatization process, the socioeconomic male bias that is evident in employment in the private sector, and the discouraging business environment.

The geographical distribution of informal economic units
The last decade witnessed several changes in the labor force growth rate, its ability to move between rural and urban areas, and its ability to move among the different kinds of economic activity:

- The labor force grew by 2.8% per annum between 1986 and 1996. The urban labor force grew by 2.58% per year and the rural labor force by 3.06%.

- There has been a continuous trend of movement toward non-agricultural activities. Over the last three censuses, employment in agricultural activities declined gradually from 47.6% of total employment in 1976 to 31.2% in 1996.

- There is clear trend of diminishing rural migration to urban areas; in fact, some estimates project that it has declined to practically zero or even reversed. The reasons for this trend include growing urban

TABLE 23   Change in geographical distribution of small enterprises by gender of owner and formality status, 1988 and 1998

	Formal			Informal		
Urban/rural	Male col %	Female col %	Total col %	Male col %	Female col %	Total col %
Urban 1988	71.2%	86.7%	74.4%	71.3%	59.3%	69.3%
Urban 1998	67.9	85.1	70.1	49.0	48.8	48.9
Rural 1988	28.7	13.2	25.6	28.6	40.6	30.6
Rural 1998	32.1	14.9	29.9	51.0	51.2	51.1
Total	100.0	100.0	100.0	100.0	100.0	100.0

Source: Authors' calculations based on ELMS 98 and LFSS 88 data files.

unemployment rates and the rising cost of living in urban areas relative to migrant wages. These combined factors—among other things—led to a change in the distribution of small and especially informal enterprises between rural and urban areas, as shown in **Table 23**. Specifically, the trend of movement of small enterprises is toward rural areas; this trend is more apparent in the case of informal enterprises; the number of informal male-owned enterprises has increased by a higher percentage in rural areas than the number of informal female-owned enterprises; and the tendency toward increasing concentration of informal economic units in rural areas is evidence of the undercurrents of continuous developments that are taking place in the Egyptian population, labor force, and labor markets.

The age of informal entrepreneurs
Since a relatively high percentage of small enterprise entrepreneurs are illiterate and therefore unable to find work in the public sector or in the formal private sector, the informal sector has presented a better and safer refuge.

Furthermore, the majority of entrepreneurs are poor individuals who either do not understand the legal procedures to license their enterprises and/or cannot afford to cover the costs of formalization. Because easy access to work, modest resources, limited initial capital, lack of access to formal credit, flexible location and markets, and dependence on family members characterize the informal sector, the age of informal entrepreneurs is likely to be younger than that of formal entrepreneurs. The data in **Table 24** bear this out:

- 1.4% of informal entrepreneurs are in the 6-14 age bracket, versus 0% among formal entrepreneurs.

- The highest frequency of informal entrepreneurs is found in a younger age bracket (30-39 years) than is the case for formal entrepreneurs (40-49 years).

- The tendency toward concentration in higher age brackets by formal entrepreneurs supports the view that ownership of a formal enterprise requires certain conditions such as knowledge of the different aspects of legal procedures, experience, capital accumulation, and an understanding of the market, which can only be acquired with time and age.

- Informal female entrepreneurs tend to fall in higher age brackets than males. This phenomenon might occur if early marriage age discourages younger females from working, while the high cost of living and raising children drives them to work later.

Certain changes took place in the context of age structure between 1988 and 1998:

- The highest concentration of all entrepreneurs was in the 20-29 age bracket in 1988. This concentration was more clearly accentuated among informal entrepreneurs, of whom 35.4% were in this age category. The change over time led to a rise in the frequency of entrepreneurs within a higher age level (30-39 years). This change could be explained by the need to accumulate more capital in order to be able to venture into an independent business and the necessity of acquiring more experience to be able to survive market complexities and drops.

- The number of child entrepreneurs in the informal sector rose from 0.89% in 1988 to 1.4% in 1998. This trend, though relatively limited, may be a reflection of growing needs within poor families driving children to work at an earlier age.

TABLE 24   Age structure of small entrepreneurs by gender and formality status, 1998

Age group	Formal			Informal		
	Male	Female	Total	Male	Female	Total
6-11	0.0	0.0	0.0	0.1	0.3	0.1
12-14	0.0	0.0	0.0	1.3	1.1	1.3
15-19	10.9	9.9	10.8	8.8	4.2	7.9
20-29	20.3	23.1	20.6	22.9	20.2	22.3
30-39	16.3	30.8	18.2	22.9	34.3	25.1
40-49	28.3	24.4	27.7	21.3	21.7	21.4
50-59	15.3	6.1	14.2	14.0	13.3	13.8
60-64	4.23	5.7	4.4	3.6	2.1	3.3
65 and over	4.6	0.0	4.1	5.0	2.7	4.5
Total	100.0	100.0	100.0	100.0	100.0	100.0

Source: ELMS 98 data files.

Economic activities of informal enterprises

Economic activities vary according to formal/informal status and gender (**Table 25**). While formal-status males are more concentrated in three main activities—namely trade, manufacturing, and services—informal male entrepreneurs are more dispersed among economic activities. Formal female entrepreneurs are concentrated mostly in two activities, services and trade, while informal female entrepreneurs operate in three main activities: trade, services, and manufacturing.

Comparing the present distribution of informal units to their distribution in 1988 (not shown in table) reveals a move out of manufacturing (37.5% in 1988) and trade (44% in 1988) and into services (10.9% in 1988). The trend toward less investment in manufacturing in the informal sector could be due to the expensive cost of investing and the need for acquisition of technology and know-how to become competitive. At the same time, the intensive growth in demand for different and new types of services may have encouraged the emergence of new service enterprises. It should be emphasized, though, that informal activities tend to be on a smaller scale than formal ones and are conducted in several cases outside establishments, e.g., itinerant retail trading of vegetables, fruits, or newspapers and mobile repair work such as plumbing, electrical, painting, and shoe repair. Manufacturing activities might include food processing, metal work, textile production, furniture production, and creation of different wood and paper products.

A survey conducted in Greater Cairo in 1998 covering a sample of 577 economic units, of which informal units represented 82% of the total, revealed similar characteristics with regard to age structure, economic activity, and educational attainment levels. This survey also found that economic units performing outside establishments accounted for 40% of total enterprises, and the number of units operating at home were close to 6% of all enterprises (El Mahdi and Powell 1999, 8-12).

Active labor market policy

The recessionary climate that started at the end of 1997 took a direct toll on the performance of the labor market and led to a continuous growth in unemployment rates. The insufficient demand for workers and the growing numbers of unemployed put substantial economic and social pressures on the Egyptian government.

In its attempt to deal with the problem, the prime minister declared, in his presentation of the Government Program in December 1999, that all efforts would be paid to create maximum employment opportunities. To realize this goal, around 650,000 work opportunities were to be created through the public sector, the private sector, the Social Fund for Development (SFD, described on the following pages), the information and communication sector, and the service sector (El Ehwany and El Laithy 2001).

The launching of the National Employment Program in mid-2000 followed this statement. The NEP consisted of five main components:

- the emergency employment scheme,

- the creation of a national training fund,

- the reformation of labor market institutions, especially among service providers,

- implementation of an informal-sector strategy, and

- the strengthening of the labor market information system.

However, the launch of the new program was not followed by serious implementation efforts.

One year later, the state budget of 2001/2002 reiterated the necessity of providing 700,000 jobs annually at the cost of LE 1.7 billion. In July 2001, the government introduced the "government employment scheme," intended to provide 800,000 work opportunities per year.

The different announcements were associated with the implementation of several employment programs by various ministries, the SFD, and nongovernmental organizations. The most important players in these efforts are described on the following pages:

Ministry of Manpower and Migration
In the past, this ministry played a major role in distributing new graduates among the different government offices, state-owned enterprises, and economic authorities. This role has diminished substantially since the mid-1980s. The new role of the ministry is limited to its attempts to create a link between available job opportunities, whether in the public or private sector, and the registered unemployed. The ministry has started lately to issue a monthly *National Employment Bulletin*, in which information regarding new opportunities is published on a regular basis.

Ministry of Social Affairs (MOSA)
MOSA acts through several programs (such as PFS; see below) to help poor families, youth, and females become engaged in productive activities (MOSA 1998).

Productive Families Scheme (PFS)
PFS is a social project designed to develop families' economic resources by putting to good use the potential of family members within their own households. It allows them access to production advances in small-size and environmental industries and handicrafts, whereby raw materials are manufactured into products needed by home-based and foreign markets. Thus, households move from receiving assistance to becoming productive units.

Training services. PFS provides training services through 3,474 centers, staffed by more than 5,700 trainers, spread all over the country. Some were established through self-financing efforts and others were financed through the MOSA investment plan.

Marketing services. Through this project, MOSA provides marketing services to families to display their products to the public in permanent marketing exhibitions set up in well-situated commercial areas.

Vocational skills formation. The vocational skills formation scheme targets youth who have completed or dropped out of the basic education stage by providing them with vocational skills of a productive nature appropriate to their aptitude. The plan also seeks to improve social behavior and provide youth with a degree of learning that ensures non-regression to illiteracy.

At present, vocational formation programs are being implemented by MOSA in cooperation with PFS and other NGOs. There is also an ambitious plan in the pipeline in cooperation with local businesspersons to upgrade vocational formation centers in the various governorates. Each center will be concerned with a specific vocation or trade such as carpentry, painting, needlework, welding, car mechanics, electro-mechanics, etc.

Ministry of Local Administration (MLA)

The MLA has an ongoing program called Shrouk, or the Egyptian National Integrated Rural Development Program (MLA 1998). It represents a new era of comprehensive political and objective vision stemming from people's participation to help them improve the quality of life in rural areas, with some necessary support by governmental resources.

Empowerment of Egyptian village communities is considered by SHROUK as the goal and means of sustained rural development. It aims at optimum utilization of human, material, and institutional resources by and for citizens living in rural areas. Community members in rural areas assess and measure their resources, prioritize their own needs, plan their future, and carry out and evaluate the output of their efforts by themselves. Village plans are multidimensional, reflecting local community needs in terms of physical infrastructure, social services, and economic opportunities. The program is trying to offer job opportunities to the rural unemployed.

Ministry of Communication and Ministry of Youth

These ministries offer training opportunities to new graduates and youth to help upgrade their skills to meet the needs of the changing labor market.

Social Fund for Development

Presidential Decree No. 40 of 1991 established the Social Fund for Development (SFD 1999; El Laithy 1999). It is financed by the Egyptian government in cooperation with the World Bank/International Development Agency, Arab Funds, the European Union, the German Financial Corporation via KFW, and multinational and bilateral donors.

SFD was established with three main objectives:

1. to help reduce poverty through supporting employment generation and community development efforts;

2. to reduce the negative impact of privatization, especially where redundant workers are concerned;

3. to provide assistance to Egyptians returning from the Gulf.

Over phase II of operations, the SFD provided LE 2.1 billion for its programs. They include the Small Enterprise Development Organization (SEDO), the Public Works Program (PWP), the Community Development Program (CDP), the Human Resources Development Program (HRDP), and the Institutional Development Program.

Recent data indicate that the SFD has been able to create 701,000 jobs (540,000 permanent jobs and 161,000 temporary jobs) during the 1992-2003 period through its different programs, especially the small and micro-finance lending program.

Despite these efforts of the government to create employment, the problem of growing unemployment persists. Several explanations have been mentioned in this respect:

The inappropriate macroeconomic policy that has been adopted since implementation of the ERSAP. The main goals of the policy were to achieve monetary and fiscal stability through implementation of an "austerity" economic stabilization program. Consequently, the budget deficit, inflation rates, and the balance-of-payments deficit were reduced; the interest rate, the exchange rate, and different prices were liberalized; and the privatization program was initiated. The contractionary fiscal and monetary policies succeeded in realizing their different goals at the expense of employment. As Samir Radwan put it:

> Traditional contractionary macroeconomic policies have always viewed the situation in terms of a trade-off between employment and inflation. The prescription was generally in favour of controlling inflation, in view of its negative impact on growth, even if it leads to unemployment.
>
> There is an emerging consensus that this argument should be turned on its head by making employment the central objective of the macroeconomic policies. (Radwan 2002, 17)

The limited skills and low productivity of new graduates, whether from universities or technical education. The educational curricula do not prepare students to the levels of skill required by private-sector companies. New graduates are not equipped with the advanced abilities that will fit them easily into the modern economy. Until now, no special progress has been achieved in the area of technical high school education or in most of the special programs offered through the government training centers. However, preliminary work on the certification of several professions and handicraft skills is under way. This project is conducted under the direction of the SFD.

The failure to consider the employment component as a special target or serious option in subsequent investment policies and laws. All investment policies, laws, and incentives that have been adopted in Egypt since the mid-1970s have failed to contain any fiscal or tax incentives that were employment sensitive; in other words, they did not encourage investments that tended to be more labor intensive. In addition, the old as well as the new labor law made it difficult for an investor to fire workers if work conditions made it necessary. Therefore, new investments were and are still usually capital intensive, and economic growth has been primarily capital intensive rather than labor intensive (Keller and Nabli 2002, 8).

The impact of the ongoing recession and the economy's failure to absorb growing numbers of workers. As the recession evolved, growing numbers of private companies downsized, and a growing number of companies went bankrupt. This situation preempted efforts to generate jobs by relying on large private-sector companies. Both the government and the informal private sector became the only remaining possibilities for finding jobs for the unemployed. However, the government is restricted by the growing budget deficit, and the informal private sector is limited by low demand in the market; thus, any jobs that are generated in the informal economy are usually associated with low wages.

Conclusion

The analysis in this chapter reveals the major role played by the informal sector in employment provision, income generation, and training. The role of the informal economy is not confined to marginal activities: it operates in all economic areas, employs workers and entrepreneurs from different educational backgrounds, and acts as a pool for trained workers who are demanded by the formal sector.

The status of informality is associated with lower wages and relatively insecure work conditions. The reasons of informality are numerous, although two factors seem to play a relevant role in this respect.

First, the institutional and legal framework in which small and micro enterprises operate is not encouraging for entrepreneurs. It does not help them register their economic units and thus become integrated in the formal economy. In fact, the transactions costs of complying with procedures are excessive, and they force the entrepreneur to operate informally, hire workers without contracts, and work without subscribing to the social security system.

In addition, the institutional and legal framework does not recognize the needs of small enterprises for technical support and fiscal incentives.

Second, the economic reform that has taken place since the early 1990s reduced the government's role in employment creation, a change that in turn left a growing responsibility to be carried out by the private sector. It was expected that the modern, large, and formal sector would assume this role, but the data reveal otherwise. The structural change did not have the expected favorable effects on the ability of modern large companies to generate employment. Furthermore, the recession that began later in the 1990s placed the goal even further out of reach. The growth rate of employment in the modern formal private sector is limited; it did not exceed 1-1.5% annually during the period 1988-98, while it exceeded 3% in the informal sector in the same period.

Obtaining a formal job is usually associated with having "helpful connections" that can ensure a secure work opportunity. Accessing informal employment is relatively easier, as data seem to indicate. Seeking work in the informal sector is therefore a result of several combined factors:

Skills mismatch, especially where illiterates and those with modest educational backgrounds are concerned. The formal private sector demands more for skillful and better-educated labor. Thus, the informal sector represents a reasonable refuge for unskillful labor, as it offers jobs, though low paid, and provides workers with new skills.

Low demand, in both the formal public and private sectors, which was deepened by the "austerity" structural adjustment program. The investment rate during the 1990s until 2002 did not exceed 19% of GDP, a definite drop compared to the 1980s when the investment rate ranged between 22% and 29% annually.

The unfavorable investment climate, which is created by the continual changing of laws; the lack of transparency and vision where investment policy is concerned; the cumbersome legal procedures of business establishment, operation, and exit; lengthy dispute settlement mechanisms; and delays in the profit transfers of foreign investors. While other developing countries in the region and elsewhere were fiercely competing for foreign direct investment by introducing vigorous changes and improvements to their institutional and legal structures, the process of change in Egypt was slow, helping to diminish the amount of inflowing FDI and the volume of domestic investment at large.

The unfavorable business climate did not only repel the formal private sector (national and foreign) but helped to strengthen the informal sector, particularly the small businesses therein. Whereas large companies were fairly surrounded by relatively encouraging laws, tax incentives, and financial access to credit and various facilities in the new industrial cities, no robust and encouraging business set-up existed to support the real "infant enterprises." This situation resulted in a tendency to act informally to evade costs, complexities in procedures, the high tax burden, and all other unaffordable expenses.

Therefore, the investment climate, the social security system, and the tax treatment of small and micro enterprises have to be revisited to help improve labor market conditions and encourage more investment and growth.

The government recently submitted to Parliament a new small and micro enterprise law that is supposed to improve the business climate for those enterprises, offer some fiscal incentives and government procurement conditions, and provide land for small business establishments.

Yet the training component is still in need of serious restructuring and redesign before it can meet the changing and sophisticated market needs of more skillful labor. So far neither the students graduating from secondary technical schools nor most of those who receive specialized training in public- or private-sector training centers are equipped with the necessary international and competitive skills. Thus, the responsibility for training development depends on the active and joint participation of both the public and private sectors.

STATISTICAL APPENDIX TABLE A1   Distribution of NAWW by gender and formality

	Formal			Informal			Total male	Total female	All
	Male	Female	Total	Male	Female	Total			
Distribution of NAWW by gender and formality									
1988	3,103,575	1,036,015	4,139,590	2,274,519	329,812	2,604,331	5,378,094	1,365,827	6,743,921
1998	4,764,183	1,657,305	6,421,488	3,063,238	340,732	3,403,970	7,827,421	1,998,037	9,825,458
Change	53.5%	60.0%	55.1%	34.7%	3.3%	30.7%	45.5%	46.3%	45.7%
Distribution of private NAWW by gender and formality									
1988	416,466	103,843	520,309	2,019,201	253,232	2,272,433	2,435,667	357,075	2,792,742
1998	664,542	108,459	773,001	2,961,415	302,541	3,263,956	3,625,957	411,000	4,036,957
Change	59.6%	4.4%	48.6%	46.7%	19.5%	43.6%	48.9%	15.1%	44.6%

Source: Authors' analysis of ELMS 1998 and LFSS 1988.

Endnotes

1.   The informal economy is defined explicitly in the first section of this chapter.

2.   The figures mentioned here refer to a large definition of economic activity that includes participation in market activities and subsistence activities (e.g., agriculture and animal husbandry for own consumption).

3.   Real wage changes are calculated on the base of nominal wages provided by the Central Agency for Public Mobilization and Statistics (CAPMAS) Establishment, Wages, and Hours of Work surveys (EWHW) and on the consumer price index of the IMF. These surveys take into account only wages of the public sector (government and public enterprises) and private-sector firms employing 10 workers or more.

4.   Beginning in 1996 in the CAPMAS, an individual receiving any kind of income, even though not working or looking for work, was no longer considered to be unemployed.

5.   The differences between LFSS figures and the two special rounds are due to differences in definitions of economic activity.

6.   El Mahdi, the Micro and Small Enterprise Survey 2003 dataset.

7.   See Table 1.

8.   The GCSS98 was conducted under the auspices of the Social Research Center in the American University in Cairo in June 1998.

9.   El Mahdi and Powell (1999).

10.   This variable has been defined as the difference between the current age of the individual and his age when he first entered the labor market. It does not take into account the potential number or years spent outside the labor market or in unemployment between the two dates.

11.   However, this result also partly reflects the age distribution of formal and informal workers. Indeed, as shown in Table 2, informal workers are younger than their formal counterparts, and this difference obviously affects the average years of experience.

12.   As for wages, we will use the ELMS 98 data to show wage differentials on the country level.

13.   Regular workers are either permanent or temporary workers. Real wages have been calculated using the inflation factor of 3.16 from 1988 to 1998, from IMF data.

14.   Gender wage ratios express female wages as a percent of male wages.

15.   The distinction between small and larger enterprises is based on the legal status of the enterprise. Therefore, only sole proprietorships and partnerships are considered as small (El Mahdi and Powell 1999).

References

Abdel-Khalek. G. 2001. *Stabilization and Adjustment in Egypt: Reform or De-Industrialization?* Edward Elgar.

Arntz, M., and R. Assaad. 2002. "Constrained Geographical Mobility and Gendered Labor Market Outcomes Under Structural Adjustment : Evidence From Egypt."

Ash, N. 1993. "Egypt Exploits Its Gulf War Bonus." *Euromoney*, April, pp. 138-41.

Assaad, R. 2002. "Transformation of the Egyptian Labor Market." In Ragui Assaad, ed., *The Egyptian Labor Market in an Era of Reform.* Cairo: American University.

Central Authority for Public Mobility and Statistics (CAPMAS). 2002.

Charmes, J. 1998. "Informal Sector, Poverty and Gender: A Review of Empirical Evidence". Background paper for the World Development Report 2001.

Central Bank of Egypt (CBE). *Annual Report.* Various issues.

CBE. *Economic Bulletin.* Various issues.

CBE. *Annual Economic Review.* Various issues, 1992-98.

Egyptian Cabinet Information and Decision Support Center (ECI & DSC). *Monthly Economic Bulletin*, Cairo.

Egyptian Ministry of Public Enterprise Sector (MPES). 1998. "Privatization Program Performance From the Start to 24-5-1998." Cairo: MPES.

El Ehwany, N., and El Laithy. 2001. "Poverty, Employment, and Policy Making in Egypt." Cairo: ILO, p. 18.

El Ehwany, N., and M. Metwally. 2001. "Labor Market Competitiveness and Flexibility in Egypt." Center for Economic and Financial Research Studies, Research Projects Volume 11. Cairo.

El Khawaga, L. 2003. "Labor and Human Resource Development." In *Egypt Country Profile*. Cairo: ERF, forthcoming.

El Laithy, H. 1999. *Evaluating the Social Fund for Development Programs to Alleviate Poverty*. Socioeconomic Policies and Poverty Alleviation Programs in Egypt Conference, organized by CEFRS, SFD, UN and SRC-AUC, Cairo, October 16-17.

El Mahdi, A. 2002, "The Labor Absorption Capacity of the Informal Labor Market in Egypt." In R. Assaad, ed., *The Egyptian Labor Market in an Era of Reform.* Cairo: American University of Cairo Press.

El Mahdi, A., and K. Powell. 1999. "The Small Entrepreneurs in Greater Cairo Community, With Special Reference to Gender and Formality." Cairo: American University, Social Research Center.

El Mahdi, A., and A. Mashhour. 1994. *The Informal Sector in Maarouf District.* Cairo: National Center for Social and Criminal Studies.

El Refaie, F. 2001. "The Combination of Monetary Policy and Fiscal Policy in Egypt." Working Paper No. 54. Cairo: ECES.

El Samalouty, G. 2003. "Fiscal Reform in Egypt: Policy and Institutional Challenges." Proceedings of the conference, "Institutional and Policy Challenges Facing the Egyptian Economy," organized by CEFRS and USAID, Cairo.

El-Said, M. 2003. "The Twin Crises: Recession and Foreign Exchange." Paper presented at the conference, "Rising to the Challenge: International Crises and Economic Management in Egypt," organized by CEFRS and USAID, Cairo.

Fergany, N. 1998. "Human Capital and Economic Performance in Egypt." Working Paper. Cairo: Al Mishkat Centre for Research.

Field, M. 1995. "The Slow Road to Privatization". *Euromoney,* Middle East.

Hassan, M. 2003. "Can Monetary Policy Play an Effective Role in Egypt?" Working Paper No. 84. Cairo: ECES.

International Organization for Migration (IOM). 2003. *Contemporary Egyptian Migration 2003.*Geneva, Switzerland.

Keller, J., and M. Nabli. 2002. "The Macroeconomics of Labor Market Outcomes in MENA Over the 1990s: How Growth Has Failed to Keep Pace With a Burgeoning Labor Market." Working Paper No. 71. Cairo: ECES, p. 8.

Kheir-El-Din, H. and S. El-Shawarby. 2003. "Trade and Foreign Exchange Regime in Egypt: A Policy Reform in Egypt." Proceedings of the conference, "Institutional and Policy Challenges Facing the Egyptian Economy," organized by CEFRS and USAID, Cairo.

Middle East Executive Reports. 1992. "Forecasts—Part One: Current Situation." Vol. 15, No. 2, February, pp. 8-12.

Ministry of Foreign Trade (MOFT). 2003. *Egypt 2003.* Cairo.

Ministry of Local Administration (MLA). 1998. *Organization for the Reconstruction and Development of the Egyptian Village.* Cairo: MLA.

Ministry of Social Affairs (MOSA). 1998. *Goals, Scope of Work, and Main Activities.* Cairo: MOSA Minister's Bureau, Information Unit.

PCSU (Privatization Coordination Support Unit). 2002a. *Labor Restructuring & Privatization: A Study of the Early Retirement Program.* Special study prepared for USAID by CARANA Corporation.

PCSU. 2002b. *Privatization in Egypt, Quarterly Review.* Prepared for USAID by CARANA Corporation.

Radwan, S. 2002. "Employment and Unemployment in Egypt: Conventional Problems, Unconventional Remedies." Working Paper No. 70. Cairo: ECES.

Roads, S. 1997. *Investing in Egypt.* London: Committee for Middle East Trade, June.

Said, M. 2002. "A Decade of Rising Wage Inequality?" In Ragui Assaad, ed., *The Egyptian Labor Market in an Era of Reform.* Cairo: American University.

Social Fund for Development (SFD). 1999. *Annual Report.* Cairo: SFD.

Timewell, S. 1991. "Egypt: It Is Time to Start Letting Go." *Banker,* Vol. 141, No. 758, July, pp. 47-48.

U.S. Department of the State. 1994. *Egypt Economic Policy and Trade Practices*. Washington, D.C.: State Department, February.

World Bank. 2001. *Egypt: Social and Structural Review.* Report No. 22397 EGT. Washington, D.C.: World Bank.

Youssef, S. 1996. "Structural Reform Program of Egyptian State-Owned Enterprises: Current Impact and Future Prospects." *Journal of Management Development*, Vol. 15, No. 5, May, pp. 88-100.

CHAPTER 2

Formal and informal employment in El Salvador: A study of labor development

by Edgar Lara López[1]

Introduction

Since the early 1980s, the disparate economies of Latin America have followed similar economic paths. Most countries have focused their efforts on promoting international trade and reducing the role of the state in economic affairs by limiting government intervention to the social and legal spheres. "Faith in the market" has become the paradigm for economic progress and the efficient distribution of resources.

In El Salvador, economic policy inspired by faith in the free market has been realized for the past decade through adjustment and stabilization reforms. These reforms have promoted free trade, a non-productive state, privatization of public services, an open financial system, a revamped tax code, indiscriminate and unilateral liberalization, a lowering of tariffs, an encouragement of exports through exchange rates, and more liberal importation policies.

Policy regarding the labor market has played a secondary role. In general the health of the labor market has been posited as a variable of automatic market adjustment, such that the creation of new jobs will result from economic growth created by exports and foreign investment. While labor market variables have not been explicitly included in recent reforms, it is undeniable that the stagnation of wages and the weakening of labor rights continue to be significant factors in preventing many businesses and sectors from integrating into the new international economic order. Furthermore, the labor market has not truly benefited from recent positive economic indicators — while unemployment has seemingly slowed, underemployment and informal employment have swelled, especially in recent years.

This chapter seeks to understand the changes and characteristics of formal and informal employment in El Salvador. It is divided into seven sections: the first analyzes El Salvador's macroeconomic context, the second examines the performance of the labor market, the next seeks to develop a methodology for a more precise definition of formal and informal employment, sections four and five discuss the characteristics of formality and informality, the sixth section offers a series of recommendations for labor market development, and the final section presents our conclusions.

Macroeconomic context in El Salvador

Economic reforms: adjustment and stabilization
The growth plan
El Salvador has undergone significant social, economic, and political changes in recent years that have altered the economy's global performance. Its macroeconomic results have been shaped by the economic reforms — structural adjustment and economic stabilization programs — implemented since the late 1980s.

These reforms were a response, in part, to the weakening of the Industrial Substitution for Imports (ISI), a protectionist plan characterized by significant state intervention in economic affairs. They were also a reaction to the need to reform existing national structures that were not conducive to new forms of global wealth accumulation. The reforms were undertaken by a right-wing government that came to power seeking to stem the economic crisis precipitated by the civil war[2] and an interventionist state.

Since 1989 and the presidency of Alfredo Cristiani,[3] economic policy in El Salvador has followed the recommendations of the "Washington Consensus," incorporating structural adjustment and economic stabilization policies. The former seek to reduce macroeconomic imbalances in variables such as inflation and the balance of payments through the liberalization of prices and trade. Structural adjustment programs are aimed at reforming the framework of the economic institution by liberalizing the economy (further opening and deregulating the market) and redefining the role of the state.

Both of these programs present as their ultimate goal the economy's attainment of its growth potential, thereby ensuring the feasibility of a balance of payments and a consequent reduction of poverty. To this end, countries are encouraged to adopt the 10 components as outlined in the Washington Consensus: fiscal discipline, reforms in public spending, tax reform, liberalization of interest rates, competitive exchange rates, trade liberalization, liberalization of foreign investment, privatization, deregulation, and intellectual property protection.[4]

In order to implement this new economic program, political alliances were established between the government, the private sector, and international financial bodies (the World Bank, the International Monetary Fund, and the Inter-American Development Bank), with the support of the United States via the U.S. Agency for International Development (Segovia 2002). The implementation of these reforms was a condition of loans and other economic aid to be provided by these organizations; in other words, the new economic direction required that the government maneuver to alter the entire scope of economic policy.

The application of these stabilization and adjustment reforms in El Salvador can be broken down into three stages (**Figure A**), all of which would theoretically bring about increased growth potential for the economy; the possibility of a balanced budget; stability in a range of macroeconomic variables; and, in the social arena, poverty reduction.

The third stage of reforms includes the most recently implemented measures as well as those that are currently underway. The free trade agreements have constituted the principal means for accelerating the process of trade liberalization, given that over the course of two years the government ratified four treaties (with Mexico, the Dominican Republic, Chile, and Panama) and is in the process of negotiating accords with the United States, Canada, and the Free Trade Area of the Americas.

As for the privatization of public services and labor flexibility, proposals have been put forth to privatize the health sector and deregulate the labor market. For example, in 2003 the government sought to reform the health sector, but was met with resistance by doctors and workers at the Salvadoran Social Security Institute, who claimed that the measures were a cover for beginning the process to privatize the health sector.

FIGURE A   Facets of structural adjustment and economic stabilization

Economic reforms

At a more detailed level, the most important reforms under the growth plan based on adjustment and stabilization are:

• *Exchange policy.* In 1990 a new liberal exchange system was adopted for the colón with respect to the dollar, as the former continued to depreciate. From 1993 to 2000, the exchange rate remained steady at around 8.75 colones to one U.S. dollar. In 2001, with the Monetary Integration Law, a new exchange policy required that "the exchange rate between the colon and the U.S. dollar shall be fixed and unalterable at 8.75 to $1.00."[5]

In addition, the new law established that the colon would circulate permanently side-by-side with the dollar, with both currencies being legal tender. In reality, though, the policy has created an accelerated process of dollarization, with a sharp drop in the circulation of the colon and, in essence, a substitution of one currency for another.

While dollarization was not one of the explicit recommendations of the Washington Consensus or structural adjustment policies, it is clear that the measure was taken to create a climate more conducive to external investment and to further link the banking establishment to foreign loans in dollars. These steps ultimately force the export sector to operate in dollars in order to remain competitive.

- *Fiscal policy and privatization.* Several reforms were introduced in the fiscal arena, specifically with regard to tax structures; these included a tax on aggregate wealth, rent tax modifications; elimination of the inheritance tax and export tax; the streamlining of fund transfers; and the modernization of administration of the Ministry of Housing.

  In terms of the reduction of the state's role and involvement in the economy, the most important measures concerned the privatization of businesses and public services. In the 1980s, the previously private central bank was nationalized, due to high debt levels, but in 1990 it was reformed and streamlined in preparation for its sale to the private sector; this occurred in 1991, with great effect on interest rates and credit lines. The central bank subsequently intervened in the open market in order to maintain a stable amount of money in circulation and control the types of exchange (Alas 2002).

  The government privatized the distribution of electrical energy in 1992, telecommunications in 1997, and the pension fund soon thereafter. The government also turned over to the private sector free-trade zones, a hotel, the Maya concrete company, and food factories and storage facilities.

  Currently, the state's role has been relegated to that of supporting the most vulnerable sectors, maintaining and modernizing infrastructure, and creating a favorable climate for foreign investment.

- *Trade liberalization.* Government efforts in this area have primarily focused on commercial policy aimed at promoting exports, the sector that currently receives the most benefits. For instance, it reaps benefits as outlined by the Caribbean Basin Initiative and the Generalized Preference System; they both allow duty-free export of certain agricultural and manufacturing products to the United States.

  Internally, throughout the 1990s to the present, the government established unilateral tax relief on prime materials, intermediary goods, and capital; removed import permits, licenses, and certificates; rolled back taxes; and launched "draw back"[6] finance programs and the Free Trade Zone Law (Alas 2002).

Compared to the 1990s, the current rate of trade liberalization is more intensive, due to free trade agreements that in addition to opening the commercial goods sector also aim to liberalize services, the public sector, and capital markets.

After almost 14 years of adjustment and stabilization, it is important to step back and ask some basic questions. What have been the macroeconomic results of the reforms? Has El Salvador reached its growth potential?

Evolution of the economy in the context of adjustment and reform

Production and prices

During the 1980s, the Salvadoran economy experienced its lowest levels of gross domestic product and real GDP growth, with an average drop of 1.7% and 0.4%, respectively. These negative growth rates can be attributed to two chief causes: the civil war throughout the decade, which led to a drop in GDP of 10.5% (11.5% per capita) in 1981, and the disintegration of trade policies between Central American countries as outlined in the Central American Common Market.

In the early 1990s, the country began to see levels of growth similar to those of the 1970s, i.e., average rates of GDP growth around 4%. Overall growth during this decade can be broken into two phases: relatively fast growth in the 1989-95 period, followed by a slowdown from 1996 through 2002 (**Figure B**). One might think that growth in the earlier period — an average annual rate of 4.9% — is a sign of the effectiveness of economic adjustment policies. Yet much of the growth was due to the signing of Peace Accords, which significantly spurred the nation's economy. It's to be expected that after a period of crisis or recession — in El Salvador's case, a civil war — an economy will rebound.[7]

In the second half of the decade, the country experienced a significant economic deceleration, leading to an average annual drop in GDP of 2.7% and a drop of GDP per capital of 0.7%. This phase was concurrent with a period of reconstruction and rehabilitation, during which the burden of encouraging growth fell on the government's economic stabilization policy. It is evident from the slow rate of economic growth that these policies had a hard time creating sustained growth.

FIGURE B   Growth of GDP and GDP per capita

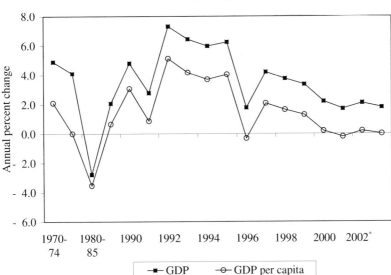

* Preliminary data.

Sources: CEPAL and BCR.

Moreover, measures aimed at reducing inflation, which were successful (**Figure C**), negatively affected economic growth.[8] A more conservative fiscal policy and stagnation in the minimum wage, aimed at controlling prices, stifled internal demand and consequently provoked a contraction of GDP (Segovia 2002, 132).

An important lesson is that while it may be necessary to take measures (including those intended to control inflation) to correct macroeconomic imbalances, such steps ought to be moderate, so that stabilization does not mean stagnation in economic growth and a deterioration of living conditions for workers.

Another problem evidenced by the Salvadoran economy is the concentrated nature of growth (see Appendix Table 3). Reforms have favored sectors involved with external trade, such as industrial manufacturing and profitable areas such as commerce and finance (Lara López 2002). These three sectors accounted for 58.6% of GDP in 2002.

During the period of adjustment and stabilization, goods production eroded, especially in farming and livestock. This sector's share of

FIGURE C   Inflation rates, 1994-2002 (annual change in the consumer price index)

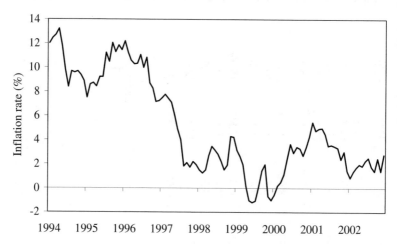

Sources: BCR.

GDP fell to 11.5% as of 2002, down from 19% in 1980. Industrial manu-facturing, on the other hand, saw considerable growth between 1989 and 2002, an average of 5%, and its share of GDP in 2002 reached 23.7%.

The importance of the manufacturing industry to GDP can be ex-plained by the performance and contribution of the assembly plant in-dustry. In 1990, this area accounted for 1.7% of manufacturing, whereas it now makes up 13.3% of industry and stands as the most dynamic area of the industrial sector. The share of assembly plants in overall GDP has grown considerably as well, from 0.4% in 1990 to 3.1% in 2001.

As we see in **Table 1**, the service sector's rate of production has been much more stable than that of the goods sector. In 2002, the ser-vice sector (both "basic services" and "other services") accounted for 54.5% of GDP; commerce and financial services were the dominant players. The significant contribution and dynamic nature of the service sector with regard to GDP serves to highlight the fact that the growth of the Salvadoran economy is dependent on services — a sector that is mostly disconnected from the rest of the economy.[9] It is noteworthy,

TABLE 1 GDP by economic sector (percentage)

Kind of economic activity	1980	1985	1990	1995	2000	2002
Goods	45.8%	43.1%	42.7%	38.9%	39.3%	39.7%
Agriculture, hunting, and forestry	19.0	18.6	17.1	13.6	12.3	11.5
Mining and quarrying	0.29	0.3	0.4	0.4	0.4	0.5
Manufacturing	22.9	20.7	21.7	21.2	23.0	23.7
Construction	3.7	3.5	3.5	3.7	3.6	3.9
Basic services	7.7%	8.4%	8.5%	8.0%	9.1%	9.5%
Electricity, gas, and water	0.9	1.1	1.2	0.5	0.6	0.6
Transport, storage, and communications	6.8	7.2	7.3	7.4	8.5	8.8
Others services	46.4%	48.5%	48.7%	46.8%	45.8%	45.0%
Wholesale and retail trade, restaurants, and hotels	17.2	18.4	18.1	20.4	19.8	19.7
Finance, insurance, and real estate	11.0	13.7	17.0	15.3	15.4	15.2
Community, social, and personal services	18.3	16.4	13.5	11.2	10.5	10.0
Total	100.0%	100.0%	100.0%	100.0%	100.0%	100.0%

Source: Author's analysis based on CEPAL and BCR data.

then, that the growth and dynamism of the financial sector has not translated into greater access to financial resources for other sectors. This is partly due to the fact that incentives are geared toward favoring tertiary activities.

The export sector

The Salvadoran economy's export sector is defined in terms of its commercial products and partnerships. Between 1989 and 2001, economic partnerships in El Salvador were significantly concentrated. Exchange with Europe deteriorated at the same time that interaction with America, especially the United States, grew (see Appendix Table 4). In 2001, 65.4% of total exports ended up in the United States. This commercial dependence on one country means that El Salvador is especially sensitive to internal or external changes in the U.S. economy.

The lack of diversity in the export sector is evidenced by the role of the assembly industry, which accounted for 57.6% of exports in 2001. Much of this activity is in clothing manufacturing, much of which is destined for the United States. Outside of this area, the majority of exports are accounted for by El Salvador's traditional main export: unroasted coffee.

In terms of the balance of trade (**Figure D**), measures taken to liberalize the commercial sector and promote export activities have not been able to reverse the trade deficit. Furthermore, the process of tariff reduction has resulted in greater dynamism for imports.

Due to the effect of family remittances, the trade deficit has not generated significant problems for the balance of payments. The increase in remittances during the 1990s has allowed external accounts to stabilize, and the commercial deficit has once again become manageable (Rubio Fabian and Lara López 2003). Between 1990 and 2001, remittances grew at an average annual rate of 21.9%. In 2002, they accounted for 13.5% of GDP.

Public finances

The second half of the 1990s saw a deterioration of public funding, which resulted in an increased fiscal deficit, growing internal and external debt, instability in revenues, a drop in the tax base, and diminished national savings (see Appendix Table 5). These last two variables, however, saw a slight improvement in 2002.

FIGURE D   Trade balance (in U.S. $ millions)

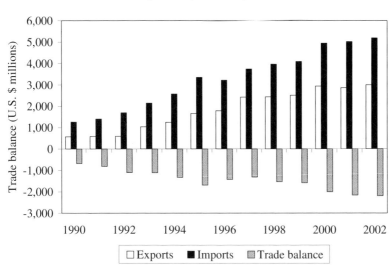

Sources: BCR.

The external debt of the non-financial public sector has grown considerably, representing some 20.8% of GDP in 1995 and growing to 27.3% in 2002. Total public debt (external and internal) has grown to account for 39.4% of GDP. El Salvador is reaching the point where it is beyond the sustainable limits of indebtedness, a serious situation that demands corrective measures.

The fiscal deficit has been another priority of adjustment policies. The goal is to have more control over the deficit, but in the past several years this has not occurred. The deficit has been unstable: in 2002 it was equivalent to 3.3% of GDP, whereas in 1995 it was only 0.1% Moreover, it is projected that the debt could grow considerably over the coming years, due to the commitments the government has made to the pension system, which over the next 15 years will be equivalent to 2% of GDP each year (UNDP 2003, 131-2).

The problems with the antiquated pension system, coupled with a drop in the tax base due to the promotion of the export sector (which began with unilateral tariff reduction but was accelerated by the Free Trade Agreements) have led to fiscal instability (**Table 2**). This situa-

TABLE 2   Tax revenue (percentage of participation)

Tax revenues	1990	1995	2000	2001	2002
Income	23.10	27.63	29.61	25.00	29.64
Patrimony	3.98	0.01	-	-	-
Property transfers	2.30	1.09	0.78	0.80	0.80
Imports	14.80	17.68	9.89	10.07	9.56
Exports	8.13	-	-	-	-
Value added tax	32.45	46.19	56.30	60.42	55.79
Consumption					
(special products)	15.19	7.34	3.42	3.43	4.11
Other	0.05	0.06	0.00	0.27	0.10
Total	100	100	100	100	100

Source: Author's analysis based on Ministry of Housing data.

tion has led to increased pressure for reforming the tax code, so that it yields increased public revenues, and rolling back the privatization or sale of state functions.

Looking at the structure of El Salvador's tax code shows that the tax reforms before and during the phase of adjustment and stabilization have tended to favor capital over labor and consumption, with the goal of attracting external investment. As Table 2 shows, taxes that fell on consumers and workers, such as income tax and the tax on aggregate value, generated 85.4% of tax revenues in 2002. In contrast, taxes on businesses and capital were minimal. Thus, the pressures to reduce the fiscal deficit have relied on raising taxes on consumption and work so as not to adversely burden capital.

Poverty and human development

In the 1990s the poverty rate[10] fell considerably, especially in urban areas (**Table 3**). Overall, poverty levels between 1992 and 2002 dropped by 22 percentage points, 23 points in urban areas and 16 points in rural areas. In 2002, 36.8% of households lived in poverty, 15.8% in extreme poverty and the remaining 21.0% in relative poverty.

However, there are some doubts as to the reliability of the poverty figure. The first incongruence relates to the link between economic growth and poverty; while it was expected that sluggish economic growth

TABLE 3 Households in poverty (percent)

Year	Total	Urban	Rural
1992	58.7	52.9	65.0
1992-93	57.5	50.5	65.3
1994	52.4	43.8	64.6
1995	47.5	40.0	58.2
1996	51.7	42.4	64.8
1997	48.1	38.7	61.6
1998	44.6	36.0	58.6
1999	41.3	33.9	56.4
2000	38.8	29.9	53.7
2001	38.8	31.3	48.5
2002	36.8	29.5	49.2

Source: Author's analysis based on Survey of Multi-Purpose Households data.

would have led to increased levels of poverty, this has not been the case (Lara López and Tolentino 2003). Second, the device for measuring poverty, the basic goods index, does not account for some basic needs it purports to cover.

There are other issues as well: the concentration of poverty in rural areas and the difficulty of measuring it casts further doubt on the official figures. Also, poverty in El Salvador disproportionately affects women: 42.9% of the population is poor, and of these 52.2% are women (see Appendix Table 7). In this sense, adjustment policies have affected men and women differently, leaving the latter more and more vulnerable.

According to the last United Nations Development Program Report on Human Development in El Salvador (UNDP 2003), the country improved its development index from 0.595 in 1975 to 0.726 in 2002. El Salvador ranks 105th out of 175 partially developed (as opposed to fully developed) countries, and it ranks second in Central America, behind Costa Rica (**Table 4**).

While in general terms the development index has improved, human development has been unequal over the 14 departments that make up the country (see Appendix Table 8). Progress has been concentrated in urban areas and among regions with industrial and assembly plants (San Salvador, La Libertad, and Cuscatlan).

TABLE 4   Human Development Index (HDI) rankings, 2001

Selected countries	HDI ranking	Development level
Costa Rica	42	High
El Salvador	105	Medium
U.S.	7	High
Egypt	120	Medium
Guatemala	119	Medium
Honduras	115	Medium
India	127	Medium
Nicaragua	121	Medium
Russia	63	Medium
South Africa	111	Medium

Source: UNDP (2003a).

Furthermore, any development as of 2002 has led to an increased concentration of wealth and greater gender inequality in the economic and political arenas, as evidence by the decline in the Index of Gender Strength between 1999 and 2002.

The decade of economic reforms has exacerbated wealth inequality. According to the UNDP's El Salvador report (2003), in 1992 the poorest 20% of households received 3.2% of national wealth, while the richest 20% accounted for 54.5% By 2002, these numbers had worsened, with the bottom fifth only receiving 2.4% and the wealthiest fifth almost 60%. This shows that not only has structural adjustment failed to ease the economic inequality in El Salvador, it has made it worse. In a general sense, then, the country has become less economically stable.

Labor market performance

Labor reforms in the context of adjustment and economic stabilization

In the first set of recommendations made by the "Washington Consensus" regarding economic growth and potential, labor was not a fundamental issue, and so the resulting reforms had no explicit labor component. Thus, any labor growth in recent years has been directly linked to those sectors targeted by the growth reforms, i.e., exports and foreign investment.

The absence of labor considerations in the stabilization programs does not mean that these programs haven't affected the labor situation in El Salvador, nor does it mean that there have been no labor reforms. The signing of the Peace Accords led to a series of labor reforms; while these reforms were intended to guarantee labor rights, they did so without addressing the structural problems of employment and unemployment. Rather, the reforms centered on guaranteeing the basic rights as prescribed by the International Labor Organization. Thus, between 1995 and 1996, several articles of the Labor Code were modified and 15 basic ILO agreements were ratified (Appendix Table 9), even aside from having to do with union freedoms (Appendix Table 10). In addition, a Labor Council was formed in 1994 to foster cooperation between employers, the government, and the labor sector.

As for wage reform, the government modified the minimum wage nine times between 1990 and 2003, but the adjustments were minimal and specific to certain sectors, areas of activity, or geographic regions. For instance, the most recent reform came after a five-year gap and only affected some sectors.

The most recent "Expanded Washington Consensus"[11] devoted some attention to the labor issue. The plan's proponents contend that labor reforms should be geared toward market flexibility, since the market's rigidity is thought to have hindered the performance of corporations, their ability to enter the international market, and their absorption of manual labor.

With the most recent wave of reforms in El Salvador, labor market flexibility has emerged as a key element if the country is to emerge from economic sluggishness. Companies trumpet the flexibility issue, consistently including it in their list of demands when negotiating with the government.

In 2000 and 2001 two key laws were proposed: a Special Law for Employment Renewal and an Emergency Law for Employment Renewal. Both seek to lower labor rights (currently regulated by the Labor Code) with regards to the work week, overtime, nighttime work, wages, and hiring practices; they would in fact legalize a flexibility within the labor market that already exists but is executed in violation of current regulations (Lara López and Tolentino 2003). By skirting the law, companies are vulnerable to demands from the labor sector — a weakness they would like to remedy.

In fact, flexibility practices in El Salvador have resulted mostly in the relaxation of monitoring, regulation, and application of labor law. This lax oversight is partly due to the weakness of the Labor and Social Services Ministry, which lacks the sufficient resources and political clout needed to effectively monitor and enforce labor legislation (FEPAD 2003, 20).

Within this context, the labor sector and human rights organizations have voiced persistent criticisms of the Labor and Social Services Ministry. A recent survey by Human Rights Watch, outlining how government institutions have failed to protect workers, concludes that:

> The Salvadoran government routinely fails its legal obligations with regards to the protection and promotion of workers human rights, in both the public and private sectors. Labor laws do not meet international standards, and that legislation which is in place is not effectively implemented. Abused workers who come to the Labor Ministry or legal system for protection have little chance of receiving aid. Employers find themselves slightly intimidated, but face little, if any, negative consequence as a result of human right violations to workers. Therefore, abuses to labor rights are common. Life for Salvadoran workers remains perilous, and it must be dealt with quickly, or workers will continue to sacrifice their rights in exchange for their paycheck. (Human Rights Watch 2003)

If reforms are to be had in El Salvador, it is critical that they be implemented with an eye toward equality between labor and capital. Reforms that continue to allow weak labor enforcement in favor of a pro-business model will be counterproductive. The objective of all labor reforms ought to be to improve conditions for El Salvador's working population.

Characteristics of unemployment

In the last 11 years (1991-2002) the open unemployment rate[12] has fallen by 28%, reaching a low of 6.2% in 2002. The drop in unemployment was widespread, occurring across geographic regions and both genders (**Table 5**). This trend is the result of an increased female presence in the workplace; overall stability in the global participation rate,[13] which remained around 50%, as well as slow growth in the working age popula-

TABLE 5   Rate of open unemployment

	Total			Men			Women		
Year	Total	Urban	Rural	Total	Urban	Rural	Total	Urban	Rural
1991	8.7%	7.9%	9.7%	9.0%	8.4%	9.4%	8.3%	7.2%	10.5%
1992	9.3	8.2	10.6	10.2	9.5	10.8	7.7	6.6	9.9
1993	9.9	8.1	12.0	11.8	9.6	13.6	6.8	6.3	7.8
1994	7.7	7.0	8.7	8.4	8.1	8.8	6.4	5.7	8.3
1995	7.6	7.0	8.6	8.7	8.6	8.8	5.9	5.0	8.0
1996	7.7	7.5	8.0	8.4	8.8	7.9	6.5	5.8	8.2
1997	8.0	7.5	8.7	9.5	9.0	10.1	5.3	5.5	4.7
1998	7.3	7.6	6.8	8.2	9.1	7.0	6.0	5.8	6.3
1999	7.0	6.9	7.0	8.5	8.9	7.9	4.6	4.6	4.7
2000	7.0	6.6	7.5	9.1	9.1	9.0	3.7	3.7	4.0
2001	7.0	7.0	7.0	8.1	8.7	7.4	5.2	4.9	6.0
2002	6.2	6.2	6.3	8.1	8.6	7.4	3.5	3.5	3.6

Source: Author's analysis based on Survey of Multi-Purpose Households data.

tion (see Appendix Table 11); and other factors that will be discussed further on.

The fact that the number of those in the workforce has not changed significantly, yet the mean working age has increased slightly, further exacerbates the unemployment situation. For example, between 1989 and 2001 the variations in the mean working age were around 3%, and the universal level of participation maintained an annual average of 52.7%. Consequently, during this 13-year period, unemployment remained steady at 7%.

The behavior of the mean working age and the global participation rate has meant that the economic slowdown has not had as much of an impact on unemployment levels as it might have otherwise. Generally, as an economy contracts, unemployment levels typically rise, as was the case in 1996 and 1997. Recently, though, slow growth in the workforce (as seen in the mean working age or the average working age), has lessened the pressure on employment levels.

The overall drop in unemployment affects the working population in rural and urban areas, and by gender, in unique ways. Rural areas have generally seen higher unemployment rates (with the exception of 1998). Nonetheless, rates have tended to converge; in the early 1990s rural unemployment was a full two points higher than that in urban areas, whereas it is currently just 0.1 point higher.

The higher rural unemployment rate is a result of economic development strategies that have favored urban activity, such as industry and exportation, at the expense of agriculture and other rural enterprises. The recent drop in rural unemployment may be explained by the migration to urban areas of rural workers, who are facing a crisis in the agricultural sector, most notably in the coffee industries.

With regard to gender, female unemployment from 1991 to 2002 fell by more than half, whereas the unemployment rate for men dropped by 10.1%. As seen in Table 5, by 2002 female unemployment had dropped to equal levels in rural and urban areas. The large drop in urban unemployment is a reflection of the large increase in jobs in urban areas in recent years. From 1991 to 2002, the average unemployment rate for women was 5.8%, in stark contrast to the 9.0% rate for men.

While a lower unemployment rate for women may be due to a change in the types of jobs available — the textile industry in particular has grown considerably — low unemployment does not always mean better economic conditions. Indeed, poverty levels among women remain high, since many of the new jobs are low paying and often unregulated.

The face of unemployment has changed considerably in El Salvador in recent years. No longer is unemployment primarily concentrated among the uneducated population. Indeed, for those without any formal education, the unemployment rate dropped from 22.1% to 12.1% between 1994 and 2002 (**Table 6**). This decline may be due in great part to an overall drop in illiteracy and greater education reforms. However, unemployment has begun to affect those with higher levels of education: 25.7% of the unemployed population has an intermediate education, including 41.4% of women in this category and 21.0% of men.

Furthermore, unemployment greatly affects younger workers and recent entrants into the workforce. In 2002, those age 20-29 made up 42.1% of the unemployed population.

From the 1990s to the present, the agricultural sector has pushed workers out; in 1994, 33.7% of the unemployed population (equivalent to 54,677 people) came from this sector (Appendix Table 12), and in 2003 they represented 18.2%. The construction sector makes up a similar percentage of the unemployed; the 18.0% rate in 2003 was the highest yet, the result of the exhaustion of the reconstruction process following the earthquakes in January and February of 2001.

TABLE 6   Unemployed population by years of schooling

Years of education completed	1994		1998		2002	
	Number	Percent	Number	Percent	Number	Percent
Total	162,298	100.0	175,723	100.0	160,192	100.0
None	35,888	22.1	21,013	12.0	19,410	12.1
1 - 3	26,973	16.6	25,691	14.6	22,075	13.8
4 - 6	33,289	20.5	39,421	22.4	32,438	20.2
7 - 9	27,257	16.8	35,227	20.0	30,511	19.0
10 - 12	28,991	17.9	41,199	23.4	41,160	25.7
13 and over	9,760	6.0	13,172	7.5	14,598	9.1
Others	140	0.1	..	..	..	..
Men	110,738	100.0	119,916	100.0	123,590	100.0
None	28,356	25.6	16,671	13.9	17,041	13.8
1 - 3	20,673	18.7	20,112	16.8	19,650	15.9
4 - 6	24,134	21.8	30,764	25.7	27,646	22.4
7 - 9	17,699	16.0	25,190	21.0	25,276	20.5
10 - 12	14,710	13.3	21,103	17.6	25,990	21.0
13 and over	5,026	4.5	6,076	5.1	7,987	6.5
Others	140	0.1	..	..	..	..
Women	51,560	100.0	55,807	100.0	36,602	100.0
None	7,532	14.6	4,342	7.8	2,369	6.5
1 - 3	6,300	12.2	5,579	10.0	2,425	6.6
4 - 6	9,155	17.8	8,657	15.5	4,792	13.1
7 - 9	9,558	18.5	10,037	18.0	5,235	14.3
10 - 12	14,281	27.7	20,096	36.0	15,170	41.4
13 and over	4,734	9.2	7,096	12.7	6,611	18.1
Others	..	..	..	..	..	..

Source: Author's analysis based on Survey of Multi-Purpose Households data.

Great numbers of jobs have also been lost in the manufacturing and commercial sectors, which include public works (including defense). Between 1994 and 2002, unemployment stemming from this sector rose steadily, totaling 49.1% and accounting for 3.3% of the unemployed population (5,238 people), 84% of whom are men.

The loss of jobs in the public works sector is tied to the rise in privatization under recent economic stabilization reforms. The privatization of the telecommunications and electric industries during the 1990s greatly affected public sector workers, especially men.

Unemployment in El Salvador appears to be short-lived, as evidenced by **Table 7**, which shows that, in 2002, 44.7% of the unemployed population had been searching for work for less than two months, an addi-

TABLE 7   Unemployed population by length of job search

Year	Less than 1 month	1-2 months	2-4 months	4 months- 1 year	1 year and over	Other
Total						
1994	20.0	13.0	12.2	11.3	7.6	35.9
1998	25.8	0.2	18.6	17.8	12.1	25.5
2002	25.6	19.1	13.4	4.5	0.3	37.1
Males						
1994	20.7	11.2	11.1	10.0	5.3	41.7
1998	26.0	0.2	19.0	15.6	10.0	29.1
2002	25.5	18.8	12.3	4.0	0.4	38.9
Females						
1994	18.6	17.0	14.5	14.1	12.5	23.3
1998	25.3	0.1	17.8	22.5	16.7	17.6
2002	25.6	20.3	16.8	6.2	-	31.1

Note: "Others" refers to those who have employment pending and those who do not seek work because they think it impossible to find or they do not know how to find it.

Source: Author's analysis based on Survey of Multi-Purpose Households data.

tional 17.9% less than a year, and 0.3% for a year or more. Nonetheless, a large segment of workers perceives a lack of jobs or are unsure of how to search for employment. Of this group — 37.1% of the unemployed in 2002 — this perception is much stronger among men, perhaps because, as was discussed earlier, many new jobs have been created in traditionally female areas of activity.

The lack of unemployment compensation, as well as the poor quality of life for those who are without work, leads many to reinsert themselves into the labor force as quickly as possible, without considering the conditions of the job they are taking or the other alternatives.

Characteristics of employment
Job creation
During the last nine years, employment rates have hovered around 92%, with a high in 2002 of 93.8% after three consecutive years at 93%. This modest increase, after several years of stagnation, is evidence of the difficulty the growth plan has had in creating new jobs. The Labor and Social Services Ministry has been unable to generate new jobs for those

FIGURE E   Job creation: people enrolled and placed each year

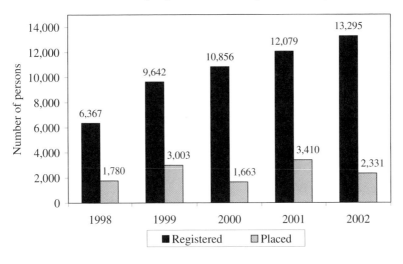

Sources: Ministry of Labor and Social Services.

participating in the Social Security and Job Creation Program; in 2002, only 17.5% (2,331 out of 13,295 applicants) found employment (**Figure E**).

Though the economy has been unable to consistently create new jobs, this trend has been ameliorated somewhat by constant foreign migration and increases in family remittances. Thus, the expected drop in the number of available jobs has not led to much growth of unemployment.

Job creation has depended on three main sectors: agriculture/cattle/forestry, commerce/hotels/restaurants, and manufacturing (**Figure F**). These groups accounted for 65.5% of the working population in 2002. The recent reforms have signaled important structural changes with regard to jobs, with employment in the third of these categories becoming more and more dynamic, less so for the second group, and dropping for the first. The implementation of policies that promote industrial exports, a drop in international coffee prices, and an overall commercial liberalization signals a worrisome situation for the agriculture and livestock sector.

Employment in El Salvador has become urbanized and feminized, with some 63% of female workers located in urban areas. Commercial

FIGURE F   Employment by economic activity (percentages)

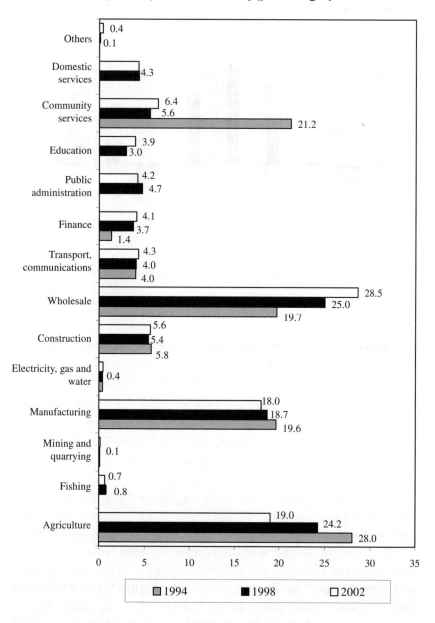

Sources: Author's analysis based on Survey of Multi-Purpose Households data.

FIGURE G Underemployment and social security coverage, urban areas (annual changes)

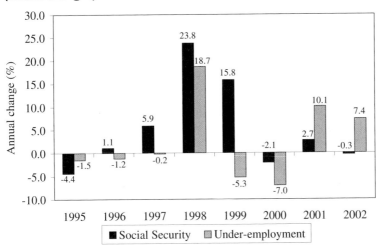

Sources: Author's analysis based on Survey of Multi-Purpose Households data.

and manufacturing jobs employ 64.6% of women (Appendix Table 13), as traditionally female jobs — such as textiles — have benefited from structural changes. Adding to this trend is increased international migration (the majority men), a decline in household incomes, and a rise in educational opportunities and civic organizations for women (CEPAL 2002, 28). This is not to say, though, that female workers in sectors such as industry and commerce are treated equally or given sufficient labor rights.

Job quality

Low levels of unemployment have been accompanied by a drop in job quality — longer hours and lower wages — as labor organizations routinely point out when negotiating labor legislation. In the past two years, underemployment[14] has grown considerably (**Figure G**); in 2002, about 30% of urban workers fell under this category. Further, almost 30% of workers work involuntarily less than 40 hours per week or more than 40 hours, yet earn less than the minimum wage.

Of the total underemployed population, 85.5% work overtime (40 or more hours per week) without earning the minimum weekly salary (invisible underemployment). Proportionally, this phenomenon predominantly affects women, though overall more men find themselves in this situation. Of women, 31.4% are underemployed, compared to 28.3% of men (Appendix Table 14). This difference is primarily due to the types of industries dominated by women, such as textiles, which are less regulated and require longer hours if one is to earn sufficient wages and meet demand.

Social security coverage has weakened. Workers have the right to social security, but in 2002 coverage dropped by 0.3%, and 54.5% of urban workers were uncovered by any social security, public or private (Appendix Table 14). The lack of social security coverage is not necessarily a result of the recent economic slowdown; indeed, during times of growth coverage continues to be low, with half the population without it. This trend is testament to the reluctance of labor institutions to fight for social security and the traditional failure of workers to make it a negotiating priority.

In conclusion, rampant underemployment, growing invisible underemployment, and decreased social security coverage highlight the fact that the drop in unemployment is due, in part, to the low quality of new jobs being created.

Trends of wages[15]

In the early 1990s El Salvador implemented a dynamic wage policy that included continual increases in the minimum wage. Between 1990 and 1995 the wage was adjusted seven times, but only twice between 1996 and 2003. The late 1990s policy of making fewer adjustments was due to the government's desire to stabilize prices by controlling inflation. Thus, inflation control has been achieved at the expense of a shrinking monetary policy and slow growth in workers' wages, among other factors.

As illustrated in **Table 8**, the raises were modest, and since 1995 ceased to be yearly; the last increase (2003) came after five years and was not generalized across sectors. It did not affect workers in the agriculture industry, whose monthly wages stayed at $74.06. In addition, a new trend targeted specific industries with wage hikes, further widening the wage gap between workers in different sectors and regions.

The rise of different minimum wages has deepened the inequality between urban and rural workers. The minimum wage earned by the major-

TABLE 8 Minimum wage and monthly averages

Minimum monthly wages in dollars and colones (nominal terms)

Years and month of change	Commerce and industry		Agriculture		Exchange rate
	U.S. dollars	Colones	U.S. dollars	Colones	
1990 April	$82.89	630.0	$45.39	345.00	7.60
1990 November	82.89	630.0	45.39	345.00	7.60
1991 May	88.13	705.0	48.75	390.00	8.00
1992 June	96.77	810.0	46.59	390.00	8.37
1993 March	106.90	930.0	55.17	480.00	8.70
1994 July	120.00	1,050.0	61.71	540.00	8.75
1995 August	132.00	1,155.0	67.89	594.00	8.75
1998 May	144.00	1,260.0	74.06	648.00	8.75

Minimum salary, effective April 2003

Kind of economic activity	Percentage change	Current salary, U.S. dollars	Previous salary, U.S. dollars
Wholesale and services	10.0%	$158.40	$144.00
Manufacturing industry	7.5%	154.80	144.00
Manufacturing, assembly	5.0%	151.20	144.00
Agriculture	0.0%	74.06	74.06

Monthly wages, mean and mode in U.S. dollars

Year	Total		Men		Women	
	Mean	Mode	Mean	Mode	Mean	Mode
Total						
1994	$153.85	$81.71	$175.60	$92.00	$125.70	$54.29
1998	224.93	93.83	249.54	100.23	192.50	59.31
2002	243.69	112.91	277.57	125.03	204.58	100.91
Urban						
1994	$181.02	$89.14	$214.15	$106.86	$143.30	$60.57
1998	264.04	125.94	304.47	140.23	216.37	97.26
2002	288.52	134.29	341.36	150.29	233.76	118.51
Rural						
1994	$92.40	$76.00	$102.60	$83.43	$74.58	$47.43
1998	135.09	81.83	141.43	87.77	124.23	51.54
2002	141.73	88.91	153.94	93.60	123.62	75.43

Source: Author's analysis based on Survey of Multi-Purpose Households and Ministry of Labor and Social Services data.

ity of rural workers is the agricultural tariff, which is roughly half of the minimum wage for urban workers. This unequal situation is evidenced even more starkly in average salaries, where the gap has increased. For example, in 1994 urban workers earned $88.62 per month more than rural workers; in 2002 the difference had grown to $146.79 per month.

The gender wage gap is a problem as well. Men earn higher salaries than women, the result of traditional Salvadoran perceptions that value women's work less than men's, even in the same jobs. Nevertheless, the gap between salaries has lessened somewhat in recent years: in 1994, women earned on average 39% less than men, while today the gap is 35%.[16]

One troublesome finding presented in Table 8 regards the modal salary, or that which is earned by the most workers. In effect, the value of the modal salary ($112.91) amounts to less than the minimum wage in non-agricultural sectors and less than the urban rate defined by the basic goods index, which is $127.04. This difference suggests that a significant population of workers are unable to meet the basic costs of food, clothing, housing, and leisure.[17]

In terms of real wages, low inflation levels have not translated into improved buying power. The minimum wage has tended to drop during the period of adjustment and stabilization (**Figure H**). The stagnation of the minimum wage since 1998 has contributed to the low buying power of workers' salaries.

Labor productivity

One of the determining factors for economic growth is labor productivity. Insofar as a country can count on high levels of productivity in its working population, it can hope to achieve satisfactory rates of growth. During the civil war (1980-91), product per worker tended to fall considerably (**Figure I**). Between 1979 and 1991, productivity fell approximately 28.4%.

During the 1990s, the rate of productivity recovered from its low in the late 1980s and has remained relatively stable, though at rates below those of the end of the 1970s. Thus, the same level of productivity requires more work than it did in 1978.

Labor productivity among different sectors or branches of economic activity is fairly heterogeneous (**Table 9**). Among the sectors with low

FIGURE H   Minimum wage, urban (1980=100)

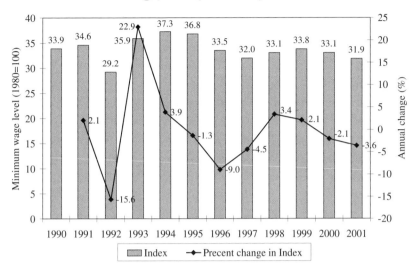

Source: Author's analysis based on ILO data.

FIGURE I   Labor productivity (product per worker in 1990 colones)

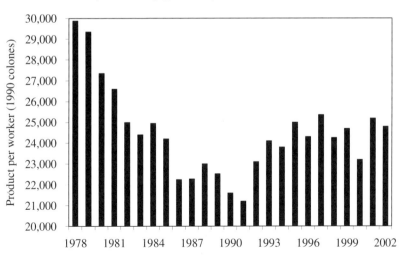

Source: UNDP (2003).

levels of productivity are agriculture, hotels/restaurant businesses, and "other" (public administration, education, social services, and domestic services). The highest levels of productivity occur in financial services and mining.

Among the sectors with intermediate and relatively stable labor productivity are manufacturing, electricity/gas/water, and transportation and communication. Productivity in commercial activity has declined steadily since 1994.

In conclusion, the data show that labor productivity during the period of structural reforms continued to be low in comparison with levels reached during the 1970s, though it has risen since the period of armed conflict. Yet two of the sectors with the greatest participation in GDP and labor generation — commercial and agriculture — have experienced low levels of productivity. As for manufacturing, labor productivity is similar to the country's overall levels of 1978-79.

Definition and measurement of informal employment

Defining informal work status

Informal sector

In general, the definition of informal employment has been linked to the concept of the *informal sector*; traditionally, the identification of informal workers has been based on the productive unit in which they work. When we speak of informal workers, we refer to people who work in the informal sector. However, this definition of the informal sector excludes many workers who could be categorized as informal because of the lack of benefits established in legislation that guarantee dignified working and living conditions. Thus, the category of informality may vary for each country, according to the political and administrative divisions.

In order to fully develop the definition of informal employment as a unit of analysis, we must ask: "What is understood by the informal sector?" in order to differentiate informal employment from the informal sector.

A wide range of possible approaches exists for defining the informal sector. While they are all related to the productive unit, they differ in their identification of the root cause of informality. Among the most important approaches are the following:[18]

TABLE 9 Productivity per worker and rate of growth (product per worker in 1990 colones and percentage change)

Kind of economic activity	1991 Production per worker	1994 Production per worker	1994 Percent change	1997 Production per worker	1997 Percent change	2000 Production per worker	2000 Percent change	2001 Production per worker	2001 Percent change	2002 Production per worker	2002 Percent change
Agriculture, cattle, fishing, and hunting	9,749	11,710	20.1	12,483	6.6	14,013	12.3	12,890	-8.0	14,466	12.2
Mining	57,219	121,433	112.2	132,996	9.5	147,032	10.6	83,141	-43.5	76,519	-8.0
Industrial manufacturing	27,177	25,473	-6.3	34,381	35.0	30,403	-11.6	31,808	4.6	32,516	2.2
Electricity, gas, and water	18,230	31,563	73.1	21,526	-31.8	39,312	82.6	33,079	-15.9	35,626	7.7
Construction	17,265	15,318	-11.3	14,456	-5.6	17,221	19.1	16,925	-1.7	17,223	1.8
Commerce, hotels, and restaurants	20,329	21,105	3.8	20,399	-3.3	18,600	-8.8	17,292	-7.0	17,040	-1.5
Transportation and comm.	45,958	44,795	-2.5	41,854	-6.6	44,436	6.2	44,110	-0.7	50,825	15.2
International finance	180,583	133,658	-26.0	128,070	-4.2	100,249	-21.7	87,046	-13.2	92,381	6.1
Others	17,016	15,589	-8.4	15,862	1.8	13,406	-15.5	13,304	-0.8	12,856	-3.4

Source: Author's analysis based on Survey of Multi-Purpose Households and BCR data.

- *Dualist approach*. This interpretation holds that the informal sector is the result of a development plan characterized by the generation of heterogeneous production activities. On the one hand are activities benefiting from capitalist modernization; they adapt intensive techniques in capital and introduce new technologies, which in turn generate an excess of manpower. On the other hand are the productive units that absorb this excess labor.

  Thus, the informal sector is made up of productive units of self-employment and/or subsistence. These units are characterized by their small scale of production; low levels of qualification, capital, skill, and organization; limited access to state benefits; low productivity; and other factors.

  According to this approach, the informal working population would include those who were self-employed and possibly not remunerated, if the worker is not the owner of the productive unit.

- *Legalist approach*. This view holds that the informal sector is the result of excessive state regulation, which can hinder the ability of productive units to respond to demand or enter new markets. Thus, the informal sector is made up of productive units that are found on the margin of legislation or that are not regulated by legal statutes, regardless of the size of the unit, its productivity, skill levels required, and capital invested.

  This definition of informal employment, like the previous approach, is based on the number of people occupied in units of production that are not being regulated. This lack of regulation may be due to the avoidance of legal obligations or non-coverage by the law.

- *Structuralist approach*. This interpretation intersects with the previous ones in that it highlights the fact that the informal sector is made up of productive units that are not regulated, that result from the process of capitalist accumulation, and that seek to increase their profits by avoiding or failing to comply with the law. Laws requiring companies to meet tax, trade, and labor regulations compel companies to increase their production costs. Thus, to reduce costs and increase profits, companies avoid their legal obligations.

  According to this approach, the informal sector is the result of productive units rejecting both syndicalism (which contributes to worker formality) and state regulations regarding salaries, taxes, and social security (which drive up the cost of labor) (Masi 2002).

Thus, because this approach to identifying informal unemployment is based on the number of people employed by non-regulated productive units, it would be possible to link informal employment to the working population that is not covered by labor legislation.

* *ILO approach.* The internationally recognized approach to calculating the informal sector is the one developed by the International Labor Organization on the occasion of the 15th International Conference on Labor Statistics in 1993. To a certain degree, this definition includes elements of the approaches described above.

   The conference defined the informal sector as comprising: "unincorporated private businesses that fall below a certain threshold determined by prevailing national conditions (normally between 5 and 10 workers), and/or are not registered according to specific national laws, such as commercial laws, business regulations, fiscal laws or social security regulations for professionals, or similar laws, regulations and decrees established by national legislative bodies" (ILO 2002).

   Specifically, the informal sector as defined by the conference is constituted, on the one hand, by productive units of self-employed workers who inconsistently employ family members and paid employees and, on the other hand, by individuals or associations that employ one or more workers in a consistent manner but that are not registered.

   This definition calculates the informal sector based on the number of establishments or small-scale productive units that are generally not registered. In the case of El Salvador, the informal sector comprises establishments of less than five workers and is limited to urban areas, following the ILO conference recommendation that, for practical reasons, takes only non-agricultural productive units into account. However, the conference recommended that countries advance their calculations of rural areas according to the resources and research methods available.

Informal employment

In the discussion above, we addressed the definition of the informal sector, which is linked to the productive unit or the size of the company but not to the characteristics or conditions of the workers. Statistically, the calculation of the informal sector is based on the worker according to employment category; however, the basic criterion for determining informality is the productive unit.

According to this definition of the informal sector, we understand informal employment as the number of workers employed in productive units classified as informal, either because of their legal status or the size of the unit. In the majority of Latin American countries, a working person is informal if he or she is employed in an establishment of between one and four, one and five, or one and 10 workers, depending on the range used by each country.

In El Salvador the criteria for determining informal employment are based on the size of the productive unit, taking into account factors such as employment category, occupational group, and the area in which the productive unit is located. Thus, according to official statistics published by DIGESTYC, informal employment (the informal sector) is the *"segment of the labor market made up of: family member wage-earners and workers in an establishment of less than five workers; self-employed workers; and owners of businesses with fewer than five workers in occupations other than professional, technical, management, and administrative."*

As we see in **Table 10**, informal employment from the perspective of the informal sector refers only to the size of the establishment. Thus, this criterion tends to exclude workers in the domestic services sector, since it is impossible to locate them via their productive unit. Because this definition does not start with the working person but rather the unit in which he or she works, it doesn't account for criteria such as security or social services and stability in work, criteria which could provide a more complete picture of the formality or informality of labor. For example, should a wage earner who works in a formal productive unit (because it has more than five employees), but who lacks any social security coverage, be considered formally employed?

One of the goals of this report is to use the worker as the unit of analysis in order to determine informality, since he or she could be working in the formal sector under informal conditions due to vulnerability, lack of access to social services, or insufficient income. From this per-

Table 10   Criteria used to calculate informal and formal employment by DIGESTYC

Criteria	Informal employment (Informal sector)	Formal employment (Formal sector)
Size of the productive unit (base criteria)	Establishment with fewer than 6 workers	Establishment with 5 or more workers
Employment category	Owner	Owner
	Self-employed	Self-employed
	Cooperative members	Cooperative members
	Non-remunerated family	Non-remunerated family
	Permanent wage earners	Permanent wage earners
	Temporary wage earners	Temporary wage earners
	Apprentice	Apprentice
	Other	Other
	Excludes domestic services	Excludes domestic services
Occupational group	Owner and self-employed in non-professional, technical, management, or administrative occupations.	Owner and self-employed in professional, technical, management, or administrative occupations.
Geographic location	Urban	Urban

Source: DIGESTYC.

spective, the definition of informal employment is linked to the quality of employment as defined by the ILO's criteria for decent work,[19] characterized as productive, secure, and respectful of worker rights, and providing social security, dignified income, and freedom of labor organizing.

Taking into consideration this definition of decent work in order to propose a new definition of informal employment that uses the working person as the unit of analysis, we understand informal employment as job status lacking in the judicial and social protections stipulated in the labor code or related to the labor market, and that thus places people in a vulnerable state reflected by increased insecurity (lack of access to social security), job instability, and low wages.

From this perspective, any worker whose rights are disrespected or who is not guaranteed the social services, job security, and income (as basic criteria of formality) that allow him or her to live in a dignified fashion falls into a state of informality, irrespective of the economic sector or size of the business.

The nature of informality in labor is determined by the factors that have given rise to the informal sector (**Table 11**), especially those pointed out by the structural approach discussed above. Yet the existence of informal labor is also the result of processes of capital accumulation, which generate an excess of labor availability, reduce workers' capacity for negotiation, and obligate workers to accept conditions established by the employer. Furthermore, since labor and trade regulation can be obstacles to the process of accumulation, they lead businesses to generate legally marginal employment in order to increase profits.

In contrast to the definition of informal employment based on the informal sector, the definition proposed here includes the entire working population (**Table 12**), not just those working in small-scale production units. Furthermore, the basic criterion is not limited to the business, but takes into account other factors affecting the quality of employment such as access to social security and contracts, among others. In addition, this criterion allows us to analyze the magnitude of informal employment at the level of the country as well as urban and rural areas.

Measuring informal employment

In order to measure informal labor using the proposed definition and having as the unit of analysis the working person, we will take into account three factors: employment category, the criteria and attributes that determine formality or informality, and the Survey of Multi-Purpose Households.

The Survey of Multi-Purpose Households

In order to determine the number of people working in an informal capacity, we use data provided by the Survey of Multi-Purpose Households (or EHPM, based on its Spanish name, Encuesta de Hogares de Propósitos Múltiples) conducted by the General Office of Statistics and Census. In El Salvador, the EHPM is the main instrument providing annual statistical information related to demographic, social, and economic conditions for the entire country and for rural and urban areas.

Table 11 Definition of informal sector and informal employment

	Informal sector	Informal employment based on the informal sector	Informal employment, proposed definition
Definition	Productive units not established in society whose size in terms of employment is under a certain level determined according to national conditions.	Number of workers employed in the productive units who are classified as informal, whether due to their legal status or size of the unit.	The group of workers who lack the legal and social protection stipulated in labor legislation or those related to the labor market, and thus find themselves in a state of vulnerability and/or uncertainty.
Unit of analysis	Productive unit or establishment according to size.	Productive unit and workers employed in these establishments.	The working person, without regard to the size of the establishment.
Causes	Characteristics of the development plan. Capital accumulation. Excessive legislation.	Characteristics of the development plan. Capital accumulation. Excessive legislation.	Characteristics of the development plan. Capital accumulation. Excessive legislation.

Source: Author's analysis.

The survey presents eight information modules: demographic characteristics, educational characteristics, residential characteristics, employment and income, productive activity, health, family remittances, and household expenditures. The employment and income module takes into account people who are 10 years old or older and produces information about the main employment variables.

To be clear, all of the statistical information to be presented in the following sections is based on DIGESTYC data in order to avoid confusion with official employment data. Nevertheless, the data for 1990-94 show slight differences from the official published data due to technical reasons: the DIGESTYC made a change in its statistical program.

Employment category
For the purposes of this study, we will use the definition proposed by the EHPM, which indicates *the relationship between an economically*

TABLE 12   Criteria for calculating informal employment

Criteria	Informal employment based on the informal sector	Informal employment Proposed definition
Base criteria	Establishment or productive unit with fewer than 5 workers	Social security Contract Salaries or income Productive unit Unionization Other
Employment category of the worker	Owner Self-employed Cooperative members Non-remunerated family Permanent wage earners Temporary wage earners Apprentice Other Excludes domestic services	Owner Self-employed Cooperative members Non-remunerated family Permanent wage earners Temporary wage earners Apprentice Domestic services Other
Occupational group	Owners and self-employed workers in non-professional, technical, management, and administrative occupations.	Entire occupational group
Geographic location	Urban	Entire country (urban and rural)

Source: Author's analysis.

active person and his or her employer. The survey presents eight categories that are defined in **Table 13**.

The aim of using occupational categories is that it allows an approximation of the characteristics (stability, social services, income) of the working person in his or her place of work, independent of the size of the company or productive unit. Furthermore, it includes the entire population and facilitates analysis of employment levels with other variables.

Attributes of informality
By attributes of informality, we consider the characteristics presented by the working person in his or her place of employment. These charac-

TABLE 13 Employment categories

Category	Definition
Owner	The person, natural or legal (anonymous society or the state), that has one or various establishments where an economic activity takes place, and that has one or more employees, who receive monetary or in-kind remuneration.
Self-employed	A person who develops an economic activity independently who does not have remunerated employees and who is not employed by anyone (he/she may have non-remunerated family members).
Cooperative member	Person who works as cooperative member.
Non-remunerated family	Person who works for a family without receiving any monetary remuneration.
Salaried - permanent	Person who works in a permanent form for an employer and receives remuneration in the form of a salary, wages, plus commissions.
Salaried - temporary	Person who works in a temporary way for an employer and receives remuneration in the form of a salary, wages, plus commissions.
Apprentice	Person who at the moment of the interview is in the process of apprenticeship for an art or office, who may or may not receive payment for this activity.
Domestic service	Person who works for a family group, performing work that is specific to the household.
Other	People not identified in any of the previous categories.

Source: Survey of Multi-Purpose Households data.

teristics allow a definition of the person as being in a situation of insecurity, instability, or low income depending on the employment category and available information.

There may be a large number of attributes; however, the availability of information can limit how many of these are useful. According to the structure and information presented by the EHPM, we have identified four attributes that allow us to identify and quantify informal employment in light of the established criteria: security and income. These attributes are size of the productive unit, salary, social security, and contract.

- *Size of the productive unit.* This attribute is the same one used to identify the informal sector and officially used to quantify informal employment (see **Table 10**). In contrast to the official calculations, we will refer only to the economically active persons who own a business in the informal sector (defined in El Salvador as having fewer than five workers) and who are identified as owners, self-employed, or cooperativist, since by definition these workers own a productive establishment.

    Thus, all of those people in the category of owners, self-employed, or cooperativist who own an establishment employing less than five people are considered informal workers/owners. While the DIGESTYC data excludes employers and self-employed workers in professional, technical, management, or administrative areas, in this study we include these workers, since even management capacity or independent work by a worker/owner does not necessarily translate into employment stability or security. In addition, it is possible to statistically compare owners of informal businesses with those who have access to social security services and thus determine how many workers find themselves in a state of informality.

- *Salaries and income.* This attribute seeks to determine informality based on the worker's earned income. Thus, workers earning salaries that do not allow them to satisfy household necessities would be in a state of informality because of the precariousness of the place of employment. According to the labor legislation stipulated in the Constitution and in the Labor Code, every worker has the right to a minimum salary that sufficiently covers normal material, moral, and cultural needs. The absence of this right places a worker in a situation of informality due to the absence of resources that would guarantee a dignified existence.

- *Social security.* Social security or social services are another right recognized in labor law. These rights are vital to the health of the labor force; their absence will inevitably lead to labor precariousness or informality. In El Salvador social security is an obligatory service, to which all workers have the right to be affiliated in order to partake of medical and hospital services and guarantee their health.

This attribute can be statistically compared with all of the occupational categories; however, with the available information it is impossible to determine social security coverage for the population working in domestic services. In general, people working in domestic capacities are not connected to the social security system and are generally considered to be informally employed, since they are at the margins of labor norms.

* *Contract.* The contract is the primary mechanism for ensuring stability in the workplace. Individual contracts, depending on national law, include the rights and obligations established by labor market legislation. The lack of contracts in a workplace places workers in a state of informality, since they lack an instrument that guarantees stability and respect for rights in the workplace.

Working proposal for the measurement of informal employment
The methodological proposal for calculating the ranks of the informally employed is summarized in **Table 14**. Every employment category has been assigned one or two attributes, which allow us to classify it as either formal or informal.

For people who work as the boss, we have indicated the size of the productive unit, since these workers' formality or informality is determined primarily by the size of the business that they lead or own or by the criteria used to define the informal sector. By these criteria, people who work as an informal boss are those who own informal businesses or businesses that employ fewer than five workers. Employers with technical or management occupations are often considered separately; however, our working definition includes employers without specifying their occupation.

With regard to the categories of self-employed, cooperative, or non-remunerated, we analyze these in light of the criteria of access to social services through social security. The reasoning behind this methodology is that the EHPM does not provide information about contracts in these employment categories, where in any case the use of contracts is rare. For self-employment and cooperativist workers, it is possible to

TABLE 14   Working proposal for defining informal employment

Employment category	Attribute of formality or informality	Informal employment	Formal employment
Owner	Size of the business	Owner-bosses of informal businesses	Owner-bosses of formal businesses (more than 5 workers)
Self-employed	Social security	Self-employed workers who are not covered by any system of social security	Self-employed workers covered by a system of social security
Cooperative member	Social security	Cooperative members not covered by any system of social security	Cooperative members covered by a system of social security.
Non-remunerated family member	Social security	Non-remunerated family member who is not covered by any system of social security	Non-remunerated family member covered by a system of social security
Salaried – permanent	Contract / Social security	Persons who have not signed a labor contract as well as those who have signed a contract, but without social security	Persons who have signed work contracts and have social security.
Salaried – temporary	Contract / Social security	Persons who have not signed a labor contract as well as those who have signed a contract, but without social security	Persons who have signed work contracts and have social security
Apprentice	Contract	Persons who have not signed an apprentice contract	Persons who have signed an apprentice contract
Domestic service		Persons who work in domestic services	
Other	Contract / Social security	Persons who have not signed a labor contract as well as those who have signed a contract, but without social security	Persons who have signed work contracts and have social security

Source: Author's analysis.

use the size of the establishment as a criterion. In the case of people who work as cooperativists, it is assumed that the cooperative is registered legally, which is one of the criteria for a cooperative's existence. One might expect that these cooperative jobs would necessarily be formal employment; however, many of these lack social services in spite of the formal nature of the productive unit.

As for the self-employed population, we leave out the criteria for the productive unit, since these workers are independent. Indeed, even when some of these self-employed workers have employees under their responsibility (remunerated or non-remunerated family members), generally these workers are not guaranteed access to social services.

For non-remunerated family members, the only attribute available in the statistics for determining informality is their affiliation to a system of public or private insurance. Indeed, if non-remunerated family members lack a mechanism for guaranteeing stability in employment and satisfactory incomes, many of these receive social security through individuals who do have some kind of public or private insurance.

Salaried workers and others have been assigned the attribute of social security and contract, which allows us to identify their level of access to social security and stability in employment. Furthermore, for this category as with the others (except family or non-remunerated workers), it would be possible to use the attribute of salaries or income, using the minimum wage as a guide. Nevertheless, because of the methodological issues raised by using the minimum wage, we will not take it into consideration in our analysis. As discussed earlier, the minimum salary varies by geographic region and productive activity and is often not enough to cover the basic needs of the working population.

For apprentices, the attribute that we consider in determining informality is the contract, since national legislation establishes that apprentices have the right to an apprentice contract stipulating that the employer is obliged to teach apprentices, pay them a fair stipend, and provide them with social services, among other requirements. Thus, apprentices with no contract are considered to be informal workers, since they lack a mechanism to guarantee employment stability, services, and income.

All people who work in domestic services are considered informally employed, since this employment category is characterized by low wages, long and demanding working hours, and a general lack of social services.

Characteristics of informal and formal employment

Magnitude of informal urban employment: a comparison of methodologies[20]

In the previous section, we related the definition of informality to the state of employment vulnerability, which is determined by insecurity or lack of social services, instability, and low wages. In order to measure the magnitude of informal employment, we put forth a working proposal based on occupational categories and respective attributes that indicate a state of employee formality or informality. The application of this working proposal to the EHPM data is shown in **Table 15**.

According to the proposed criteria, 899,466 urban workers, or 59.1% of the total employed urban population, find themselves in a state of informality. Thus, more than half of the working urban population lacks stability and/or access to social services in the workplace.

By comparison, the methodology used by DIGESTYC shows informal employment in urban areas at 49.7%, 1.3% lower than formal employment. The results of our proposed methodology, however, show informal urban employment to be much higher (59.1%), or 18.2% greater than formal employment.

One of the reasons why the calculation of informal work using our proposed methodology is higher than the DIGESTYC calculation is that DIGESTYC excludes from its analysis certain employment categories such as domestic workers and some non-remunerated family employees. Also, the use of the productive unit as the basic attribute of formality or informality falls short as an indicator of real working conditions, as we have argued in this chapter.

Another finding suggested by our proposed methodology is that, in the period between 1991 and 2002, the magnitude of informal employment has been consistently higher than formal employment. The DIGESTYC analysis finds the opposite, but with a smaller gap between each type of work, as we can see in **Table 16**.

Evolution and characteristics of formal and informal employment
Trends of informal employment
Between 1991 and 2002, the size of the informal workforce tended to move in step with the overall labor market, while formal employment

TABLE 15 Formal and informal employment according to urban employment category, 2002

Occupation	Characteristic of formal or informal employment	Informal employment Definition	Number	Formal employment Definition	Number
Owner	Size of the establishment	Private owners of informal businesses	66,510	Private owners of establishments with 5 or more employees	10,191
Self-employed	Social security	Self-employed with no social security coverage	385,514	Self-employed but covered by social security	35,329
Cooperative member	Social security	Cooperative members with no social security coverage	110	Cooperative members covered by social security	
Family non-remunerated	Social security	Non-remunerated family with no social security coverage	85,162	Non-remunerated family covered by social security	6,006
Salaried-permanent	Contract, Social security	Employees with or without a contract but with no social security coverage	141,384	Employees with a contract and covered by social security	537,743
Salaried-temporary	Contract, Social security	Employees with or without a contract but with no social security coverage	157,973	Employees with a contract and covered by social security	32,623
Apprentice	Contract	Apprentices without a contract	4,658	Apprentices with a contract	57
Domestic services		Domestic workers	55,794		
Others	Contract, Social security	Employees with or without a contract but with no social security coverage	2,361	Employees with a contract and covered by social security	74
Total			899,466		622,023

Source: Author's analysis based on DIGESTYC calculations.

TABLE 16   Informal and formal urban employment according to
methodology (as a percentage of the working population)

	Proposed method[1]		Official calculation[2]	
Year	Informal	Formal	Informal	Formal
1991	65.4	34.6	..	..
1992	64.0	36.0	..	..
1993	64.4	35.6	..	..
1994	63.5	36.5	48.8	51.2
1995	64.7	35.3	47.1	52.9
1996	65.9	34.1	47.4	52.6
1997	64.8	35.2	49.5	50.5
1998	57.9	42.1	46.6	53.4
1999	56.7	43.3	46.5	53.5
2000	58.5	41.5	47.7	52.3
2001	59.1	40.9	49.4	50.6
2002	59.1	40.9	49.7	50.3

[1] Calculation by FUNDE, based on official statistics (DIGESTYC).
[2] Calculation by DIGESTYC.

Source: Author's analysis based on Survey of Multi-Purpose Households data.

demonstrated a heterogeneous tendency. As shown in **Table 17** (see also Appendix Table 15), the variations in informal employment are related to the behavior of the overall working population, while formal employment has a more disparate pattern.

The consistent relationship demonstrated by informal employment (on the national level as well as in urban and rural regions specifically) and overall employment reveals that newly generated jobs in El Salvador consist mainly of informal employment opportunities. As can be seen in **Figure J**, the similar pattern of informal employment and overall employment shows that the economy generally absorbs the growing working population into precarious or informal jobs. In other words, the generation of labor seems to rely on informal employment, while formal employment shows a weaker relation to overall employment (in the past few years, though, formal employment has tracked overall employment more closely).

Another finding here is that there have been overall reductions in unemployment and informal employment and a rise in formal employ-

TABLE 17   Employed population by type of employment

Year	Total employment		Informal employment			Formal employment		
	Number of persons	Growth (%)	Number of persons	Rate* (%)	Growth (%)	Number of persons	Rate* (%)	Growth (%)
Total								
1991	1,781,562	..	1,383,159	77.6%	..	398,403	22.4%	..
1992	1,753,147	-1.6%	1,345,349	76.7	-2.8%	407,798	23.3	2.3%
1993	1,802,586	2.8	1,382,604	76.7	2.7	419,982	23.3	2.9
1994	1,950,998	8.2	1,442,542	73.9	4.2	508,456	26.1	17.4
1995	1,973,017	1.1	1,478,690	74.9	2.4	494,327	25.1	-2.9
1996	2,056,450	4.2	1,558,069	75.8	5.1	498,381	24.2	0.8
1997	2,066,523	0.5	1,545,201	74.8	-0.8	521,322	25.2	4.4
1998	2,227,471	7.8	1,530,429	68.7	-1.0	697,042	31.3	25.2
1999	2,274,728	2.1	1,539,988	67.7	0.6	734,740	32.3	5.1
2000	2,322,697	2.1	1,603,670	69.0	4.0	719,027	31.0	-2.2
2001	2,451,317	5.5	1,707,996	69.7	6.1	743,321	30.3	3.3
2002	2,412,785	-1.6	1,667,308	69.1	-2.4	745,477	30.9	0.3
Urban								
1991	947,145	..	619,588	65.4	..	327,557	34.6	..
1994	1,170,968	21.2	743,448	63.5	16.3	427,520	36.5	19.6
1995	1,172,884	0.2	758,335	64.7	2.0	414,549	35.3	-3.1
1997	1,235,612	1.6	800,369	64.8	-0.1	435,243	35.2	4.8
1999	1,427,410	3.4	809,431	56.7	1.3	617,979	43.3	6.0
2000	1,464,611	2.6	857,266	58.5	5.6	607,345	41.5	-1.8
2001	1,522,871	4.0	900,205	59.1	4.8	622,666	40.9	2.5
2002	1,521,489	-0.1	899,466	59.1	-0.1	622,023	40.9	-0.1
Rural								
1991	834,417	..	763,571	91.5	..	70,846	8.5	..
1994	780,030	-6.7	699,094	89.6	-8.7	80,936	10.4	5.9
1995	800,133	2.6	720,355	90.0	3.0	79,778	10.0	-1.5
1997	830,911	-1.2	744,832	89.6	-1.6	86,079	10.4	2.4
1999	847,318	0.0	730,557	86.2	-0.1	116,761	13.8	0.7
2000	858,086	1.3	746,404	87.0	2.1	111,682	13.0	-4.5
2001	928,446	8.2	807,791	87.0	7.6	120,655	13.0	7.4
2002	891,296	-4.0	767,842	86.1	-5.2	123,454	13.9	2.3

* Rate: Percentage of total employment.

Source: Author's analysis based on calculations by DIGESTYC using the proposed working definition of informal employment.

ment in 1991. Yet in periods of slight growth of unemployment, formal employment falls while informal employment tends to grow by the same magnitude as unemployment, allowing the unemployment rate to remain stable (at around 7%), as we have seen since 1994.

As **Figure K** shows, the reductions in formal employment are accompanied by an increase in the level of informal employment, which indicates the existence of a persistent mobility between types of em-

FIGURE J   Trends of working population by type of work (percent changes)

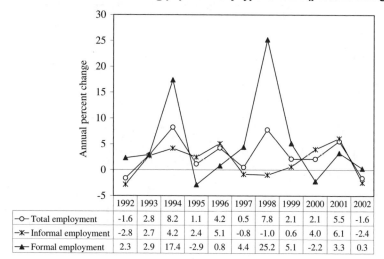

	1992	1993	1994	1995	1996	1997	1998	1999	2000	2001	2002
–○– Total employment	-1.6	2.8	8.2	1.1	4.2	0.5	7.8	2.1	2.1	5.5	-1.6
–✳– Informal employment	-2.8	2.7	4.2	2.4	5.1	-0.8	-1.0	0.6	4.0	6.1	-2.4
–▲– Formal employment	2.3	2.9	17.4	-2.9	0.8	4.4	25.2	5.1	-2.2	3.3	0.3

Source: Author's analysis based on the working proposal for the definition of informal employment.

ployment. Thus, when formal employment increases, informal employment decreases significantly. However, once that period is over, formal employment falls considerably but does not result in significant increases in the unemployment rate, due to the absorption of workers into informal employment. This process may occur through the establishment of small productive units or the generation of self-employment and precarious jobs which don't guarantee worker stability or security; in order to survive, workers are obliged to accept any type of employment, even those that put them at risk.

As we noted at the beginning of this section, informal employment is higher than formal employment. As Table 17 shows, during the entire period analyzed informal employment is 75.3% greater than formal employment (annual average). However, slight reductions are evident in the level of informal employment in certain years: in 1991, the working population in informal conditions represented 77.6% of all workers; this share fell to 69.1% in 2002.

During the economic high point of the early 1990s, the level of informal employment fell 3.5% while formal employment increased 12.0%.

FIGURE K   Changes in rate of formal and informal employment and unemployment

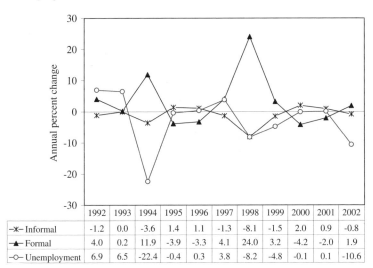

	1992	1993	1994	1995	1996	1997	1998	1999	2000	2001	2002
–✱– Informal	-1.2	0.0	-3.6	1.4	1.1	-1.3	-8.1	-1.5	2.0	0.9	-0.8
–▲– Formal	4.0	0.2	11.9	-3.9	-3.3	4.1	24.0	3.2	-4.2	-2.0	1.9
–○– Unemployment	6.9	6.5	-22.4	-0.4	0.3	3.8	-8.2	-4.8	-0.1	0.1	-10.6

Source: Author's analysis based on the working proposal for the definition of informal employment.

When the economy slowed during the 1996-2002 period, the rate of informal employment tended to increase and then stalled for the last three years due in part to slow job growth.

The troubling magnitude of informal employment in relation to formal employment, as well as the increases in recent years, leads us to conclude that the economic growth plan has contributed little to the improvement of employment quality. Furthermore, the low levels of unemployment are due to the generation of informal or precarious jobs.

Location of informal employment
Of all formal jobs in 2002, 53.9% were found in urban areas and 46.1% in rural. During the period under study, the share of total informal employment found in rural areas has fallen (**Figure L**). This reduction is not fully explainable by the existence of measures aimed toward improving entry of rural people into the labor force; the pattern reflects a greater urbanization of employment and the erosion of agricultural activities, which has generated labor mobility from rural to urban areas.

FIGURE L Informal employment by geographic region (as percentage of total employment in country)

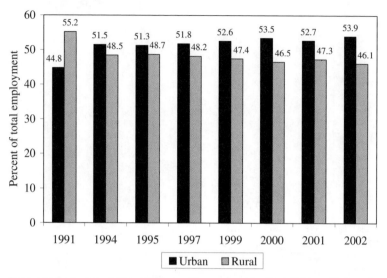

Source: Author's analysis based on the working proposal for the definition of informal employment.

In terms of the population that is employed in each area, the analysis reveals that unemployment is more informal in rural areas. In 2002, 86.1% of rural workers were informally employed vs. 13.9% in formal employment, meaning that informal work is six times more common than formal work in rural areas. As noted above, in urban areas informal employment was 59.1% in 2002, 18.2% greater than formal employment. These figures demonstrate once again that the present plan for economic growth marginalizes rural development because of its focus on export-oriented production, which is overwhelmingly concentrated in urban areas.

In terms of informal employment according to employment category, the self-employed, temporary salaried, and non-remunerated family populations account for 74% of informal employment in the country (**Table 18**); this share is roughly the same in all geographic areas. As Table 18 shows, informal employment is concentrated in the self-employed category, accounting for 41.1% of informal employment in 2002; this share grew in the period under consideration. In every other cat-

TABLE 18 Informal and formal employment by geographic area and employment category (as percentages of informal and formal employment for each year)

By status in employment	Total				Urban				Rural			
	1991		2002		1991		2002		1991		2002	
	Informal	Formal	Informal	Formal	Informal	Formal	Informal	Formal	Informal	Formal	Informal	Formal
Employer	7.0%	7.6%	5.9%	1.7%	6.7%	4.3%	7.4%	1.6%	7.2%	22.8%	4.1%	2.0%
Men	5.9	6.6	4.4	1.5	4.9	3.6	5.1	1.4	6.7	20.8	3.6	0.2
Women	1.1	0.9	1.5	0.2	1.9	0.7	2.3	0.2	0.6	2.0	0.5	0.0
Own account	32.3	0.0	41.1	5.6	37.3	0.0	42.9	5.7	28.2	0.0	39.1	5.5
Men	15.7	0.0	19.6	1.7	13.5	0.0	16.5	1.6	17.5	0.0	23.2	2.1
Women	16.6	0.0	21.6	4.0	23.8	0.0	26.4	4.1	10.7	0.0	15.9	3.4
Cooperatives	0.6	0.0	0.0	0.0	0.0	0.0	0.0	0.0	1.0	0.0	0.1	0.2
Men	0.5	0.0	0.0	0.0	0.0	0.0	0.0	0.0	0.9	0.0	0.1	0.0
Women	0.0	0.0	0.0	0.0	0.0	0.0	0.0	0.0	0.1	0.0	0.0	0.0
Unpaid workers	13.5	0.0	12.8	1.0	8.5	0.0	9.5	1.0	17.5	0.0	16.6	1.3
Men	8.8	0.0	7.8	0.4	3.4	0.0	3.7	0.4	13.2	0.0	12.7	0.7
Women	4.7	0.0	4.9	0.6	5.2	0.0	5.8	0.6	4.3	0.0	3.9	0.6
Permanent wage earners	17.6%	86.1%	12.8%	85.9%	20.8%	90.4%	15.7%	86.5%	15.0%	65.9%	9.3%	83.2%
Men	13.4	55.1	9.0	47.5	14.1	55.2	10.4	46.1	12.7	54.5	7.4	54.2
Women	4.3	31.0	3.7	38.4	6.7	35.2	5.3	40.3	2.3	11.4	1.9	29.0
Temporary wage earners	22.6%	6.3%	20.1%	5.6%	16.0%	5.3%	17.6%	5.2%	27.9%	11.3%	23.0%	7.6%
Men	17.2	4.9	17.2	3.6	11.9	3.8	14.1	3.1	21.5	10.1	20.9	6.1
Women	5.4	1.4	2.9	2.0	4.0	1.5	3.5	2.1	6.4	1.3	2.2	1.5

(continued)

TABLE 18 (cont.) Informal and formal employment by geographic area and employment category (as percentages of informal and formal employment for each year)

By status in employment	Total				Urban				Rural			
	1991		2002		1991		2002		1991		2002	
	Informal	Formal	Informal	Formal	Informal	Formal	Informal	Formal	Informal	Formal	Informal	Formal
Apprentices	1.0%	0.0%	0.4%	0.0%	1.8%	0.0%	0.5%	0.0%	0.4%	0.0%	0.2%	0.0%
Men	1.0	0.0	0.4	0.0	1.7	0.0	0.5	0.0	0.4	0.0	0.2	0.0
Women	0.1	0.0	0.0	0.0	0.1	0.0	0.0	0.0	0.0	0.0	0.0	0.0
Domestic workers	5.4	0.0	6.2	0.0	8.7	0.0	6.2	0.0	2.6	0.0	6.3	0.0
Men	0.3	0.0	0.6	0.0	0.4	0.0	0.5	0.0	0.3	0.0	0.7	0.0
Women	5.0	0.0	5.7	0.0	8.4	0.0	5.7	0.0	2.3	0.0	5.6	0.0
Other	0.1	0.0	0.7	0.0	0.1	0.0	0.3	0.0	0.0	0.0	1.3	0.0
Men	0.1	0.0	0.7	0.0	0.1	0.0	0.2	0.0	0.0	0.0	1.2	0.0
Women	0.0		0.0	0.0	0.0		0.0	0.0	0.0	0.0	0.1	0.0

Source: Author's analysis based on the working proposal of the definition of informal employment.

egory except domestic services in rural areas, levels of informality dropped.

To a certain extent, self-employment has become the most immediate option for absorbing unemployed labor from the formal sector of the economy (which is the least difficult population to insert into the labor market). Nevertheless, self-employment as a subset of the informal sector is characterized by the lack of measures that provide decent employment. Based on the definition of informal employment, the levels of informality are high in this sector: in 2002, 94.2% (the equivalent of 685,604 people) of the workers in this category were informal and 5.8% were formal (see Appendix Table 16).

Furthermore, self-employment is the category in which women are second-most represented, next to domestic employment. Self-employed women represent 26.4% of informal employment in urban areas, while self-employed men make up 16.4% (**Table 18**). In El Salvador, self-employment or independent work led by women has become a way to complement household income. This kind of work still obligates women to simultaneously undertake household responsibilities, which are traditionally relegated to women.

The self-employed working population has increased its participation in the formal sector. In 2002, it represented 5.6% of total formal employment, up from 0.01% in 1991. As is the case with informal employment, self-employed women have greater participation in formal employment, except in rural areas where men have higher participation due to the (traditionally male) agricultural nature of most independent activities.

According to Table 18, the population with the highest level of formality is the permanent salaried category, which represented 85.9% of formal employment in 2002. These workers are the ones who most benefit from labor legislation guaranteeing stability, employment security, and income. From the perspective of the definition of the informal sector, these are workers who are for the most part employed by large registered businesses.

Although permanent salaried workers make up the largest part of formal employment, in recent years the growth in percentage terms has been light. In comparison with 1991, these workers' participation in urban areas has been especially reduced. Another important change observed in this category is that salaried women have increased their participation while men's participation has fallen. In 1991, permanent salaried women represented 31.0% of formal employment while men made up 55.1%; in 2002, the percentage for women rose to 38.4% and for men it fell to 47.5%.

Greater participation by women in the category of permanent salaried workers is explained by the promotion of export-oriented industrial activities, which in El Salvador has benefited textile manufacturing. Due to the nature of this industry and the sexual division of labor, this type of work has been more open to women. For example, women are estimated to represent approximately 88% of the population employed in this sector, and the majority of these women are heads of household (see Alvarenga 2001); thus, their work extends beyond their place of employment to their home.

In the category of employers, informality is determined according to the size of the establishment (by the number of workers based on the definition of the informal sector). In the period under consideration, the percentage of owner-employers in formal businesses fell while the number of informal businesses or informal employers rose (Table 18). This trend indicates that during this period there has been a proliferation of people working as employers but with the high degree of vulnerability that characterizes small productive units.

Economic activities employing formal and informal labor
Among the different sectors or branches of activity, some stand out as especially generating either formal or informal employment, while others generate both types. Sectors linked to the state generate employment that provides worker stability and security (in other words, formal employment). These sectors include public administration and defense, education, and social services and health, which made up 31.3% of formal employment for 2002 (**Table 19**).

It is natural that these sectors would provide the highest degree of formality, since the state acts both as employer and guarantor of economic well-being and social justice of the population, including workers. Nevertheless, the percentage of these workers who are informal has increased slightly: in administration and public defense they make up 0.5% of the workforce, with most of these being permanent salaried workers in rural areas.

While the sectors linked to the state generate a significant percentage of formal employment, during the period under consideration we

TABLE 19 Employed population by type of employment and branch of economic activity (percentages of participation according to each type of employment)

Kind of economic activity	1991			1994			1997		
	Total	Formal	Informal	Total	Formal	Informal	Total	Formal	Informal
Total	100.0%	100.0%	100.0%	100.0%	100.0%	100.0%	100.0%	100.0%	100.0%
1. Agriculture, hunting, and forestry	35.2	7.7	43.1	27.6	3.2	36.2	25.5	2.8	33.2
2. Fishing	0.7	0.2	0.8	0.4	0.1	0.5	0.8	0.2	1.0
3. Mining and quarrying	0.1	0.2	0.1	0.1	0.1	0.1	0.1	0.2	0.0
4. Manufacturing	17.3	24.2	15.3	19.6	27.0	17.0	16.1	25.3	13.0
5. Electricity, gas, and water	0.6	2.6	0.1	0.4	1.5	0.0	0.7	2.1	0.3
6. Construction	4.5	5.4	4.3	5.8	7.3	5.2	6.7	7.8	6.3
7. Wholesale and retail trade, restaurants, and hotels	19.6%	13.4%	21.3%	22.2%	16.2%	24.3%	24.6%	19.2%	26.4%
8. Transport, storage, and communications	3.4%	4.5%	3.1%	4.0%	4.4%	3.8%	4.6%	3.7%	5.0%
9. Finance, insurance, and real estate	2.0	5.7	0.9	2.7	6.8	1.3	3.0	8.1	1.3
10. Public administration	4.4	16.9	0.8	4.2	14.2	0.7	4.4	14.5	1.0
11. Education	2.5	9.0	0.6	2.8	9.3	0.6	3.3	5.8	2.4
12. Community, social, and personal services	5.3%	9.7%	4.1%	6.0%	9.6%	4.7%	5.7%	10.0%	4.2%
13. Home work (domestic services)	4.1	0.0	5.3	4.1	-	5.6	4.4	-	5.8
14. Others	0.1	0.3	0.1	0.1	0.3	0.0	0.1	0.2	0.0

(continued)

TABLE 19 (cont.) Employed population by type of employment and branch of economic activity (percentages of participation according to each type of employment)

Kind of economic activity	2000			2001			2002		
	Total	Formal	Informal	Total	Formal	Informal	Total	Formal	Informal
Total	100.0%	100.0%	100.0%	100.0%	100.0%	100.0%	100.0%	100.0%	100.0%
1. Agriculture, hunting, and forestry	20.9	2.7	29.0	21.2	2.4	29.4	19.0	2.4	26.4
2. Fishing	0.7	0.1	1.0	0.5	0.1	0.7	0.7	0.1	0.9
3. Mining and quarrying	0.1	0.1	0.1	0.1	0.1	0.2	0.1	0.1	0.2
4. Manufacturing	18.7	26.9	15.0	17.6	26.4	13.8	18.0	27.3	13.8
5. Electricity, gas, and water	0.4	1.0	0.1	0.4	1.3	0.1	0.4	1.2	0.1
6. Construction	5.1	4.5	5.4	5.4	4.1	6.0	5.6	4.8	6.0
7. Wholesale and retail trade, restaurants, and hotels	26.3%	19.0%	29.6%	27.2%	19.8%	30.5%	28.5%	19.6%	32.5%
8. Transport, storage, and communications	4.7%	4.4%	4.8%	4.6%	4.9%	4.5%	4.3%	3.8%	4.5%
9. Finance, insurance, and real estate	3.8	8.2	1.8	4.1	9.6	1.7	4.1	9.4	1.7
10. Public administration	5.3	15.7	0.7	4.0	11.8	0.6	4.2	12.4	0.5
11. Education	3.0	8.3	0.7	3.6	10.0	0.8	3.9	10.5	1.0
12. Community, social, and personal services	6.7%	9.0%	5.6	6.3%	9.4%	5.0%	6.4%	8.5%	5.5%
13. Home work (domestic services)	4.3	-	6.3	4.7	-	6.7	4.3	-	6.2
14. Others	0.1	0.1	0.0	0.1	0.1	0.0	0.4	0.1	0.6

Source: Author's analysis based on the working proposal for the definition of informal employment.

have seen a reduction in these sectors' participation in formal employment. In 1991, the three aforementioned sectors — public administration and defense, education, and social services and health — made up 35.6% of formal employment, while in 2002 their share fell to 31.3%. This reduction is due to the implementation of structural adjustment and privatization measures intended to reduce public spending. These measures have led to a reduced capacity to generate employment in public institutions.

The sector in which informal employment predominates is households with domestic servants, who are by definition informal due to the vulnerability this type of work entails. The agricultural/cattle raising/ hunting sector is also predominately informal, with 69.1% of these workers in an informal employment situation. This sector accounts for just 2.4% of total national formal employment and 26.4% of informal employment (see Appendix Table 18). This situation can be explained by the fact that labor legislation guarantees little stability or security to agricultural workers. It is common to find clauses in labor market legislation that make exceptions for agricultural and domestic workers, granting them lower labor standards than other workers.

The sectors with a significant presence of formal as well as informal labor are manufacturing and commercial/hotels/restaurants. During the period of structural adjustment, labor generation has largely been left to these sectors, especially commercial activities. However, these sectors are characterized by a greater degree of informality in employment; informal employment is 171% greater than formal employment. This is also the category with the most self-employed, legally marginal workers.

As for manufacturing, the gap between informal and formal employment is 13.6%. The participation of this sector in formal employment is 27.3%, compared to 13.8% in informal employment. In terms of the overall population in manufacturing, there are more informal workers (53.2%) than formal workers (see Appendix Tables 17 and 18). It is important to note that this sector includes the *maquilladora* industry, which has been repeatedly criticized for creating precarious jobs that fall short of the definition of decent employment. In many cases *maquilladora* owners make selective use of the law in order to avoid their responsibilities to workers.

In terms of gender, women in informal employment tend to be located in the commercial sector and manufacturing; these activities make up 70.3% of informal female employment (**Figure M**). It is important to note that 3.6% of female informal workers are found in activities that have traditionally been assigned to men (agriculture); these women generally labor as non-remunerated family members and temporary salaried workers.[21]

As we have noted, the greater presence of women in commercial activities and manufacturing is due to traditional cultural patterns and/ or the potential for combining these types of work with household duties. The primary sectors in which formal female employment is found are industry (32.1%), commerce (21.4%), education (14.4%), and social services (11.7%).

As for men in informal employment, 41.9% work in the agricultural/cattle farming/hunting sector and to a lesser degree in commerce, manufacturing, and construction. Among the primary activities employing men in formal arrangements are industry, commerce, public administration, and construction.

Remuneration and poverty

The informal working population is characterized by a low level of remuneration (Appendix Table 19) that is below monthly minimum salaries (with the exception of the agricultural minimum salary). According to our calculations, in 2002 62% of informal jobs (the equivalent of 1,033,796 workers, including those who are non-remunerated) paid less than US $114 per month, as did 13.6% of formal jobs. In terms of gender, the percentage of informally employed women with incomes below US $114 (63.4%) is slightly higher than that of men (61.1%).

The percentage of informal employees with remunerations less than US $114 is 49.0% in urban areas and 77.2% in rural ones. These results are troubling, since they represent a significant number of people who do not have the necessary income to satisfy basic needs. In other words, 49% of informal urban workers receive a salary that does not even cover the cost of their basic food needs, which were estimated in 2002 to be US $127.04 per month.

Low income levels have had an impact on the poverty levels of informal workers;[22] as **Table 20** shows, informal workers have higher levels of poverty than formal workers. In 2002, 42.7% of informal workers were living in poverty,[23] 18.0% in extreme poverty. These indicators are

**FIGURE M   Informal employment by gender and economic activity
(as percentage of total informal employment for each gender)**

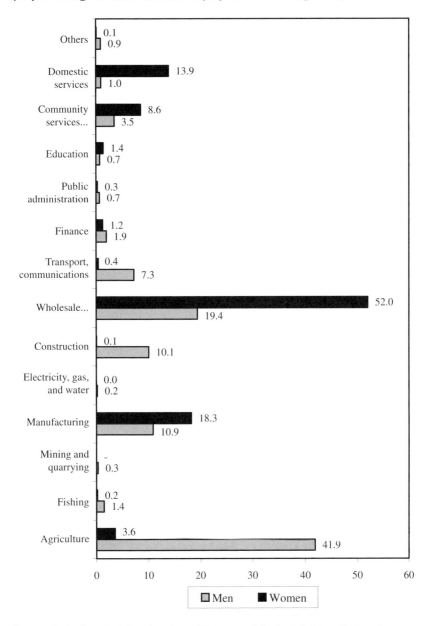

Sources: Author's analysis based on the working proposal for the definition of informal
employment.

TABLE 20 Formal and informal employment by poverty status, 2002 (as a percentage of total informal and formal employment in each area of the country)

	Total			Urban			Rural		
	Total	Formal	Informal	Total	Formal	Informal	Total	Formal	Informal
Total	100	100	100	100	100	100	100	100	100
Poverty	33.6	13.3	42.7	25.7	12.7	34.7	47.1	16.4	52.1
Extreme poverty	13.3	2.9	18.0	7.8	2.8	11.3	22.7	3.2	25.8
Relative poverty	20.3	10.4	24.7	17.8	9.9	23.4	24.4	13.2	26.2
Not poor	66.4	86.7	57.3	74.3	87.3	65.3	52.9	83.6	47.9
Men	100	100	100	100	100	100	100	100	100
Poverty	37.4	14.4	46.8	26.0	13.2	35.2	51.8	19.3	56.7
Extreme poverty	16.5	3.1	22.0	8.4	2.8	12.3	26.9	4.1	30.3
Relative poverty	20.9	11.3	24.8	17.6	10.4	22.9	24.9	15.2	26.4
Not poor	62.6	85.6	53.2	74.0	86.8	64.8	48.2	80.7	43.3
Women	100	100	100	100	100	100	100	100	100
Poverty	28.3	11.9	36.6	25.3	12.1	34.2	36.5	10.9	41.2
Extreme poverty	8.9	2.6	12.0	7.3	2.8	10.3	13.2	1.6	15.3
Relative poverty	19.5	9.3	24.6	18.0	9.3	23.9	23.3	9.3	25.9
Not poor	71.7	88.1	63.4	74.7	87.9	65.8	63.5	89.1	58.8

Source: Author's analysis based on proposed working definition for informal employment.

even greater in rural areas, where more than half of informal workers are poor.

In summary, employment in El Salvador is characterized by high levels of informality. Close to 70% of the employed population is vulnerable in its place of work, whether because of limited access to loans, employment instability, or the precariousness of owning small productive units. This population receives low pay and works in economic sectors in which labor law is selectively enforced. Furthermore, during the 1990s, sectors that generated formal employment in the past reduced their capacity to do so due to structural adjustment reforms.

State of the imbalance of skills and training in the labor market

Training and the development of skilled employees are fundamental to the success and growth of a technical-professional sector, especially with regard to jobs that provide stability and security. The overall lack of training and the low availability of skilled employees is due to the fact that more of the working population is faced with unequal opportunities, landing them in low-level, unstable, and unregulated jobs, a situation further decreasing their opportunity to learn new skills and acquire the training necessary to move up.

One of the key factors in the success and competitiveness of a country or business is the demand for and acquisition of skilled labor. This same issue often determines the formality or informality of employment. Skilled workers are concentrated in stable, regulated industries, while unskilled workers must settle for more precarious working conditions.

Following an exploration of the skills and training that contribute to the formation of and a growing gap between formal and informal employment, this section outlines some indicators that give us a picture of the training of the Salvadoran workforce in the sectors we have been discussing.

Levels of experience

One variable that can serve as an indicator of the skill level of a worker is age, as we assume that skill and competency is acquired over time. As evidenced by **Figure N**, the experience factor as measured by age is important in determining the make-up of formal and informal employ-

FIGURE N   Employed population by age and type of employment, 2002 (as percentage of the total for each respective type of employment)

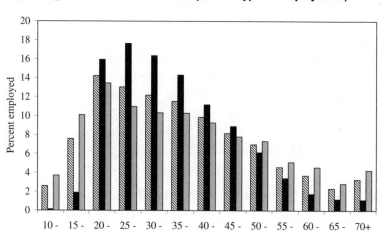

Source: Author's analysis based on the working proposal for the definition of informal employment.

ment. For instance, those between 10 and 19 years old enter easily into the informal sector, and represent some 13.8% of it, whereas they make up only 2.0% of the formal sector. Another way to look at this statistic is to note that 90% of these youngest workers have informal status and about 9% formal, wherein they have access to social services.

The formal sector is made up primarily of workers with mid-level experience, ages 20-44. There is a drop-off, though, in formal employment among the next level of experience and age. We must keep in mind, though, that many of these older workers are self-employed or have some other sort of arrangement that cannot be considered formal since it lacks stability and access to regulation and services.

Educational levels

Another indication of a worker's skill is his or her level of education, measured by the number of years of schooling completed. According to recent calculations, 20.7% of informal workers lack schooling, 63.3% have 1-9 years of formal education, and those with further schooling

FIGURE O   Employed population by type of work and years of schooling, 2002 (as percentage of the total for each respective type of employment)

Source: Author's analysis based on the working proposal for the definition of informal employment.

make up 16.0% (**Figure O**). In the formal sector, the numbers are markedly different: just 2.3% lack any education, whereas 61.5% have completed intermediary school or higher.

An analysis by geographic region reveals notable differences in education levels and employment. In 2002, 5.1% of the rural informal sector was made up of those with higher levels of education, whereas this demographic group made up 25.3% of the urban informal sector (not shown in figure). While these levels may seem counterintuitive, it speaks to the nature of employment in El Salvador. To receive higher levels of education many move from rural to urban areas, which feature a higher concentration of schools and universities. Additionally, those who achieve higher education levels often leave rural areas in search of better and more suited work. Consequently, rural areas are left without educated workers, and urban areas often cannot provide them jobs.

The same imbalance exists for those holding a degree: 80.7% of informal workers have no degree, compared to 48.5% of formal workers (**Table 21**).

TABLE 21 Employed population by type of work and educational degree (as a percentage of the total for each respective type of employment)

Degree earned	2000			2001			2002		
	Total	Formal	Informal	Total	Formal	Informal	Total	Formal	Informal
TOTAL	100.0	100.0	100.0	100.0	100.0	100.0	100.0	100.0	100.0
None	74.5	52.0	84.6	72.8	48.5	83.4	70.7	48.5	80.7
High school	17.9	30.9	12.0	19.8	34.1	13.5	21.9	35.0	16.1
University	3.5	8.3	1.4	3.7	8.9	1.4	3.8	9.0	1.5
Post-graduate	0.1	0.2	0.0	0.1	0.2	0.0	0.0	0.2	0.0
Military	0.3	0.6	0.1	0.1	0.3	0.1	0.1	0.2	0.1
Teaching	1.0	2.0	0.5	1.3	3.0	0.6	1.1	2.4	0.6
Nursing	0.2	0.6	0.1	0.3	0.7	0.1	0.2	0.4	0.1
Social work	0.1	0.1	0.0	0.0	0.1	0.0	0.0	0.0	0.0
University seminars	2.3	4.9	1.1	1.8	4.0	0.8	1.9	4.0	0.9
Other	0.2	0.4	0.1	0.1	0.2	0.1	0.2	0.4	0.1
Male	100.0	100.0	100.0	100.0	100.0	100.0	100.0	100.0	100.0
None	77.3	56.3	86.1	76.0	52.9	85.1	74.7	53.3	83.5
High school	16.1	29.1	10.6	17.9	32.9	12.0	19.5	33.2	13.8
University	3.1	7.4	1.3	3.2	7.8	1.3	3.0	7.2	1.3
Post-graduate	0.1	0.1	0.0	0.0	0.2	0.0	0.1	0.3	0.0
Military	0.4	0.9	0.1	0.2	0.4	0.0	0.1	0.2	0.1
Teaching	0.8	1.5	0.5	0.9	2.2	0.5	0.8	1.8	0.4
Nursing	0.2	0.4	0.1	0.2	0.4	0.1	0.1	0.2	0.1
Social work	0.0	0.1	0.0	0.0	0.1	0.0	0.0	0.0	0.0
University seminars	1.8	3.9	1.0	1.4	2.9	0.8	1.5	3.2	0.8
Other	0.2	0.3	0.1	0.1	0.2	0.1	0.2	0.4	0.1

(continued)

TABLE 21 (cont.) Employed population by type of work and educational degree (as a percentage of the total for each respective type of employment)

Degree earned	2000			2001			2002		
	Total	Formal	Informal	Total	Formal	Informal	Total	Formal	Informal
Female	100.0	100.0	100.0	100.0	100.0	100.0	100.0	100.0	100.0
None	70.5	46.3	82.4	68.1	43.1	80.6	65.2	42.7	76.5
High school	20.4	33.2	14.2	22.4	35.6	15.9	25.3	37.0	19.4
University	4.1	9.6	1.5	4.5	10.3	1.6	4.9	11.3	1.8
Post-graduate	0.1	0.3	0.0	0.1	0.2	0.0	0.0	0.0	0.0
Military	0.2	0.2	0.2	0.1	0.1	0.1	0.1	0.1	0.1
Teaching	1.2	2.7	0.5	1.8	4.1	0.7	1.6	3.0	0.8
Nursing	0.3	0.8	0.1	0.4	1.0	0.1	0.3	0.6	0.2
Social work	0.1	0.2	0.0	0.0	0.0	0.0	0.0	0.0	0.0
University serninars	2.9	6.3	1.2	2.3	5.4	0.8	2.4	5.0	1.0
Other	0.2	0.4	0.1	0.1	0.2	0.0	0.2	0.2	0.2

Source: Author's analysis based on proposed working definition for informal employment.

Among those workers in the formal and informal sector who have degrees or diplomas, the majority has a high school diploma (35.0% of formal and 16.1% of informal). Only 9.2% of formal and just 1.5% of informal workers have received a university or post-graduate degree.

The figures in **Table 21** show that female workers — both formal and informal — generally hold higher levels of education than males, especially with regard to high school and university education.

Though women generally have higher levels of education, this status does not translate to an advantage in the workforce. Cultural norms persist that devalue women's work, and females are compensated disproportionately and have less access to loans, services, and other advantages.

Unskilled workers

The EHPM household survey enables a breakdown of the working population by specific occupation as well as by skill level and type of specialization acquired on the job or in training. Thus, workers in military sectors, farming or livestock, craftsmanship, public works, scientific and technical employment, commercial services, and machine operation can be identified. Those not falling into these basic categories — which are outlined in the ISCO (International Standard Classification of Occupations) — are said to be unskilled workers[24] in that they participate in activities that do not require specific skills or advanced training.

The CIUO lets us identify three basic types of work by skill level. The first are those high-level jobs that require significant training, among them academic, scientific, public sector work, and the professional sector. The next are mid-level skill jobs: merchants, service workers, agriculture, fishing and livestock, and artists. The third is the group with minimal refined skill needed in their work.

The most recent figures show that the informal sector has a high level of unskilled workers compared to the formal sector; 39.5% of informal workers are employed in unskilled jobs, compared to 15.2% of the formal sector (**Table 22**). This is consistent with the trend of informal workers being less educated and finding themselves in more labor-intensive jobs.

With regard to gender, types of training and subsequent skill levels follow existing cultural norms: women are skilled in traditionally fe-

TABLE 22 Employed population by type of employment and acquired skill level, 2002 (as a percentage of the total for each respective type of employment)

Acquired skill level	Total			Men			Women		
	Total employment	Formal	Informal	Total employment	Formal	Informal	Total employment	Formal	Informal
Totals	100.0	100.0	100.0	100.0	100.0	100.0	100.0	100.0	100.0
Armed forces	0.2	0.6	0.0	0.3	1.1	0.0	0.0	0.0	0.0
Legislators, senior officials, and managers	1.0	2.4	0.4	1.3	3.1	0.6	0.6	1.5	0.2
Professionals	3.1	8.1	0.8	2.8	7.6	0.9	3.4	8.6	0.7
Technicians and associate professionals	8.3	21.3	2.5	7.7	19.8	2.8	9.1	23.1	2.1
Clerks (office employed)	5.2	13.6	1.4	3.1	8.0	1.0	8.1	20.2	2.0
Service workers and shop and market sales workers	17.6	13.4	19.4	9.4	10.2	9.1	28.9	17.3	34.7
Skilled agricultural and fishery workers	8.9	1.3	12.3	14.7	2.3	19.8	0.7	0.1	1.0
Craft and related trades workers	15.9	8.8	19.0	16.3	12.8	17.7	15.2	3.9	20.9
Plant and machine operators and assemblers	8.0	15.4	4.7	8.7	13.5	6.8	6.9	17.6	1.6
Elementary occupations (unskilled Workers)	32.0	15.2	39.5	35.6	21.5	41.3	27.0	7.6	36.8

Source: Author's analysis based on proposed working definition for informal employment.

male areas such as commerce and certain industries (textiles, for instance), while men are trained and reach high skill levels in agriculture, livestock, machine operation, etc. Note that the percentage of unskilled male workers is higher.

During the period analyzed the number of formal workers trained and skilled in public administration and defense has dropped. They represented 16.89% of formal employment in 1991, 14.52% in 1997, and 12.3% in 2002. This trend is a result of the economic reforms, which have restructured the labor market such that fewer and fewer public sector jobs are available.

Gaps in skill, training, and experience are significant with regard to the economy's ability to develop and expand. The wide gap between these factors in the formal and informal sectors reverberates throughout the entire economy, denying access to jobs and stunting overall growth. Both the individual worker and the economy as a whole are left in a perilous condition.

Policies for labor market development

The need for a labor market policy

The development of a progressive labor policy requires a strong democratic state, with governance over all political, economic, and social sectors. A state that maintains strong services (health, infrastructure, education), organizations (legal system, police, security, external relations), and other auxiliary duties will be positioned to promote a strong economic structure (Salazar 1991, 487).

The definition and development of labor policy with regards to the different parties involved (the state, the labor sector, private enterprise) must keep in mind the following principles:

- Employment is a pillar of an effective development strategy that seeks to combat poverty. Household incomes must be stable and sufficient.

- Gender gaps must be closed, with female workers reaching equal footing with their male counterparts.

- Working conditions and the role of the state in promoting a stable and just job market cannot be subject to the fluctuation of the economy. Labor policy must remain above demand-and-supply issues.

• Job policy must recognize national and international labor rights in order to guarantee adequate conditions for all workers.

• In addition to recognizing the role of labor legislation, job policy must also support institutions and measures taken to promote job creation.

With these basic principles in mind, along with ideas put forth by economic and labor organizations, we present below some recommendations for development in the institutional, legal, and production sectors.

Recommendations for the development of the labor force[25]
Labor development and mediation
Labor placement services. One of the functions of the Labor and Social Services Ministry is that of a clearinghouse: it manages a web site where workers can post their resumes and employers can post openings. Thus, the ministry serves to place workers and find them jobs. However, as discussed earlier, this system has grown inefficient, and the ministry no longer effectively finds opportunities for workers. This situation requires significant improvement.

A recent analysis of this problem (Mazza 2003) concluded that several measures ought to be taken: private placement agencies ought to be supervised effectively; coordination between these services and job creation programs must be better managed; technology must be updated; clearer and more thorough information must be obtained for workers regarding types of employment, services, wages, private and public sector work, etc. (**Table 23**).

In El Salvador two models of worker placement have been developed: public monopoly by the Labor and Social Services Ministry and privately provided services that have been implemented by the Foundation for Integral Education of El Salvador with the support of the ministry.

In spite of having two systems of worker placement, the results have been minimal; as discussed earlier, the ministry's mediation program had trouble providing employment to the population covered by the program. Of the total number of people signed up in 2002, only 17.5% were placed. Only 3.2% of people signed up in the private system had

TABLE 23 Models of labor placement services

Model	Characteristics
Public monopoly	The need for the public sector to take on this role is fundamentally based on the theory of market imperfections that lead to an insufficient provision of employment services for certain kinds of workers. In the framework of the model based on the public sector, there is a single national public service, generally dependent on a department of labor or other executive body, to which all workers have access without charge.
National employment service that competes with private providers	Employment agencies and services of private employment are permitted, but the private and public services act independently of one another. The private employment agencies can be regulated by the public service or other body, or operate solely by market forces. The coexistence of private and public providers is beneficial because competition will increase the quality of mediation and promote innovation.
Partnerships between public and private employment services	In this model, the association is defined as a non-competitive, collaborative relationship, for which public and private institutions share, among other things, resources, information, services, and users.
Tripartite autonomous services and participation of key social actors	These services are neither exclusively public nor private; they function independently and make decisions about the action of the offices and the provision of services. Generally, these receive significant public financing via subsidies and payment for capacity-building services, but the day-to-day administration is independent of the public sector.
Network based on competence, with public financing	This institutional model is strongly determined by achievements, since the organization (whether it is public, private, or non-profit) receives a certain sum of money for every unemployed person it places, and an extra sum if the person had been unemployed for a long time.
Services based on the private sector	In this model, there are no public providers. Nevertheless, the public sector can provide financing to private providers in order to promote its own objectives.

Source: Mazza (2003).

found employment by December 2003. This situation requires a revision of the existing labor mediation services.

In order to improve the effectiveness of labor placement models — and in the process reduce levels of informality — the institutions charged with this service should consider the following recommendations: promotion of efficiently supervised private agencies, coordination of the placement program with training programs, incorporation of new advances in information technology, institutional coordination, clear definition of the profile of people to be placed, and evaluation and monitoring of private as well as public services (see Samaniego 2002).

Furthermore, as Mazza proposes, when informal employment is high the labor placement programs should take the challenges of this sector into account so that the programs are more suited to the country's reality (Mazza 2003, 182). Thus, programs or models should pay special attention to those sectors that have a hard time with labor placement and those workers who are inserted into jobs that don't guarantee labor stability and security.

Professional training. The process of commercial expansion that the country is currently undergoing requires a workforce that is able to meet the demands of new industries that compete both internally and externally. The development of a qualified professional class is key, then, if domestic businesses are to enter the international market. In addition, the development of such a class would allow for certain citizens who are unsuited for traditional activities to be absorbed into the workforce. In the effective development and training of a professional class, we ought to bear in mind these recommendations:

• Professional training ought to be in line with socioeconomic development strategies and the internal and external needs of the production sector.

• The Education Ministry, the Ministry of Labor and Social Services, the Economic Ministry, the Salvadoran Institute for Professional Development, and the Ministry of Agriculture and Livestock need to coordinate their services in order to take advantage of their various resources and knowledge.

• The Institute for Professional Development should be thoroughly reformed with the goal of strengthening its power, making it more efficient, and allowing it to perform its duties more effectively.

- Training and educational methods should be reviewed to ensure that they are in line with the country's strategies and meet the needs of the production sector.

- Training within businesses should be promoted through programs that facilitate professional development.

- Measures need to be taken to promote gender equity and fairness in training.

- Training centers should be coordinated with the Salvadoran Institute for Women's Development and other organizations that look to promote training and education, both formal and informal.

- Experts should reassess curriculum designs and monitor courses, lessons, and examinations.

- Design training programs that are geared towards specific geographic regions, and encourage the participation of local women.

Institutional framework for labor
Revitalization of the Ministry of Labor and Social Services.[26] Given the fact that informality is determined by access to social services and legal resources and protection, it follows that the ministry plays an important role in determining the nature of the informal sector in El Salvador. Several studies, though, have shown that the ministry not only provides inadequate legal regulation and enforcement, but is in fact a major violator of labor rights. In light of this, it is fundamental that an effective work policy rescues the ministry and restores it to an effective advocate of the labor sector. This can be done in several ways:

- Evaluate the personnel who govern and work at the ministry to ensure they are qualified and experienced in economic and labor policy issues and familiar with the nature of the El Salvadoran labor market.

- Make the General Labor Inspection Board more effective — and purge it of recently revealed corruption — so that it is able to perform its duties as outlined by mandate.

- Create means for workers and their organizations to supervise and monitor the ministry to ensure that it is free of corruption and illegal activity.

- Make the operations of the ministry more transparent, allowing access to workers and unions so that they may understand how their proposals are handled and how policy is determined.

- Develop methods that allow for more efficient mitigation of disputes between workers and employers.

- Raise expectations that the ministry performs its duties and actively enforces labor policy.

Enforcement by the attorney general for labor rights. Given that the role of the Office of the Attorney General for the Defense of Human Rights is to ensure that human rights are protected in El Salvador by public services and that violations are punished, its attorney general for labor rights should take on the responsibility of supervising and funding the labor ministry in its duties as mandated by labor law. Thus, if the ministry is found to be delinquent in its duties, it would be subject to both financial penalty and the will of the labor rights officer in correcting the infraction.

Full representation on the Superior Labor Council. The role of the council is to institutionalize and promote economic and social dialogue between government, workers, and the business sector. Given this, it follows that the council should be representative of these different constituencies. Greater access needs to be granted to labor organizations, and the council should become more transparent in its elections and appointments. These moves would promote a more just and balanced discussion regarding labor policy.

Institutionalization of gender equity. In order to promote and advance fair social and economic opportunities for both men and women, the state and especially the labor ministry need to institutionalize fairness and equity in job creation. Furthermore, the Fourth World Women's Conference, held in 1995 in Beijing (El Salvador was a participant), recommended that countries work toward integrating the concept of equality in all state functions: legislation, policy, programs, etc.

The Beijing accords led to the creation of the Salvadoran Institute for Women's Development and the National Female Policy, directed by the institute and created to promote equal opportunity. While there are some institutional links between the institute and the labor ministry, the two do not interact sufficiently and visibly enough, and they ought to work together to take concrete steps toward equality and fairness.

In order to assure equal employment opportunity and the promotion of job creation measures, a Gender Council ought to be created within the labor ministry, charged with the task of promoting fairness in job creation and coordinating with the Institute for Women's Development and nongovernmental organizations in promoting female equality and professional opportunities.

Legal framework

Unemployment aid. With the implementation of measures that guarantee some stability and aid for unemployed workers, the pressure on the unemployed to accept substandard jobs and diminished working conditions can be relieved, as can the proliferation of informal businesses. To that effect, below are three basic proposals for providing unemployment aid:

UNIVERSAL COMPENSATION

In light of the fact that, for one reason or another, workers leave their jobs and are not compensated accordingly, it is necessary to create an effective universal compensation law that grants workers their rights under the El Salvador Constitution.

Such compensation would involve an economic benefit given to a worker upon the termination of his or her contract, whether that occurred through firing, resignation, or mutual consent. Section 12 of Article 38 of the Constitution says that workers who resign ought to be compensated for their service according to current wages and length of service. This compensation ought to be equivalent to the basic wage for 70 days of pay for every year of service (including fractions of a year) that the employee worked in the business from which he or she is resigning. In calculating such payment, wages ought not to be less than 100 colones per day.

In order to implement this compensation plan effectively, it is necessary that the employer comply with the following:

1. At the beginning of any contract, the employer should create an account under the employee's name in which a monthly

amount is deposited toward the universal compensation fund. Such a fund would be non-negotiable and would be monitored by the Labor Ministry. At the end of the agreed-upon contract or upon resignation, the employee would be able to retrieve this amount.

2. If the contract is terminated, an employer should present to the employee a detailed account of the terms of service, completed service, wages paid, and the cause for termination. With regard to compensation, the employee ought to have legal recourse with the Labor Ministry if he or she is not compensated properly.

3. The document, to be signed by both employer and employee, can serve alone as evidence and grant the employee access to the amount deposited in his or her compensation fund.

4. An employer's refusal to accept the resignation of an employee would constitute unjust firing and the compensation would have to be paid.

5. The obligations of the employee and rights of the worker as outlined above would also apply if the worker were to become permanently incapacitated or die, in which case the beneficiaries of the worker would be able to seek compensation from the employer.

UNEMPLOYMENT INSURANCE

Unemployment benefits would have as their objective the financial, temporary compensation of workers who have lost their jobs involuntarily or by extraneous circumstance.

Involuntary unemployment can be defined in the following ways:

1. The downsizing of the number of employees in a company resulting from reduced production demand.

2. Retirement due to valid health reasons that limit the worker's ability to perform his or her duties.

3. Retirement as a result of poor working conditions or a lack of rights within the workplace.

4. Retirement due to relocation.

The termination of a contract due to poor performance would not be considered involuntary unemployment.

The cost of unemployment assistance would be divided among the employer, the worker, and the government, and upon the implementation of a universal compensation plan the business would also contribute to this fund. The unemployment fund would last for one year, as long as the beneficiaries can prove that they are looking for employment. This process would be monitored by a government office, the same office through which benefits would be distributed.

Compensation would be set at a minimum of 60% of the current minimum wage, with this figure dropping to 30% for the last six months. This percentage would be adjusted according to the needs of each candidate, and would be tax exempt. The administration of the program should exist within the public sector, and the profits from the program would be reinvested in government social programs.

GUARANTEE OF LABOR OBLIGATIONS[27]

Commercial legislation in El Salvador obliges businesses to account for their labor obligations. The supervision of this law is in the hands of the Mercantile Industries Superintendent, but the agency enforces the law inadequately, and many businesses do not meet their obligations.

In order to avoid labor fraud, businesses must be held accountable for meeting their social security, salary, compensation, and labor responsibilities as well as their obligations to their retired. To this end, the Office of the Superintendent must be given greater power.

Measures to strengthen labor organization. In order to ensure the negotiation power and promotion of the interests of the labor sector in its fight for better working conditions and against informal employment, mechanisms need to be implemented that guarantee the basic rights and freedoms of labor organizations.

The ILO has proposed eight pacts to be ratified and enforced by all of its member states: Pact 87, regarding union freedoms and protections; Pact 98, regarding union collective negotiation; Pact 29, regarding forced labor; Pact 105, regarding the abolition of forced labor; Pact 111, regarding discrimination; Pact 100, regarding equal compensation; Pact 138, regarding minimum working age; and a final pact regarding child labor abuses.

Of these eight basic accords, El Salvador has failed to ratify 87 and 98, those regarding union freedoms, on the grounds that they contradict the Constitution. Though many legal scholars suggest this is not the case, the Constitution should be amended to allow the adoption of these pacts.

Once these constitutional issues are dealt with, these two pacts and the following additional ILO pacts regarding union freedoms ought to be ratified:[28]

- Pact 87: Union Freedoms and Protections
  This pact asserts that all workers and employers have the right to organize freely to promote and defend their interests. Public authorities are barred from interfering from such organization, and must respect the autonomy of these groups.

- Pact 98: Union Rights and Collective Negotiation
  This pact protects workers from persecution for their affiliation with a union. It also encourages and fosters voluntary collective negotiation.

- Pact 135: Labor Representatives
  Offers protection for labor leaders from retribution or prejudice. This protection would apply for all activities related to legally recognized unions and activities.

- Pact 141: Rural Workers Organizations
  This pact establishes the right of rural workers to organize unions and freely operate them. These are the same rights as outlined in Pact 89. In addition, it states that national policy should promote and reserve a place for such organizations in economic development plans.

- Pact 151: Relations With Public Administration
  This pact protects public employees unions from interference by public authorities.

Minimum wage. Article 144 of the Labor Code states that all workers have a right to a minimum wage that sufficiently covers normal household costs. Article 145 directs that the minimum wage be determined by the overall cost of living and differences in geography, employment, and other criteria. Nonetheless, the minimum wage is inadequate when one takes into account the real cost of basic necessities, not simply food.

The following proposal should be adopted to guarantee a real living wage:

- The Labor Ministry should determine the process used to set the minimum wage. This process ought to be transparent and available to the public.

- The method for determining the basic cost index must be revised so that it accurately represents the actual costs of living.

- Given the determinants outlined in Article 145, the benchmark for the minimum wage should be the expanded cost index (roughly twice the basic good index). This measure would ensure that costs are met for food, clothing, and education.

- Alternatively, the Labor Ministry could conduct a yearly study to determine the actual costs of living, taking into account both basic costs as outlined in Article 146 and the average food, clothing, and education costs for a working family. The survey would look to realistically determine a living wage and any adjustments that would have to be made to the minimum wage.

- Article 159, which currently states that "by law, fixed minimum wages ought to be revised every three years at least," should be revised to read that "by law, fixed minimum wages ought to be revised yearly."

- Reform Article 152, section "a", to read: "It is the duty of the Council (National Council on the Minimum Wage) to "present to the Executive branch, the Labor Branch and Social Services, each year, a plan for the adjustment and setting of the minimum wage."

Measures to create employment
Subsidies to promote job growth. Job subsidies can be defined as money contributed by a government to businesses in order to combat unemployment or alleviate informality in work status. Such subsidies can take several forms, including a fixed monetary contribution, tax credit on business revenue, or relief in rent payments.

It is proposed that employment subsidies integrate the following:

- Subsidies could be delivered in the form of rent exemptions. In other words, businesses that create new jobs would receive a refund of some of their rent payments from the government.

- The percentage of exemption should fall within a range, with the state determining a minimum and maximum amount of financial relief. The government would revise this range each fiscal year.

- The program should be structured to benefit only those businesses that have generated a certain number of long-term jobs.

- The amount of relief should be adjusted to the relative number of jobs created. For instance, a business would qualify for a higher credit if it created more jobs than the average number of jobs created in its sector or industry that year.

- The subsidy could be reinvested in the business, to improve working conditions, purchase new equipment, technology, etc.

Another approach to the subsidy could be to direct it to employers who hire workers from a certain population, workers who have had difficulty finding employment, those with little access to the job market, etc.

Promotion of labor-intensive sectors. The sectoral analysis by Matriz Insumo Producto allows a determination of which sectors are creating the most jobs. These sectors could be targeted with financial incentives, technical assistance, professional training, and other related programs in order to promote competition and allow businesses within that sector to create demand for workers.

Promotion of small business and self-employment. Self-employment and small businesses provide important relief for unemployment, and they ought to be supported by government programs. This step would require an assessment of the role of the National Commission on Self-Owned and Small Businesses, and a re-evaluation of the effects of current policy on such businesses. Government support could include employment programs, technical assistance, financial support, market assistance, etc.

Conclusion

Economic policy in El Salvador, as in other Latin American countries, has adhered to the Washington Consensus by promoting concrete stabilization and economic adjustment reforms. After 15 years of these policies, the results for the Salvadoran economy have been less favorable than expected. Since the 1990s, the country has been in a period of economic deceleration, and it has looked to liberalization policy and commercial treaties to revive production.

But the growth policies have changed the structure of the El Salvadoran economy, gearing it toward less and less intervention on the part of the state, a focus on economic liberalization that favors the external sector at the expense of traditional sectors (agriculture), the development of industrial sector exports, and the promotion of highly profitable sectors such as financial and commercial services. In effect, El Salvador's economy has become a service economy, with even industry performing more service than production by merely assembling parts for export rather than generating real and lasting wealth.

With regard to humanitarian development, certain indicators have improved, but development has been unequal across regions. The three urban sectors, with the highest industrial concentration, show the most growth, and they are generating further income for those already in the wealthiest sector. These statistics reveal a dualistic nature in both the Salvadoran economy and society.

The labor market has not been immune to the effects of the growth schemes. In a general sense, labor issues have been neglected in favor of promoting the external sector. Thus, the only real labor progress has occurred in that sector, while the majority of the domestic labor sector has been marginalized and seen little policy aimed at stabilizing and promoting the life of Salvadoran workers.

Furthermore, recent policies aimed at redefining the role of the state in economic affairs — policies that favor a select few groups and concentrate power among those already in a position of wealth — have weakened government influence and promoted a pro-business labor climate.

With job creation concentrated only in manufacturing and commerce (those sectors favored by the growth plan) the presence of female workers has risen, especially in the textile industry. These sectors, however, are characterized by poor working conditions and a lack of labor rights. The job-creating capacity of the agricultural and public sectors has been diminished: in agriculture because the state has abandoned it as not strategic, and in public sectors because structural changes have reduced labor demand.

In light of these structural adjustments the labor market has been characterized by low levels of employment, due primarily to a drop in the working-age population and growth in sub-employment and informal employment. Especially in recent years, then, the jobs that have been created are precarious ones.

According to figures from studies aimed at determining the nature of informal work in El Salvador, much of the employment in this country qualifies as informal — informal employment is more prevalent than formal. While informal employment dropped between 1991 and 1998, 1999 saw an increase. Further investigation reveals that rural employment is about 80% informal, urban employment about 59%.

The geographic distribution of informal employment has changed fundamentally. From 1991 to 1993, more than 50% of the informal population was found in rural areas. Since then, more and more informal employment has become concentrated in urban areas. This phenomenon is evidence of the deterioration of rural activities (agriculture) and the growth of commerce and industry in urban areas. Urban industry has absorbed traditionally rural informal employment.

Informal employment consists mainly of those self-employed or employed unofficially, active mainly in the commercial, industry, and agricultural areas. More that 80% of formal workers are permanent employees and concentrated in industry, commerce, public administration, and education.

It is important to note that the commercial and industrial sectors feature prevalent formal and informal employment, and a higher presence of women. In addition, those areas linked to the state, which traditionally generate formal employment, have seen increased levels of informality and decreased job creation, due to privatization and other restructuring.

Training and skill levels among workers differ greatly between the formal and informal sectors, with informal workers being generally unqualified. About 80% of these workers have no educational degree, and about 21% have no formal training. By contrast, only about 48% of formal sector employees lack a degree, and 60% have more than 10 years of formal education. These statistics reveal the difficulty informal sector employees have in finding stable employment and better working conditions.

The nature of informality in employment is not necessarily related to the size of the business, nor does it relate to whether a worker is the manager or owner of his or her business. Informality and formality are linked to a worker's labor conditions; the less stable a position, and the less access a worker has to social security and other protections, the more informal a worker's status.

Given these criteria, a worker employed in a large, longstanding business (which under the general definition of the formal sector would lead one to think that the worker would be formally employed), but without security or social protections, would be informally employed. It is possible, then, to argue that the proliferation of informal employment is not solely linked to the number of informal businesses; rather, informal employment can exist outside the informal sector.

Under this reworked paradigm, informal employment in El Salvador is linked to three elements: economic performance, the cost of labor for businesses, and the labor institution. These elements, moreover, have been determined primarily by economic policy in this country.

In keeping with these outlined characteristics of formal and informal employment, it follows that, during the peak economic years, levels of informality dropped, while during the recent slowdown, formal employment dropped and informality grew.

If we concede that, during times of growth, businesses expand their benefits and worker security, then we must also acknowledge that, during times of economic sluggishness, businesses back away from their promises to workers in an effort to reduce labor costs and fight recession. This tendency naturally leads to precarious situations and increased informality for the labor force.

Ultimately, given the fact that formality and informality are linked to measures that guarantee security and stability for workers, and that these measures are ostensibly stipulated in formal labor legislation, much of the blame for rising levels of informality must lie with the weakness of this country's labor institutions, which do not adequately guarantee decent conditions for their workers.

This weakness exists because the state is uninterested in intervening in labor issues, opting instead to spend public resources in the promotion of the private sector and deny the basic needs of labor. It is critical, then, that the state embark in a new direction with regard to labor policy in order to strengthen labor's position, reduce informal employment, and guarantee decent conditions for all Salvadoran workers.

APPENDIX TABLE 1   Economic growth in El Salvador (gross domestic product, total and per capita, constant 1990 colones)

Year	GDP	GDP per capita
1970-74	4.9%	2.1%
1975-79	4.1	1.8
1980-85	-2.8	-3.5
1985-90	2.1	0.7
1980-90	-0.4	-1.5
1990-2002*	4.1	2.1
1981	-10.5	-11.5
1982	-6.3	-7.0
1983	1.5	1.0
1984	1.3	0.7
1985	0.6	-0.3
1986	0.2	-0.9
1987	2.5	1.3
1988	1.9	0.5
1989	1.0	-0.5
1990	4.8	3.1
1990	4.8	3.1
1991	2.8	0.9
1992	7.3	5.1
1993	6.4	4.2
1994	6.0	3.7
1995	6.2	4.0
1996	1.8	-0.3
1997	4.2	2.1
1998	3.8	1.6
1999	3.4	1.3
2000	2.2	0.2
2001**	1.7	-0.2
2002**	2.1	0.2

*   Author's calculation based on data from CEPAL and BCR.
** Preliminary data.

Source: CEPAL and BCR.

APPENDIX TABLE 2 Growth rate of GDP by sector (constant 1990 colones)

Sector	1989	1990	1991	1992	1993	1994	1995	1996	1997	1998	1999	2000	2001*	2002*
Total	1.0%	4.8%	3.6%	7.5%	7.4%	6.0%	6.4%	1.7%	4.2%	3.7%	3.4%	2.2%	1.7%	2.1%
Agriculture, hunting, forestry, and fishing	-0.6%	6.5%	-0.3%	8.0%	-2.6%	-2.4%	4.5%	1.3%	0.4%	-0.7%	7.7%	-3.1%	-2.6%	0.2%
Mining and quarrying	4.3	-1.0	9.6	5.2	10.6	10.9	6.7	1.0	6.5	5.3	0.4	-4.7	11.7	7.0
Industry and manufacturing	2.6	4.9	5.9	9.9	-1.5	7.4	6.9	1.7	8.0	6.6	3.7	4.1	4.0	2.9
Electricity, gas, and water	0.8	5.6	-50.6	5.2	9.4	4.7	5.0	17.1	4.2	6.1	2.7	-2.3	4.7	5.5
Construction	3.6	-12.8	10.3	6.4	3.6	11.5	6.1	2.7	6.2	8.5	-1.8	-3.4	9.6	4.6
Wholesale and retail trade, restaurants, and hotels	3.3%	3.0%	7.0%	11.5%	6.4%	8.6%	9.9%	0.4%	2.9%	4.0%	2.0%	3.6%	1.9%	1.0%
Transport, storage, and communications	1.2%	6.3%	4.7%	9.4%	6.6%	6.0%	5.5%	1.9%	7.7%	4.2%	9.5%	6.1%	4.3%	3.7%
Financial and insurance	-9.5	2.0	-3.7	21.4	10.7	20.7	16.4	2.7	12.6	9.6	12.0	7.7	1.6	1.3
Real estate and management services	-		8.3%	3.7%	0.9%	5.7%	5.9%	3.3%	4.4%	2.8%	0.2%	1.5%	1.9%	2.0%
Rental housing	2.4%	2.5%	1.0	1.5	1.5	1.8	1.8	1.7	1.8	2.0	0.5	1.5	-2.9	5.0
Community, social, and personal services	1.5%	1.8%	2.9%	3.2%	2.8%	4.7%	5.9%	0.5%	3.0%	2.1%	0.3%	1.4%	1.1%	1.2%
Government services	-1.1	1.6	0.6	-3.5	0.4	2.6	4.3	4.2	3.8	0.3	1.6	0.9	0.1	-2.5

* Preliminary data.

Source: BCR.

APPENDIX TABLE 3   GDP by components of economic activity (constant 1990 colones)

Sector	1985	1990	1995	2000*	2001*	2002*
GDP**	100.0%	100.0%	100.0%	100.0%	100.0%	100.0%
Goods	43.1%	42.7%	38.9%	39.3%	39.7%	39.7%
Agriculture	18.6	17.1	13.6	12.3	11.8	11.5
Mining	0.3	0.4	0.4	0.4	0.4	0.5
Industry and manufacturing	20.7	21.7	21.2	23.0	23.5	23.7
Construction	3.5	3.5	3.7	3.6	3.9	3.9
Basic services	8.4%	8.5%	8.0%	9.1%	9.2%	9.5%
Electricity, gas, and water	1.1	1.2	0.5	0.6	0.6	0.6
Transportation, storage, and communications	7.2	7.3	7.4	8.5	8.6	8.8
Other services	48.5%	48.7%	46.8%	45.8%	45.2%	45.0%
Wholesale and retail trade, restaurants, and hotels	18.4	18.1	20.4	19.8	19.8	19.7
Finance, insurance, real estate, and management services	13.7	17.0	15.3	15.4	15.0	15.2
Community, social, and personal services	16.4	13.5	11.2	10.5	10.4	10.0

*   Preliminary data.

** Includes the effect of the removal of import duties, an imputation for adjustments for banking services, and, after 1993, the value-added tax.

Source: CEPAL, based on official data.

APPENDIX TABLE 4   Share of exports by trading partner

Country or region	1989	2000	2001
Central America	32.29%	25.06%	25.22%
Costa Rica	8.07	2.91	3.30
Guatemala	20.62	10.84	11.29
Honduras	3.06	7.65	6.43
Nicaragua	0.54	3.65	4.20
Other America*	43.06%	68.24%	69.63%
Mexico	0.68	0.45	0.86
United States**	35.88	65.26	65.42
Canada	2.52	0.22	0.17
Chile	-	0.05	0.06
Dominican Republic	-	0.42	0.43
Panama	-	1.33	1.71
Other	3.98	0.52	0.97
Asia	3.04%	0.38%	0.29%
Europe	21.47%	5.17%	2.79%
Africa	-	0.29%	0.00%
Oceania	-	0.00%	0.00%
Other	0.14%	0.85%	2.06%
Total	100.00%	100.00%	100.00%

*   Canal Zone excluded 1986-91, included 1992-98.
** Includes maquila exports.

Source: BCR.

APPENDIX TABLE 5   Fiscal indicators, in percentages

	1995	1996	1997	1998	1999	2000	2001	2002
Central Government								
Tax burden	12.0%	10.6%	10.3%	10.2%	10.2%	10.2%	10.5%	11.2%
Total expenditures plus CNdP/GDP	14.3%	14.9%	12.9%	13.6%	13.5%	14.3%	15.6%	15.7%
Fiscal deficit/GDP	-0.5%	-2.0%	-1.1%	-2.0%	-2.1%	-2.3%	-3.6%	-3.1%
Internal debt/GDP	9.9%	8.7%	7.7%	7.1%	7.4%	9.3%	11.9%	11.3%
External Debt								
Balance/GDP	16.6%	16.6%	17.7%	16.7%	18.1%	17.6%	19.2%	24.2%
Service/GDP	1.5	1.3	6.9	3.9	3.8	2.4	3.5	4.7
Annual growth (in millions of U.S. dollars)								
Current income	$28.3	$12.9	-$1.9	-$87.7	$0.5	$6.8	$7.4	$9.2
Current expenditure	13.7	22.2	-3.2	-87.4	7.0	11.8	2.5	2.6
Public/Nonfinancial sector								
Total expenditures plus CNdP/GDP	18.1%	19.5%	17.1%	17.6%	17.8%	18.8%	18.6%	18.9%
Fiscal deficit/GDP	-0.1%	-2.5%	-1.8%	-2.6%	-2.8%	-3.0%	-3.7%	-3.3%
Internal debt/ GDP	10.8%	9.4%	8.5%	7.2%	7.5%	9.5%	12.2%	12.1%
External debt								
Balance/GDP	20.8%	22.0%	24.2%	22.0%	22.5%	20.4%	22.0%	27.3%
Service/GDP	3.1	2.8	8.0	5.4	4.4	2.6	3.7	4.9
Annual growth (in millions of U.S. dollars)								
Current income	$26.2	$11.1	-$3.4	-$87.9	$3.4	$6.5	$2.0	$5.5
Current expenditure	17.0	23.1	-5.2	87.1	9.6	12.2	-4.6	2.5
Current savings (in millions of U.S. dollars)			$212.8	$121.0	$22.6	-$80.1	$53.7	$115.2

CNdP = Net Borrowing Approval.

Source: BCR.

APPENDIX TABLE 6 Households by poverty and condition, in percentages

Poverty Level	1992	1992-93	1994	1995	1996	1997	1998	1999	2000	2001	2002
Total country											
Extreme poverty	27.66%	27.0%	23.94%	18.2%	21.9%	18.5%	18.9%	17.5%	16.0%	16.13%	15.8%
Relative poverty	31.03	30.5	28.47	29.3	29.8	29.6	25.7	25.0	22.8	22.67	21.0
Total poor	58.69	57.50	52.41	47.53	51.69	48.05	44.61	42.47	38.79	38.8	36.8
Not poor	41.31	42.50	47.59	52.47	48.31	51.95	55.39	57.60	61.21	61.19	63.23
Total urban											
Extreme poverty	21.87%	20.8%	16.33%	12.4%	14.5%	12.0%	12.9%	10.9%	9.3%	10.2%	10.3%
Relative poverty	30.99	29.6	27.51	27.6	27.9	26.7	23.1	23.0	20.6	21.0	19.15
Total poor	52.86	50.45	43.84	40.02	42.44	38.69	36.01	33.90	29.85	31.26	29.45
Not poor	47.14	49.55	56.16	59.98	57.56	61.31	63.99	65.80	70.15	68.74	70.55
Total rural											
Extreme poverty	33.97%	33.8%	34.78%	26.5%	32.3%	27.9%	28.7%	28.2%	27.2%	26.1%	25.02%
Relative poverty	31.07	31.47	29.84	31.74	32.5	33.7	29.9	28.2	26.6	25.46	24.15
Total poor	65.04	65.25	64.62	58.20	64.84	61.61	58.64	56.40	53.73	48.53	49.17
Not poor	34.96	34.75	35.38	41.80	35.16	38.39	41.36	43.70	46.27	47.27	50.83

Source: Author's calculations with data from EHPM.

APPENDIX TABLE 7   Population in poverty according to gender

Poverty levels by gender	1998	1999	2000	2001	2002
Total	6,046,257	6,154,079	6,272,353	6,428,672	6,510,348
Poverty	3,052,977	2,910,322	2,801,192	2,852,831	2,795,847
Extreme poverty	1,369,363	1,232,558	1,206,314	1,245,844	1,247,343
Relative poverty	1,683,614	1,677,764	1,594,878	1,606,987	1,548,504
Not poverty	2,993,280	3,243,757	3,471,161	3,575,841	3,714,501
Men	2,891,875	2,932,509	3,002,068	3,052,986	3,084,625
Poverty	1,456,007	1,383,370	1,340,950	1,358,116	1,336,468
Extreme poverty	647,609	593,561	585,887	605,781	606,486
Relative poverty	808,398	789,809	755,063	752,335	729,982
Not poverty	1,435,868	1,549,139	1,661,118	1,694,870	1,748,157
Women	3,154,382	3,221,570	3,270,285	3,375,686	3,425,723
Poverty	1,596,970	1,526,952	1,460,242	1,494,715	1,459,379
Extreme poverty	721,754	638,997	620,427	640,063	640,857
Relative poverty	875,216	887,955	839,815	854,652	818,522
Not poverty	1,557,412	1,694,618	1,810,043	1,880,971	1,966,344

Source: EHPM.

APPENDIX TABLE 8   Indicators by geographical region, 2002

Regions	Poverty Extreme poverty (%)	Poverty Relative poverty (%)	HDI 2002	GDP per capita (US$, PPP) Urban	GDP per capita (US$, PPP) Rural
Ahuachapan	29.31%	24.45%	12	4,111.0	2,284.0
Santa Ana	18.06	24.17	4	6,098.0	2,574.0
Sonsonate	18.29	26.17	6	6,321.0	2,250.0
Chalatenango	28.7	19.94	10	5,456.0	2,140.0
La Libertad	10.6	16.2	2	9,844.0	3,308.0
San Salvador	8.34	17.25	1	7,756.0	3,053.0
Cuscatlan	14.92	21.96	3	5,372.0	2,877.0
La Paz	19.85	24.81	8	5,377.0	2,614.0
Cabanas	30.66	26.53	14	5,026.0	1,676.0
San Vicente	27.75	26.88	9	4,870.0	1,847.0
Usulutan	21.69	25.61	7	5,691.0	2,451.0
San Miguel	20.1	22.7	5	5,696.0	2,391.0
Morazan	27.18	24.42	13	6,056.0	2,357.0
La Union	17.43	24.73	11	5,986.0	3,079.0

Source: EHPM and PNUD (2003a).

APPENDIX TABLE 9   International Labour Organization ratified agreements

Agreement	Date ratified
C12 Compensation in case of accident related to work (Agriculture) Convention, 1921	Oct. 11, 1955
C29 Forced labor Convention, 1930	June 15, 1995
C77 Child medical examination (Industry) Convention, 1946	June 15, 1995
C78 Child Medical Examination (Non-industry) Convention, 1946	June 15, 1995
C81 Convention on the Inspection of Labour, 1947	June 15, 1995
C88 Convention on employment services, 1948	June 15, 1995
C99 Agreement on the Methods for Determining the Minimum Wage (Agriculture), 1951	June 15, 1995
C100 Equal Remuneration Convention, 1951	Oct. 12, 2000
C104 Abolition of Penal Sanctions (Indigenous Workers) Convention, 1955	Nov. 18, 1958
C105 Abolition of Forced Labor Convention, 1957	Nov. 18, 1958
C107 Indigenous and Tribal Populations Convention, 1957	Nov. 18, 1958
C111 Discrimination (Employment and Occupation) Convention, 1958	June 15, 1995
C122 Employment Policy Convention, 1964	June 15, 1995
C129 Labour Inspection (Agriculture) Convention, 1969	June 15, 1995
C131 Minimum Wage Fixing Convention, 1970	June 15, 1995
C138 Minimum Age Convention, 1973	Jan. 23, 1996
C141 Rural Workers' Organisations Convention, 1975	June 15, 1995
C142 Human Resources Development Convention, 1975	June 15, 1995
C144 Tripartite Consultation (International Labour Standards) Convention, 1976	June 15, 1995
C150 Labour Administration Convention, 1978	Feb. 2, 2001
C155 Occupational Safety and Health Convention, 1981	Oct. 12, 2000
C156 Workers with Family Responsibilities Convention, 1981	Oct. 12, 2000
C159 Vocational Rehabilitation and Employment (Disabled Persons) Convention, 1983	Dec. 19, 1986
C160 Labour Statistics Convention, 1985	April 24, 1987
C182 Worst Forms of Child Labour Convention, 1999	Oct. 12, 2000

Source: OIT.

APPENDIX TABLE 10 Fundamental ILO ratifications in selected countries

County	Forced labor		Union freedom		Discrimination		Forced labor	
	C. 29	C. 105	C. 87	C. 98	C. 100	C. 111	C. 138	C.182
Costa Rica	6/2/1960	5/4/1959	6/2/1960	6/2/1960	6/2/1960	3/1/1962	6/11/1976	9/10/2001
Egypt	11/29/1955	10/23/1958	11/6/1957	7/3/1954	7/26/1960	5/10/1960	6/9/1999	5/6/2002
El Salvador	6/15/1995	11/18/1958	-	-	10/12/2000	6/15/1995	1/23/1996	10/12/2000
United States	-	9/25/1991	-	-	-	-	-	12/2/1999
Guatemala	6/13/1989	12/9/1959	2/13/1952	2/13/1952	8/2/1961	10/11/1960	4/27/1990	10/11/2001
Honduras	2/21/1957	8/4/1958	6/27/1956	6/27/1956	8/9/1956	6/20/1960	6/9/1980	10/25/2001
India	11/30/1954	5/18/2000	-		9/25/1958	6/3/1960		-
Nicaragua	4/12/1934	10/31/1967	10/31/1967	10/31/1967	10/31/1967	10/31/1967	11/2/1981	11/6/2000
Russia	6/23/1956	7/2/1998	8/10/1956	8/10/1956	4/30/1956	5/4/1961	5/3/1979	3/25/2003
South Africa	3/5/1997	3/5/1997	2/19/1996	2/19/1996	3/30/2000	3/5/1997	3/30/2000	6/7/2000

Note: C = Convention.
Source: ILO

APPENDIX TABLE 11 Population old enough to work, by gender and location

Gender and year	Entire country			Urban			Rural		
	Labor force[1]	Global rate of participation on the PEA[2]	Economically Inactive Population rate[3]	Labor force[1]	Global rate of participation on the PEA[2]	Economically Inactive Population rate[3]	Labor force[1]	Global rate of participation on the PEA[2]	Economically Inactive Population rate[3]
Total									
1991	—	51.6	—	—	54.2	—	—	49.0	—
1992	—	50.8	—	—	53.0	—	—	48.6	—
1993	—	52.2	—	—	54.5	—	—	49.8	—
1994	3.0	53.4	46.6	2.9	55.5	44.5	3.1	50.5	49.5
1995	6.6	52.4	47.6	6.5	54.1	45.9	6.7	50.2	49.8
1996	1.6	51.3	48.7	1.5	52.9	47.1	1.9	49.1	50.9
1997	1.8	50.9	49.1	6.4	53.0	47.0	-4.4	48.0	52.0
1998	3.4	53.5	46.5	3.9	55.7	44.3	2.6	50.2	49.8
1999	2.9	52.6	47.4	3.2	55.0	45.0	2.4	49.0	51.0
2000	3.5	52.2	47.8	3.9	54.5	45.5	3.0	48.8	51.2
2001	1.6	53.3	46.7	2.0	54.8	45.2	1.0	51.0	49.0
2002		51.2	48.8		53.2	46.8		48.1	51.9
Men									
1991	—	70.6	—	—	66.2	—	—	74.7	—
1992	—	70.2	—	—	64.7	—	—	75.3	—
1993	—	70.2	—	—	65.6	—	—	74.6	—
1994	3.4	71.2	28.8	3.6	67.1	32.9	3.2	76.2	23.8
1995	6.5	70.6	29.4	6.9	66.5	33.5	5.9	75.6	24.4
1996	2.0	69.2	30.8	2.1	64.8	35.2	1.8	74.7	25.3
1997	1.8	83.9	31.5	6.2	64.6	35.4	-3.6	73.3	26.7
1998	2.8	69.6	30.4	3.4	67.0	33.0	1.9	73.3	26.7
1999	3.2	68.1	31.9	3.5	65.6	34.4	2.8	71.7	28.3
2000	2.7	67.7	32.3	2.8	65.0	35.0	2.6	71.4	28.6
2001	1.2	69.2	30.8	1.6	65.7	34.3	0.6	74.2	25.8
2002		65.8	34.2		63.0	37.0		69.8	30.2

(continued)

Good jobs, bad jobs, no jobs

APPENDIX TABLE 11 (cont.) Population old enough to work, by gender and location

Gender and year	Entire country			Urban			Rural		
	Labor force[1]	Global rate of participation on the PEA[2]	Economically Inactive Population rate[3]	Labor force[1]	Global rate of participation on the PEA[2]	Economically Inactive Population rate[3]	Labor force[1]	Global rate of participation on the PEA[2]	Economically Inactive Population rate[3]
Women									
1991	—	35.0	—	—	44.5	—	—	24.7	—
1992	—	33.8	—	—	43.5	—	—	23.3	—
1993	—	36.4	—	—	45.6	—	—	26.3	—
1994	—	37.9	62.1	—	46.1	53.9	—	26.1	73.9
1995	2.6	36.5	63.5	2.3	43.9	56.1	3.1	26.0	74.0
1996	6.6	35.6	64.4	6.1	43.0	57.0	7.4	25.1	74.9
1997	1.4	35.3	64.7	1.0	43.2	56.8	2.0	24.4	75.6
1998	1.7	39.3	60.7	6.6	46.3	53.7	-5.1	28.2	71.8
1999	3.9	39.1	60.9	4.4	46.3	53.7	3.2	27.7	72.3
2000	2.6	38.7	61.3	3.0	45.8	54.2	1.9	27.4	72.6
2001	4.3	39.5	60.5	4.9	45.8	54.2	3.3	29.1	70.9
2002	2.0	38.6	61.4	2.4	45.2	54.8	1.5	27.7	72.3

[1] Growth rate of the Labor Force (PET).
[2] Ratio between Economically Active Population (PEA) and Labor Force (PET).
[3] Ratio between Economically Inactive Population (PEI) AND PET.

Source: EHPM.

APPENDIX TABLE 12 Unemployment by economic activity of last job performed

Sector	1994	1995	1996	1997	1998	1999	2000	2001	2002
Total (thousands of people)	162,298	163,433	170,959	178,896	175,723	170,231	173,668	183,483	160,192
Agriculture, hunting and forestry	54,677	52,399	44,455	59,200	34,109	39,601	43,870	37,509	29,099
Fishing	0	0	0	672	1,152	702	705	2,493	442
Mining and quarrying	196	75	136	118	103	285	275	256	174
Manufacturing	22,228	22,245	22,487	20,977	23,160	24,777	23,033	27,244	27,493
Electricity, gas, and water	423	881	1,256	444	1,307	1,247	266	421	411
Construction	14,854	17,007	21,499	20,373	25,514	21,650	23,189	26,008	28,783
Wholesale and retail trade, restaurants, and hotels	15,082	14,538	15,072	19,199	19,085	21,300	23,142	28,644	19,345
Transport, storage, and communications	5,408	4,713	6,207	5,900	8,239	8,031	10,585	8,722	8,655
Finance, insurance, and real estate	1,431	1,571	1,854	2,952	5,481	5,167	5,945	6,144	5,801
Public administration	0	0	0	3,514	5,704	3,910	5,212	5,027	5,238
Education	0	0	0	2,273	2,557	2,186	1,938	869	3,143
Community, social, and personal services	20,179	18,363	23,302	4,240	4,780	6,500	3,531	5,319	5,099
Domestic servant	0	0	0	3,441	7,065	4,293	3,235	5,611	4,124
Other	231	0	0	0	423	0	325	0	—
Never worked	27,589	31,641	34,691	35,593	37,044	30,582	28,417	29,216	22,385

(continued)

APPENDIX TABLE 12 (*cont.*) Unemployment by economic activity of last job performed

Sector	1994	1995	1996	1997	1998	1999	2000	2001	2002
Total (in percents)	100.0	100.0	100.0	100.0	100.0	100.0	100.0	100.0	100.0
Agriculture, hunting, and forestry	33.7	32.1	26.0	33.1	19.4	23.3	25.3	20.4	18.2
Fishing	-	-	-	0.4	0.7	0.4	0.4	1.4	0.3
Mining and quarrying	0.1	0.0	0.1	0.1	0.1	0.2	0.2	0.1	0.1
Manufacturing	13.7	13.6	13.2	11.7	13.2	14.6	13.3	14.8	17.2
Electricity, gas, and water	0.3	0.5	0.7	0.2	0.7	0.7	0.2	0.2	0.3
Construction	9.2	10.4	12.6	11.4	14.5	12.7	13.4	14.2	18.0
Wholesale and retail trade, restaurants, and hotels	9.3	8.9	8.8	10.7	10.9	12.5	13.3	15.6	12.1
Transport, storage, and communications	3.3	2.9	3.6	3.3	4.7	4.7	6.1	4.8	5.4
Finance, insurance, and real estate	0.9	1.0	1.1	1.7	3.1	3.0	3.4	3.3	3.6
Public administration	-	-	-	2.0	3.2	2.3	3.0	2.7	3.3
Education	-	-	-	1.3	1.5	1.3	1.1	0.5	2.0
Community, social and personal services	12.4	11.2	13.6	2.4	2.7	3.8	2.0	2.9	3.2
Domestic servant	-	-	-	1.9	4.0	2.5	1.9	3.1	2.6
Other	0.1	-	-	-	0.2	-	0.2	-	..
Never worked	17.0	19.4	20.3	19.9	21.1	18.0	16.4	15.9	14.0

Source: Author's calculation from EHPM data.

APPENDIX TABLE 13 Workers by economic activity, gender, and location, 2002 (percentage of participation)

Sectors	Entire country			Urban			Rural		
	Total	Men	Women	Total	Men	Women	Total	Men	Women
Total	100.0%	100.0%	100.0%	100.0%	100.0%	100.0%	100.0%	100.0%	100.0%
Agriculture, hunting, and forestry	19.0	30.8	2.6	4.5	8.1	0.6	43.7	59.7	7.7
Fishing	0.7	1.0	0.1	0.3	0.5	0.0	1.3	1.8	0.3
Mining and quarrying	0.1	0.2	0.0	0.0	0.1	-	0.3	0.5	0.0
Manufacturing	18.0	14.5	22.9	21.0	19.2	23.0	12.8	8.5	22.5
Electricity, gas, and water	0.4	0.6	0.1	0.5	0.9	0.2	0.3	0.4	0.1
Construction	5.6	9.3	0.5	5.8	10.5	0.7	5.5	7.8	0.1
Wholesale and retail trade, restaurants, and hotels	28.5	19.0	41.8	34.6	27.6	42.0	18.2	8.2	41.0
Transport, storage, and communications	4.3	6.7	0.9	5.3	9.0	1.2	2.6	3.8	0.1
Finance, insurance, and real estate	4.1	4.5	3.5	5.6	6.5	4.5	1.5	1.8	0.7
Public administration	4.2	5.1	2.8	5.2	6.6	3.6	2.5	3.2	0.7
Education	3.9	2.6	5.7	5.5	4.2	6.9	1.2	0.6	2.6
Community, social, and personal services	6.4	4.1	9.7	8.1	6.1	10.2	3.7	1.7	8.2
Domestic servant	4.3	0.7	9.3	3.6	0.5	7.0	5.4	0.9	15.5
Others	0.4	0.7	0.1	0.1	0.2	0.0	0.9	1.3	0.2

Source: Author's calculations from EHPM data.

Appendix Table 14   Workers by labor condition and social security availability, urban areas

	Workers	% employed	% under-employed	In which: % invisible	% visible	Social security coverage % covered	% uncovered
Total							
1994	1,110,224	67.3%	32.7%	—	—	40.9%	59.1%
1995	1,121,751	68.1	31.9	—	—	38.4	61.6
1996	1,157,788	69.4	30.6	—	—	37.9	62.1
1997	1,181,234	70.1	29.9	—	—	38.7	61.3
1998	1,320,819	68.3	31.7	10.6%	89.4%	43.8	56.2
1999	1,365,438	70.9	29.1	13.4	86.6	48.5	51.5
2000	1,404,871	73.7	26.3	14.0	86.0	45.8	54.2
2001	1,458,975	72.2	27.8	13.8	86.2	46.4	53.6
2002	1,465,695	70.2	29.8	14.5	85.5	45.5	54.5
Men							
1994	624,577	70.3%	29.7%	—	—	42.6%	57.4%
1995	637,321	72.9	27.1	—	—	39.7	60.3
1996	663,757	73.6	26.4	—	—	38.5	61.5
1997	675,203	74.5	25.5	—	—	39.2	60.8
1998	740,411	70.6	29.4	12.1%	87.9%	45.2	54.8
1999	750,670	72.1	27.9	13.3	86.7	47.0	53.0
2000	769,819	74.8	25.2	13.5	86.5	44.8	55.2
2001	802,488	73.0	27.0	13.8	86.2	44.3	55.7
2002	782,142	71.7	28.3	15.0	85.0	44.1	55.9
Women							
1994	485,647	63.3%	36.7%	—	—	38.6%	61.4%
1995	484,430	61.8	38.2	—	—	36.5	63.5
1996	494,031	63.8	36.2	—	—	37.1	62.9
1997	506,031	64.2	35.8	—	—	38.0	62.0
1998	580,408	65.3	34.7	8.9	91.1	41.8	58.2
1999	614,768	69.4	30.6	13.6	86.4	50.3	49.7
2000	635,052	72.5	27.5	14.5	85.5	47.1	52.9
2001	656,487	71.1	28.9	13.7	86.3	49.2	50.8
2002	683,553	68.6	31.4	14.1	85.9	47.0	53.0

Source: Author's calculations with EHPM data.

APPENDIX TABLE 15   Amount of formal and informal employment in urban areas according to various characteristics

Occupational category	Attribution of formality or informality	Informal employment			Informal employment		
		Definition	Number[1]	Number[2]	Definition	Number[1]	Number[2]
Employer	Size of establishment	Employers who own informal enterprises.	166,510	66,510	Employers who own formal enterprises (over 5 workers).	10,191	10,191
Self-employed	Social security	Self employed workers with out social security benefits.	385,514	385,514	Self-employed workers receiving some social security benefits.	35,329	35,329
Members of cooperatives	Social security	Cooperative members not covered by any system of social security.	110	110	Cooperative members covered by any system of social security.		
Unpaid Family member	Social security	Unpaid family member who does not receive any social security benefit.	85,162	85,162	Unpaid family member receiving some social security benefit.	6,006	6,006
Permanent with salary	Contract social security	Workers not receiving social security benefits, regardless of their contract status.	451,622	141,384	Workers that have signed a job contract and enjoy social security benefits.	227,505	537,743
Temporary with salary	Contract social security	Workers not receiving social security benefits, regardless of their contract status.	178,522	157,973	Workers that have signed a job contract and enjoy social security benefits.	12,074	32,623
Apprenticeship	Contract	Workers that have not signed apprenticeship contract.	4,658	4,658	Workers that have signed an apprenticeship contract.	57	57
Domestic services		Workers in domestic services.	55,794	55,794	Workers in domestic services.		
Others	Contract social security	Workers not receiving social security benefits, regardless of their contract status.	2,361	2,361	Workers that have signed a job contract and enjoy social security benefits.	74	74
Total			1,230,253	899,466		291,236	622,023

[1] Calculations regarding paid permanent, temporary, formal, and informal workers have been done using attribution of social security crossed with "contract" attribution.
[2] Calculations regarding permanent, temporary, formal, and informal paid workers have been done with only the attribution social security.

APPENDIX TABLE 16   Informal and formal employment by geographical area and job category (number of employed workers)

	1991		1997		2002	
	Informal	Formal	Informal	Formal	Informal	Formal
Total country						
Employer	96,875	30,156	88,246	15,333	98,149	12,901
Men	81,035	26,472	68,245	12,290	73,924	11,310
Women	15,840	3,684	20,001	3,043	24,225	1,591
Self-employed	446,734	42	589,262	16,128	685,604	42,114
Men	217,278	0	300,215	4,016	326,113	12,577
Women	229,456	42	289,047	12,112	359,491	29,537
Members of cooperatives	7,712	0	3,848	916	733	287
Men	7,207		3,685	916	634	287
Women	505		163		99	
Family member w/o salary	186,470	0	166,167	888	212,831	7,570
Men	121,355		111,477	444	130,568	3,129
Women	65,115		54,690	444	82,263	4,441
Salaried, permanent	243,609	342,831	190,116	440,883	212,871	640,482
Men	184,670	219,523	130,068	269,339	150,491	353,969
Women	58,939	123,308	60,048	171,544	62,380	286,513
Salaried, temporary	312,104	25,261	409,126	46,952	334,953	41,992
Men	237,960	19,537	336,660	32,112	287,101	27,031
Women	74,144	5,724	72,466	14,840	47,852	14,961
Apprentice	14,466		6,040		6,147	57
Men	13,770		5,822		6,147	57
Women	696		218			
Domestic services	74,215		90,221		104,011	
Men	4,507		4,097		9,570	
Women	69,708		86,124		94,441	
Other	974	113	2,175	222	12,009	74
Men	933	113	1,521		11,438	74
Women	41		654	222	571	
Total country	1,383,159	398,403	1,545,201	521,322	1,667,308	745,477
Total country, urban						
Employer	41,709	14,018	59,447	10,664	66,510	10,191
Men	30,074	11,726	42,762	8,740	45,966	8,882
Women	11,635	2,292	16,685	1,924	20,544	1,309
Self-employed	231,311	42	328,788	15,218	385,514	35,329
Men	83,740		137,038	3,935	148,205	9,962
Women	147,571	42	191,750	11,283	237,309	25,367
Members of cooperatives	226				110	
Men	226				110	
Women						
Family member w/o salary	52,912		57,319	888	85,162	6,006
Men	20,861		22,401	444	32,975	2,253
Women	32,051		34,918	444	52,187	3,753
Salaried, permanent	128,769	296,163	125,027	376,907	141,384	537,743
Men	87,456	180,920	77,200	224,220	93,446	287,054
Women	41,313	115,243	47,827	152,687	47,938	250,689
Salaried, temporary	99,017	17,221	169,768	31,344	157,973	32,623
Men	73,938	12,396	133,709	19,742	126,843	19,461
Women	25,079	4,825	36,059	11,602	31,130	13,162

(continued)

APPENDIX TABLE 16 *(cont.)* Informal and formal employment by geographical area and job category (number of employed workers)

	1991 Informal	1991 Formal	1997 Informal	1997 Formal	2002 Informal	2002 Formal
Total country, urban *(cont.)*						
Apprentice	11,050		4,319		4,658	57
Men	10,622		4,259		4,658	57
Women	428		60			
Domestic Services	53,994		54,378		55,794	
Men	2,183		1,821		4,105	
Women	51,811		52,557		51,689	
Other	600	113	1,323	222	2,361	74
Men	559	113	753		2,196	74
Women	41		570	222	165	
Total country, urban	619,588	327,557	800,369	435,243	899,466	622,023
Total country, rural						
Employer	55,166	16,138	28,799	4,669	31,639	2,710
Men	50,961	14,746	25,483	3,550	27,958	2,428
Women	4,205	1,392	3,316	1,119	3,681	282
Self-employed	215,423		260,474	910	300,090	6,785
Men	133,538		163,177	81	177,908	2,615
Women	81,885		97,297	829	122,182	4,170
Members of cooperatives	7,486		3,848	916	623	287
Men	6,981		3,685	916	524	287
Women	505		163		99	
Family member w/o salary	133,558		108,848		127,669	1,564
Men	100,494		89,076		97,593	876
Women	33,064		19,772		30,076	688
Salaried, permanent	114,840	46,668	65,089	63,976	71,487	102,739
Men	97,214	38,603	52,868	45,119	57,045	66,915
Women	17,626	8,065	12,221	18,857	14,442	35,824
Salaried, temporary	213,087	8,040	239,358	15,608	176,980	9,369
Men	164,022	7,141	202,951	12,370	160,258	7,570
Women	49,065	899	36,407	3,238	16,722	1,799
Apprentice	3,416		1,721		1,489	
Men	3,148		1,563		1,489	
Women	268		158			
Domestic services	20,221		35,843		48,217	
Men	2,324		2,276		5,465	
Women	17,897		33,567		42,752	
Other	374		852		9,648	
Men	374		768		9,242	
Women			84		406	
Total country, rural	763,571	70,846	744,832	86,079	767,842	123,454

Source: Author's calculations with EHPM data.

APPENDIX TABLE 17   Employed population by type and economic activity, number of employed workers

	1991		1997		2002	
	Formal	Informal	Formal	Informal	Formal	Informal
COUNTRY						
TOTAL	398,403	1,383,159	521,322	1,545,201	745,477	1,667,308
Agriculture, livestock, hunting	30,739	595,766	14,693	512,649	17,599	440,833
Fishing	911	10,877	1,083	15,581	421	15,554
Mining	766	1,873	1,048	634	549	2,973
Industry and manufacturing	96,564	212,204	131,821	201,069	203,192	230,825
Electricity, gas, and water	10,382	1,143	10,911	4,159	8,954	1,749
Construction	21,650	59,348	40,793	96,738	35,681	100,565
Businesses, hotels, restaurants	53,563	295,035	99,953	408,226	146,172	542,311
Transportation and communication	17,860	43,154	19,178	76,719	28,418	74,999
Finance/real estate	22,705	12,264	42,194	20,450	70,300	27,715
Public administration and defense	67,282	11,597	75,708	15,992	92,108	8,409
Education	35,990	8,468	30,476	36,981	78,116	16,401
Social services, health	38,581	56,665	52,285	65,264	63,103	92,304
Households/domestic services	71	73,789	0	90,221	0	103,151
Other	1,339	976	1,179	518	864	9,519
MALE	265,645	868,715	319,117	961,790	408,434	995,986
Agriculture, livestock, hunting	27,590	504,360	11,988	460,069	15,787	416,929
Fishing	827	9,376	1,083	14,856	364	14,378
Mining	624	1,683	988	634	469	2,973
Industry and manufacturing	62,196	105,225	70,043	104,307	95,047	108,303
Electricity, gas and water	8,956	717	9,883	4,032	7,590	1,638
Construction	20,757	58,435	37,823	95,673	30,989	100,197
Businesses, hotels, restaurants	32,559	100,297	53,201	144,103	74,211	193,161
Transportation and communication	15,290	41,197	15,836	73,487	22,012	72,278
Finance/real estate	12,770	9,286	25,946	15,402	43,230	19,338
Public administration and defense	51,370	8,361	55,427	12,558	65,203	6,654
Education	15,055	2,923	14,645	12,652	29,449	7,097
Social services, health	16,666	21,912	21,297	19,458	23,523	34,517
Households/domestic services	71	4,380	0	4,097	0	9,570
Other	914	563	957	462	560	8,953
FEMALE	132,758	514,444	202,205	583,411	337,043	671,322
Agriculture, livestock, hunting	3,149	91,406	2,705	52,580	1,812	23,904
Fishing	84	1,501	0	725	57	1,176
Mining	142	190	60	0	80	0
Industry and manufacturing	34,368	106,979	61,778	96,762	108,145	122,522
Electricity, gas, and water	1,426	426	1,028	127	1,364	111
Construction	893	913	2,970	1,065	4,692	368
Businesses, hotels, restaurants	21,004	194,738	46,752	264,123	71,961	349,150
Transportation and communication	2,570	1,957	3,342	3,232	6,406	2,721
Finance/real estate	9,935	2,978	16,248	5,048	27,070	8,377
Public administration and defense	15,912	3,236	20,281	3,434	26,905	1,755
Education	20,935	5,545	15,831	24,329	48,667	9,304
Social services, health	21,915	34,753	30,988	45,806	39,580	57,787
Households/domestic services	0	69,409	0	86,124	0	93,581
Other	425	413	222	56	304	566

(continued)

APPENDIX TABLE 17 *(cont.)*   Employed population by type and economic activity, number of employed workers

	1991 Formal	1991 Informal	1997 Formal	1997 Informal	2002 Formal	2002 Informal
URBAN						
TOTAL	327,557	619,588	435,243	800,369	622,023	899,466
Agriculture, livestock, hunting	8,329	76,967	4,909	69,937	7,513	61,098
Fishing	405	2,784	1,000	5,771	379	3,713
Mining	561	313	1,048	273	251	186
Industry and manufacturing	80,837	139,478	104,750	137,311	161,024	158,999
Electricity, gas, and water	8,707	617	9,465	3,001	7,164	781
Construction	17,262	35,536	26,990	58,821	26,222	61,357
Businesses, hotels, restaurants	49,129	211,370	91,020	302,703	130,292	395,694
Transportation and communication	15,883	32,038	17,590	58,860	25,244	54,739
Finance/real estate	21,273	10,112	38,703	17,147	60,836	23,948
Public administration and defense	55,004	8,117	63,811	11,567	73,595	4,962
Education	32,811	7,122	27,694	33,064	70,482	13,230
Social services, health	36,218	40,676	47,167	47,280	58,350	64,198
Households/domestic services	71	53,736	0	54,378	0	55,287
Other	1,067	722	1,096	256	671	1,274
MALE	205,155	309,659	257,081	419,943	327,743	458,504
Agriculture, livestock, hunting	7,016	62,179	4,363	63,027	6,582	57,331
Fishing	321	2,515	1,000	5,493	322	3,489
Mining	419	207	988	273	251	186
Industry and manufacturing	49,879	68,643	56,817	70,303	76,127	74,816
Electricity, gas, and water	7,418	309	8,437	2,874	6,049	754
Construction	16,369	34,773	24,326	58,321	21,639	61,031
Businesses, hotels, restaurants	29,657	78,471	46,532	114,405	65,766	151,121
Transportation and communication	13,447	30,318	14,605	55,628	19,019	52,018
Finance/real estate	11,713	7,321	22,947	12,754	34,683	16,690
Public administration and defense	40,264	5,954	44,504	8,296	48,478	3,465
Education	13,062	2,498	13,194	11,560	26,929	6,046
Social services, health	14,827	13,870	18,494	14,988	21,338	26,343
Households/domestic services	71	2,224	0	1,821	0	4,105
Other	692	377	874	200	560	1,109
FEMALE	122,402	309,929	178,162	380,426	294,280	440,962
Agriculture, livestock, hunting	1,313	14,788	546	6,910	931	3,767
Fishing	84	269	0	278	57	224
Mining	142	106	60	0	0	0
Industry and manufacturing	30,958	70,835	47,933	67,008	84,897	84,183
Electricity, gas, and water	1,289	308	1,028	127	1,115	27
Construction	893	763	2,664	500	4,583	326
Businesses, hotels, restaurants	19,472	132,899	44,488	188,298	64,526	244,573
Transportation and communication	2,436	1,720	2,985	3,232	6,225	2,721
Finance/real estate	9,560	2,791	15,756	4,393	26,153	7,258
Public administration and defense	14,740	2,163	19,307	3,271	25,117	1,497
Education	19,749	4,624	14,500	21,504	43,553	7,184
Social services, health	21,391	26,806	28,673	32,292	37,012	37,855
Households/domestic services	0	51,512	0	52,557	0	51,182
Other	375	345	222	56	111	165

(continued)

APPENDIX TABLE 17 *(cont.)* Employed population by type and economic activity, number of employed workers

	1991		1997		2002	
	Formal	Informal	Formal	Informal	Formal	Informal
RURAL						
TOTAL	70,846	763,571	86,079	744,832	123,454	767,842
Agriculture, livestock, hunting	22,410	518,799	9,784	442,712	10,086	379,735
Fishing	506	8,093	83	9,810	42	11,841
Mining	205	1,560	0	361	298	2,787
Industry and manufacturing	15,727	72,726	27,071	63,758	42,168	71,826
Electricity, gas, and water	1,675	526	1,446	1,158	1,790	968
Construction	4,388	23,812	13,803	37,917	9,459	39,208
Businesses, hotels, restaurants	4,434	83,665	8,933	105,523	15,880	146,617
Transportation and communication	1,977	11,116	1,588	17,859	3,174	20,260
Finance/real estate	1,432	2,152	3,491	3,303	9,464	3,767
Public administration and defense	12,278	3,480	11,897	4,425	18,513	3,447
Education	3,179	1,346	2,782	3,917	7,634	3,171
Social services, health	2,363	15,989	5,118	17,984	4,753	28,106
Households/domestic services	0	20,053	0	35,843	0	47,864
Other	272	254	83	262	193	8,245
MALE	60,490	559,056	16,917	488,979	80,691	537,482
Agriculture, livestock, hunting	20,574	442,181	4,985	367,378	9,205	359,598
Fishing	506	6,861	0	9,183	42	10,889
Mining	205	1,476	0	182	218	2,787
Industry and manufacturing	12,317	36,582	2,687	27,222	18,920	33,487
Electricity, gas, and water	1,538	408	522	604	1,541	884
Construction	4,388	23,662	6,186	36,262	9,350	39,166
Businesses, hotels, restaurants	2,902	21,826	1,256	25,188	8,445	42,040
Transportation and communication	1,843	10,879	343	14,711	2,993	20,260
Financial/real estate	1,057	1,965	401	1,029	8,547	2,648
Public administration and defense	11,106	2,407	274	1,501	16,725	3,189
Education	1,993	425	0	406	2,520	1,051
Social services, health	1,839	8,042	180	2,858	2,185	8,174
Households/domestic services	0	2,156	0	2,276	0	5,465
Other	222	186	83	179	0	7,844
FEMALE	10,356	204,515	5,186	190,764	42,763	230,360
Agriculture, livestock, hunting	1,836	76,618	1,874	42,273	881	20,137
Fishing	0	1,232	0	447	0	952
Mining	0	84	0	0	80	0
Industry and manufacturing	3,410	36,144	2,662	27,437	23,248	38,339
Electricity, gas, and water	137	118	0	0	249	84
Construction	0	150	0	366	109	42
Businesses, hotels, restaurants	1,532	61,839	650	72,786	7,435	104,577
Transportation and communication	134	237	0	0	181	0
Finance/real estate	375	187	0	330	917	1,119
Public administration and defense	1,172	1,073	0	0	1,788	258
Education	1,186	921	0	970	5,114	2,120
Social services, health	524	7,947	0	12,588	2,568	19,932
Households/domestic services	0	17,897	0	33,567	0	42,399
Other	50	68	0	83		

Source: Author's calculations with EHPM data.

APPENDIX TABLE 18   Population employed according to type of employment and economic activity (number of employed workers and participation by percentage of formal and informal labor with respect to each activity)

	1991		1997		2002	
	Formal	Informal	Formal	Informal	Formal	Informal
TOTAL	398,403	1,383,159	521,322	1,545,201	745,477	1,667,308
Agriculture, livestock, hunting	30,739	595,766	14,693	512,649	17,599	440,833
Fishing	911	10,877	1,083	15,581	421	15,554
Mining	766	1,873	1,048	634	549	2,973
Industry and manufacturing	96,564	212,204	131,821	201,069	203,192	230,825
Electricity, gas, and water	10,382	1,143	10,911	4,159	8,954	1,749
Construction	21,650	59,348	40,793	96,738	35,681	100,565
Businesses, hotels, restaurants	53,563	295,035	99,953	408,226	146,172	542,311
Transportation and communication	17,860	43,154	19,178	76,719	28,418	74,999
Finance/real estate	22,705	12,264	42,194	20,450	70,300	27,715
Public administration and defense	67,282	11,597	75,708	15,992	92,108	8,409
Education	35,990	8,468	30,476	36,981	78,116	16,401
Social services, health	38,581	56,665	52,285	65,264	63,103	92,304
Households/domestic services	71	73,789	0	90,221	0	103,151
Other	1,339	976	1,179	518	864	9,519
MALE	265,645	868,715	319,117	961,790	408,434	995,986
Agriculture, livestock, hunting	27,590	504,360	11,988	460,069	15,787	416,929
Fishing	827	9,376	1,083	14,856	364	14,378
Mining	624	1,683	988	634	469	2,973
Industry and manufacturing	62,196	105,225	70,043	104,307	95,047	108,303
Electricity, gas, and water	8,956	717	9,883	4,032	7,590	1,638
Construction	20,757	58,435	37,823	95,673	30,989	100,197
Businesses, hotels, restaurants	32,559	100,297	53,201	144,103	74,211	193,161
Transportation and communication	15,290	41,197	15,836	73,487	22,012	72,278
Finance/real estate	12,770	9,286	25,946	15,402	43,230	19,338
Public administration and defense	51,370	8,361	55,427	12,558	65,203	6,654
Education	15,055	2,923	14,645	12,652	29,449	7,097
Social services, health	16,666	21,912	21,297	19,458	23,523	34,517
Households/domestic services	71	4,380	0	4,097	0	9,570
Other	914	563	957	462	560	8,953
FEMALE	132,758	514,444	202,205	583,411	337,043	671,322
Agriculture, livestock, hunting	3,149	91,406	2,705	52,580	1,812	23,904
Fishing	84	1,501	0	725	57	1,176
Mining	142	190	60	0	80	0
Industry and manufacturing	34,368	106,979	61,778	96,762	108,145	122,522
Electricity, gas, and water	1,426	426	1,028	127	1,364	111
Construction	893	913	2,970	1,065	4,692	368
Businesses, hotels, restaurants	21,004	194,738	46,752	264,123	71,961	349,150
Transportation and communication	2,570	1,957	3,342	3,232	6,406	2,721
Finance/real estate	9,935	2,978	16,248	5,048	27,070	8,377
Public administration and defense	15,912	3,236	20,281	3,434	26,905	1,755
Education	20,935	5,545	15,831	24,329	48,667	9,304
Social services, health	21,915	34,753	30,988	45,806	39,580	57,787
Households/domestic services	0	69,409	0	86,124	0	93,581
Other	425	413	222	56	304	566

(continued)

APPENDIX TABLE 18 *(cont.)* **Population employed according to type of employment and economic activity (number of employed workers and participation by percentage of formal and informal labor with respect to each activity)**

	1991		1997		2002	
	Formal	Informal	Formal	Informal	Formal	Informal
PERCENTAGES						
TOTAL	22.36%	77.64%	25.23%	74.77%	30.90%	69.10%
Agriculture, livestock, hunting	4.91	95.09	2.79	97.21	3.84	96.16
Fishing	7.73	92.27	6.50	93.50	2.64	97.36
Mining	29.03	70.97	62.31	37.69	15.59	84.41
Industry and manufacturing	31.27	68.73	39.60	60.40	46.82	53.18
Electricity, gas, and water	90.08	9.92	72.40	27.60	83.66	16.34
Construction	26.73	73.27	29.66	70.34	26.19	73.81
Businesses, hotels, restaurants	15.37	84.63	19.67	80.33	21.23	78.77
Transportation and communication	29.27	70.73	20.00	80.00	27.48	72.52
Finance/real estate	64.93	35.07	67.36	32.64	71.72	28.28
Public administration and defense	85.30	14.70	82.56	17.44	91.63	8.37
Education	80.95	19.05	45.18	54.82	82.65	17.35
Social services, health	40.51	59.49	44.48	55.52	40.60	59.40
Households/domestic services	0.10	99.90	0.00	100.00	0.00	100.00
Other	57.84	42.16	69.48	30.52	8.32	91.68
MALE	23.42%	76.58%	24.91%	75.09%	29.08%	70.92%
Agriculture, livestock, hunting	5.19	94.81	2.54	97.46	3.65	96.35
Fishing	8.11	91.89	6.79	93.21	2.47	97.53
Mining	27.05	72.95	60.91	39.09	13.63	86.37
Industry and manufacturing	37.15	62.85	40.17	59.83	46.74	53.26
Electricity, gas, and water	92.59	7.41	71.02	28.98	82.25	17.75
Construction	26.21	73.79	28.33	71.67	23.62	76.38
Businesses, hotels, restaurants	24.51	75.49	26.96	73.04	27.76	72.24
Transportation and communication	27.07	72.93	17.73	82.27	23.34	76.66
Finance/real estate	57.90	42.10	62.75	37.25	69.09	30.91
Public administration and defense	86.00	14.00	81.53	18.47	90.74	9.26
Education	83.74	16.26	53.65	46.35	80.58	19.42
Social services, health	43.20	56.80	52.26	47.74	40.53	59.47
Households/domestic services	1.60	98.40	0.00	100.00	0.00	100.00
Other	61.88	38.12	67.44	32.56	5.89	94.11
FEMALE	20.51%	79.49%	25.74%	74.26%	33.42%	66.58%
Agriculture, livestock, hunting	3.33	96.67	4.89	95.11	7.05	92.95
Fishing	5.30	94.70	0.00	100.00	4.62	95.38
Mining	42.77	57.23	100.00	0.00	100.00	0.00
Industry and manufacturing	24.31	75.69	38.97	61.03	46.88	53.12
Electricity, gas, and water	77.00	23.00	89.00	11.00	92.47	7.53
Construction	49.45	50.55	73.61	26.39	92.73	7.27
Businesses, hotels, restaurants	9.74	90.26	15.04	84.96	17.09	82.91
Transportation and communication	56.77	43.23	50.84	49.16	70.19	29.81
Finance/real estate	76.94	23.06	76.30	23.70	76.37	23.63
Public administration and defense	83.10	16.90	85.52	14.48	93.88	6.12
Education	79.06	20.94	39.42	60.58	83.95	16.05
Social services, health	38.67	61.33	40.35	59.65	40.65	59.35
Households/domestic services	0.00	100.00	0.00	100.00	0.00	100.00
Other	50.72	49.28	79.86	20.14	34.94	65.06

Source: Author's calculations with EHPM data.

APPENDIX TABLE 19 Employed population by type of employment and levels of remuneration (number of employed workers)

	1991		1997		2002	
	Formal	Informal	Formal	Informal	Formal	Informal
COUNTRY						
TOTAL	398,403	1,383,159	521,322	1,545,201	745,477	1,667,308
None	130	156,666	888	155,394	73,387	445,751
Under 400	14,214	460,175	2,931	120,119	5,920	161,379
400-999	162,676	550,158	22,576	509,338	22,414	426,666
1,000-1,499	119,219	86,434	151,522	239,628	159,417	255,448
1,500-1,999	52,122	30,524	69,989	107,408	115,241	140,400
2,000-2,499	15,675	13,706	65,743	56,658	65,836	63,829
2,500-2,999	9,888	12,220	41,285	39,044	54,197	52,859
3,000-3,999	9,108	6,756	66,274	56,015	107,600	42,315
4,000-4,999	4,523	5,135	27,755	18,745	54,237	23,633
5000-5,999	2,086	2,922	17,135	16,798	27,377	16,305
6,000-6,999	1,522	1,178	10,086	6,815	18,196	10,636
7,000 and more	5,205	4,720	27,012	15,490	41,655	28,087
Unaccounted for	2,035	52,565	18,126	203,749	0	0
MALE	265,645	868,715	319,117	961,790	408,434	995,986
None	89	103,109	444	102,426	44,934	344,609
Under 400	10,730	245,449	1,142	30,184	1,315	61,640
400-999	104,098	370,084	10,839	274,928	6,856	202,233
1,000-1,499	78,295	59,952	78,321	146,266	69,473	140,223
1,500-1,999	33,394	22,149	49,961	72,161	67,000	93,155
2,000-2,499	11,524	8,602	45,274	42,870	40,744	42,723
2,500-2,999	7,125	8,484	25,364	21,819	33,899	34,974
3,000-3,999	7,593	5,023	40,132	37,238	62,300	24,834
4,000-4,999	3,760	3,604	17,269	14,679	25,964	14,860
5,000-5,999	1,683	1,829	10,487	11,435	14,816	10,481
6,000-6,999	1,327	1,019	7,724	5,981	10,630	7,269
7,000 and more	4,506	3,260	20,022	10,801	30,503	18,985
Unaccounted for	1,521	36,151	12,138	191,002	0	0
FEMALE	132,758	514,444	202,205	583,411	337,043	671,322
None	41	53,557	444	52,968	28,453	101,142
Under 400	3,484	214,726	1,789	89,935	4,605	99,739
400-999	58,578	180,074	11,737	234,410	15,558	224,433
1,000-1,499	40,924	26,482	73,201	93,362	89,944	115,225
1,500-1,999	18,728	8,375	20,028	35,247	48,241	47,245
2,000-2,499	4,151	5,104	20,469	13,788	25,092	21,106
2,500-2,999	2,763	3,736	15,921	17,225	20,298	17,885
3,000-3,999	1,515	1,733	26,142	18,777	45,300	17,481
4,000-4,999	763	1,531	10,486	4,066	28,273	8,773
5,000-5,999	403	1,093	6,648	5,363	12,561	5,824
6,000-6,999	195	159	2,362	834	7,566	3,367
7,000 and more	699	1,460	6,990	4,689	11,152	9,102
Unaccounted for	514	16,414	5,988	12,747	0	0

(continued)

APPENDIX TABLE 19 *(cont.)* **Employed population according to type of employment and levels of remuneration (number of employed workers)**

	1991		1997		2002	
	Formal	Informal	Formal	Informal	Formal	Informal
URBAN						
TOTAL	327,557	619,588	435,243	800,369	622,023	899,466
None	61	45,086	888	54,723	62,149	143,973
Under 400	5,332	184,467	2,076	61,078	4,544	79,120
400-999	128,941	254,838	14,352	218,918	16,500	217,712
1,000-1,499	99,609	61,943	113,588	159,214	117,255	166,199
1,500-1,999	47,720	20,150	56,505	81,741	89,115	99,609
2,000-2,499	14,577	9,946	58,311	45,581	56,402	48,821
2,500-2,999	9,704	11,323	34,430	33,518	46,909	41,279
3,000-3,999	8,278	3,738	60,902	50,187	94,740	34,008
4,000-4,999	4,247	4,212	27,117	17,219	49,542	20,133
5,000-5,999	1,884	2,650	16,821	15,356	26,073	14,040
6,000-6,999	1,285	606	9,812	6,041	17,646	9,208
7,000 and more	4,628	4,002	26,496	15,153	41,148	25,364
Unaccounted for	1,291	16,627	13,945	41,640	0	0
MALE	205,155	309,659	257,081	419,943	327,743	458,504
None	20	19,957	444	21,148	35,914	80,911
Under 400	3,290	62,059	529	15,332	885	25,016
400-999	76,529	141,385	5,722	82,434	3,328	81,626
1,000-1,499	60,925	40,071	53,524	87,938	47,533	82,440
1,500-1,999	29,161	14,935	38,513	53,396	48,216	64,000
2,000-2,499	10,495	5,862	39,851	32,576	33,215	32,751
2,500-2,999	6,941	7,656	19,735	18,381	27,877	27,814
3,000-3,999	6,763	2,566	35,841	32,918	53,033	19,309
4,000-4,999	3,484	2,955	16,631	13,551	23,474	12,250
5,000-5,999	1,481	1,641	10,173	10,575	13,914	8,735
6,000-6,999	1,090	565	7,450	5,207	10,358	6,307
7,000 and more	4,081	2,764	19,506	10,622	29,996	17,345
Unaccounted for	895	7,243	9,162	35,865	0	0
FEMALE	122,402	309,929	178,162	380,426	294,280	440,962
None	41	25,129	444	33,575	26,235	63,062
Under 400	2,042	122,408	1,547	45,746	3,659	54,104
400-999	52,412	113,453	8,630	136,484	13,172	136,086
1,000-1,499	38,684	21,872	60,064	71,276	69,722	83,759
1,500-1,999	18,559	5,215	17,992	28,345	40,899	35,609
2,000-2,499	4,082	4,084	18,460	13,005	23,187	16,070
2,500-2,999	2,763	3,667	14,695	15,137	19,032	13,465
3,000-3,999	1,515	1,172	25,061	17,269	41,707	14,699
4,000-4,999	763	1,257	10,486	3,668	26,068	7,883
5,000-5,999	403	1,009	6,648	4,781	12,159	5,305
6,000-6,999	195	41	2,362	834	7,288	2,901
7,000 and more	547	1,238	6,990	4,531	11,152	8,019
Unaccounted for	396	9,384	4,783	5,775	0	0

(continued)

APPENDIX TABLE 19 *(cont.)* **Employed population according to type of employment and levels of remuneration (number of employed workers)**

	1991		1997		2002	
	Formal	Informal	Formal	Informal	Formal	Informal
RURAL						
TOTAL	70,846	763,571	86,079	744,832	123,454	767,842
None	69	111,580	0	100,671	11,238	301,778
Under 400	8,882	275,708	855	59,041	1,376	82,259
400-999	33,735	295,320	8,224	290,420	5,914	208,954
1,000-1,499	19,610	24,491	37,934	80,414	42,162	89,249
1,500-1,999	4,402	10,374	13,484	25,667	26,126	40,791
2,000-2,499	1,098	3,760	7,432	11,077	9,434	15,008
2,500-2,999	184	897	6,855	5,526	7,288	11,580
3,000-3,999	830	3,018	5,372	5,828	12,860	8,307
4,000-4,999	276	923	638	1,526	4,695	3,500
5,000-5,999	202	272	314	1,442	1,304	2,265
6,000-6,999	237	572	274	774	550	1,428
7,000 and more	577	718	516	337	507	2,723
Unaccounted for	744	35,938	4,181	162,109	0	0
MALE	60,490	559,056	62,036	541,847	80,691	537,482
None	69	83,152	0	81,278	9,020	263,698
Under 400	7,440	183,390	613	14,852	430	36,624
400-999	27,569	228,699	5,117	192,494	3,528	120,607
1,000-1,499	17,370	19,881	24,797	58,328	21,940	57,783
1,500-1,999	4,233	7,214	11,448	18,765	18,784	29,155
2,000-2,499	1,029	2,740	5,423	10,294	7,529	9,972
2,500-2,999	184	828	5,629	3,438	6,022	7,160
3,000-3,999	830	2,457	4,291	4,320	9,267	5,525
4,000-4,999	276	649	638	1,128	2,490	2,610
5,000-5,999	202	188	314	860	902	1,746
6,000-6,999	237	454	274	774	272	962
7,000 and more	425	496	516	179	507	1,640
Unaccounted for	626	28,908	2,976	155,137	0	0
FEMALE	10,356	204,515	24,043	202,985	42,763	230,360
None	0	28,428	0	19,393	2,218	38,080
Under 400	1,442	92,318	242	44,189	946	45,635
400-999	6,166	66,621	3,107	97,926	2,386	88,347
1,000-1,499	2,240	4,610	13,137	22,086	20,222	31,466
1,500-1,999	169	3,160	2,036	6,902	7,342	11,636
2,000-2,499	69	1,020	2,009	783	1,905	5,036
2,500-2,999	0	69	1,226	2,088	1,266	4,420
3,000-3,999	0	561	1,081	1,508	3,593	2,782
4,000-4,999	0	274	0	398	2,205	890
5,000-5,999	0	84	0	582	402	519
6,000-6,999	0	118	0	0	278	466
7000 and more	152	222	0	158	0	1,083
Unaccounted for	118	7,030	1,205	6,972	0	0

Source: Author's calculations with EHPM data.

Endnotes

1.   This report was prepared for the Global Policy Network (GPN) as part of the Workforce Development project. It has benefited from the oversight and advice of José Ángel Tolentino and the collaboration of Rosa Inés Arrivillaga, who worked on systematizing the statistical information and the research. Also appreciated is the help of Roxana Palacios y Martha García in organizing the data. The opinions put forth in this report are the responsibility of the author.

2.   At the end of the 1970s El Salvador fell into a civil war that ended with the signing of the Peace Accords in 1992.

3.   The presidential election of March 1989 gave a victory to Alfredo Cristiani and the rightist Alianza Republicana Nacionalista (ARENA) party.

4.   For an analysis of the agreement, see Williamson (2003).

5.   Art. 1 in the Monetary Integration Law.

6.   Refund of 6% of the export value of products destined for outside the Central American region.

7.   For example, Segovia (2002, 32) argues: "The period of high growth registered in the first half was tied to the expansion of domestic demand associated with the end of the war and the consequent process of reconstruction and its positive effects for public and private investment."

8.   One of the main successes attributed to the structural adjustment programs was that they managed to lower rates of inflation, which fell from 24.7% in the 1980s to 2.3% between 1998 and 2002 (Lara López 2002).

9.   For an analysis of the levels of constraints or activity in the productive economy of El Salvador, see Rubio Fabian and Lara López (2003).

10.   In El Salvador, poverty levels are measured by comparing income with the value of the basic goods index. Thus, a home or person is considered to be in a condition of extreme poverty when their income is less than the value of the basic goods index (the poverty line). The value of the index varies according to place of residence, whether rural or urban. Relative poverty occurs when income is greater than the value of a given basic goods index but less than the *Canasta Ampliada*, which is double the index.

11.   The "Expanded Washington Consensus" incorporates 10 initial recommendations as well as the following: corporative governance, fighting corruption, flexible labor markets, equality in WTO agreements, strengthening of financial regulation and supervision, prudent tightening of capital accounts, no intermediary systems of types of exchange, monetary stability guaranteed by the Independent Central Bank, social security networks, and strategies to reduce poverty (UNDP 2003).

12.   "Relationship which measures the volume of unemployment or unemployed people in the economically active population during a given period, representing the percentage of the labor market which is not absorbed by the economic system" (DIGESTYC 2002).

13.   "Relationship between average working age is economically active population] and working-age population. Indicates the proportion of working-age people in the country who are economically active. Denotes the precise level of economic activity in the country" (DIGESTYC 2002).

14. In El Salvador, the underemployed population is made up of visible and invisible underemployed people. By "visible underemployment" we mean the employed population that is working involuntarily less than 40 hours a week. "Invisible underemployment" includes people who work involuntarily for fewer than 40 hours a week and who receive salaries lower than the legal minimum salary.

15. See Lara López and Tolentino (2003).

16. It is important to note that the salary gap between men and women is greater when analyzed in terms of functions or skills (which are comparable or which either men or women can carry out under the same conditions) that both sexes carry out within the same sector. For example, in 2002 men working as directors and/or functionaries earned $428.09 per month more than women who carried out the same work or who had the same skills. At the level of certain different economic sectors or functions, the gap tends to be smaller, and in some sectors women earn a higher average salary than men.

17. A closer look shows that, in 2002, 47.1% (1,135,517 people) of the employed population earned salaries lower than $114.17; of this group, 534,015 people did not receive any salary.

18. See Trejos (2001).

19. In this study, we understand dignified work to be "employment which respects the rights of workers and around which forms of social protection are developed; also, work which is carried out under conditions of freedom, equity, security, and human dignity" (ILO 2001).

20. In order to render the data from each year comparable and to enable an analysis of informal and formal labor tendencies between 1991 and 2002, the categories of permanent salaried, temporary workers, etc. have been determined by using the attribute of social security solely. The attribute of "contract" has been taken into account in the Survey of Multi-Purpose Households only since 1998, which makes it difficult to compare to previous years. Calculations using both attributes estimate urban informal unemployment at 1,230,253 people; that is, 80.9% of the employed urban population (see Appendix 15).

21. For 2002, 39.4% of workers in the country who were employed in agribusiness worked as unremunerated family members, 29.5% as temporary salaried workers, 18.1% as self-employed, 5.3% as owners, and 0.4% as cooperativists.

22. Poverty of the working population is determined by comparing income to the value of the basic goods index per person.

23. That is, below the poverty line, determined by the value of the basic goods index.

24. According to the CIUO, this large group includes occupations that require general knowledge and experience, manual tools, sometimes considerable physical effort, and (except for rare cases) low initiative or capacity for judgment. Tasks include selling goods in the streets; providing transportation and guarding services for property; laundering clothing; simple mining, agricultural, and fishing activities; construction or public works; and manufacturing.

25. This claim follows, in part, that of Lara López (2004).

26. This section takes up the conclusions proposed by Cardona (2003).

27. Proposal taken from Iniciativa Mesoamericana de Comercio Integración y Desarrollo Sostenible (2003).

28. ILO (1990).

Bibliography

Alas de Franco, Carolina. 2002. Commercial Policy and the Evolution of the Export Sector During the Nineties in El Salvador. Investigative Series. El Salvador: FUSADES.

Acevedo, Carlos. 2000. *El Salvador 1999: Macroeconomic Stabilization and Structural Reforms.* San Salvador, El Salvador: FLACSO.

Alvarenga, Ligia. 2001. *The Economic-Labor Situation in Maquila Factories in El Salvador: An Análisis by Gender.* Chile: CEPAL.

Cardona, Amílcar. 2003. "Toward a Policy in Defense of Labor and Union Rights." . *Reality: Journal of the Social Sciences and Humanities.* No. 93. El Salvador: UCA.

CEPAL (Comisión Económica Para América Latina y el Caribe). 2002. Styles of development and changes in the labor sector in Northern Latin America. México: CEPAL.

DIGESTYC. 2002. Survey of Multi-Purpose Households. El Salvador: DIGESTYC.

FEPAD (Fundación de Estudios Para la Aplicación del Derecho). 2003. Achievement and Monitoring of Economic, Social, and Cultural Rights in El Salvador. El Salvador: FEPAD.

Human Rights Watch. 2003. Intentional Indifference: The El Salvadoran Government's Inaction in Workers' Rights Protection. Human Rights Watch. Vol. 15, No. 5(B). http://www.org/spanish/informes/2003/elsalvadorl203/

Mesoamerican Initiative for Trade Integration and Sustainable Development. 2003. *Regional Labor and Agricultural Proposal in the FTA Negotiations Between the U.S. and Central America.* www.iniciativacid.org.

ILO. 1990. Summary of International Labor Norms. Second Edition. Geneva: ILO.

ILO. 1993. *Resolution Regarding Employment Statistics in the Informal Sector, Adopted by the 15th International Conference on Work Statistics.* www.ilo.org/public/spanish/bureau/stat/download/res/infsec.pdf

ILO. 2001. *Formation for Decent Work.* Montevideo, México: CINTERFOR.

ILO. 2002. Report VI: *Dignified Work and the Informal Economy.* International Conference on Work, 90th Meeting, Geneva.

Lara López, Edgar. 2002. *El Salvador at 13 Years of Economic Adjustment and Stabilization Policies. Theory and Practice.* No. 2. San Salvador, El Salvador: Universidad Don Bosco.

Lara López, Edgar. 2004. "Steps for a National Employment Policy in El Salvador." *Alternatives for Development.* Nos. 85, 86. El Salvador: FUNDE.

Lara López, Edgar, and José Tolentino. 2003. *Performance of the Labor Market in El Salvador 2002/2003.* Washington, D.C.: Global Policy Network (GPN). www.gpn.org.

Masi, Fernando. 2002. *Informal Sector and Private Accounts in Paraguay.* Paraguay: Office of Statistics, Surveys, and General Census. www.deec.gov.py

Mazza, Jacqueline. 2003. "Labor Mediation Services for Latin America and the Caribbean." *Revista de la CEPAL.* No. 80. Chile: CEPAL.

Oscar, Peñate, Edgar Lara, and María Ochoa. 2003. *El Salvador, mundo laboral y sindicatos.* El Salvador: Friedrich Ebert – Centra.

Rubio Fabian, Roberto, and Edgar Lara López. 2003. Winning and losing sectors with the CAFTA signing: Perspectives for the Future, El Salvador Case. Mimeo. Costa Rica: CIDH.

Salazar, José Manuel. 1991. "The Role of the State and the Market in Economic Development." In O. Sunkel, ed., *Development From the Inside: A Structuralist Focus for Latin America,* p. 487.

Samaniego, Norma. 2002. Labor Market Policies and Their Evolution in Latin America. Chile: CEPAL.

Segovia, Alexander. 2002. *Structural Transformation and Economic Reform in El Salvador.* Guatemala: F & G Editores, pp. 32-33.

Trejos, Juan Diego. 2001. *Dignified Work and the Informal Sector in Central American Countries.* ILO, Office for Central America, Panama, and the Dominican Republic. www.ILO.or.cr/ILO/papers/trab_dec_sect_inf_ca.pdf

UNDP (United Nations Development Program). 2003. *Report on Human Development in El Salvador: Challenges and Options in an Era of Globalization.* New York, N.Y.: UNDP.

UNDP (United Nations Development Program). 2003a. *Report on Human Development in El Salvador.* New York, N.Y.: UNDP.

Williamson, John. 2003. "There Is No Consensus in the Agreement." *Finances and Development.* (IMF) Vol. 40, No. 3.

CHAPTER 3

Economic reforms and employment in India

by Mridula Sharma

Introduction

The world economy underwent radical change in the late 1980s. A large number of countries switched from planned to market economies and from command economies to free ones, and the movement toward privatization of public sector activities, deregulation of industries, and opening up of economies for foreign direct investment significantly changed the planning and economic development processes of almost all the world's developing countries. India has been no exception. Responding to the sense that excessive control and over-protection of domestic markets had resulted in slow economic development and unsatisfactory performance in the post-independence period, the Indian government introduced structural reforms — specifically liberalization, privatization, and globalization — that were considered essential to achieving macroeconomic stability and putting the economy on a faster growth path. These reforms primarily affected trade, industry, finance, and fiscal policy.

In the traded sector, reforms included:

- reductions in export tariffs from 300% to 40% and in import tariffs from 87% to 20%;

- abolition of the import licensing system;

- withdrawal of the Crash Compensatory Scheme for exports;

- two separate devaluations of the rupee;

- abolition of a real exchange rate system;

- liberalization of foreign exchange; and

- relaxation in the licensing regime, leading to a shift of a large number of items from the restricted list to the open general license.

Industrial sector reforms included:

- policies promoting capital mobility;

- relaxation of the Monopoly Restricted Trade Practices Act;

- opening up of industries to the private sector (e.g., the privatization of foreign direct investment (FDI) and foreign portfolio investment);

- relaxation of the Foreign Exchange Regulation Act; and

- approval for foreign investments of up to 51% of equity in 34 industries.

Under the financial sector reforms, the cash reserve ratio and statutory liquidity ratio were lowered, effecting less government access to the resources of commercial banks. Other financial sector reforms included the deregulation of interest rates, the abolition of the controller of capital issues post, the establishment of a Security Exchange Board of India, and an increase in the level of foreign portfolio investment.

Fiscal policy reforms called for:

- reduction in the fiscal deficit;

- widening of the tax base;

- increases in relative importance of direct vs. indirect taxes (1.3% to 3%);

- introduction of presumptive taxation;

- reduction in the bank credit to the government by 40%;

- reduction in the central government budget deficit (financed by the Reserve Bank of India, or RBI) from 15.6% to 9.0% of gross domestic product;

TABLE 1   Economic indicators for India, 1990-91 to 1999-2000 (in percent)

Indicators	1990-91	1993-94	1999-2000
Real growth in GDP at factor cost	-	5.9	6.1
Exports as a percentage of GDP	5.8	-	9.8
Imports as a percentage of GDP	8.8	-	13
Exports (Rs. in Crores)	-	69751	203571
Imports (Rs. in Crores)	-	73101	230873
Trade balance (Rs. in Crores)	-	(-) 3350	(-) 27302
Foreign currency reserves (in billion US $)	1	-	27.4
FDI inflows (in billion US $)	0.135	-	3
Investment rate	-	23.1	25.3
Saving rate	-	22.5	24.5
Annual rate of inflation	17	-	6.5

Source: Reserve Bank of India (2003).

- a significant decline in net borrowing;

- increases in corporate and income taxes from 2% to 3% of GDP;

- decline in the share of customs and excise duties from 9% to 7% of GDP;

- reduction in non-interest expenditures from 16% to 13% of GDP; and

- reductions of subsidies.

The introduction of these reforms generated intense debate on their impact on growth, poverty, and employment. Those opposed to the reforms believe that they have weakened the link between economic growth, poverty reduction, and employment. The pro-reformers, however, argue that these reforms have benefited investment, output, and employment. The performance of the economy over the last decade has provided arguments for both sides (**Table 1**). On the positive side, GDP growth rose from 5.9% in fiscal year 1993-94 to 6.1% in 1999-2000. Inflation fell while investment and saving rates rose, and inflows of FDI increased. At the same time, however, the rate of growth of employment fell, the trade balance deteriorated, and the growth in exports was less than anticipated.

TABLE 2   Indices of nominal and real effective exchange rate (REER)

Nominal effective exchange rate (NEER) of the Indian rupee
(Five country trade-based weights)

(Base year 1991-92 = 100)

Year	NEER	REER
1991-92 (base year)	100	100
1993-94	76.02	85.85
1999-2000	56.42	74.22

Source : Reserve Bank of India, March 2003.

The country now also faces a problem of sustaining its desired 7% growth rate in the future to absorb new entrants into the workforce.

The nominal effective exchange rate and real effective exchange rate declined from the 1993-94 to the 1999-2000 period, indicating a decline in the value of the rupee (**Table 2**).

According to the United Nation Development Program's Human Development Report for 1994, India's human development index increased from 0.206 in 1960 to 0.382 in 1992. In 1999, the country ranked 132 out of 174 countries. The National Human Development Report of the government's Planning Commission shows improvements in economic, educational, and health indicators from 1983-84 to 1999-2000, but rates of employment and unemployment growth were not favorable in the same period. Furthermore, a comparison of the human development indicators of India with those of East and Southeast Asian countries like China, Indonesia, the Republic of Korea, Malaysia, the Philippines, and Thailand shows India lagging behind (**Tables 3** and **4**).

The following sections analyze four major facets of India's economy and offer a set of policy recommendations. The first section deals with the structure and quality of employment in the organized and unorganized sectors of India's labor market. The next section provides information about the educational composition of the workforce and the system of imparting education and skill formation. The third section examines the incidence of unemployment, particularly among educated youth. The final section provides details on the fixing of wages

TABLE 3   Human development indicators, 1983-84 to 1999-2000

Economic indicators	1983-84	1993-94	1999-2000
Per capita net state domestic product	1,790	2337	2840
Per capita consumption expenditure	125.13	328.18	590.98
Growth in employment	2.1	-	1.6
	(1983-93 – 1999		(1993-94 – 1999-2000)
Incidence of unemployment	2.0	2.0	2.3
Percentage of population			
below poverty line	44.8	35.97	26.0
	(Poverty line = Rs. 89.5)	(Poverty line = Rs. 208.84)	(Poverty line = Rs. 327.56)

Education attainment	1981	1991	2001
Literacy in India	43.57	52.21	65.20
School drop-out rate			
(Class I-V)	53.5	45.01	39.53
			(1998-99)
(Class I-VIII)	72.10	61.10	56.82
			(1998-99)
(Class I-X)	82.3	72.93	67.44
			(1998-99)
Teacher/pupil ratio			
Primary	40	45	42
			(1997-98)
Upper primary	34	43	37
			(1997-98)
Secondary	29	29	29
			(1997-98)
Number of schools per			
thousand population			
Primary	5.70	5.75	5.04
			(1997-98)
Upper primary	2.44	6.69	2.75
			(1997-98)

Indicators of health	1981-85	1991-95	1992-96
Life expectancy at birth	55.5	60.3	60.7
Life expectancy at one year of age	60.9	64.5	64.9
Persons not expected to survive			
beyond age 40 (per thousand)	23.0	18.0	-
	(1981)	(1991)	
Infant mortality rate per thousand	115	77	-
	(1981)	(1991)	
Death rate (per thousand)	12.5	9.7	8.9
	(1981)	(1991)	(1997)
Maternal mortality ratio	408	-	407
(per hundred thousand)	(1997)		(1998)
Overall sex ratio females	934	927	933
Per thousand males			
Birth attended by health professionals	32.2	25.5	33.6
	(1992-93)	(1992-93)	(1998-99)
Total fertility rate	4.5	3.7	3.4
	(1980-82)	(1990-92)	(1995-97)

Source: National Human Development Report, Planning Commission, Government of India, March 2002.

TABLE 4   Human development indicators for India and some Asian countries

Country	Life expectancy at birth (years)	Infant mortality rate (per thousand births)	Adult literacy rate (%)
India	62.4	71	62
Kerala State (India)	72.0	12	93
Bangladesh	58.1	81	39
China	69.8	38	83
Indonesia	65.1	45	85
Korea, Republic	72.4	6	97
Malaysia	72.0	10	86
Pakistan	64.0	95	41
Philippines	68.3	32	95
Thailand	68.8	31	95

Source: Economic Survey, 1999-2000, Government of India.

and the provision of social security for workers in the organized and unorganized sectors. This chapter ends with summary findings, concluding observations, and suggested interventions.

The Indian labor market

The Indian labor market can be viewed as having two segments: organized and unorganized, or formal and informal. It is difficult to draw a clear-cut distinction between the two sectors, yet attempts have been made.

The first National Commission on Labor stated in 1969 that unorganized labor was:

> [a] group of workers who cannot be identified by a definition but could be described as those who have not been able to organize themselves in pursuit of a common objective, because of constraints such as: (a) casual nature of employment; (b) ignorance and illiteracy; (c) small size of establishments with low capital investment per person employed; (d) scattered nature of establishment; and (e) superior strength of the employer operating singly or in combination.

The commission drew up an illustrative list of unorganized workers comprising the following:

- contract labor, including construction workers;

- casual labor;

- labor employed in small-scale industry;

- handloom/power-loom workers;

- bidi and cigar workers;

- employees in shops and establishments;

- sweepers and scavengers;

- tannery workers;

- tribal labor; and

- other unprotected labor.

The second National Commission on Labor in 2001 recognized the following characteristic features of the unorganized sectors in India:

- low level of organization;

- small in scale usually employing fewer than 10 workers, and often from the immediate family;

- heterogeneity in activities;

- entry and exit from the labor market easier than in the organized sector;

- capital investment usually minimal, and little or no division between labor and capital;

- work that is mostly labor intensive, requiring low-level skills; there is usually no formal training, and instead workers learn on the job;

- labor relations based on casual employment and or social relationships as opposed to formal contracts; the employer/employee relationship is often unwritten and informal, and it specifies few or no rights; and

- isolation and invisibility of workers, helping them to be unaware of their rights and leaving them with little negotiating power and few options for organizing.

The commission saw the organized sector as having barriers to entry, utilizing foreign capital, operating as a capitalist enterprise, utilizing important technology, offering formal training, operating in a regulated market and within the confines of government policy, and employing an often unionized workforce. By contrast, it saw the informal sector as having ease of entry, relying on indigenous resources, operating as a family enterprise, utilizing adaptive technology and labor-intensive work methods, relying on skills acquired outside of formal education, operating in unregulated and competitive markets outside of government control, and employing a mostly non-unionized workforce.

The basic point as emphasized by the commission is that the unorganized sector is not a homogeneous group—there is great diversity within it. It is also a growing sector, coming at the expense of the shrinking organized sector.

The division between the organized and unorganized sectors is not watertight; there are strong linkages between them, and no description or definition can capture this complexity fully. It may be simplest to say that the entire workforce outside of the organized sector is the unorganized sector.

The 1993 System of National Accounts of the Government of India refers to the unorganized sector as productive institutional units characterized by: (1) low-level organization, (2) little or no division between labor and capital, and (3) labor relations based on casual employment and or social relationships as opposed to formal contracts. It delineated three types of units within the unorganized sector: (1) own-account enterprises, which are mainly operated by family members without any regularly employed workers; (2) non-directory establishments, enterprises that employ five workers or fewer, including family members, and at least one is a regularly employed worker; and (3) directory establishments, units that employ six or more workers of which at least one is hired. Own-account enterprises constitute the vast majority (up to 85%) of total establishments in the unorganized sector, and they do not maintain regular accounts and are mostly outside the purview of statute and regulation.

The 1993 National Account also describes unorganized work (or the definitional absence of it) by economic sector (discussed in Bhalla 2002 and various rounds of the National Sample Survey Organization (NSSO)):

Manufacturing. The unorganized manufacturing segment includes all units using power and employing fewer than 10 workers or not using power but employing fewer than 20 workers.

Trade. All government and public sector trading enterprises are excluded from the unorganized sector. Within the private sector, unorganized trading segments are not determined by the size of the units. In the absence of any clear-cut size stipulations, large trading units of manufacturing concerns are sometimes considered part of the unorganized segment when these units have a separate and distinct identity. For example, the sales shops of Delhi Cloth Mills and Bata Shoes are considered part of the unorganized trade segment.

Service. According to a report of the 34th round of the NSSO, the unorganized service sector includes "all institutions for which no regular accounts were available." All public sector enterprises owned by the central and state government, local bodies, public cooperatives, and public undertakings, along with all enterprises registered under the Banking Companies Act, are excluded from the unorganized service sector. In the education sector, all unrecognized institutions are classified under the unorganized sector.

Transport. Public sector enterprises — namely rail and air transport and other enterprises owned or run by government or quasi-government institutions — are excluded from classification in the unorganized segment, although cooperatives are not. The unorganizcd transport scctor can include both mechanized and non-mechanized goods and passenger transport by land, waterways, or sea. It can also include a wide range of activities covered under the heading "services incidental to transport."

Storage and warehousing. The method for determining whether a storage and warehousing enterprise is classified as part of the unorganized labor market is somewhat different from the usual method of determining coverage. The definition includes not only storage and warehousing activities under private and cooperative ownership without any restrictions on the size of employment, but it can also include, as a special case, the community grain goals/dharma goals maintained by village panchayats. Storage and warehouse facilities available on hire to farmers, dealers, traders, processors, and manufacturing enterprises, as well as the storage and warehousing activities undertaken by an enterprise whose main or auxiliary activity is trade, manufacturing, or transport, are designated as part of the unorganized segment. However, the storage of a farmer's or manufacturer's own goods in his or her own inventory is not included under the definition of unorganized activity.

Communications. In general, the unorganized communications sector includes all those activities that are identified by the 1987 national industrial classification codes 750, 751, and 759. These codes identify postal, telegraph, wireless, and signal communications businesses as unorganized enterprises. It is, however, difficult to conceive of examples of these enterprises where provision by the unorganized sector is significant.

Public sector enterprises owned by local government bodies and public undertakings are excluded from the unorganized communications sector. The organized sector consists of the group of enterprises (public, private, and governmental) in which workers are protected in an effective manner by legislation. These units are registered under the Factories Act of 1948, and data are regularly collected under the annual survey of industries. The working conditions for this sector are clearly defined, and wages are relatively higher.

Employment

The annual growth rate of employment declined from 2.04% during the period from 1983-84 to 1993-94 to 0.98% during the 1993-94 to 1999-2000 period. The growth rate declined both in rural and urban areas. The annual growth rate of both the population and the labor force also declined (**Table 5A**).

However, the decline in the labor force's annual growth rate between 1983-84 and 1999-2000 was much sharper than that of the decline in the annual growth rate of the population during the same period. This sharper decline can be explained by the drop in labor force partici-

TABLE 5A Growth rates of population, labor force, and employment (annual percent)

Period	Population growth rate	Labour force growth rate (UPSS)	Employment growth rate (UPSS)
1983 to 1987-88	2.14	1.74	1.54
1987-88 to 1993-94	2.10	2.29	2.43
1983-84 to 1993-94	2.12	2.05	2.04
1993-94 to 1999-2000	1.93	1.03	0.98

Source: Report of the Planning Commission, Govt. of India on Labour and Employment, 2002.

pation rates (LFPR) for all age groups between the 1993-94 period and the 1999-2000 period. The decline in the LFPR for younger workers was mainly due to a shift in the activity status of this group toward education, while the decline in the LFPR for those age 50 and older could be due to some definitional problems, as LFPRs for this group during the 1993-94 period were significantly higher than the usual long-term trend would suggest (**Table 5B**).

Employment in primary, secondary, and tertiary sectors

The primary, secondary, and tertiary sectors represent broad divisions in economic activity. The primary sector represents agriculture, forestry, fishing, hunting, mining, and quarrying, all of which provide tangible raw goods. The secondary sector consists of industries involved in manufacturing, gas, electricity, and the water supply. And the tertiary sector includes activities involving education, health care, public administration, transport, storage, insurance, communication, finance, and personal and community services and trade. The nine-digit classifications in the census industrial category provides detailed subcategories for each of these sectors.

Total employment in the year 1983-84 was 302.8 million. Of this, the primary sector accounted for 68.7%, the secondary sector 13.3%, and the tertiary sector 18.8% (**Table 6**). Total employment increased to 397.0 million in 1999-2000, by which time the primary sector's share of total employment declined to 61.7%, while the shares of secondary and tertiary sectors increased to 15.8% and 22.5%, respectively. A larger share of women than men are employed in the primary sector, but the

TABLE 5B Labour force participation rates by sex and age, 1993-94 to 1999-2000

Age group	Rural male		Rural female		Urban male		Urban female	
	1993-94	1999-2000	1993-94	1999-2000	1993-94	1999-2000	1993-94	1999-2000
5-9	11	7	14	7	4	3	4	2
10-14	139	93	142	96	71	52	47	37
15-19	598	532	371	314	404	366	142	121
20-24	902	889	470	425	772	755	230	191
25-29	980	975	528	498	958	951	248	214
30-34	988	987	587	557	983	980	283	245
35-39	992	986	610	579	990	986	304	289
40-44	989	984	607	586	984	980	320	285
45-49	984	980	594	566	976	974	317	269
50-54	970	953	543	515	945	939	287	264
55-59	941	930	468	450	856	811	225	208
60+	699	640	241	218	443	402	114	94
All Ages	561	540	331	302	542	542	164	147

Source: Planning Commission Report on Labour and Employment, Government of India, 2002.

TABLE 6 Percentage distribution of total employment by economic sector

Sector	All			Male			Female		
	1983	1993-94	1999-2000	1983	1993-94	1999-2000	1983	1993-94	1999-2000
Primary	68.7	64.6	61.7	62.3	58.3	54.9	81.1	77.8	76.2
Secondary	13.3	14.2	15.8	15.0	15.9	17.8	12.5	10.9	11.8
Tertiary	18.0	21.2	22.5	22.7	25.8	27.3	9.1	11.4	12.0
Total	100.0	100.0	100.0	100.0	100.0	100.0	100.0	100.0	100.0

Note: Figures relate to usual status of individuals. Workforce covers those involved in gainful activity regularly plus those involved in gainful activity occasionally.

Source: National Sample Survey Organisation; Sarvekshana Vol. V, July 77-June 78, 32nd Round; Sarvekshana Vol. XI, Jan. Dec. 1983, 38th Round; Sarvekshana special No., July 87-June 88, 43rd Round; Sarvekshana Vol. XX, July 93-June 94, 50th Round; Report No. 458, July 99-June 2000, 55th Round.

opposite is the case in the tertiary sector, where nearly twice as many men as women are employed. The decline in the male employment share in the primary sector from 1983-84 to 1999-2000 was larger than that for women. The gender difference was not very significant, however, in the secondary sector.

The details of sectoral share in urban employment were indicative of the dominance of the tertiary sector in total urban employment from 1983-84 to 1999-2000: the tertiary sector accounted for more than half of total urban employment (**Table 7**). By contrast, the share in the primary sector was small, and it declined from 15.6% in 1983-84 to 8.6% in 1999-2000. Gender differences were significant in the primary sector, as compared to the secondary sector, in 1983-84, but they had become less so in the primary sector and more so in the secondary sector by 1999-2000.

The primary sector accounted for more that 80% of total rural employment during 1983-84 (**Table 8**). Its share had declined slightly, though it still remained the highest, by 1999-2000. The shares of secondary and tertiary sectors were small but increased from 1983-84 to 1999-2000. Relatively higher percentages of females than males were employed in the primary sector in rural areas, but their respective shares declined during the period under consideration here. The percentage share of both males and females increased in the secondary and tertiary sectors from 1983-84 to 1999-2000.

The decline in employment in the primary sector and increases in the tertiary sector from 1983-84 to 1999-2000 were perhaps the outcome of a declining share of the primary sector in GDP and a correspondingly increasing share of the tertiary sector. The share of the primary sector in GDP at 1993-94 prices declined from 38.1% to 26.1% from 1980-81 to 2000-01, and employment in this sector declined from 68.7% to 61.7% during the same period. The share of the tertiary sector in GDP at 1993-94 prices increased from 36.0% to 49.0% from 1983-84 to 1999-2000, and employment in the sector increased from 18.0% to 22.5%.

Employment by activities
An analysis of employment by activity shows that the annual rate of growth of employment in the activities of the primary sector (agriculture, mining and quarrying) not only declined but also became negative

TABLE 7 Urban employment by economic sector

Sector	All			Male			Female		
	1983	1993-94	1999-2000	1983	1993-94	1999-2000	1983	1993-94	1999-2000
Primary	15.6	13.5	8.6	11.4	10.3	6.6	31.7	25.2	17.7
Secondary	32.3	30.9	32.2	32.9	31.7	32.8	30.1	28.5	29.3
Tertiary	52.1	55.6	59.2	55.7	58.0	60.6	38.2	46.3	52.9
Total	100.0	100.0	100.0	100.0	100.0	100.0	100.0	100.0	100.0

Note: Figures relate to usual status of individuals. Workforce covers those involved in gainful activity regularly plus those involved in gainful activity occasionally.

Source: National Sample Survey Organisation; Sarvekshana Vol. V, July 77-June 78, 32nd Round; Sarvekshana Vol. XI, Jan. Dec. 1983, 38th Round; Sarvekshana special No., July 87-June 88, 43rd Round; Sarvekshana Vol. XX, July 93-June 94, 50th Round; Report No. 458, July 99-June 2000, 55th Round.

TABLE 8 Rural employment by economic sector

Sector	All			Male			Female		
	1983	1993-94	1999-2000	1983	1993-94	1999-2000	1983	1993-94	1999-2000
Primary	81.7	79.0	76.2	78.1	74.8	71.4	87.8	86.6	85.3
Secondary	8.5	9.6	11.3	9.4	10.5	12.6	7.1	7.9	9.0
Tertiary	9.8	11.4	12.5	12.5	14.7	16.0	5.1	5.5	5.7
Total	100.0	100.0	100.0	100.0	100.0	100.0	100.0	100.0	100.0

Note: Figures relate to usual status of individuals. Workforce covers those involved in gainful activity regularly plus those involved in gainful activity occasionally.

Source: National Sample Survey Organisation; Sarvekshana Vol. V, July 77-June 78, 32nd Round; Sarvekshana Vol. XI, Jan. Dec. 1983, 38th Round; Sarvekshana special No., July 87-June 88, 43rd Round; Sarvekshana Vol. XX, July 93-June 94, 50th Round; Report No. 458, July 99-June 2000, 55th Round.

TABLE 9 Gross domestic production (GDP) and sectoral shares

	Gross domestic product (Rs. in Cores)		Sectoral share in GDP (percent)		
	At factor cost	At market prices	Primary	Secondary	Tertiary
At current prices					
1980-81	130,176	143,362	38.1	25.9	41.1
1990-91	510,954	568,674	34.0	24.9	41.1
2000-01	107,724	2,104,298	37.3	24.2	48.5
At 1993-94 prices					
1980-81	401,128	439,201	38.1	25.9	36.0
1990-91	692,871	771,295	34.9	24.5	40.6
2000-01	1,196,685	1,316,340	26.1	24.9	49.0

Source: Tata Services Ltd. Department of Economics and Statistics.

between 1983-84 and 1999-2000. Conversely, a number of activities in the tertiary sector (construction, trade transport, storage and communication) saw annual rates of employment growth rise (**Tables 9** and **10**). The decline in the annual rate of growth of total employment from 1983-84 to 1999-2000 may therefore may be attributed to the negative rates of growth of employment in agriculture and allied activities of the primary sector, which have the highest labor-absorbing capacities. Although the rate of employment in tertiary activities increased, it was not significant enough to offset the impact of the declining rate of growth of employment in agriculture and allied activities. As a result, total employment declined.

A rural-urban breakdown of employment by activities shows that the share of agriculture and allied services declined in both rural as well as urban employment, but the decline was more in urban areas (**Table 11A**). In general, agriculture dominated the share of total rural employment, while services and manufacturing accounted for a relatively higher share of total urban employment during 1983-2000. A matter of concern here is the decline in the share of agricultural and allied activities during 1983-2000; these are the main employment-generating activities in India.

An important point to be noted in the context of the agriculture sector is that this sector has the highest number of illiterate workers. Only 8.8% of workers in this sector had a secondary or higher education (**Table 11B**).

TABLE 10   Employment by activities (UPSS)

Name of the industry	Employed workers (in millions)			Annual growth rate (in percent)	
	1983	1993-94	1999-2000	1983-94	1994-2000
Agriculture	207.23	242.46	237.56	1.51	-0.34
Mining and quarrying	1.76	2.70	2.27	4.16	-2.85
Manufacturing	34.03	42.50	48.01	2.14	2.05
Electricity, gas, and water	0.85	1.35	1.28	4.50	-0.88
Construction	6.78	11.68	17.62	5.32	7.09
Trade	19.22	27.78	37.32	3.57	5.04
Transport storage and communication	7.39	10.33	14.69	3.24	6.04
Financial services	1.70	3.52	5.05	7.18	6.20
Community social and personal services	23.80	32.13	33.20	2.90	0.55
Total employment	302.76	374.45	397.00	2.04	0.98

Source: Report of the Planning Commission, Govt. of India, Labour and Employment, 2002.

TABLE 11A   Employment distribution by rural/urban location and industry

Industry division	Rural			Urban		
	1983	1993-94	1999-2000	1983	1993-94	1999-2000
Agriculture, forestry, fishing & hunting	81.2	78.4	76.3	14.6	12.3	8.6
Mining and quarrying	0.5	0.6	0.5	1.0	1.2	0.8
Manufacturing	6.7	7.0	7.3	26.7	23.6	22.7
Electricity, gas & water	0.1	0.2	0.2	0.9	1.0	0.7
Construction	1.7	2.4	3.3	4.7	6.3	8.0
Wholesale and retail trade & restaurant and hotels	3.5	4.3	5.1	18.4	19.4	26.9
Transport storage & communication	1.1	1.4	2.1	8.1	8.0	8.7
Services	4.9	5.7	5.2	25.0	28.2	23.6
Activities not classified	0.3	-	-	-	0.5	-
Total	100.0	100.0	100.0	100.0	100.0	100.0
Total employment (in millions)	243.1	290.3	300.8	59.6	81.8	96.0

Note: Figures relate to usual status of individuals. Workforce covers those involved in gainful activity regularly plus those involved in gainful activity occasionally.

Source: National Sample Survey Organisation; Sarvekshana Vol. V, July 77-June 78, 32nd Round; Sarvekshana Vol. XI, Jan. Dec. 1983, 38th Round; Sarvekshana special No., July 87-June 88, 43rd Round; Sarvekshana Vol. XX, July 93-June 94, 50th Round; Report No. 458, July 99-June 2000, 55th Round.

TABLE 11B   Distribution of workers (principal status) by education, 1999-2000

Sector description	Illiterate	Primary	Middle	Secondary and above
Total agriculture	56.8%	23.1%	11.2%	8.8%
Repair services	-	-	2.5	97.5
Whole sale trade (NEC)	7.9	12.1	12.2	67.8
Air transport	0.2	3.8	2.7	93.3
Services incidental to transport	16.5	19.5	19.7	44.4
Communication service	0.7	6.2	18.1	75.0
Banking services	0.4	3.5	12.2	83.8
Provident and insurance	-	1.7	3.5	94.8
Legal services	0.4	1.9	3.5	94.1
Business services NEC	2.7	5.2	11.3	80.9
Finance, insurance & real estate	2.3	5.6	11.5	80.6
Education, scientific, etc.	3.2	4.3	6.2	86.2
Medical and health, etc.	5.4	8.3	10.3	76.0

Source: NSSO, Household level data, CD-ROM, 1999-2000.

Absorption of the labor force

The labor absorption capacity of the Indian economy is assessed here in terms of employment elasticities in different activities during 1993-2000. The elasticities of employment have shown a declining trend in agriculture, mining and quarrying, and even manufacturing (**Table 12**). This raises a question for the reform agenda because it was expected that liberalization would alter the structure of production in favor of labor-intensive industries and help increase employment intensities.

Gross domestic product per worker

GDP per worker is used here as a crude proxy for productivity per worker. **Table 13** lists productivity per worker and its rates of growth, before and after reforms. It is interesting to note that the sectors which have shown a decline in employment have shown higher productivity; agriculture and mining and quarrying are typical examples. Labor productivity in construction, which attracted the maximum labor force from 1993-94 to 1999-2000, became negative (-1.0) in that period.

Employment in organized and unorganized sectors

Out of total employment of 388.34 million during 1999, the share of the

TABLE 12   Elasticity of employment by sector*

Sector	1983 to 1987-88	1987-88 to 1993-94	1993-94 to 1999-2000
Agriculture	1.91	0.36	0.07
Mining and quarrying	0.85	0.34	-1.28
Manufacturing	0.38	0.26	0.20
Electricity, gas, & water	0.97	0.39	-0.14
Construction	3.95	-0.86	1.18
Trade & transport	0.78	0.54	0.79
Service	0.42	0.57	0.18
Total	0.41	0.35	0.20

* Elasticity of employment is derived by dividing percentage change in employment by percentage change in GDP at 1980-81 prices for each inter-round period.

Source: Sudha Desh Pande, Reforms and Labour Market in India – Paper in Reforms and Employment, IAMR, New Delhi, 2002.

organized sector was only 7.24%. The remaining 93% fell into the unorganized sector (**Table 14A**).

Tables **14B**, **14C**, and **14D** show the rate of growth of employment and net domestic product (NDP) in organized and unorganized sectors. Though the organized sector had slower rates of employment growth than the unorganized sector, it accounted for a higher rate of NDP growth from 1993-94 to 1999-2000.

The changes in rates of growth of employment in different activities of the organized and unorganized sectors are shown in **Table 15**. The annual rate of employment growth in the unorganized sector (1.12%) was low, but still higher than annual growth in the organized sector (0.56%) during 1994-2000. A comparison of the annual rates of growth of the two sectors by activities indicates that: (1) the annual rate of employment growth in agriculture was very low (0.03%) in the unorganized sector, and (2) it has become negative in the organized sector. This means that the job-providing capacity of the economy has declined, as agriculture is the main job-providing sector in India. A negative annual rate of growth of employment in mining and quarrying in both the organized and unorganized sectors was indicative of a saturation of job possibilities in these activities. Activities of the tertiary sector, namely transport, storage, and communications and financing, insurance, and real

TABLE 13   GDP per worker at 1980-81 prices by sector of origin (in rupees)

Sector	1977-78	1983	1987-88	1993-94	1999-2000
Agriculture	2,710	2,888	2,853	3,373	3,968
Mining and quarrying	13,643	14,050	14,503	18,302	23,968
Manufacturing	7,971	9,082	10,608	13,433	19,346
Electricity, gas & water	30,920	35,795	36,141	47,428	78,549
Construction	13,742	10,647	7,117	9,794	9,251
Trade & transport	11,974	13,906	14,647	16,960	18,519
Services	8,195	8,733	10,209	11,923	17,379
GDP per worker	4,713	5,277	5,849	7,204	9,756
GDP per capita	1,791	1,979	2,154	2,693	3,559

Compound rates of growth per annum (in percentage)

Sector	1977-78 to 1983	1983 to 1987-88	1983 to 1993-94	1993-94 to 1999-2000
Agriculture	1.1	-0.3	2.8	2.7
Mining and quarrying	0.5	0.7	3.9	4.5
Manufacturing	2.2	3.5	3.9	6.1
Electricity, gas & water	2.4	0.2	4.5	8.4
Construction	-4.3	-9.0	5.3	-1.0
Trade & transport	2.5	1.2	2.4	1.5
Services	1.1	3.5	2.5	6.3
GDP per worker	1.9	2.3	3.5	5.1
GDP per capita	1.7	1.9	3.7	4.6

Source: Sudha Desh Pande, Reforms and Labour Market in India – Paper in Reforms and Employment, IAMR, New Delhi, 2002.

TABLE 14A   Employment in organized and unorganized sector (in millions)

Year	Organized sector	Unorganized sector	Total	Percentage of organized sector to total
1983	24.01	217.48	302.70	7.93
1994	27.38	278.69	372.10	7.36
1999	28.11	360.23	388.34	7.24

Source: IAMR Paper Proceedings of the Workshop on Contemporary Issues in Public Policy and Governance, Oct. 2001.

TABLE 14B　Growth rates of employment and NDP in organized and unorganized sectors (1993-94 to 1999-2000)

	Per annum growth of employment current daily status (CDS) (%)	Per annum growth of net domestic product (NDP) at factor cost (%)
1　Organized	0.56	8.50
2　Unorganized	1.12	5.27
3　Total	1.07	6.52

Source: Planning Commission Report on Labour and Employment, Government of India, 2002.

estate, showed higher rates of employment growth in the unorganized sector than in the organized sector. The same was true of construction and trade, hotels, and restaurants; in construction, as noted above, employment fell in the organized sector. The community and social and personal services sector shows complete saturation of employment generation in the unorganized sector. In general, the traditional major activities of employment generation in the organized sector have shown either declining or negative annual rates of employment growth in 1994-2000.

Though 93% of the total workforce in India belongs to the unorganized sector, they produce on average only one-eighth the income generated per worker in the organized sector. **Table 16** shows that the 93.0% of workers employed in the unorganized sector produced 60.4% of NDP while the remaining 7.0% of workers in the organized sector generated 39.6% of NDP during 1997-98. The table also provides a breakdown of employment and income, generated in agricultural and non-agricultural activities, within the organized and unorganized sector.

Unorganized agriculture and allied activities accounted for 60.0% of total employment but shared only 28.8% of the total income generated in India during 1997-98. Unorganized non-agricultural activities accounted for about 33.0% of the total employment and 31.6% of NDP. The role of organized agriculture and allied activities in terms of providing employment and income generation was negligible, but organized non-agricultural activities, though providing employment to a small number of persons, contributed more than 38.5% to NDP during

TABLE 14C Growth rate of net domestic product by sector, 1993-94 and 1999-2000

S. No.	Industry	1994-2000 At current prices			1994-2000 At 1993-94 prices		
		Organized	Unorganized	Total	Organized	Unorganized	Total
1	Agriculture, forestry and fishing	9.67	11.35	11.30	1.52	3.08	3.03
2	Mining & quarrying	13.06	12.90	13.04	5.54	5.39	5.53
3	Manufacturing	11.65	13.79	12.46	5.40	7.30	6.12
4	Electricity, gas & water supply	17.36	12.87	17.07	9.09	4.92	8.81
5	Construction	15.07	19.45	17.41	4.11	8.08	6.23
6	Trade, hotels & restaurants	27.70	14.06	16.05	20.19	7.36	9.22
7	Transport, storage & communication	13.73	20.85	17.35	6.59	13.27	9.80
8	Financing, insurance, real estate & business services	20.14	11.87	16.28	12.09	4.37	8.52
9	Community, social & personal services	18.88	15.50	18.27	9.27	6.17	8.72

Note: Growth rates are calculated from the data in the Table 14D.

Source: Authors' calculations from Planning Commission Report on Labour and Employment, 2002.

TABLE 14D Net domestic product by sectors (Rs. in Crores)

Industry	1993-94 At current prices			1993-94 At 1993-94 prices			1999-2000 At current prices			1999-2000 At 1993-94 prices		
	Organized	Un-organized	Total	Organized	Un-organized	Total	Organized	Un-organized	Total	Organized	Un-organized	Total
1 Agriculture, forestry & fishing	8,046	221,783	229,829	8,046	221,783	229,829	13,999	422,844	436,843	8,808	266,050	274,858
2 Mining & quarrying	13,861	1,089	14,950	13,861	1,089	14,950	28,944	2,255	31,199	19,156	1,492	20,648
3 Manufacturing	65,774	37,965	103,739	65,774	37,965	103,739	127,387	82,419	209,806	90,168	57,953	148,121
4 Electricity, gas & water supply	8,169	632	8,801	8,169	632	8,801	21,350	1,307	22,657	13,766	843	14,609
5 Construction	18,929	19,820	38,749	18,929	19,820	38,749	43,941	57,580	101,521	24,107	31,589	55,696
6 Trade, hotels & restaurants	10,865	85,762	96,627	10,865	85,762	96,627	47,110	188,888	235,998	32,751	131,313	164,064
7 Transport, storage & communication	21,000	16,721	37,721	21,000	16,721	37,721	45,437	52,088	98,525	30,801	35,309	66,110
8 Financing, insurance, real estate & business services	39,706	40,835	80,541	39,706	40,835	80,541	119,377	80,032	199,049	78,739	52,788	131,527
9 Community, social & personal services	70,499	16,536	87,035	70,499	16,536	87,035	198,997	39,257	238,254	120,033	23,679	143,712

Source: Planning Commission Report on Labour and Employment, Government of India, 2002.

TABLE 15 Structural growth of employment in organized and unorganized sector, 1994-2000 (annual percent)

Activities	Organized sector growth	Unorganized sector growth
Agriculture	- 1.00	0.03
Mining & quarrying	- 1.30	- 2.40
Manufacturing	0.87	2.95
Electricity, gas & water supply	0.51	- 17.00
Construction	- 0.69	5.85
Trade, hotels & restaurants	1.43	5.79
Transport, storage & communication	0.21	7.59
Financial services, real estate & business services	1.27	8.30
Community & social personal services	0.80	- 3.56
All sectors	0.56	1.12

Source: Report of Planning Commission, Govt. of India on Labour and Employment, 2002.

1997-98. In general, agriculture and allied activities dominated in terms of providing jobs in India in the 1990s, but did not contribute much in terms of income generation.

Employment within the unorganized sector

Agriculture, which accounts for the largest share of work in the unorganized sector, ceased to provide new jobs in the 1990s due to: (1) a deceleration in the rate of growth of output of the crop sector, (2) a decline in the growth rate of infrastructure investment in agriculture over a prolonged period, (3) the increasing capitalization of agriculture, (4) technological stagnation, and (5) diversification of the rural economy. Manufacturing seems to be a lost cause in terms of both employment and income generation. A study conducted by Shiela Bhalla (2002) revealed that the share of manufacturing in the unorganized sector declined both in rural and urban areas (**Table 17**). The category lost four million jobs in the 10 years from 1984 to 1995. The rate of growth of employment in unorganized trade dwindled in rural areas but improved in urban areas, while the gross value addition improved in both rural and urban areas. The services, transport, and hotels and restaurants categories, however, recorded substantial gains not only in employment and number of enter-

TABLE 16   Share of unorganized and organized sectors in employment and net domestic product (all India)

Segment and sector	Shares in employment		Shares in net domestic product
	1993-94	1999-2000	1997-98
Unorganized agriculture	63.56	59.95	28.84
Unorganized non-agriculture	29.17	33.00	31.62
All unorganized	92.73	92.95	60.45
Organized agriculture	0.39	0.35	1.08
Organized non-agriculture	6.88	6.70	38.47
All organized	7.27	7.05	39.55
Organized and unorganized segments combined	100.00	100.00	100.00
All sectors	374,271,353 persons	398,441,131 persons	Rs.1,233,920 crores

Notes:
1. The organized sector employment estimates are derived from the Quarterly Employment Review, published by the Directorate General of Employment and Training (DGE & T). The figures given all as the mid-points of the NSS Rounds. These figures are known to be underestimates because: (i) establishments employing 10 to 24 persons in the private sector in the metropolitan areas of greater Mumbai and Calcutta are not covered at all; (ii) the data for these smaller establishments in other places are collected "on a voluntary basis"; (iii) part-time employees are excluded; and (iv) new establishments may be left out of the list of establishments maintained at the Employment Exchanges (EE).
2. The unorganized sector employment estimates are derived as a residual by subtracting organized sector estimates from usual principal and subsidiary status (UPSS) employment estimates interpolated for the mid-points of the NSS Rounds.
3. The "all sectors" employment figures are derived as the sum of the separate sectoral estimates. These figures differ from the "all workers" figures by the number of workers counted in the NSS UPSS estimates for all workers, but not classified by sector and sub-sector.
4. Net Domestic Product (NDP) figures are derived from the Table on page 9 of "Measurement of Informal Sector – the Indian Experience – Country Paper India," Fourth meeting of the Group on Informal Sector Statistics, Doc. 14, ILO, Geneva 28-30 August 2000.

Source: Shiela Bhalla (2002).

prises but also in gross value addition. Much of the above restructuring in unorganized employment was due to: (1) improvement in transport facilities, leading to exploitation of rural resources and the integration of villages with the rest of the economy, (2) improvement in technology, and (3) efforts of increasing scale of operation for reducing costs. The entire process of economic restructuring no doubt increased the productivity of manufacturing enterprises but reduced their labor absorption capacities.

TABLE 17 Sectoral and sub-sectoral restructuring of the unorganized segment, 1984-85 to 1994-95, by location (percent of sub-sector in all sectors)

Location and year	Manufact-uring	Trade	Hotels & restaurants	Transport	Services	All sectors
Enterprises						
Rural						
1984-85	60.79	23.36	2.51	1.46	11.88	100.00
1990-91	46.13	28.94	2.81	3.13	18.99	100.00
1994-95	37.89	27.35	3.22	5.94	25.60	100.00
Urban						
1984-85	40.37	33.58	4.66	3.74	17.65	100.00
1990-91	28.63	39.19	5.76	5.32	21.10	100.00
1994-95	24.00	42.09	5.77	6.18	21.96	100.00
Employment						
Rural						
1984-85	63.94	20.77	3.30	1.16	10.83	100.00
1990-91	53.19	23.49	3.53	2.39	17.41	100.00
1994-95	45.76	21.99	3.76	4.54	23.95	100.00
Urban						
1984-85	40.69	32.34	7.18	2.90	16.89	100.00
1990-91	35.73	32.82	8.58	3.93	18.94	100.00
1994-95	32.02	33.60	8.80	4.94	20.62	100.00
Cross value added						
Rural						
1984-85	59.79	32.64	1.63	3.40	2.54	100.00
1990-91	49.37	33.05	3.89	5.15	8.53	100.00
1994-95	34.17	34.28	6.06	7.47	18.01	100.00
Urban						
1984-85	34.60	55.77	1.66	4.79	3.18	100.00
1990-91	31.64	45.18	5.73	6.85	10.60	100.00
1994-95	24.90	40.22	8.95	7.66	18.27	100.00

Source: Shiela Bhalla (2002).

Employment within the organized sector

Employment in the organized sector increased from 24.01 million in 1983 to 28.11 million in 1999-2000, but the annual growth rate of employment declined from 1.20% to 0.53% during 1983-2000, due mostly to a sharp decline in the annual rate of growth of public sector employment from 1993-94 to 1999-2000 (**Table 18**). In fact, annual growth of public sector employment become negative (-0.03) during 1999-2000 as a result of the downsizing policies of the government and public sector industrial units. The rate of employment growth increased, though,

TABLE 18   Employment in organized sector

Sector	Employment in million			Rate of growth (annual percent)	
	1983	1994	1999-2000	1983-94	1994-2000
Total employment	302.75	374.45	397.00	2.04	-0.98
Organized sector	24.01	27.37	28.11	1.20	0.53
Public sector	16.46	19.46	19.46	1.523	-0.03
Private sector	7.55	7.39	8.70	0.45	1.87

Source: Report of Planning Commission, Govt. of India on Labour and Employment, 2002.

in the private sector during 1983-2000, but it was not significant enough to offset the slow growth of public sector employment; note that the private share in the organized sector is only about one-third.

Public sector share in GDP

Though employment in the public sector declined in 1999-2000, the public sector share of GDP, at one-fourth, was the same as a decade before (**Table 19**). But in terms of the country's fixed capital stock, the public share fell between 1993-94 and 1999-2000; in terms of gross domestic saving, the public share became negative (-4.3%) during 1999-2000. The contrasting trends in the public sector's shares in GDP and capital stock reflect perhaps the transitional phase that the economy is passing through. The declining share of the public sector in the fixed capital stock indicates the withdrawal of the public sector from some activities.

Quality of employment

Quality of employment is generally assessed in terms of the availability of social security coverage, favorable working conditions, and high wages, benefits usually available to regular salaried workers but not to casual workers and the self-employed. Hence, a crude measure of quality of employment can be made by analyzing the composition of employment in terms of casual work, regular work, and self-employment. The larger the portion of regular workers, the better the quality of employment. As **Table 20** shows, more than half of employment in India during 1983-2000 comprised self-employed persons. The share declined

TABLE 19 Percentage of public sector in gross domestic product (GDP), gross domestic saving (GDS), and gross domestic capital formation (GDCF)

	Share of public sector	
	1993-94	1999-2000
GDP at current prices	25.2	25.5
GDS	2.8	-4.3
GDCF	38.8	29.3

Source: National Accounts Statistics, Central Statistical Organization.

in the rural areas and slightly increased in urban areas over this period. Casual workers accounted for about one-third of total employment, and their share increased in rural areas and declined in urban areas. Regular workers constitute only about 14% of total employment, and their shares were almost exactly the same in 1999-2000 as in 1983. The analysis thus gives a picture of the low quality of employment in India.

A report by the Planning Commission supports this conclusion. It found that, while the unemployment rate was only 7% in 1999-2000, the share in poverty was 26%, suggesting that large numbers of those currently employed earn income levels insufficient to take them above the poverty line. A study by Ghose (1999) on the quality of employment in India during the pre- and post-reform periods reveals that: (1) quality of employment is highest in services and lowest in agriculture, (2) employment quality deteriorated in the aggregate economy and in all three main sectors, and (3) the deterioration in the aggregate economy has been greater for males than females (**Table 21**).

Since few micro-level studies are available on this question, one has to depend on the results of the limited number of studies for reaching conclusions. A study of a small-scale industry (Lock Manufacturing Industry at Aligarh) by Mridula (2002) shows that casualization increased between 1994-95 and 1999-2000. Working conditions were not favorable, and social security coverage was lacking for a majority of the workers. The paucity of studies notwithstanding, the simple distribution of workers by organized or unorganized sector (93% work in the latter) supports the conclusion that quality of employment in India is poor.

TABLE 20 Employment growth by employment category (in percentage)

	Employment category								
	Self-employment workers			Regular salaried workers			Casual workers		
Year	Rural	Urban	Total	Rural	Urban	Total	Rural	Urban	Total
1983	61.0	41.8	57.4	7.5	40.0	13.9	31.5	18.2	28.7
1987-1988	59.4	42.8	56.0	7.7	40.3	14.9	32.9	16.9	29.6
1993-1994	58.0	42.3	54.8	6.4	39.4	13.2	35.6	18.3	32.0
1999-2000	56.0	42.1	52.9	6.7	40.1	13.9	37.3	17.8	33.2

Source: NSSA, household-level data, 32nd, 42nd, and 50th rounds.

TABLE 21   Employment quality index, 1997-98 to 1993-94

	1977-78	1983	1987-88	1993-94
Males	0.737	0.731	0.725	0.717
Females	0.687	0.680	0.686	0.675
Aggregate economy	0.723	0.717	0.715	0.706
Agriculture	0.694	0.688	0.687	0.675
Industry	-	0.749	-	0.715
Service	-	7.91	-	0.782

Note: Employment Quality Index is constructed by applying weights to the types of employment (regular, self-employed, casual labour).

Source: Based on Ajit K. Ghose (1999), "The Question on Employment Security in India: A Note", Paper presented at the Conference on Social Security in India, New Delhi, April 15-17.

Education and skill formation of India's workforce

The liberalization of economic policies together with globalization and improvement in technology not only changed the occupational profile of the workforce but also changed the demand for education and skills in the labor market. The strategies of education and skill formation of India's workforce therefore have to take into consideration the changing needs of the labor market in order to reduce increasing unemployment.

Due to a lack of data, it is not possible to comprehensively assess the current status of skill formation of the labor force in India. We have therefore tried to assess the educational development and educational composition of the workforce.

The education system
The system of education in India works at three levels — the school level, the college level, and the university level. Within this system are polytechnic and technology institutes offering technical education at the certificate, diploma, and up to the doctorate level. General education consists of social science, arts, commerce, and science. Professional education includes all types of engineering, medical, agriculture, and management courses. **Table 22** lists the types of number of institutions for the years 1981, 1991, and 2000.

TABLE 22   Number of educational institutions

Type	1981	1991	2000*
Pre-primary schools	10,281	15,877	37,288
Primary/junior basic schools	494,503	560,935	638,738
Middle/senior basic schools	118,555	151,456	206,269
High/higher secondary schools/			
pre-degree junior colleges	51,006	79,796	126,047
Universities/deemed universities/			
institutions of national importance	132	184	254
Degree standards and above			
professional and technical institutions for:	3,421	4,862	7,929
(a) Agriculture & forestry	61	80	NA
(b) Engineering/technology/ architecture	171	351	880
(c) Medicine**	249	346***	NA
(d) Veterinary science	22	27	NA
(e) Teacher's training	341	474	834
Below degree level professional/ vocational			
and technical institutions	4,808	5,739	6,855

*   As on September 30 of relevant year.
**   Medicine includes Allopathy, Homeopathy, Ayurveda and Unani.
*** DGHS—Health Information of India—1993.

Sources: 1. Ministry of Human Resource Development: (i) Education in India, (ii) A Hand Book of Educational and Allied Statistics, (iii) Selected Educational Statistics, (iv) All India Council for Technical Education, 2. University Grant Commission.

Enrollments expanded tremendously at all levels during last two decades (**Table 23**). The increase in the number of institutions of general education as well as enrollments there out-stripped the increases among institutions of professional education.

The system of higher education consists of 18 central universities, 178 state universities, 52 deemed-to-be universities, 12 institutions of national importance, and 13,150 colleges (**Table 24**). Total enrollment in universities and colleges increased more than threefold between 1981 and 2000 (**Table 25**). The rate of increase for women was much higher than that of men, though more men were enrolled than women throughout the period.

Roughly 80% of enrollment in higher education is at the undergraduate level. Few move up to the Ph.D. level, but the share of women at this level is higher than at the undergraduate level (**Table 26**). As for enrollment by subject, the arts predominate (**Table 27**), especially among

TABLE 23   Enrollment by level of education

Stage	1981	1991	2000*
General education			
Pre-primary	1,158	1,635	2,617
Primary	73,774	97,375	113,827
Middle	20,724	34,026	42,810
High/higher secondary	8,807	14,365	18,993
Post-secondary but below degree level**	3,079	3,658	9,851
Degree and above	2,320	3,672	8,626
Professional/technical/vocational education			
School level	524	527	NA
Post-secondary but below degree level***	519	666	987
Degree and above:	623	901	1,337
(a) Engineering/technology/ architecture	130	241	530
(b) Medicine****	121	179	261
(c) Agriculture/ Forestry	40	55	62
(d) Education	75	92	122
(e) Veterinary science	7	13	17
(f) Others	250	321	345

*   As on September 30 of relevant year.
**   Pre-Degree/Junior College.
***   Includes Teacher Training Schools, Polytechnic and Art & Craft Schools.
****   Medicine includes Allopathy, Homeopathy, Ayurveda and Unani.

Sources: 1. Ministry of Human Resource Development: (i) Education in India, (ii) Selected Educational Statistics, 2. University Grant Commission.

TABLE 24   Types of higher education institutions, 2001-02

	Type of institutions	Number of institutions
1	Central universities	18
2	State universities	178
3	Deemed to be universities	52
4	Institutions established under state legislative act	5
5	Institutions of national importance	12
6	Colleges	13,150

Source: University Grants Commission (UGC), New Delhi, Annual Report 2001-02.

women, though gender differences by subject have declined over the years. Enrollments and graduation from professional courses pales in comparison to enrollments in arts, science, and commerce (**Table 28**). The system today turns out about 75,000 engineering degrees and 92,000

TABLE 25   Enrollment in universities and colleges, 1981-2000

	1981	1991	2000
Male	1,631,628	2,403,036	4,960,894
Female	688,788	1,264,781	2,976,363
Total	2,320,406	3,667,807	7,937,257

Source: University Grants Commission (UGC), New Delhi, various annual reports.

engineering diplomas per year. In 1991 (the latest year for which data are available), the system turned out only 14,300 doctors. Outturn in paramedical courses (**Table 29**) has remained low throughout the last two decades. In 1998, the country produced only 13,331 nurses, 3,725 midwives, 4,988 health workers, and 412 health visitors. The outturn of midwives, health workers, and health visitors rose during 1980-90 but declined significantly during 1990-98.

Educational composition of the workforce
Data about the educational attainment of workers in India age 15 and above indicates that about 44% of the workforce is illiterate (**Table 30**). The level of illiteracy among the workers in the unorganized sector is even higher than among workers overall. Though macro-level data on this question is not available, a micro-level study (Mridula 2003) revealed that illiteracy among workers in an industry in the unorganized sector was as high as 72%. Data on the literacy levels of workers indicates that only 22.7% have an education up to primary level, and another third up to secondary level. More females were illiterate (69.3%) than males (32.9%), and more rural workers (51.3%) than urban (21.5%). Within rural areas, many more women are illiterate (74.0%) than men (39.6%). Furthermore, the share of female workers with a middle-level education was much lower than the share of males.

Marketable skills and vocational training
In the 1993-94 survey, the NSSO on employment and unemployment provided information on the possession of 30 specific marketable skills

TABLE 26   Enrollment by education level in 1981, 1991, and 2000

Level of education	1981			1991			2000		
	Male	Female	Total	Male	Female	Total	Male	Female	Total
Ph.D.	16,805	7,572	24,377	18,696	9,129	27,815	29,149	15,855	45,004
Post-graduate	1,76,803	7,758	2,54,361	2,37,928	1,16,288	3,54,216	3,99,359	2,47,979	6,47,338
Graduate	14,38,020	84,994	20,41,668	21,46,412	2,42,936	32,85,776	45,32,386	5,29,858	72,44,915
Total	16,31,628	100324	23,20,406	24,03,036	368353	36,67,807	49,60,894	793692	79,37,257

Source: University Grants Commission (UGC), New Delhi, various annual reports.

TABLE 27 Higher education enrollment by level, 1981, 1991, and 2000

Level of education	1981			1991			2000		
	Male	Female	Total	Male	Female	Total	Male	Female	Total
Arts	743,849	445,863	1,189,712	743,849	692,289	1,737,179	2,954,974	1,672,569	4,764,743
Science	398,097	154,530	552,627	523,403	305,384	828,787	822,004	581,711	1,528,841
ommerce	489,682	88,385	578,067	816,047	257,979	1,074,026	1,029,641	569,028	1,598,669
nrollment for which break up of science, arts, and commerce is not given	-	-	-	18,696 -1	27,825 -2	9,129	29,149 -1	15,855 -1	45,004
Total	1,631,628	688,788	2,320,406	2,101,995	1,283,477	3,667,807	4,835,768	2,839,163	7,937,257

Source: University Grants Commission (UGC), New Delhi, various annual reports.

TABLE 28 Admission and turnout in select professional courses, 1981, 1991, and 2000

| | Engineering | | | | Medical (allopathy) | | Dental | |
| | Degree | | Diploma | | | | | |
	Admission	Turnout	Admission	Turnout	Admission	Turnout	Admission	Turnout
1981	34,835	19,012	61,114	35,487	11,431	12,170	705	501
1991	70,481	44,724	117,835	65,325	14,700*	14,300*	2,160*	1,500*
2000	197,071	74,223**	159,555	92,323**	NA	NA	NA	NA

* Corrected to account for non-responding institutions.
** Estimated.

Source: (i) Ministry of Human Resource Development, Technical Education in India-Survey.

TABLE 29   Turnout in selected paramedical courses, 1980, 1990, and 1998

	Nurses (diploma certificate holders)	Midwives	Auxiliary nurse-midwives (health workers female)	Health visitors
1980	7,256	6,541	4,264	483
1990	11,032	9,366	12,377	1,185
1998	13,331	3,725	4,988	412

Source: Indian Nursing Council.

TABLE 30   Composition of workers age 15 years and over, by education level, 1999-2000 (in percentage)

	Not literate	Literate & schooling up to primary level	With schooling up to middle & higher level	Total	Share in workforce
Rural areas					
Male	39.6	27.3	33.1	100	49.74
Female	74	15.5	10.5	100	25.77
Person	51.3	23.3	25.4	100	75.51
Urban areas					
Male	16	21.9	62	100	19.72
Female	43.9	17.6	38.5	100	4.76
Person	21.5	21.1	57.4	100	24.49
All areas					
Male	32.9	25.8	41.3	100	69.46
Female	69.3	15.8	14.9	100	30.54
Person	44	22.7	33.2	100	100

Source: National Sample Survey on Employment and Unemployment, 55th Round.

by persons in the labor force (**Table 31A**). The percentage of persons with marketable skills is low: in rural areas only 10.1% of males and 6.3% of females had some marketable skills. The shares were barely higher in urban areas. A profile of persons having some marketable skill by type of skill possessed is presented in **Table 31B**.

The vocational training system is not sufficient to cater to the growing needs of the labor market. India's 4,274 industrial training institutes

TABLE 31A   Distribution of marketable skills, 1993-94

Possessing	Rural		Urban	
	Male	Female	Male	Female
No skill	89.9	93.7	80.4	88.8
Some skill	10.1	6.3	19.6	11.2
Total	100	100	100	100
Sample persons	183,464	172,835	109,067	99,283

Source: NSO Report No. 409 on result of 50th Round, 1993-94, Survey on Employment and Unemployment.

have a seating capacity of 6,028,189 per year, an insufficient number to cover the country's needs (**Table 32**).

Vocational training is provided through apprenticeships as well as technical institutes. But data on the available vacancies of apprenticeships and their utilization during the last two decades indicates that a number of vacancies remained unutilized (**Table 33**), even those for minorities and women. This would seem to indicate a mismatch between the demand and supply of skill in the labor market.

The training system in India

The central and state governments share responsibility for vocational training. At the national level, the Director General of Employment and Training (DGET) in the Ministry of Labor is responsible for formulating policies, laying down standards, and conducting testing and certification. DGET runs a number of institutions directly. State government departments are responsible for vocational training programs as well. The National Commission for Vocational Training (NCVT), a tripartite body comprising representatives of employers, workers, and the government, advises the government on vocational policy.

A report of the Planning Commission (2002) provides details on methods of providing skills and training to the labor force. The primary methods are discussed below:

Training through family members

Workers in most industrial units in the unorganized sector have acquired

TABLE 31B   Number of workers per 1,000 with marketable skills, by skill type, 1993-94

Skill	Code	Rural		Urban	
		Male	Female	Male	Female
Typist/Stenographer	1	3	2	14	10
Fishermen	2	5	-	2	-
Miner, quarryman	3	2	-	1	-
Spinner including Charkha operator	4	1	3	2	3
Weaver	5	6	10	11	8
Tailor cutter	6	6	18	15	54
Shoemaker, cobbler	7	1	-	2	-
Carpenter	8	6	-	8	-
Mason, bricklayer	9	5	-	9	-
Moulder	10	-	-	1	-
Machine man	11	2	-	8	-
Fitter die maker	12	1	-	6	-
Welder	13	1	-	4	-
Blacksmith	14	2	-	2	-
Goldsmith	15	1	-	4	-
Silversmith	16	-	-	1	-
Electrician	17	2	-	8	-
Repairer of electronic goods	18	1	-	5	-
Motor vehicle driver, tractor driver	19	11	-	27	1
Boatman	20	-	-	-	-
Potter	21	2	1	1	-
Nurse midwife	22	-	-	-	2
Basket maker, wicker product maker	23	3	4	1	1
Toy maker	24	-	-	-	-
Brick maker, tile maker	25	2	1	-	-
Bidi maker	26	3	7	-	7
Bookbinder	27	-	-	2	-
Barber	28	3	-	3	-
Mud house builder & thatcher	29	9	1	1	1
Others	30	24	15	57	21
Any skill possessed (sub-total)	31	102	62	195	108
No skill possessed		898	938	805	892
Total		1,000	1,000	1,000	1,000

Source: NSSO Report No. 409 on Results on 50th round (1993-94) survey on Employment and Unemployment.

skills and craftsmanship from family members. Children of workers organized in traditional family-based crafts (like weaving and pottery) and other small businesses (like tailoring, hair cutting, repair work, lock manufacturing) acquire their skills from parents while helping them in the family profession.

TABLE 32   ITIs seating capacity by state/union territory, 2000

State/union territories	Number of ITIs			Seating capacity		
	Government	Private	Total	Government	Private	Total
Andhra Pradesh	82	470	552	22,395	83,580	105,975
Arunachal Pradesh	2	0	2	374	0	374
Assam	24	3	27	4,536	84	4,620
Bihar	33	19	52	12,820	3,404	16,224
Delhi	14	32	46	8,772	1,428	10,200
Goa	11	4	15	492	420	2,912
Gujarat	130	90	220	54,016	8,202	62,218
Haryana	78	23	101	13,157	1,380	14,537
Himachal Pradesh	41	2	43	3,771	88	3,859
Jammu & Kashmir	37	0	37	4,044	-	4,044
Karnataka	94	355	449	15,374	25,024	40,398
Kerala	46	454	500	12,520	41,401	53,921
Madhya Pradesh	129	20	149	21,426	1,720	23,146
Maharashtra	347	269	616	66,216	30,724	96,940
Manipur	7	0	7	540	0	540
Meghalya	5	2	7	622	304	926
Mizoram	1	0	1	294	0	294
Nagaland	3	0	3	404	0	404
Orissa	23	109	132	5,540	10,148	15,688
Punjab	103	29	132	13,999	1,724	15,723
Rajasthan	79	12	91	8,256	892	9,148
Sikkim	1	0	1	140	0	140
Tamil Nadu	53	603	656	17,200	59,200	76,400
Tripura	7	0	7	400	0	400
Uttar Pradesh	179	93	272	38,148	7,204	45,252
West Bengal	47	12	59	11,436	612	12,048
Union territories						
Andaman Nicorbar	1	0	1	198	0	198
Chandigarh	2	0	2	904	0	904
Dadra & Nagar Haveli	1	0	1	228	0	228
Daman and Diu	2	0	2	388	0	388
Lakshadweep	1	0	1	96	0	96
Pondicherry	1	0	1	96	0	96
India	1,654	2,620	4,274	349,310	278,879	628,189

Note: As on December 12, 2000.

Source: Ministry of Labor, Annual Report, 2000-01.

On-the-job training

On-the-job training is given both in small industrial units as well as in medium and large industrial units. Workers join an organization as unskilled workers but acquire skills while working with skilled and trained persons. Some large industrial units formalized this system.

TABLE 33   Number of vacancies available and utilized for apprentices in various trades

	Vacancy		Vacancy utilized by			
	Available	Utilized	SC	ST	Minorities	Women
1985	189,013	134,074	13,101	3,781	15,296	3,457
1993	208,465	138,300	15,590	5,475	13,118	3,654
2000*	227,501	165,474	21,910	7,024	10,964	4,997

Note: Data relate to September 30. SC = Schedule Caste, ST = Scheduled Tribe.
* As on of June 30 in a given year.

Source: Ministry of Labour, Various Annual Report.

Formal apprenticeships

Formal apprenticeships were introduced in the Apprenticeship Act of 1961, which requires employers in specific industries to engage apprentices in specified ratios in relation to the workforce. Apprentices obtain training for periods ranging from six months to four years, and at the end of the period they are trade-tested by the National Council for Vocational Training. Successful candidates receive national apprenticeship certificates. Of the 227,000 seats for apprenticeship training, only 165,000 were utilized during the year 2000.

Special training for the informal sector

"Tool rooms" have been set up to provide technical training and other support to the industrial units working in the informal sector. For example, the Central Institute of Hand Tools at Jallandhore was established by the government to provide training and other support to units engaged in the manufacturing of hand tools at Punjab. Similarly, a tool room at Nagaur is expected to provide training and support to the industries producing hand tools there. The Department of Women and Child Development has also institutionalized vocational training for the informal sector.

Training through the formal education system

The formal education system in India meets some of the demand of the employment market. The system produces engineers, doctors, lawyers, managers, administrators, teachers, etc. The graduates and postgraduates of the formal system are either directly absorbed into the job market or are absorbed after some training.

Vocational training in specialized institutions
The 4,274 industrial training institutes impart training in 43 engineering and 24 non-engineering trades. Of these, 1,654 are run by the state governments while 2,620 are private. The total seating capacity in these institutes is 628,000. In addition, six advanced training Institutes (ATIs) are run by the central government; two of them offer long and short courses for training of skilled personnel at technical levels in the fields of industrial, medical, and consumer electronics and process instrumentations. Apart from the industrial training institutes, there are private proprietary institutes, organized as businesses, that provide training in areas such as computer applications, hardware maintenance, refrigeration, air-conditioning, electronics, catering, etc. Training provided by these institutions varies in quality.

The globalization of trade and structural adjustments in the organized and unorganized sectors continue to focus attention on technological upgrading, skill development, and training. The introduction of new technology can make certain skills obsolete, and downsizing can lead to redundancy of skilled personnel, regardless of sector. These types of changes call for the provision of multi-skill training programs. At present the situation is not favorable: the numbers of facilities for education and training are insufficient to meet the growing demand for an educated and skilled labor force.

The data in **Table 34** are drawn from different years and therefore are subject to error. In any case, the total capacity is only about 1.7 million, against the 12.3 million expected to enter the labor force per year.

According to the estimates of the Planning Commission, every year 5.5 million students pass out of Class X. Of these, 3.3 million go to Class XI, leaving behind 2.2 million. Another category is dropouts after Class VIII — about 19.0 million do not pursue further studies. These are the people who look for vocational training and self-employment. Therefore, around 21.0 million students every year need some training to the employed, yet the available formal training capacity of the country is only 2.3 million, a gap of about 19.0 million.

TABLE 34   Facilities for education and training in applied courses

		Thousands (year)
1	**Industrial training**	
	Apprentices from industrial establishments	227.0 (2001)
	Seats in ITIs	628.0 (2001)
2	**Para-medical courses**	
	Nurses out-turn	11.4 (1996)
	Mid-wives	6.3 (1996)
	Health workers (female)	6.5 (1996)
	Health visitors	0.5 (1996)
3	**Engineering**	
	Admission at degree level	138.4 (1997)
	Admission at diploma level	186.2 (1997)
4	**Medical**	
	Admission to degree level in allopathy & dental	17.0 (1992)
5	**Agriculture and forestry courses**	
	Enrollment	45.0 (1987)
6	**General education courses**	
	Enrollment	188.6 (1999)
7	**Veterinary science colleges**	
	Enrollment	22.2 (1999)
8	**Journalism, library science, social work, physical education, and others**	
	Enrollment at graduate level	272.9 (1987)
	Total	1,750

Source : 1. IAMR Manpower profile India (2000) unless otherwise stated. 2. Ministry of Labour (Director General of Employment and Training).

Unemployment

The unemployment rate is higher in urban areas than in rural areas (**Table 35**). This may be partly due to the dominance of the organized sector (which has more formalized reporting of unemployment) and partly due to the absence of low-productivity subsidiary employment in urban areas. The rate of unemployment declined both in rural and urban areas between 1983 and 1999-2000. This could be due to a shift in the composition of employment away from self-employment toward casual work, under which disguised unemployment is non-existent. The difference in the unemploy-

TABLE 35   Unemployment by gender (percent of labour force)

Survey period	Rural areas			Urban areas		
	Male	Female	Persons	Male	Female	Persons
1983	7.5	9.0	7.9	9.2	11.0	9.5
1993-94	5.3	5.6	5.6	6.7	10.5	7.4
1999-2000	7.2	7.3	7.2	7.2	9.8	7.7

Source: NSSO Surveys (unemployment rate on current daily status basis).

ment rates of urban and rural areas had narrowed by 1999-2000. The reason for this was a sharp increase in the unemployment rates of both males and females in rural areas from 1993-94 to 1999-2000. The rates of unemployment were found to be higher among females than in males in both rural and urban areas. However, the differences were narrowed down in urban areas and were almost eliminated in the rural areas (Table 35).

The highest rate of unemployment (19%) was for urban youth age 15-19 during 1999-2000, a reflection of large entries of that group into the labor market and another sign of the mismatch between availability of jobs and expectations of the workforce (**Table 36**).

Unemployment by household expenditure class

Table 37A examines unemployment rates by the usual principal and subsidiary status method, while **Table 37B** looks at unemployment rates by the current daily status method. Each shows different unemployment rates for lower expenditure groups. According to Table 37A, unemployment rates among low expenditure groups are lower than those for higher expenditure groups, most likely because the lower expenditure groups cannot wait for the appropriate job and accept whatever is available to them. The high unemployment rate by current daily status method indicates the intensity of employment, i.e., low-income groups become the victims of the uncertainties of demand for casual labor.

Unemployment by education level

Unemployment rates are higher the higher the level of education. Unemployment among illiterates was only 0.2%, compared to 8.8% among

TABLE 36   Unemployment* across age groups, 1999-2000

Age in years	Unemployment rate		
	Rural	Urban	Combined
15-19	13.3	19	14.4
	(8.8)	(16.6)	(10.3)
20-24	11.0	18.7	13.5
	(9.8)	(19.2)	(12.0)
25-29	8.7	10.9	9.2
	(7.4)	(10.4)	(8.1)
Sub-group (15-29)	11.0	15.5	12.1
	(8.6)	(15.0)	(10.1)
30-34	6.1	4.9	5.8
35-39	5.0	3.7	4.6
40-44	4.8	2.7	4.2
45-49	4.6	2.4	3.9
50-54	4.5	2.1	3.9
55-59	4.6	2.0	4.0
60 and above	3.5	3.8	3.5
All age groups	7.2	7.7	7.3
	(5.6)	(7.4)	(6.0)

* Unemployment rate on current daily status basis.
Note: Figures in parentheses give the comparative estimates for 1993-94.

Source: NSSO 50th (1993-94) and 55th (1999-2000) Round Surveys.

graduates and 7.8% among persons with higher secondary education. These figures suggest a large mismatch between expectations and the availability of jobs for more-educated persons compared to less-educated persons. The mismatch becomes even more noticeable when we analyze unemployment rates among educated youth (**Table 38**). Though unemployment rates declined for educated youth (both general and technical) during the 1983 to the 1999-2000 period, the incidence of unemployment in the group, even in 1999-2000, is high (14.8% for general education and 23.7% for technical education). Apparently, the aspirations of educated youth are not matching the available jobs.

Migration
The mismatch between the demand and supply of skills and education in the labor market has led to an outflow of educated manpower from

TABLE 37A   Unemployment rates by monthly per capita household income, 1999-2000 (calculated on usual principle and subsidiary status basis)

Monthly per capita (rupees)		Unemployment rate (percent of labor force)	
Rural	Urban	Rural	Urban
0-225	0-300	1.06	2.91
225-255	300-350	1.02	5.21
255-300	350-425	1.27	4.08
300-340	425-500	0.98	5.43
340-380	500-575	1.20	5.81
380-420	575-665	1.43	8.20
420-470	665-775	1.59	5.85
470-525	775-915	1.79	4.95
525-615	915-1,120	1.78	5.08
615-775	1,120-1,500	2.21	4.21
775-950	1,500-1,925	2.44	3.49
950 and above	1,925 and above	2.54	2.99
All	All	1.43	4.63

Source: NSSO Survey 55th Round (1999-2000).

TABLE 37B   Unemployment rates by monthly per capita household income, 1999-2000 (calculated on current daily status basis)

Monthly per capita (Ruppes)		Unemployment rate (percent of labor force)	
Rural	Urban	Rural	Urban
0-225	0-300	11.31	9.61
225-255	300-350	9.62	9.67
255-300	350-425	8.12	8.20
300-340	425-500	7.46	9.20
340-380	500-575	6.56	9.20
380-420	575-665	6.18	8.63
420-470	665-775	6.48	8.19
470-525	775-915	6.14	7.18
525-615	915-1,120	5.60	6.65
615-775	1,120-1,500	6.06	5.68
775-950	1,500-1,925	5.57	4.67
950 and above	1,925 and above	5.25	4.10
All	All	7.21	7.65

Source: NSSO Survey 55th Round (1999-2000).

TABLE 38   Unemployment rates* among educated youth

| | Secondary education and above | | | | | |
| | General | | | Technical | | |
Period	Rural	Urban	Combined	Rural	Urban	Combined
1983	20.4	30	20.7	25	23.9	24.4
	(2.5)	(10.7)	(4.2)			
1987-88	15.9	16.6	16.2	24	20.7	22.1
	(3.8)	(12.1)	(5.4)			
1993-94	17.0	20.8	18.5	29	25.9	27.3
	(2.9)	(10.8)	(4.6)			
1999-2000	12.5	18.3	14.8	22.8	24.4	23.7
	(3.7)	(11.2)	(5.4)			

* On usual status basis.
Note: i) Technical education comprised of of additional diplomas or certificates in agriculture, engineering/technology, medicine, crafts, and other subjects. ii) Youth means age group 15-29. iii) Figures in the parentheses show the unemployment rate among youth as a whole.

Source: Report of the Planning Commission, Government of India, Labour Employment, 2000.

India (**Table 39**). During 1991-92, 7,353 male and female students left the country; the number declined to 3,461 in 1994-95 but rose to 8,030 in 1998-99. The highest numbers of migrants were recorded for commerce, business administration, and business management in 1998-99. The situation was just the reverse during 1991-92, when the largest number of migrants were engineering and architect graduates. The number of migrants in medicine, pharmacy, and veterinary science almost doubled between 1991 and 1998-99, though the migration of scientists is declining.

Table 40 shows the countries these youth are leaving for. The United States is the biggest market for Indian students, absorbing 2,580 in 1998-99, mostly engineers, scientists, administrators, and managers. Europe and Oceania are other big draws.

Wages and social security

Wages
About 90% of workers in India work in the unorganized sector and have no collective bargaining power. The government enacted the Minimum

TABLE 39   Number of Indian students going abroad, by field of study and gender

Field of study	Sex	1991-92	1994-95	1998-99
Engineering and Architect	Male	2,390	792	1,156
	Female	158	68	113
Science	Male	1,384	340	921
	Female	231	63	158
Technology and industry	Male	121	141	540
	Female	17	43	86
Commerce, business administration, business management	Male	946	646	2,342
	Female	122	55	293
Arts	Male	204	111˙	351
	Female	94	33	158
Agriculture and forestry	Male	94	16	6
	Female	17	3	2
Medicine, pharmacy & veterinary science	Male	350	327	645
	Female	94	50	87
Law	Male	26	18	66
	Female	5	6	20
Bank/Banking institutions	Male	14	2	35
	Female	3	-	7
Fine arts	Male	30	42	46
	Female	14	24	18
Others	Male	905	548	810
	Female	130	133	170
Total	Male	6,466	2,983	6,918
	Female	887	478	1,112

Source: Ministry of Human Resource Development, Indian Students and Trainees Going Abroad, 1998-99.

Wages Act of 1948 to save and protect workers from exploitation. Though detailed data about minimum wages as fixed by the government for various professions and types of labor are not available, **Table 41** provides some data for the minimum wages fixed and/or revised by the government in some employment areas. The table shows the wide variation in the minimum wages fixed by the government in 1998. The highest minimums are found in agriculture.

TABLE 40   Number of Indian students going aboard, by field of study and continent, 1998-99

Field of study	America	Europe	Asia	Oceania	Others	Total
Engineering and architect	707	160	94	189	6	1,156
Science	552	147	22	184	16	921
Technology and industry	118	73	14	332	3	540
Commerce, business administration, management	577	467	64	1,208	26	2,342
Arts	193	98	5	49	6	351
Agriculture and forestry	3	1	-	2	-	6
Medicine, pharmacy, dentistry, and veterinary sciences	73	37	481	42	12	645
Law	17	43	-	5	1	66
Banking services	9	10	1	14	1	35
Fine arts	33	2	-	10	1	46
Others	298	121	23	319	49	810
Total	2,580	1,159	704	2,354	121	6,918

Source: Ministry of Human Resource Development, Indian Students and Trainees Going Abroad, 1998-99.

A comparison of prevailing wage rates with minimum fixed wage rates is difficult because different sources provide data on prevailing wages rates in different formats. The NSSO provides some estimates about annual compensation for hired workers in the unorganized manufacturing sector. According to these estimates, a hired worker on average earns less than 2,000 rupees per month (**Table 42**). The Ministry of Labor also provides figures for the average daily wages of workers in non-agricultural occupations (**Table 43**). The annual survey of industry provides data on compensation for the workers in the organized and unorganized sectors combined (**Table 44**).

Table 45 provides data for average daily earnings in agricultural operations in agricultural rural labor households. The table shows clearly that prevailing wage rates in agricultural operations in rural India are much lower than the minimum wages fixed by the government. Women receive lower wages than men, and children, as might be expected, receive the lowest wages of all.

Table 46 shows the differences in average daily earnings of workers in various occupations in India during 1958-59 to 1985-92. Planta-

TABLE 41   Minimum wages fixed/revised as of Dec. 31, 1998 in Scheduled Employment Central Sphere

	Name of scheduled employment	Basic	D.A.**	Total
		Minimum wages fix/revised per day as of Dec. 1998 (in Rs.)		
	Central sphere			
1	Agriculture	26	42.4	68.4
		33	42.4	75.4
2	Construction and maintenance of roads and building operations	28	14.02	42.02
		36	17.13	53.13
3	Stone breaking or crushing	28	14.02	42.02
		36	17.13	53.13
4	Maintenance of buildings	28	14.02	42.02
		36	17.13	53.13
5	Construction and maintenance of runways	28	14.02	42.02
		36	17.13	53.13
6	Mines	28	14.02	42.02
		34	17.13	51.13
7	Loading, unloading in railways sheds and in ports and docks	29	14.13	43.31
		42	20.55	62.55
8	Ashpit cleaning on railways	29	14.31	43.31
		42	20.55	62.55
9	Local authority	*		
10	Tanneries and leather manufacturing	*		

* Wages fixed as per wage board recommendation and not revised under.
** Dearness Allowance (i.e., a cost of living adjustment).

Source: Ministry of Labour, Labour Bureau, Government of India, 2004.

TABLE 42   Estimated annual emoluments per unorganized hired worker in the informal sector, 2000-01

		Rural	Urban	Total
1	NDME	13,034	19,365	17,320
2	DME	13,104	24,264	19,216
3	NDME + DME	13,082	2,213	18,488

Source: NSSO – Unorganized Manufacturing Sector in India 2000-01.

TABLE 43   All-India average daily wage rates in non-agricultural occupations during the year 2002-2003 (occupation-wise)

	Occupation	Men	Women	Children
1	Carpenter	105.81	-	*
2	Blacksmith	83.31	-	*
3	Cobbler	60.9	-	*
4	Mason	116.34	41.86	*
5	Tractor driver	78.33	-	-
6	Sweeper	50.08	49.74	*
7	Unskilled laborers (unspecified)	57.75	43.42	29.19

-   = Not reported
* Quotations are less than five.

Source: Wage rate in rural India (2002-03), Labour Bureau, Ministry of Labour, Government of India, Shimla, 2004.

TABLE 44   Wages and employments in organized and unorganized sector

Year	Wages per worker (Rs. 000)	Employment per employee
1993-94	2.7	3.3
1995-96	3.7	4.5
1997-98	4.1	5.2
1999-2000	4.2	5.9

Note: Results for factory sector (registered units). Figures for the year 1999-2000 are calculated on the basis of the data of workers, wages, and salaries from the Annual Survey of Industries, Ministry of Statistics and Program Implementation, Central Statistical Organization, Industrial Statistics Wing, Kolkata, 1999-2000.

Source: Annual Survey of Industries, 1993-94 to 1997-98. EPW Research Foundation, 2002, Bombay.

TABLE 45   Average daily earnings in agricultural operations in agricultural/rural labor households

All agricultural operations	Agricultural labor households		
	1983	1987-88	1993-94
Man	4.72	9.42	21.34
Women	3.56	7	15.18
Child	2.32	6.01	12.45

Source: Indian Labour Year Book, 2000 and 2001, Government of India, Labour Bureau.

TABLE 46 Average daily earnings of workers in various rounds of occupational wage surveys

	Industry	Average daily earnings in (Rs. 00) OWS Rounds			
		First (1958-59)	Second (1963-65)	Third (1974-79)	Fourth (1985-92)
1	Tea plantations	1.66	2.15	3.6	15.86
2	Coffee plantations	1.32	1.56	4.16	11.58
3	Rubber plantations	1.88	2.17	6.37	21
4	Coal mines	3.46	4.6	14.82	67.34
5	Iron ore mines	1.86	3.93	11.81	38.8
6	Managanese mines	1.96	2.,08	5.33	20.18
7	Mica mines	1.65	2.19	5.86	15.68
8	Cotton textiles	3.94	5.69	11.99	42.22
9	Jute textiles	3.27	3.78	14.69	42.21
10	Synthetic textiles	*	*	*	40.67
11	Woollen textiles	3.47	4.84	10.04	35.84
12	Silk textiles	3.89	4.67	9.61	28.93
13	Textile garments (including wearing apparel)	2.67	4.25	10.29	25.85
14	Ship building and repairing	6.16	6.6	16.77	84.7
15	Manufacture of locomotives, railway wagons, coaches and parts	4.17	5.51	16.48	55.34
16	Manufacture of motor vehicles and parts	3.49	4.61	20.48	65.54
17	Manufacture of motor cycles, scooters, and parts	-	-	-	61.63
18	Manufacture of bicycles, cycle rickshaws, and parts	4.6	6.7	10.06	29.31
19	Manufacture of air craft and parts	4.9	12.49	19.72	87.13
20	Castings and forgings (Ferrous)	3.26	3.79	18.25	45.49
21	Iron and steel	6.15	6.91	14.28	42.46
22	Manufacture of agricultural machinery, equipment, and parts	2.94	3.74	9.93	34.3
23	Manufacture of textile machinery and jute machinery	4.5	5.24	10.4	42.01
24	Manufacture of machine tools, their parts and accessories	3.89	4.02	10.4	48.69
25	Manufacture of electrical apparatus, appliances, and other parts excluding repairs	3.96**	6.44**	12.92	41.4
26	Manufacture of electrical industrial machinery, apparatus, and parts	3.96**	6.44**	16.55	88.71
27	Manufacture of basic industrial organic, inorganic chemicals and gases	3.27***	5.31	18.07	71.46
28	Manufacture of fertilizers (inorganic, organic, and mixed)	4.96	6.24	17.27	82.84
29	Manufacture of drugs and medicines	3.27***	5.05	11.29	75.43
30	Manufacture of matches	1.49	5.65	4.59	20.01
31	Manufacture of cement	3.38	5.42	17.24	64.12
32	Manufacture of footwear (excluding repair) except vulcanized moulded or rubber or plastic footwear	3.73	6.51	11.4	58.9
33	Petroleum refineries	6.49	11.2	43.43	110.93

(continued)

TABLE 46 *(cont.)* Average daily earnings of workers in various rounds of occupational wage surveys

	Industry	Average daily earnings in (Rs. 00) OWS Rounds			
		First (1958-59)	Second (1963-65)	Third (1974-79)	Fourth (1985-92)
34	Manufacture of toilet soap, washing soap, and soap powder	5.29	5.89	19.81	40.97
35	Manufacture of glass and glass products	2.9	3.15	9.79	45.59
36	Manufacture of refining of sugar	2.28****	3.17****	11.86	54.39
37	Paper and paper products	3.5	4.32	12.83	62.21
38	Printing and publishing of newspapers, periodicals, books, journals, atlases, maps, etc.	3.35	4.2	12.01	66.5
39	Cashew nut shelling, processing, and packing	0.98	1.5	5.63	16.44
40	Manufacture of hydrogenated oils, vanaspati ghee, etc.	3.72	5.25	16.9	55.28
41	Manufacture of cigarette and cigarette tobacco	6.46	5.74	21.09	106.16

* Synthetic textiles was included subsequent to the third round; manufacture of motor cycles, scooters, and parts was included in the fourth round.
** A combined industry group "Manufacture of Electrical Machinery and Appliances" was covered during the First and Second Rounds which was split into two industries viz. (I) Electrical Industrial Machinery and (ii) Electrical Apparatus & Appliances from the Third Round of survey.
*** Industries namely (I) Manufacture of Basic Industrial Organic, Inorganic Chemicals and Gases and (ii) Manufacture of Drugs and Medicines was covered as a single industry during the First Round.
**** Manufacture and Refining of Sugar and Manufacture of Khandsari Sugar were covered as a single industry under the First and Second Rounds of the Survey. Manufacture of Khandsari Sugar industry has been replaced with "Manufacture of Plastic Articles" in the Fifth round Note: For the remaining 15 industries please consult the respective reports.

Source: Statistics, Occupational Wages Surveys, Ministry of Labour, Labour Bureau,Government of India, 2004.

tions provided the lowest earnings in 1985-92, ranging from 11.58 to 21.00 rupees for one-day work. By comparison, wages for workers in petroleum refineries and cigarette and tobacco manufacturing were over 100 rupees per day. In all, of the total occupations listed in the table only seven paid wages more than 70 rupees per day; another nine provided wages between 59 and 70 rupees per day. Wages in most occupations ranged between 20 and 45 rupees per day during 1985-92.

In general, available data on wages show that wages received by workers are usually less than official minimum fixed wage rates. Employers usually fix these wages on their own, and workers have little power to change them. Exceptions are those workers whose skills are in demand.

Social security and labor legislation

India at present has no declared or well-defined policy on social security. Various government schemes have been taken up in this regard, but they have been implemented piecemeal and are restricted to the organized sector, i.e., only 7-8% of the total labor force in India. The remaining 92-93% of the labor force has no protection under labor laws nor any kind of social security benefits.

Protection for workers in the organized sector

About 47 labor-related statutes enacted by the central governmental provide social security, stipulating minimum wages and other benefits concerning accidental death, maternity, conditions of employment, dismissal, disciplinary action, formation of trade unions, industrial disparities, etc. for workers in the organized sector. A number of state statutes also provide social protection to different segments of the labor force.

- *The Industrial Dispute Act* (1947) provides protection to workers against retrenchment, lay off, and closure. Chapter V-B of the act has made retrenchment and closure very difficult for employers. Retrenchment requires three months written notice, plus prior permission from the government or appropriate authorities. Closure requires the prior permission of the government. Termination in the organized sector is almost impossible in the absence of proven misconduct.

- *The Contract Labor* (Regulation and Abolition) *Act* (1970) was originally enacted to regulate the practice of contract labor. Two landmark judgments by the Supreme Court in 1995 and 1996 made it obligatory on the part of a public sector undertaking to absorb contract labor in service for more than one year. A 2001 judgment of the Supreme Court held that a contract laborer hired to comply with statuary obligations could also become a direct employee. The act however, permits an organization to outsource jobs of non-core activities.

- ***The Factory Act*** (1948) provides social security for workers in the organized sector. Each state's director of industrial safety and health is in charge of administration of the act. Main provisions of the act relate to health, safety measures, welfare facilities, working hours, overtime, leave, and the employment of women.

- ***The Trade Union Act*** (1926) is one of the oldest labor laws, and it has been retained so far without major amendments. The act provides for registration of trade unions by groups of seven or more workers. It also allows half the number of trade union officers to be outsiders.

- ***The Minimum Wage Act*** (1948) mandates the "appropriate government" to fix minimum wages for the scheduled employments falling under the purview of the act. The primary criteria for an employment to be included in the schedule are that the number of employees in the employment should be more than 1,000. So far there are 1,140 categories of employment in respect to state government, 40 in respect to central government, and 20 in respect to union territories. The rates of minimum wages are revised from time to time as per the provisions of the act.

- ***The Workman's Compensation Act*** (1923) provides protection to workers in case of loss of earning capacity due to an accident arising out of or in the course of employment. The act is applicable to all manufacturing units, railways, transport, establishments engaged in construction, plantations, and other employment listed in the second schedule of the act.

Social security measures

Apart from protection under labor laws, the organized sector is also benefited by the social security scheme. Civil servants benefit from two major social security schemes: pension on contribution basis, and health insurance, which provides health services free of charges. Other organized private and public sector workers are covered under employer's social insurance (ESI), which is based on contributions from employers, employees, and the government. The rates of contribution since 1997 have been 4.75% of wages by employers and 1.75% by employees. Some workers in the organized sector are also covered under the employers provident fund (EPF), an old-age benefit scheme under which both employees and employers contribute during the service period of the employee. The contributed amount plus interest is given to the employee at retirement.

Protection of workers in the unorganized sector

Currently more than 150 pieces of legislation have been enacted either by Parliament or by the state legislatures relating to the unorganized sector. But in actual practice workers have scarcely benefited from these laws. The socioeconomic complexities of the unorganized labor market and the rigidities of the legislation leave the workers of the unorganized sector to their own fate.

- *The Workmen's Compensation Act* (1923). Under this act protection was provided to workers in case of loss of earnings capacity due to any accident arising out of employment. The loss of earnings capacity may be either by death or disability. The act applies to all manufacturing units, and every worker engaged for the purpose of an employer's business, either directly or through a contractor, is entitled to the benefits of the act. In practice, however, few registered units provide compensation to workers in the case of death and/or disability. Moreover, casual workers do not come under the coverage of the act.

- *The Minimum Wages Act* (1948). This and other similar laws for the protection of unorganized labor emerged after continuous pressure from various quarters, including the International Labour Organization. The welfare nature of the government of the early post-independence era also compelled it to promote the interests of workers in the unorganized sector as a whole.

    The act mandates the "appropriate government" to fix minimum wages for the scheduled employment falling under the purview of the act. But there are no fixed criteria to set minimum wages, with the result that minimum wages for an unskilled worker vary today from 600 to 1,800 rupees in various states and various industries. Minimum wages are to be revised every two years or after every rise of 50 points in the consumer price index. But the procedure is so cumbersome that the wages are not revised in certain states' industries for eight to 10 years. There is no remedy available to workers to contest a failure to revise minimum wages.

- ***The Contract Labor (Regulation and Abolition) Act*** (1970). The act makes a principal employer responsible for ensuring that legal provisions are implemented. It also requires that the same wages and service conditions should be provided for the same or similar jobs. But contract workers are deprived of pension benefits and if the contractor is frequently changed workers do not get the benefit of the gratuity.

- ***The Equal Remuneration Act*** (1976). This act states that men and women performing the same work should be paid equally. However, in practice, the provisions have failed to guarantee such equality.

- ***The Inter-State Migrant Worker Act*** (1978 and 1979). These acts attempt to safeguard the interests of migrant workers and regulate their conditions of service and other matters. The act deals only with migrant workers who have migrated through contractors; individual workers who have migrated have no protection. In practice, migrant laborers are paid less than local laborers and live in slums without basic facilities such as safe drinking water, sanitation, and drainage. Many instances have come to light showing that even the worker's compensation due on death is not paid to migrant workers.

- ***The Beedi & Cigar Workers' Act.*** The acts requires that all beedi and cigar workers be issued identity cards so that they can be entitled to the facilities of the welfare scheme. There are about 7 million beedi workers in the country, but only 4 million have been issued identity cards.

Labor laws applicable to agricultural workers
The most important legislation applicable to agricultural workers is the Minimum Wages Act of 1948. Both the central and state governments have determined minimum wage rates for agricultural workers, ranging from about 35 to 90 rupees per day. Another important law with far-reaching impact for agricultural workers is the Bonded Labor System (Abolition) Act of 1976. In addition, a number of laws are applicable to plantation labor and have enabling provisions to extend them to agricultural workers:

- the Payment of Wages Act of 1936;

- the Employees State Insurance Act of 1948;

- the Maternity Benefit Act of 1961;

- the Personal Injuries (Compensation Insurance) Act of 1963; and

- the Payment of Gratuity Act of 1972.

In addition, the Workmen's Compensation Act of 1923, the Employees Provident Fund and Miscellaneous Provision Act of 1952, the Contract Labor (Regulation and Abolition) Act of 1970, the Equal Remuneration Act of 1976, the Inter-State Migrant Worker Act of 1979, and the Child Labor (Prohibition and Regulation) Act of 1986 are also applicable to agricultural workers in one form or another.

Their enactment notwithstanding, in practice none of the above laws are able to safeguard the interests of agricultural workers adequately, nor have they been able to provide for security of employment. The acts do not clearly provide for specific hours of work, machinery for settlement of disputes, social security measures, or a system of identification of agricultural laborers so that specific welfare measures can be directed to their benefit.

Existing schemes of social security for agricultural workers
The existing schemes of social security that directly or indirectly benefit agricultural laborers can be broadly classified into two groups: (1) promotional social development schemes, and (2) protective social security schemes. Promotional social development schemes are those that aim to provide employment opportunities such as:

- Swarnjayanti Gram Swarozgar Yojana;

- Jawahar Gram Samridhi Yojana;

- Employment Assurance Scheme;

- Draught Prone Area Program;

- Desert Development Program;

- Integrated Waste Land Development Program;

- Employment Guarantee Scheme (Maharashtra);

- Accelerated Rural Water Supply Program;

- Minimum Needs Program; and

- Rural Sanitation Program.

Examples of protective social security schemes include the following:

- The National Social Assistance Program, which includes the earlier schemes of the National Old Age Pension and the National Maternity Benefit Scheme. Apart from the National Old Age Pension Scheme, certain states like Gujarat, Maharashtra, Karnataka, Kerala, and Tamil Nadu operate their own old-age pension schemes, which are also extended to agricultural workers.

- Financial assistance is given by states like Gujarat, Kerala, and Tamil Nadu to destitute/deserted widows and divorced women.

- Pensions are given to handicapped persons by states like Gujarat, Kerala, Haryana, Nagaland, and West Bengal.

- The government of Kerala has introduced a death/retirement benefit scheme for artisans and skilled workers. Under this scheme, a retirement benefit is paid on completion of 40 years of enrollment; if the beneficiary dies before the completion of this period, the benefit is paid to their families.

- A comprehensive insurance scheme called Janashree Bima Yojana has been introduced in rural areas. Persons below the poverty line and between the ages of 18 and 60 are covered.

The above schemes have no doubt benefited a few agricultural workers, but the coverage is relatively insignificant. A majority of workers are ignorant of these schemes, and there are many inherent problems in the mechanism of their implementation, making the schemes ineffective and limited in coverage. Therefore, unless awareness of these schemes is enhanced and the mechanism of implementation is improved, the importance of these schemes for workers will be minimal.

Latest welfare scheme for agriculture workers
Because comprehensive legislation for agricultural laborers has not been enacted, a proposal to formulate a specific scheme for the benefit of agricultural workers covering life/accident insurance and other benefits was prepared in consultation with the Insurance Division, the Ministry of Finance, and other government agencies. The scheme aims to bridge the gap in the various welfare schemes of the government. The scheme would provide both life insurance and accident insurance, plus annuity benefits to help agricultural laborers when they are past productive age and need money to meet basic requirements.

Social security schemes for cultivators
The discussion in the National Consultation on Social Security held in 2001 concluded that cultivators, who are also called farmers, are basically self-employed persons. They are exposed to vagaries of weather and subject to the operation of market forces. Famine, drought, floods, and other natural calamities affect their income, as does the fluctuation in the supply of and demand for agricultural commodities. Schemes designed for promoting or protecting the interests of cultivators included the Crop and Livestock Insurance Scheme, the Minimum Support Price Scheme, the Fertilizer Subsidy, and the Subsidy on Sale of Electricity. But the problem again is that poor cultivators are not able to benefit from these schemes if they are ignorant of them or if implementation methods are so cumbersome that poor farmers fail to receive coverage.

Protection under law — small-scale industry workers
Some special laws have been enacted to protect the interest of workers in small-scale industries (SSI). But these laws accomplish little in practice. For instance, the Factory Act of 1948 provides for protection of workers against exploitation and for the improvement of working conditions within the factory premises. But in reality, unhygienic working conditions remain. Many SSI work units have insufficient light and fresh air. In some the air is injurious to health. Units operating from residences are able to regulate their own air, but the provision of health safety measures, welfare safety measures, and safety measures against occupational diseases have no relevance to these units. Laws enacted to cover SSIs include:

- ***The Industrial Establishment (Standing Orders) Act of 1946*** seeks to regulate the conditions of recruitment, discharge, disciplinary action, holidays, etc. of workers employed in industrial undertakings and establishments. It is applicable to industrial establishments employing 50 or more workers in the preceding 12 months. Central and state governments can make this act applicable to establishments employing fewer than 30 persons; West Bengal has done so. In Assam it is applicable to establishments employing 18 or more workers. But the basic problem again is that SSI units do not work in a regularized way in which the laws related to regulation of recruitment, discharge, disciplinary action, etc. are needed. Most of the units are not registered. Moreover, there is no recruitment process in practice, and, when work is over, the workers leave the units. If any social security is to be provided to the workers in these units, the first step would be to understand their functioning and the socioeconomic conditions under which the work is done. Without an understanding of such conditions, any amendment in legislation or provision of social security will be a waste of resources.

- ***The Payment of Wages Act of 1936*** was enacted to ensure regular and prompt payment of wages and to prevent the exploitation of wage earners by prohibiting arbitrary fines and deductions from wages. Considering the current functioning of SSI units, the act has no relevance for providing any protection. Most of the workers are daily wage workers, employed on a job or per-piece basis.

- ***The Employees/Provident Fund Act of 1952***, which makes provisions for the future of industrial workers after they retire or for their dependents in the case of early death, is applicable only to factories and establishments employing 10 or more workers. Thus, the majority of SSI units, which employ between two and seven workers, are uncovered. Moreover, the provisions of the act demand contributions from employers and employees, but employers of most SSI units work on a subsistence level and are unable or unwilling to contribute their share; similarly, workers come and go and are unlikely to participate. A similar shortcoming is evident in the ***Payment of Gratuity Act of 1972***. As the act is applicable to establishment/units employing 10 or more persons, a majority of SSIs remain out of its coverage. Moreover, the benefits of the act go only to those workers who have put in five years of continuous service at the time of their termination; in most SSI units such tenure is rare.

- *The Employees' State Insurances Act of 1948* provides cash benefits to employees in cases of sickness, maternity, and employment injury. It is applicable to employees in a wide range of establishments drawing monthly wages up to 1,000 rupees. Dependents are covered for medical benefits and pension if a worker dies from an employment-related injury. But again, the problems of organizing workers of SSI units make them unaware of these benefits. At present only a few workers within SSI units are aware of the schemes and are reaping their benefits.

- *The Payment of Bonus Act of 1985* provides a statutory obligation for payment of a bonus to persons employed in certain establishments on the basis of profits or productivity. Most SSI units are not covered under this act because they employ fewer than 10 workers, but in any case profits at SSIs are rare, thanks in part to the increasing availability of competing foreign goods.

- *The Trade Union Act of 1926* confers legal and corporate status on registered trade unions. It is applicable to associations of employees and extends to the whole of India. An insignificant number of SSI units are covered under the trade union act, as the job of organizing workers of SSI units spread all over India is a difficult task.

Promotion of welfare funds

Welfare funds represent one of the models developed in India for providing social security protection to workers in the unorganized sector. Under this mechanism, funds are raised by levying an assessment on the production, sale, or export of specified goods or by collecting contributions from various sources including employers, employees, and the government. The question of whether welfare funds could be established to benefit all classes of workers in the unorganized sector was examined by a study group set up by the National Commission on Labor. It concluded that a welfare fund could be set up for major employment sectors with large number of persons employed, such as agriculture, building and construction, beedi workers, handlooms, power looms, and fishing. But for minor employment sectors a welfare fund for each was considered impractical. Rather, the study group concluded, an umbrella fund should serve all smaller employment categories.

The government has set up welfare funds for mine workers, beedi workers, dock workers, and a few others. The Building and Other Construction Workers (Regulation of Employment and Conditions of Services) Act of 1996 provides for the establishment of one or more welfare funds for the benefit of workers in the building industry. There is a proposal to set up one or more welfare funds for agricultural workers under the Agricultural Workers Bill presently under consideration.

Conclusion and policy recommendations

The post-reform period in India has witnessed the casualization and informalization of the workforce. The number of part-time jobs rose, as did the share of the unorganized sector in total employment. Although no systematic cause-and-effect relationship study on this trend has been undertaken, an analysis of the statistical data in this chapter suggests the following reasons for the increase in the informalization of the Indian economy during the last decade:

- Huge fiscal deficits carried over the years compelled the government to cut public expenditure by adopting policies of downsizing and retrenchment in both the government itself and in public sector undertakings. These cuts resulted in the decline of regular salaried jobs in the public sector.

- Adoption of market-friendly policies by the government in the post-reform period promoted privatization and disinvestment. The process of privatization and disinvestment was associated with increasing effort by private entrepreneurs to enhance cost effectiveness, mainly through a reduction in labor costs. To this end, they have preferred contract, part-time, and piece-rate labor to regular salaried jobs.

- An increase in the productivity of agriculture during the post-reform period released workers from the rural farm sector. Rural poverty compelled these landless unemployed workers to migrate to urban areas in search of employment, but high productivity in manufacturing and tertiary activities diminished the supply of jobs. In such a situation, the informal sector worked as a repository for these migrated workers. The result was an expansion of the urban unorganized sector.

The post-reform period has generated low-quality employment:

- Casualization has increased and regular salaried jobs have declined. The number of part-time, contractual, and piece-rate jobs has increased.

- Major employment has been generated in the unorganized sector, where per capita earnings are low, working conditions are unfavorable, and job and social security are non-existent.

- Although only about 7% of the workforce is unemployed, about 26% of the population is below the poverty line, suggesting very low levels of earnings for the majority of currently employed persons.

- Employment growth in the organized sector, particularly in the public sector, was slow during the 1980s and 1990s. Market distortions and the adoption of capital-intensive technology led to sluggishness in employment growth in the organized industrial sector. Given limited labor demand in this sector, the urban unorganized sector absorbed as much surplus labor as it could, at lower wages.

- Women's employment shifted from home-based activities to market- and commercial-based activities, but their wages remain low relative to men's. The employment of women at lower wages is an indication of the exploitation of women workers by employers.

It is not the growth but the composition of growth that helps in solving the problem of unemployment. The post-reform growth in the Indian economy has been led by the tertiary sector. Because the value-added from the tertiary sector cannot be treated on par with the value-added from the commodity-producing sector, the predominance of the tertiary sector in the growth of a developing country like India can only produce a heavy burden on the commodity-producing sector. This burden results in an adverse balance-of-payment situation and an increase in the rate of inflation.

The problem of unemployment in India is a problem not just of the demand side of the labor market but of the supply side as well. The system of education and skill formation in India still works along traditional lines; it has not yet responded to the changing education and skills needs of the labor market. As a result, the country faces a problem of the growing mismatch between the demand and supply of education and skills in the labor market. The trades and skills provided by the industrial training institutes have failed to keep pace with the improved technology of the industrial units. As a result, many seats at the institutes remain unutilized. The absence of a well-planned and well-developed education and training system for the workforce has not only become the cause of increasing unemployment, it has also become the cause of prevailing low productivity, particularly in the unorganized sector. Micro-level studies indicate that the illiteracy of workers and lack of training facilities are the main cause of low output and low productivity in the unorganized sector and in small-scale industries.

Suggested interventions

- A well-planned and well-developed system of education and skill formation, which can address the changing needs of the globally competitive enterprises of the organized and unorganized sectors.

- A survey of the educational and skill-development needs of the various professions and of the employment/income generation programs for restructuring the present system of education and skill formation in India.

- Provision of minimum social security to workers in the unorganized sector. Such a benefit will contribute positively to the growth and productivity of enterprises in this sector.

- Government support (technical, financial, and skill development) for improving the operations of small-scale industries.

- Effective implementation of employment/income generation programs for the development of villages and towns.

- Planning and implementation of infrastructure development programs.

Bibliography

Bhalla, G.S., and Hazell Peter. 2003. "Rural Employment and Poverty: Strategies to Eliminate Rural Poverty Within a Generation." *Economic and Political Weekly*, August 16.

Bhalla, Shiela. 2002. "The Restructuring of the Unorganized Sector in India." Report submitted to the Planning Commission, Institute of Human Development, New Delhi.

Central Statistical Organization. 2003. National Accounts Statistics, Ministry of Statistics and Programme. New Delhi: Government of India.

Country Paper, India. 2000. "Measurement of Informal Sector: The Indian Experience." Fourth Meeting of the Group of Informal Sector Statistics, Doc. 14, International Labour Organization, Geneva, August 28-30.

Ghose, Ajit K. 1999. "The Question on Employment Security in India: A Note." Paper presented at the Conference on Social Security in India, New Delhi, April 15-17.

Government of India. 2002. Report of the National Statistics Commission. New Delhi: CSO.

IAMR. 2001. Labor Laws and Contemporary Issues: Workshop on Contemporary Issues in Public Policy and Governance. New Delhi: IAMR.

Indian Year Book. 2002. Manpower Profile. New Delhi: IAMR.

Kundu, Amitabh, and Alakh N. Sharma, eds. 2001. *Informal Sector in India: Perspective and Policies.* New Delhi: IAMR, IHD.

Kundu, Amtabh. 2003. "Urbanization and Urban Governance: Search for a Perspective Beyond Neo-Liberalization." *Economic and Political Weekly*, July 19-25.

Mathur, Ashok. 2002. National and Regional Growth Performance in the Indian Economy: A Sectoral Analysis in Reform and Employment. New Delhi: IAMR.

Mitra, Arup. 2002. *Growth and Employment With Special Reference to Organized Industry in Reforms and Employment.* New Delhi: IAMR.

Mridula, Sharma. 1992. "Labor Market Reforms: Social Security in Organised and Unorganized Sectors." Background paper presented at the National Seminar on Labor Market Reforms, IAMR, New Delhi.

Mridula, Sharma. 2003. *Impact of Economic Reforms on Small Scale Industries: A Study of Lock Manufacturing Industry in Aligarh.* New Delhi: IAMR.

Mridula, Sharma. 2004. *Impact of Economic Reform on Small Scale Industry: A Study of Handtool Manufacturing Industry at Jallandhar and Nagaur.* New Delhi: IAMR.

National Commission on Labor. 2001. National Consultation on Social Security. Vols. I and II. New Delhi: NCL.

Panchmukhi, P.R. 2002. *Social Sector Developments and Economic Reforms: A Focus on the Education Sector in Reform and Employment.* New Delhi: IAMR.

Pande, Sudha Desh, and Lalit Desh Pande. 2002. "Reforms and Labor Market in India." In *Reforms and Employment.* New Delhi: IAMR.

Planning Commission. 1990. "Employment Trends and Prospects for 1990s." Working Paper. New Delhi: Government of India.

Planning Commission. 1992. Eighth Five-Year Plan, 1992-93. Vol. I. New Delhi: Government of India.

Planning Commission. 2001. Report of the Task Force Employment Opportunities. New Delhi: Government of India.

Planning Commission. 2002. Special Group on Targeting Ten Million Employment Opportunities Per Year. New Delhi: Government of India.

CHAPTER 4

Informal labor markets and the Russian workforce: strategies for survival

by Oksana Sinyavskaya and Daria Popova

Background

For more than 10 years Russia has undertaken the difficult and inconsistent path of economic transition, moving from a planned economy to a market one. This shift has involved a transformation of almost all the institutions and modes of regulation that existed previously. As a result, Russia's transition to a market economy was followed by a period of economic decline, as well as periods of high inflation.

Since the beginning of the reform, there has been a sharp decrease in gross domestic product (GDP) that has not been overcome until recently (see **Table 1**). During the 1990s, the economic situation was unstable. Some researchers have explained this instability as a result of inconsistent stabilization policies (Gaidar et al. 1998). Others suggested that it was the excessively single-minded focus on macroeconomic stabilization that *kept* policy makers from recognizing the risk of a financial crisis, such as the one that occurred in August 1998 (Avdasheva et al. 1999). Russia's economic situation changed in 1999 when a substantial ruble devaluation in combination with high oil prices allowed for a rather quick recovery of the national economy following the crisis of 1998. Since that time, the Russian economy has grown every year; the budget is in a surplus, and inflation has declined slowly but steadily. This economic improvement was caused mainly by devaluation and the high price of natural resources rather than by active economic policy aimed at improving the investment attractiveness of Russia (Avdasheva et al. 2002). By 2002, output in Russia comprised almost three-quarters

TABLE 1 Different estimates of Russia's GDP, 1980-2003

Year	GDP, World bank (million USD)	Nominal GDP in current prices (billion RUR; trillion RUR before 1998)	GDP index in constant prices (2000=100)	Growth rate of GDP to the same period of previous year**,***** (%)	GDP in 2000 prices, seasonally smoothed data (billion RUR; trillion RUR before 1998)	GDP per capita, RUR *,** (thousands RUR before 1998)	GDP per capita in 2000 prices (thousands RUR before 1998)	GDP per capita measured by purchasing power parity (PPP) *** (USD)
1980						2.3		
1981								
1982								
1983								
1984				0.0				
1985				2.3		2.8		
1986				3.3		2.8		
1987				2.9		2.9		
1988				5.5		3.1		
1989				3.0		3.2		
1990		0.6	148.8	-3.0	10,869.1	4.3	73.2	
1991	$542,100.0	1.4	141.3	-5.0	10,325.6		69.3	
1992		19.0	120.8	-14.5	8,828.4		59.0	
1993		171.5	110.3	-8.7	8,060.3		54.2	
1994		610.7	96.3	-12.7	7,036.7		47.7	
1995	850,000.0	1,428.5	92.4	-4.1	6,748.2	10,398.8	44.2	5,700.0

(continued)

TABLE 1 (cont.) Different estimates of Russia's GDP, 1980-2003

	GDP, World bank (million USD)	Nominal GDP in current prices (billion RUR; trillion RUR before 1998)	GDP index in constant prices (2000=100)	Growth rate of GDP to the same period of previous year**,***** (%)	GDP in 2000 prices, seasonally smoothed data (billion RUR; trillion RUR before 1998)	GDP per capita, RUR *,** (thousands RUR before 1998)	GDP per capita in 2000 prices (thousands RUR before 1998)	GDP per capita measured by purchasing power parity (PPP) *** (USD)
1996		2,007.8	89.0	-3.6	6,504.9	14,523.2	43.4	4,370.0
1997		2,342.5	90.3	1.4	6,594.6	16,826.4	44.8	6,508.0
1998	282,434.6	2,629.6	85.4	-5.3	6,242.2	18,659.0	43.0	7,473.0
1999	193,616.8	4,823.2	90.9	6.3	6,638.6	32,580.6	45.2	
2000	259,596.5	7,305.6	100.0	10.0	7,305.6	50,168.3	50.3	
2001	309,951.2	9,039.4	105.0	5.0	7,674.4	62,457.1	53.1	
2002	346,519.9	10,863.4	109.6	4.3	8,004.4		55.7	
2003*****		2,599.0		6.8				

* 1980 data are for the USSR.
** Data for 1980-1989 are taken from: Narodnoe khosiajstvo in 1990 (National Economy in 1990), Statistical yearbook, Moscow, Finances and statistics (1991, p. 7).
*** In 1998 the Russia's state statistical agency (Goskomstat) changed the methodology of calculating the PPP in accordance with international requirements.
**** First quarter 2003.
***** Data for 2003 are taken from Russian Economic Trends.

Source: Russian Bureau of Economic Analysis.

of 1991 output levels, but the speed of growth has declined since 2000. Many structural imbalances remain, including a high degree of dependence on exporting raw materials and goods, primarily energy resources, which has led to the high dependence of the Russian economy on energy resources whose prices fluctuate widely on global markets.

Although the crisis helped to improve the average financial situation of firms and enterprises by driving many weaker ones out of business, a lot of ineffective enterprises still exist.[1] Experts suggest that in order to develop more rapidly, Russia has to develop comparative advantage in skills- and technology-based production, which among other things means more investment in human capital (Maleva 2002). Further structural reforms are also vital for economic development (Yassin et al. 2000).

The Soviet economy was too concentrated on industry and production of goods, while production of market services was under-represented (**Tables 2a and 2b**). As expected, transition to a market economy has increased demand for market services. The most significant decline in terms of GDP production was observed in agriculture, while the most considerable growth was in trade. The share of production of nonmarket services has decreased since 1999.

At the same time, the process of economic restructuring was not stable or fully effective. The nonmarket sector represents a significant share of the economy, and includes mostly budgetary sponsored branches (education, health care, culture) as well as (1) ineffective firms of industry, agriculture, and other branches producing negative value-added; (2) housing and communal services, mainly financed from budgets; (3) natural monopolies preserving administered prices and cross-subsiding; (4) households using free of charge or cheap services and receiving understated wages and salary (Avdasheva et al. 2002, p. 30). The absence of a real bankruptcy procedure remains the main problem. Even in 2001 40.6% of transport enterprises, 48.0% of agriculture firms, and 61.4% of those providing housing and communal services were unprofitable (Avdasheva et al. 2002, p. 17).

In the Soviet era, prices were regulated—along with the only official exchange rate set by the state bank of the USSR—on the base of the gold content of currencies. The state had a monopoly on currency trade. But as early as the end of 1980s, enterprises were allowed to enter the market themselves without state mediators. This was followed by cur-

TABLE 2A GDP sectoral composition, 1990-2002

Year	GDP in current prices (billion RUR; trillion RUR before 1998)	Including: Production of goods (billion RUR; trillion RUR before 1998)	Production of market services (billion RUR; trillion RUR before 1998)	Production of nonmarket services (billion RUR; trillion RUR before 1998)	Shares of GDP in current prices (%)	Production of goods (%)	Including: Production of market services (%)	Production of nonmarket services (%)
1990	0.64	0.39	0.13	0.08	100.0%	60.9%	20.3%	12.5%
1991	1.40	0.86	0.35	0.16	100.0	61.4	25.0	11.4
1992	19.0	9.4	8.4	1.6	100.0	49.5	44.2	8.4
1993	171.5	82.4	59.5	19.9	100.0	48.0	34.7	11.6
1994	610.7	285.6	221.3	79.8	100.0	46.8	36.2	13.1
1995	1428.5	596.9	591.6	146.6	100.0	41.8	41.4	10.3
1996	2007.8	855.1	777.6	200.7	100.0	42.6	38.7	10.0
1997	2342.5	965.7	915.0	254.6	100.0	41.2	39.1	10.9
1998	2629.6	1047.3	1061.5	280.8	100.0	39.8	40.4	10.7
1999	4823.2	1959.5	1995.1	384.7	100.0	40.6	41.4	8.0
2000	7305.6	2939.6	3041.3	549.5	100.0	40.2	41.6	7.5
2001	9039.4	3463.6	3872.5	738.4	100.0	38.3	42.8	8.2
2002	10863.4	3963.1	4912.0	957.2	100.0	36.5	45.2	8.8

Source: *Annual Review of Economic Policy in Russia in 2002*. Bureau of Economic Analysis (2003, p. 469).

TABLE 2B   GDP sectoral composition, 1980-2003: GDP structure by branches

Year	Production of goods, including:	Industry	Construction	Agriculture	Production of services, including:	Transport, communication	Trade	Total production
1980	63.0%	42.0%	8.0%	13.0%	37.0%	6.0%	13.0%	100.0%
1985	62.0	37.0	8.0	17.0	38.0	6.0	14.0	100.0
1988	62.0	34.0	10.0	18.0	38.0	6.0	12.0	100.0
1989	60.0	32.0	10.0	18.0	40.0	6.0	12.0	100.0
1990	65.5	38.0	9.6	16.6	34.5	10.0	5.6	100.0
1991	64.1	39.0	9.6	14.3	35.9	11.4	12.2	100.0
1992	50.5	35.0	6.5	7.4	49.5	7.6	29.9	100.0
1993	52.7	35.7	8.0	8.3	47.3	8.7	19.4	100.0
1994	50.8	34.2	9.5	6.5	49.2	9.9	19.2	100.0
1995	48.4	31.0	8.9	7.8	51.6	11.3	18.7	100.0
1996	46.3	29.8	8.3	7.4	53.7	13.4	15.7	100.0
1997	43.4	28.5	8.0	6.3	56.6	12.2	17.4	100.0
1998	43.3	29.9	7.1	5.6	56.7	10.8	19.5	100.0
1999	45.6	31.2	6.2	7.7	54.4	9.6	21.6	100.0
2000	47.2	32.7	6.7	7.3	52.8	8.5	21.1	100.0
2001	50.4	—	—	—	49.6	—	—	100.0
2002	47.6	—	—	—	52.4	—	—	100.0
2003	36.5	27.6	5.9	2.2	63.5	10.1	23.5	100.0

Source: *Annual Review of Economic Policy in Russia in 2002.* Bureau of Economic Analysis (2003, p. 469).

TABLE 3   Dynamics of prices, 1990-2002

Year	Consumer Price Index (CPI), total *	CPI for food *	CPI for nonfoods *	CPI for services *	Deflator of retail turnover	Composite index of producers' prices *
1990	0.005	0.010	0.010	0.001	—	—
1991	0.01	0.01	0.02	0.002	0.02	—
1992	0.40	0.39	0.55	0.05	0.20	—
1993	3.4	3.5	4.1	1.3	1.9	—
1994	10.6	11.1	11.0	7.8	7.6	—
1995	25.5	24.8	23.9	26.0	22.5	—
1996	29.8	28.8	31.4	21.2	33.7	—
1997	33.1	31.3	37.0	25.0	38.9	39.6
1998	61.0	62.4	60.6	55.8	48.2	48.1
1999	83.2	84.8	84.4	74.8	82.0	75.2
2000	100.0	100.0	100.0	100.0	100.0	100.0
2001	118.6	117.1	112.7	136.9	120.7	114.8
2002	136.5	130.0	125.0	186.5	139.9	132.3

Note: December 2000 = 100.
* By the end of a year.

Source: Annual Review of Economic Policy in Russia in 2002. Bureau of Economic Analysis (2003, p. 498-500).

rency auctions of Vneshtorgbank (the bank of external economic links) in 1990, and then by currency auctions of the state bank of the USSR in April 1991. In the beginning of the 1990s, Russia undertook a complex liberalization policy. Prices were mostly freed from strict regulation, a change that resulted in the period of higher inflation in the early 1990s and following the crisis of 1998 (**Table 3** and **Figure A**).

Russia's currency remains convertible (i.e., can be freely exchanged for other currencies), although monetary authorities do manage its value within a fairly narrow band (**Table 4**). Different exchange rate policies have been applied since mid-1992. The current official exchange rate is calculated as a mean rate between declared rates of purchasing and selling of Central Bank of Russia (CBR). The financial crisis of 1998 resulted in a large devaluation of the Russian ruble. Experts agree that after the crisis of 1998, monetary and credit policy has accommodated the devaluation of the ruble by keeping interest rates low (Avdasheva et al. 2002, p. 110). The Central Bank of Russia conducted

FIGURE A   Growth rate of total Current Price Index, 1991-2002*

* Log scale.

Sources: *Annual Review of Economic Policy in Russia in 2002*. Bureau of Economic Analysis (2003, p. 498-500).

a so-called "dirigible floating" policy with frequent interventions, a policy which is commonly used in developing and transitioning economies highly dependent on external shocks in order to keep a stable exchange rate.

In the administrative Soviet economy, ownership rights were not determined practically; there was almost no private ownership and only a small number of non-governmental organizations existed, while state ownership was the most widespread. The institute of private ownership was renewed by the Law on Ownership in RUFSR (Russian republic) in 1990. And after the adoption of the Law on Enterprises and Entrepreneurial Activity (1990) new legal forms of firms became possible. Bearing in mind that ownership is the basis of an economic system, it is understandable that one of the main objectives of transition to a market economy is retrenchment of the public sector. This public-sector overhaul could be done in one of two ways: increasing the number of newly created private firms, on the one hand, and privatization of previously existing public firms, on the other hand. At the beginning, two of the most popular methods of privatization were used:

TABLE 4   Exchange rates, 1990-2004

Year	Exchange rate (MICE), average for a period* (RUR/USD)	Exchange rate (MICE), end of a period (RUR/USD)	Real exchange rate, average for a period** (Dec. 1995=100)
1990	0.019	0.022	—
1991	0.063	0.169	4.2
1992	0.228	0.415	14.6
1993	1.018	1.247	110.4
1994	2.205	3.550	88.5
1995	4.562	4.640	134.3
1996	5.126	5.570	112.8
1997	5.785	5.974	101.4
1998	9.965	21.140	102.6
1999	24.836	26.959	98.4
2000	28.145	28.163	101.2
2001	29.258	30.137	103.6
2002	31.355	31.784	107.6

*   Denominated rubles.
**   Increase of indicator means increase in exchange rate of ruble (real exchange rate was obtained by weightening of real exchange rate to USD (40%), DM (40%), urkainian grivna (20%).

Source: *Annual Review of Economic Policy in Russia in 2002.* Bureau of Economic Analysis (2003, p. 524)

vouchers for primary privatization and direct sales for secondary privatization. The law limited the possibility of land right selling. Despite the critics of privatization, one can hardly assess its direct social outcomes separated from the consequences of other reforms. Meanwhile, it has been acknowledged that privatized and state enterprises do not change significantly in terms of employment conditions, but newly created private firms do differ from all others by this parameter.

The private-sector share in GDP increased from 50% in 1994 to 70% in 1997 (European Bank for Reconstruction and Development data), while budget income from privatization (e.g., from selling state firms in auctions, from emission of shares, etc.) grew from 0.11% of GDP to 0.90% over the same period. **Table 5** presents the dynamics of growth of private firms and privatization and shows that the public sector was reduced to 10.3% of total enterprises by the end of 2002.

TABLE 5   Number of firms and organizations in Russia, 1992-2002

	Number of organizations* (thousands)	Number of organizations owned by states and municipalities* (thousands)	Share of private organizations in its total number * (%)	Enterprises privatized for a period (items)
1992	—	—	—	47,041
1993	1,245	—	—	42,929
1994	1,946	496	74.51%	21,905
1995	2,250	520	76.89	10,125
1996	2,505	384	84.67	4,997
1997	2,727	287	89.48	2,743
1998	2,890	283	90.21	2,129
1999	3,087	295	90.44	1,536
2000	3,347	367	89.03	2,274
2001	3,594	386	89.26	2,287
2002	3,845	396	89.70	2,557

* By the end of a year.

Source: *Annual Review of Economic Policy in Russia in 2002*. Russian Bureau of Economic Analysis (2003, p. 516).

In addition, **Table 6** shows that slightly more than a third of all employed people worked for state or municipal organizations in 2001. A comparison of data from Table 5 and Table 6 shows that small and medium enterprises prevail among those in private ownership. As shown by sociological surveys and detailed later in this chapter, trade and catering sectors prevail among new private enterprises, while industry dominates among state and privatized firms (Kabalin and Clark 1999, p. 30).

During last three years, several major structural reforms have been launched in Russia, including adoption of a new tax code aimed at reducing the complexity of the tax system, which eliminates various tax privileges and reduces the tax burden on firms and enterprises. In the course of tax reform contribution payments for four budget funds (state Pension Funds, state Employment Funds, Fund of Social Security, and that of Mandatory Medical Insurance) were replaced by a Single (unified) Social Tax (or SST), which had a regressive tax scale. The maximum SST rate is 35.6% for employees (26.4% for individual entrepreneurs) with annual remuneration up to 100 thousand rubles; the minimum SST rate is 5% (2% since January 2003) for employees with annual

TABLE 6 Structure of annually employed population by forms of ownership, 1980-2001 (%, total employment=100)

			Type of ownership		
	State and municipal	Private	Public-service and religious organizations (associations)	Mixed Russian	Foreign, mutual Russian, and foreign
1980	90.4%	9.6%	...	...	...
1985	91.1	8.9	...	...	...
1990	82.6	12.5	0.8%	4.0%	0.1%
1995	42.1	34.4	0.7	22.2	0.6
1996	42.0	35.6	0.6	21.0	0.8
1997	40.0	39.9	0.6	18.3	1.2
1998	38.1	43.2	0.7	16.4	1.6
1999	38.2	44.3	0.8	14.9	1.8
2000	37.9	46.1	0.8	12.5	2.7
2001	37.4	47.6	0.8	11.6	2.6

Source: Labor and Employment in Russia in 2001 (Goskomstat 2002, 55).

incomes over 600 thousand rubles. In addition, the progressive scale of income tax for individuals was replaced by a flat tax rate of 13% of individual incomes that introduced some social deductions (for education, health care, etc.). All these measures were aimed at reducing the scope of hidden remuneration of labor. At the same time, the new tax code obliged individual entrepreneurs to pay value-added taxes (VAT). In 2001 profit tax was reduced to 24%, but most of the previously existing privileges and deductions were eliminated. Small firms can simplify their accounting system and taxation further if they choose the less-complex released procedure of taxation, which has been in place since 2003. The Russian government is currently discussing additional amendments to tax regulation aimed at lowering the tax burden, which are expected to be implemented by 2005.

Poverty and inequality in Russia

The incidence of poverty increased sharply during Russia's period of economic transition. Official measurement of the poverty rate is based on the absolute concept of poverty with the subsistence minimum as a poverty line (**Table 7**). The methodology of subsistence minimum assessment changed in 1992 and 2000, leading to incomparability of official poverty rates (**Figure B**).

Depending on the indicator that is being compared with the poverty line (either money income or disposable resources) as well as on the data source used, there are variations even in official poverty rates (**Figure C**). Early evidence shows that the poverty rate depends on the following factors:

- *Geographical position.*

- *Type of settlement*—rural and urban citizens differ substantially in access to jobs and incomes; people from single-industry towns and small hamlets have limited access to the labor market.

- *Age and gender*—these two factors, both in themselves and as characteristics of household composition, determine the potential number of employed and dependant members within the household and indicate poverty risk.

- *Employment status*—determines degree of access to incomes and social guarantees.

- *Education*—important both in terms of access to higher stages of education and access to education of higher quality, which determines the further transition from education to the labor market.

- *Health and disability*—including living standards and styles of living that substantially influence health.

- *Housing quality type and ownership*—in terms of cost issues, ownership, and rental status opening out poverty differentials more sharply as rents rise.

- *Transport availability*—access to services, earnings opportunities, and access to livelihood.

It is significant that, despite its high degree of incidence, much of the poverty in Russia is relatively transitory, with nearly 55% of the poor escaping poverty on their own over the one-year period between

TABLE 7 Personal incomes and subsistence minimum in Russia, 1990-2002

	Monthly personal income per capita * (RUR)	Official subsistence minimum ** (RUR)	Ratio of average income to subsistence minimum ** (times)	Share of population with incomes below subsistence minimum ** (%)	Real personal income per capita*** (2000=100)	Growth rate to a previous period (%)
1990	—	0.1	—	—	145.9	—
1991	0.5	0.2	3.0	—	188.2	29.0
1992	4.0	1.9	2.1	33.5	92.8	-50.7
1993	44.8	20.6	2.2	31.5	111.3	19.8
1994	206.4	86.6	2.4	22.4	128.4	15.4
1995	514.9	264.1	2.0	24.7	109.8	-14.5
1996	769.1	369.9	2.1	22.0	111.3	1.4
1997	941.0	411.2	2.3	21.2	118.9	6.8
1998	1,010.6	493.3	2.1	24.6	100.7	-15.3
1999	1,655.8	907.8	1.8	33.2	87.7	-12.9
2000	2,275.2	1,030.5	2.2	26.4	100.0	14.0
2001	3,052.0	1,248.9	2.4	19.5	110.5	10.5
2002	3,938.1	1,468.2	2.7	18.5	121.6	10.1

*   According to the concept of Russia's state statistical agency.

**   Quarter estimates follow new methodology of subsistence minimum calculation (introduced in 2000). For comparative purposes annual data are provided by the former methodology.

*** According to the Goskomstat concept, taking into account dynamics of CPI.

Source: *Annual Review of Economic Policy in Russia in 2001*; Russian Bureau of Economic Analysis (2002, p. 352); *Annual Review of Economic Policy in Russia in 2002*; Russian Bureau of Economic Analysis (2003, p. 477).

FIGURE B Share of population with incomes below subsistence minimum (SM) measure by different methodologies, 1991-2001 (%)

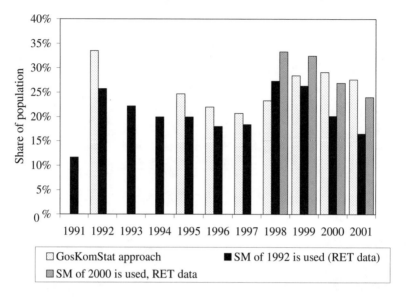

Note: RET=Russian Economic Trends.

Sources: *Russia's Statistical Yearbook* (2002, p. 591); *Russia in Figures* (2003, p. 338).

1995 and 1996 (Office of the U.N. 2002, p. 8). This implies that the potential for reducing poverty broadly and rapidly via economic growth is high. Indeed, independent research suggests a decrease in the incidence of poverty in Russia over the last three years was driven largely by significant economic growth. According to the UN Common Country Assessment, as the economy experienced real growth for the first time in many years in 1999 and 2000, "the incidence of poverty declined sharply—from 38% in 1998 to 29% in 2000—implying that nearly 13 million Russians escaped poverty during this two-year period.[2] Since the distribution of income actually deteriorated slightly during this time (with the Gini coefficient rising from 39.4% to 40.1%), the decline in poverty appears to have been driven entirely by economic growth" (Office of the UN 2002, p. 6).

Nevertheless, the so-called "underclass" does exist in modern Russia. As the World Bank (2000) found, 14% of Russia's population remained consistently poor over the four-year period from 1994 to 1998,

FIGURE C   Variation in official poverty rates between sources, 1992-2001

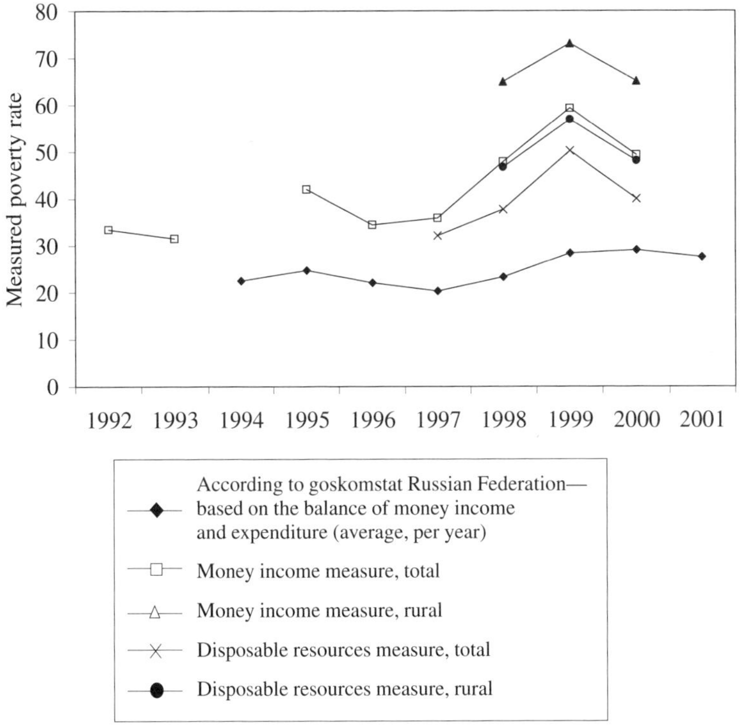

Legend:

—◆— According to goskomstat Russian Federation—based on the balance of money income and expenditure (average, per year)

—□— Money income measure, total

—△— Money income measure, rural

—✕— Disposable resources measure, total

—●— Disposable resources measure, rural

Sources: *Review of Economic Policy in Russia in 2002* (2003, p. 503).

among which nearly 75% live in households with four or more members (World Bank 2000).[3]

It has been acknowledged that job quality plays an important role in a person's well-being, and, accordingly, further dynamics of poverty will depend on the number and quality of jobs created in the course of economic growth. One of the main features of Russia's transition labor market is the expansion of the number of jobs paying poverty-level wages concentrated in the public sector (public education, health care, social services, etc.).

As far as living standards are concerned, economic reforms have resulted not only in a decline in real income but also in a sharp increase in wage differentiation. Additionally, increased income inequality has resulted in part from a shift of income from wages to income from own-

TABLE 8   Structure of personal money incomes in Russia (in billions of rubles), 1990-2001

	Money incomes, including:*				
	Remuneration**	Social transfers	Ownership income	Other income***	Total money income
1990	76.3	15.8	2.6	5.3	100.0
1991	62.7	16.9	13.3	8.4	100.0
1992	73.2	14.1	1.4	11.3	100.0
1993	61.1	15.0	3.0	21.0	100.0
1994	64.5	13.5	4.5	17.5	100.0
1995	60.7	12.7	6.3	20.3	100.0
1996	64.5	13.7	5.2	16.6	100.0
1997	65.2	14.9	5.7	14.1	100.0
1998	64.7	13.1	5.5	16.7	100.0
1999	65.4	13.6	7.4	13.6	100.0
2000	65.6	13.4	7.2	13.8	100.0
2001	64.5	14.9	5.5	15.1	100.0

*   In accordance with the Goskomstat concept.
**   Since 1992, remuneration includes the hidden wage.
*** Other income, calculated by residual method, includes entrepreneurial income.

Source: *Annual Review of Economic Policy in Russia in 2001*; Russian Bureau of Economic Analysis (2002, p. 349).

ership, which is typically distributed more unequally than wage income (**Table 8**).

Table 9 shows official data from Goskomstat (the Russian government's statistical agency) that provide estimates for income differentiation; however, it should be noted that most researchers do not agree with these estimates and believe the real differentiation to be much higher. This problem has been considered in detail in the Human Development Report for 2001 (UNDP 2001), in which the authors have argued that the actual level of wage differentiation in Russia was two times higher than the Goskomstat report shows.

Human development

At the beginning of 1990s, a new concept of human development was developed by experts of the United Nations Development Program (UNDP). This approach focused on the potential for human development by means of increasing life expectancy, providing better access to educa-

TABLE 9   Distribution of total money income, coefficients of differentiation, and concentration of income, 1991-2000

	Total money income	First quintile (lowest incomes)	Second quintile	Third quintile	Fourth quintile	Fifth (highest incomes)	Decile coefficient of differentiation
1991	100.0%	11.9%	15.8%	18.8%	22.8%	30.7%	4.5%
1992	100.0	6.0	11.6	17.6	26.5	38.3	8.0
1993	100.0	5.8	11.1	16.7	24.8	41.6	11.2
1994	100.0	5.3	10.2	15.2	23.0	46.3	15.1
1995	100.0	5.5	10.2	15.0	22.4	46.9	13.5
1996	100.0	6.2	10.7	15.1	21.6	46.4	13.0
1997	100.0	5.9	10.2	14.1	21.6	47.5	13.2
1998*	100.0	6.2	10.4	14.8	21.2	47.6	13.8
1999	100.0	6.1	10.4	14.7	20.9	47.9	14.0
2000	100.0	6.0	10.4	14.8	21.2	47.6	13.7
2001	100.0	5.6	10.4	15.4	22.8	45.8	13.8
2002	100.0	5.6	10.4	15.4	22.8	45.8	13.8
First half of 2003 **	100.0	5.5	10.3	15.2	22.7	46.3	14.6

* Data for 1988 are taken from the *National Economy of the USSR in 1988* (p. 94).
** Data for 2002 and 2003 are taken from the Current Statistical Survey, No. 3 (46) (2003, p. 21).

Source: *Annual Review of Economic Policy in Russia in 2001*; Russian Bureau of Economic Analysis (2002, p. 349).

tion, and facilitating income growth. In this way, human development is treated as both a goal and means of social progress. The index for measuring human development, published in 1990, varies from 0 to 1. The closer the value of the index to 1, the more opportunities a country provides for human development. Indices of human development of Russia are presented in **Table 10.** According to the values of these indices, Russia is a country with a medium level of development. For the purposes of this report it should also be noted that 100% of Russia's population are literate, and nearly three-fourths of people between the ages of seven and 24 are students. Russia is a country with a high level of education, which was of very good quality during the Soviet era. The transition period saw a remarkable growth in the number of students and institutions within the higher education system. The number of students more than doubled between 1990 and 2002 (from 2.825 million people in 1990 to 5.948 million in 2002), and the number of graduates almost doubled (401,000 and 753,000 in 1990 and 2002, respectively) (Goskomstat 2003, p. 328).

Simultaneously, the number of institutions of higher education (academies, institutes, universities) has almost doubled; there were 1,039 institutions in 2002-03, two-thirds were owned by the state (Russia in Figures 2003, p. 119). But the number of institutions and students at the primary occupational education level (i.e., in basic trade schools) has slightly decreased for the same period, while the number of students at secondary vocational educational institutions was near constant. These changes in the vocational education structure certainly had an effect on the labor market. There are too many people with higher education and not sufficient number of young people with primary or secondary vocational grounding. The changing economy in Russia makes it more difficult for those with a college education to find jobs. Another consequence is a different profile of informal employment in Russia compared to that in the developing world.

Labor market regulation and trends

Regulation
The Labor Code regulates employment at all types of organizations in Russia. The New Labor Code acts were established in February 2002, while before that the Code of 1971 was used. Since 1991, employment

TABLE 10   Indices of human development, 1985-2003

	GDP per capita (in U.S. dollars) *	Life expectancy at birth (in years)	Ratio of students in population of 7 to 24-year-olds	Share of literate people among adult population	Index of human development (HDI)	Rank by HDI
1985	—	68.1	—	—	—	—
1986	—	69.3	—	—	—	—
1987	—	70.1	—	—	—	—
1988	—	69.9	—	—	—	—
1989	—	69.6	—	—	—	—
1990	—	—	—	—	—	—
1991	—	69.0	—	—	—	—
1992	—	67.9	—	—	—	—
1993	—	65.1	—	—	0.804	57
1994	—	64.0	—	—	—	—
1995	$5,700.0	64.6	—	98.4%	0.760	52
1996	—	—	—	—	0.693	67
1997	4,370.0	66.6	77%	99.0	0.766	71
1998	6,508.0	67.0	71.4	100.0	0.766	62
1999	7,473.0	65.9	74.0	100.0	0.771	—
2000	—	65.3	—	100.0	0.771	—
2001	—	65.3	—	99.8	0.775	—
2002	—	64.8	—	99.8	0.781	—
2003	—	—	—	99.8	—	63

* In 1998, Goskomstat changed the methods of calculating purchasing power parity in accordance with international standards.

Source: Human Development Index, United Nations Development Program (UNDP 2003).

has been regulated by the Law on Employment of Population of Russian Federation. When compared with the labor legislation in other OECD members, Russia's labor norms are rather strict. In Soviet times such rigidity of labor regulation tended to keep labor mobility at very low levels. In the beginning of the 1990s, complicated procedures of mass dismissal were introduced because of the anxieties of high unemployment. As a result, an employer's actions are substantially limited both in the areas of layoffs for economic reasons and the conclusion of fixed-terms contracts. The former are permitted only if submitted to labor unions and the other parties involved in collective agreements and announced in writing two or three months before the actual layoff. Moreover, employers are required to pay dismissed employees remuneration for three months. Other types of employment terminations are also difficult for an employer; for example, employers are required to form a special commission to approve that an employee is inadequate for a job. All of these barriers increase costs of dismissals for an employer.

The New Labor Code kept a set of previous restrictions on fixed-term labor contracts. Such contracts can be concluded only if there are serious causes for termination, cannot last more than five years, and cannot be renewed. These norms increase the costs of hiring.

Contrary to the labor legislation in many developing countries, there are a lot of social guarantees afforded employees in Russia. Some of these guarantees strengthen discrimination against certain social groups in the labor market. For instance, some legally mandated benefits for women with children provided at the expense of the employer prevent employers from hiring women into executive positions.

The discrepancy between the institutional structure supported by legislation and that formed in the course of transformation provoked employers into violating the labor legislation. The most obvious form of illegal labor practices is informal hiring based on verbal agreements. One of the most popular of these "gray remuneration" schemes involved payments made either in cash or though special insurance of private pension programs. During the 1990s, direct transgressions of labor legislation—such as wage arrears and longer durations of working hours—were widespread. Even by September 2003 wage arrears at medium and large enterprises comprised 30.7 billion rubles and covered 5.3 million employees.

The New Labor Code strengthened sanctions for irregular remuneration payments, although overall, according to expert estimates, the magnitude of employers' social liabilities has even grown after the new code introduction (Maleva et al. 2001). Kapelyushnikov and Gimpelson, for example, have demonstrated that after two years of implementation, the New Labor Code did not seriously change the employment policy of industrial enterprises. Enforcement of these labor laws seems to be insufficient (Kapelyushnikov and Gimpelson 2004).

Unions

The notion of social partnership emerged with liberalization and the development of new influences on Russia's labor market. The following laws regulate the relationship between unions and employers: Collective Treaties and Agreements (1992); On Procedure of Settlement of Collective Disputes (1995); On Trade Unions, Their Rights and Guarantees of Their Activity (1996); and On Russian Tripartite Commission on Regulation of Social and Labor Relations (1999). All of these documents are aimed at regulating labor relations between employees and with their representatives, including trade unions.

Although trade unions existed in Soviet enterprises, their role was completely different from that in developed market economies. Membership in trade unions was obligatory and absolutely formal. Trade unions were very large and had wide latitude, but normally advocated for employers and were concentrated on social and cultural arrangements.

During the period of transition, labor unions could not adequately answer the challenges of new economic realities, and their role diminished. According to a Carnegie Moscow Center (CMC) survey, at the end of 2000 only 4.6% of respondents between the ages of 18 and 54 (for women) and the ages of 18 and 59 (for men) participated in trade unions actively; 53.1% of respondents were not trade union members, while the other 10.4% did not know whether they were members or not.

After the decade of reform, no official trade unions existed in the new private sector, but some informal and unstable unions of employees arose for solving current disputes with employers or for defending employees' rights in some areas. In the public sector, trade unions still exist, but their role is very limited and passive, fully focusing on the cultural life of employees. Activities of trade unions at privatized industrial enterprises are the most diversified and include participation in settling many employment-related issues. But even in private industry the role of trade unions has diminished during the period of reform. According to a sociological survey conducted by Zaslavskaya and her colleagues in 2001, only 5% of budgetary-sponsored employees and 7.5% of employees from industrial privatized enterprises considered trade unions as capable of influencing an employer (Zaslavskaya 2002, p. 247-9).

Trends in employment

Because the idea of mandatory total employment was supported during the Soviet era, there was no information on activity rates and unemployment in Russia until 1992. Hence, we cannot compare how activity rates changed between the end of 1980s and the 1990s. Official data, obtained by means of Labor Force Surveys (LFS), showed decreases in activity rates of all age groups from 1992 to 1998. The number of labor force participants decreased despite a moderate increase in the number of people of working age. As more detailed trends of economic activity show, labor force participation rates decreased faster for two age groups at either end of the spectrum: the youngest (age 15-19) and the oldest (age 60-72). As will be discussed later, it has been shown that both groups tend to have informal or occasional work more often than other age groups. Activity rates for these (and other) groups increase after taking into account their involvement into household activities, including subsistence farming (Maleva et al. 2002, p. 31). There is no accurate quantitative evidence on the dynamics of economic activity during the late 1980s and early 1990s, but researchers have made a number of findings regarding Russia's economic situation. Gimpelson (2002) suggests that declining accessibility of infant schools (i.e., kindergartens) along with increasing demand for vocational education and the growth of the reservation wage were the main reasons that young people were pushed out of the labor market. Gimpelson found that a number of factors contributed to lower labor market participation for older workers: falling demand for education and labor market experience, early retirement programs, and pension reforms that withheld pension income from people still working (Maleva et al. 2002, p. 34). Increased demand for higher education can also be interpreted as a response to the low likelihood of young labor market entrants finding decent work in the Russian labor market. For pensioners (a group which includes almost all people 60 years of age and older), inactivity could also be related to growth of real pensions in relation to real wages during the first half of the 1990s.

There was a noticeable increase in labor market activity rates in 1999 (**Table 11**). This increase in labor force participation had two possible causes. First, it can reflect an income effect, in which a sharp decline in real incomes pushed people into the labor market. Second, increased rates of labor force participation could be due to changes in the methodology used by Russia's state statistical agency (Goskomstat), which changed the LFS sample by beginning to include employment within the household for productive purposes in measures of overall employment (Vishnevskaia et al. 2002, p. 30). We cannot test how the shift from annual to quarterly surveys and the changes in the sample reflected on the activity rates. **Table 11** shows the difference between old and new methods of measuring activity. There were 71.8 million

TABLE 11 Labor market indicators, 1970–2002*

Year	Active population ages 15-72 (in millions)**	Economically active population (in millions)	Employed population (in millions)***	Unemployment according to the ILO (in millions)	Hours worked (in billions)	Labor productivity (2000 = 100)****
1970	NA	NA	64.0	NA	NA	NA
1980	NA	NA	73.3	NA	NA	NA
1985	NA	NA	74.9	NA	NA	NA
1989	105.4	NA	75.6	NA	NA	NA
1990	106.1	NA	75.3	NA	NA	NA
1991	106.9	NA	73.8	NA	NA	NA
1992	107.4	74.9	72.1	3.9	NA	NA
1993	107.9	72.9	70.9	4.3	NA	NA
1994	108.5	70.5	68.5	5.7	NA	NA
1995	109.2	70.9	66.4	6.7	NA	NA
1996	109.6	69.1	66.0	7.2	NA	NA
1997	109.9	68.1	64.7	8.1	NA	NA
1998	110.3	67.3	63.8	8.9	NA	NA
1999	110.7	70.4	64.0	9.1	126.6	NA
2000	110.8	NA	64.3	NA	130.5	NA
2001	NA	NA	64.7	NA	NA	NA
2002*****	110.7	71.9	65.4	6.2	NA	NA

(*continued*)

TABLE 11 (cont.) Labor market indicators, 1970-2002*

Year	Active population ages 15-72 (in millions)**	Economically active population (in millions)	Employed population (in millions)***	Unemployment according to the ILO (in millions)	Hours worked (in billions)	Labor productivity (2000 = 100)****
*Data taken from BEA Annual Economic Review:******						
1999	110.2	71.8	62.5	9.3	142.6	92.7
2000	110.3	71.8	64.3	7.5	145.5	100.0
2001	110.4	70.8	64.4	6.4	150.6	101.5
2002	110.4	71.8	66.1	5.7	153.3	103.9

*   Data on economically active population and unemployment for the period until 1999 are for the fourth quarter of a year, and measured by the old methodology of LFS.

**   At the beginning of a year.

***   Data on employment in 1989-2000 measured by the method of balance of labor resources.

*****   Real GDP per one hour of work.

******   Estimates by Goskomstat (Labor and Employment in Russia).

*******   Data on labor force, employment, and unemployment are average figures from quarter observations, measured by new methodology (including HH production); data for 2001-02 are based on incomparable methodology.

Sources: *Annual Review of Economic Policy in Russia in 2002*; Russian Bureau of Economic Analysis (2003, p. 481); *Employment Outlook in Russia*, Issue 1 (2002, pp. 16, 72, 241, 243); *Labor and Employment in Russia* (Goskomstat 2003, p. 31, 35, 105, 181).

employed people in Russia in 2002. It is notable that activity rates for women, although reduced, remained at a relatively high level even compared to developed economies (Table 11).

Employment
The data on the dynamics of employment at firms, enterprises, and organizations during Russia's economic transition was obtained from different sources, including enterprises' accounts (census), the LFS, and the balance of labor resources (BLR)[4] provide different estimates. For instance, in 2000 employment measured by the LFS comprised 56.6 million people; by the BLR, 52.7 million (1999 data); and by the census of enterprises, 51.2 million. The decline is the largest according to accounting statistics and the smallest as measured by LFS. Experts explain such differences either by statistical error in the LFS or by an expanded definition of the term "enterprise" by respondents in the LFS. According to the latter hypothesis, in 1999-2000 estimates of employment by the LFS covered employment at unofficial, not registered, informal enterprises. Growth in employment after the crisis of 1998 occurred mostly due to an increase in the informal component (Maleva et al. 2002, p. 61-2).

The data on employment presented in Table 11 are based on the BLR method of measurement. Figures exclude military personnel but include people employed at subsistence plots and shadow—i.e., unofficial—employment. There is evidence that current estimates of employment based either on the balance method or on the LFS provide a similar employment picture up until 1999, when the LFS underestimated employment because it ignored employment within the household (e.g., subsistence farming). Table 1 and Table 11 show that the decline in employment was much less than the drop in output.

The unemployment rate
The unemployment rate is one of the best indicators of the situation of a nation's labor market. Among the four approaches to measuring unemployment proposed by the International Labor Organization, the following two are most popular in Russia: 1) the rates of so-called "general unemployment" as measured on the base of the LFS according to the ILO criteria, and 2) measures of registered (by Employment Fund) unemployment. Data on both measures have been available only since the beginning of the 1990s. The two measures of unemployment show sub-

stantially different unemployment rates in Russia (**Figure D**). The ratio of registered unemployment dramatically underestimates actual unemployment. For instance, it does not include people younger than 16, people who were discouraged from looking for further work, students, pensioners, etc. The rate of registered unemployment depends heavily on regulation. For instance, in 1996 new amendments to the Law on Employment, aimed mostly at toughening the rules of registering people as unemployed, were introduced. Additionally, the worsening financial situation of the Employment Fund since mid-1995 meant that most of the Fund's resources were used to pay benefits (which still did not prevent benefit arrears). These factors have caused declines in the number of registered unemployed people since 1996.

In accordance with the ILO criteria, a person is deemed to be unemployed if he or she has no job, but is searching for a job and is ready to start work within a short period of time (two weeks in Russia). The data on the unemployment rate according to these criteria are available for people between 15 and 72 years old, including students and pensioners. Thus, general unemployment is a better estimator of unemployment in Russia, and further figures will refer to this measure. From Figure G, one can see that, unlike other transition countries, Russia's unemployment rose slowly and smoothly and has never reached dramatic values. Contrary to the dynamics of registered unemployment, the general unemployment grew throughout most of the 1990s, then peaked with a lag after the crisis of 1998, and—owing to economic growth—has constantly decreased since 1999.

Long-term unemployment (unemployment lasting more than a year) comprised 11.1% of all unemployment in 1992 and 42.3% in 2000, covering 4.2% of the total labor force in 2000 (**Figure E**). In 2001 long-term unemployment comprised 36.9% of total unemployment. Compared with other countries, this rate is not bad, especially taking into account that it is decreasing as the economic recovery progresses (Maleva et al. 2002, p. 110). The problem is that persistent unemployment is geographically concentrated in certain regions, especially those that have experienced little economic growth (UN 2002, p. 6). Figures on extended unemployment are not inflated by generous benefits: they are capped at one year (**Figure F**).

Another important issue is the unequal dispersion of unemployment among different socio-economic groups. Unemployment among women,

FIGURE D   General and registered unemployment for men and women (as a percentage of Russia's labor force), 1992-2002

Source: ILO and authors' calculations using Goskomstat data.

for example, is almost the same as among men in Russia (Figure H). Moreover, there are fewer women counted as unemployed by the ILO, but more of them are among the ranks of the registered unemployed. The gap between urban and rural employment in Russia is small by international standards, at 9.6% and 11.6%, respectively. Russian unemployment among youth, as in other countries, is much higher than other groups, reaching 19.6% in 2000. At the same time, in so far as the duration of unemployment indirectly indicates the level of access to jobs, it becomes clear that the ratio of long-term unemployment is higher for women, rural citizens, and senior citizens, while young people account mainly for short-term unemployment. Moreover, young people as a group show the largest discrepancy between registered and general unemployment.

Both the level and the duration of unemployment are in general negatively correlated with education (**Table 12**). Unemployment among people without general education was 17.6% in 2000, and job searches for this group often lasted up to three years (Maleva et al. 2002, p. 121).

FIGURE E   Structure of general unemployment by its duration, 1992-2001

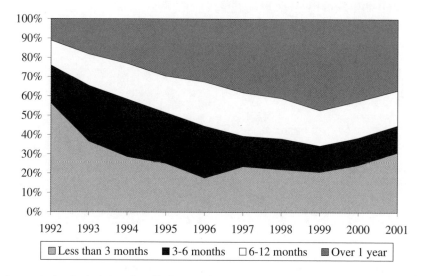

Source: Authors' calculations from Goskomstat data.

FIGURE F   Structure of registered unemployment by its duration

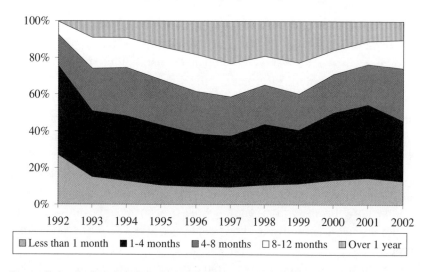

Source: Authors' calculations from Goskomstat data.

TABLE 12   Rate of general unemployment by education level, 1992-2002

Year*	Higher education	Not finished higher education	Specialized secondary	Primary vocational	Secondary	General	Lower than general
Data taken from ILO							
1992	3.3%	9.9%	4.5%	—	5.9%	6.6%	4.0%
1993	3.5	10.4	5.3	—	6.7	7.8	4.1
1994	4.8	11.2	7.3	—	9.5	10.7	6.4
1995	5.0	13.5	8.3	—	11.6	12.9	7.3
1996	4.5	12.8	8.6	—	11.7	14.1	7.7
1997	5.7	14.2	10.2	15.9	14.2	17.6	15.9
1998	7.1	16.5	11.4	17.3	16.2	19.4	17.5
1999	7.1	14.8	10.6	15.5	16.1	19.9	23.4
2000	5.3	9.0	7.9	11.4	13.5	16.5	17.6
*Data taken from Russia's state statistical agency (Goskomstat)**:*							
1999	7.1%	14.7%	10.5%	15.3%	15.7%	18.2%	16.9%
2000	5.3	8.9	7.8	11.3	13.2	15.0	11.7
2001	4.3	11.1	7.3	9.9	12.5	15.1	9.9
2002	4.0	9.3	6.7	9.5	12.2	16.5	12.5

*   Employment Outlook figures.
** Author's calculation by average annual data taken from LFS and published by Goskomstat.

Sources: *Employment Outlook in Russia*, Issue 1 (2002, p. 116); *Labor and Employment in Russia* (Goskomstat 2003, pp. 67, 133).

Extremely low unemployment benefits given for only 12 months can cause so-called *hidden unemployment*, which refers to people on forced administrative leaves or involuntarily employed part time as well as people with episodic and irregular work or those who want work but have given up actively seeking a job because they are discouraged about the prospects of finding one. These groups of people may enter the informal labor market. As **Table 13** shows, the share of discouraged workers has increased over the last decade.

As employment decreased less than output, excessive employment at enterprises may have resulted in expanded *underemployment* of employees. **Table 14** shows the dynamics of overall underemployment measured by combining different methods. Underemployment picked up in the beginning of economic reforms. Although the problem persists, it has been decreasing since 1999.

TABLE 13   Economically inactive population by groups, 1992-2000

Year	All inactive population (in millions)	Inactive population ages 16-59 (in millions)	Wanted to work	Did not want to work	Did not want to work, including discouraged workers	Ratio of discouraged people in inactive population of working ages, %
1992	31.6	13.1	—	—	172	1.31%
1993	34.12	14.8	—	—	294	1.99
1994	37.4	15.6	—	—	587	3.77
1995	38.4	16.5	—	—	731	4.43
1996	39.6	17.6	—	—	931	5.29
1997	41.2	19.1	14,674	4,388	962	5.05
1998	42.6	20.1	15,571	4,496	1092	5.44
1999	39.9	18.6	12,587	6,045	1386	7.44
2000	40.6	19.0	13,182	5,805	1259	6.63

Source: *Employment Outlook in Russia*, Issue 1 (2002, p.137).

Another way of adjusting to excessive employment is *wage arrears*, which appeared in the beginning of the 1990s. Wage arrears still exist even now, despite several years of economic growth and toughening sanctions for back pay. The practice seems to be growing again as the economic situation in Russia becomes worse.

More to the point, some economists explain growth in *employment in the public sector*, including state employees, as a way to absorb excessive labor resources. In Russia the number of state and municipal employees increased during all the periods of reform. Even between 1994 and 2002 the number of state and municipal employees increased from 1.0 million people to 1.3 million, totaling 1.5% and 1.9% of employment, respectively.[5]

Labor productivity

As set forth by Maleva et al. (2002, pp. 244-45), experts mark out four periods in the dynamics of labor productivity during the transition decade (**Table 15**). The first, spanning 1990-91, was characterized by a reduction of all figures, including output and employment; productivity was stable as a result. Across 1992-94, output slumped, while employment and average hours worked also diminished but to a lesser degree. Therefore, labor productivity slightly decreased in the early 1990s. During the third period of change in labor productivity, between 1995 and

TABLE 14   Underemployment in Russia as a percentage of total employment, 1992-2000

Year	Under-employment level	Voluntary under-employment	Forced under-employment	Forced under-employment due to economic reasons
1992	3.1%	0.6%	2.5%	2.3%
1993	3.9	0.6	2.7	2.4
1994	5.5	0.6	4.4	4.1
1995	5.2	0.6	4.1	3.7
1996	6.0	0.5	5.0	4.5
1997	3.1	0.2	2.9	2.6
1998	4.0	0.2	3.8	3.5
1999	3.3	0.3	2.5	2.1
2000	2.0	0.3	1.4	1.0

Source: *Employment Outlook in Russia*, Issue 1 (2002, p. 179).

1998, rates of decline of GDP were less than in the previous period, but rates of reduction of employment and working hours were at least the same, which resulted in an increase in productivity. In 1996, labor productivity in Russia was equal to 26.5% of that in the United States and 32.7% of that in Japan (Goskomstat of Russia). Finally, in the final period between 1999 and 2000, the economy had recovered from the crisis of 1998, and output, employment, and working hours had increased. However, as a consequence of growth in employment and working hours lagging behind GDP growth, reported figures on labor productivity have strongly improved, especially in industry. **Table 15** also shows that productivity in the overall economy is less than in industry, with an increasing gap during the last few years. Productivity is declining if employment at small firms and secondary employment arc taken into account.

It has already been shown that employment in the private sector rose over all the periods of reforms (Table 6). The most significant changes in employment structure covered shifts across branches. The number of people employed in industry and construction significantly decreased, while employment in commercial services such as trade or finance services and administration, increased (**Table 16** and **Figure G**).

TABLE 15   Annual figures of labor productivity per hour in industry, 1989-2000 (RUR per hour)

Year	Industry*	Economy**
1989	81.3	—
1990	83.7	—
1991	82.4	—
1992	73.0	65.4
1993	66.8	63.4
1994	64.2	59.2
1995	66.1	58.1
1996	69.1	58.5
1997	75.1	59.5
1998	74.9	57.3
1999	77.2	59.1
2000	82.8	62.9

*   Productivity is a quotient from division of employment (measured by Balance of Labor Resources) by hours worked (by large and medium enterprises).
** Productivity is measured by LFS and includes data on secondary employment.

Source: *Employment Outlook in Russia*, Issue 1 (2002, p. 243).

The transition to a market economy resulted in shifts from employment in large and medium enterprises to employment in small ones. For the period from 1991 to 2000, employment in large and medium enterprises fell 30%, which was much higher than the decline in overall employment. Nevertheless, even in 2000, according to enterprise accounts, nearly two-thirds of employment was concentrated in this segment of the labor market (Maleva 2002, p. 52). A majority of large and medium enterprises are found in industry, especially in the power and fuel industry and ferrous and non-ferrous metallurgy.

The definition of a "small firm" for the purposes of Russian statistics has been changed several times and is extremely complicated. In addition to the different number limitations (varying by branches), legislation has introduced restrictions on activity (only commercial activity is taken into account) and the structure of the authorized capital stock of such organizations. In regards to the number of employees, regulations state that small firms should not have more than 100 people in the industries of construction, and transport; 60 people in agriculture and R&D; 30 people in retail trade and consumer services; and 50 employ-

TABLE 16 Structure of annual employment in economy by branches, 1980-2002 (%)

	1980	1990	1991	1992	1993	1994	1995	1996	1997	1998	1999	2000	2001	2002
Industry	32.50	30.28	30.34	29.59	29.36	27.12	25.84	24.82	23.04	22.19	22.35	22.61	22.70	22.50
Agriculture	14.63	12.91	13.18	14.02	14.26	15.01	14.67	14.04	13.28	13.67	13.28	13.01	12.26	11.68
Forestry	0.39	0.32	0.32	0.33	0.34	0.37	0.39	0.37	0.37	0.37	0.38	0.37	0.41	0.41
Construction	9.57	11.97	11.49	10.94	10.08	9.91	9.35	8.91	8.76	7.98	7.95	7.78	7.75	7.83
Transport	8.29	6.55	6.60	6.62	6.44	6.55	6.59	6.60	6.61	6.29	6.35	6.43	6.36	6.42
Communication	1.32	1.17	1.18	1.20	1.19	1.27	1.32	1.32	1.31	1.31	1.34	1.36	1.39	1.41
Wholesale and retail trade, catering	8.27	7.79	7.62	7.88	9.00	9.47	10.05	10.30	13.49	14.59	14.57	14.65	15.45	15.94
Housing and communal services	3.89	4.27	4.28	4.15	4.21	4.41	4.49	4.86	5.19	5.34	5.25	5.16	5.04	5.02
Health care, physical training, social security	4.81	5.63	5.83	5.87	5.99	6.42	6.69	6.87	6.83	6.99	7.03	7.00	7.00	7.07
Education	6.84	8.05	8.31	8.90	8.70	9.12	9.30	9.39	9.30	9.28	9.28	9.13	9.05	9.06
Culture, art	1.37	1.55	1.54	1.54	1.52	1.66	1.71	1.70	1.74	1.75	1.77	1.78	1.79	1.81
Science	4.06	3.72	3.75	3.20	3.16	2.68	2.54	2.30	2.21	2.04	1.89	1.87	1.83	1.84
Finance, credit, insurance	0.52	0.53	0.59	0.69	0.82	1.09	1.23	1.21	1.20	1.15	1.16	1.15	1.22	1.25
Administration	1.57	2.13	2.07	1.89	2.13	2.24	2.85	4.03	3.99	4.35	4.47	4.55	4.45	4.47
Other branches	1.98	3.12	2.88	3.21	2.81	2.70	2.97	3.29	2.68	2.69	2.93	3.17	3.29	3.31
Total*	100	100	100	100	100	100	100	100	100	100	100	100	100	100

* Totals may not sum exactly to 100 due to rounding.

Source: Russian Bureau of Economic Analysis.

FIGURE G   Redistribution of employment across branches, 1990-2002

Source: Authors' calculations from Goskomstat data.

ees in wholesale trade and other branches and activities. According to official statistics, in 2002 the number of organizations with 100 employees or fewer in construction was 95.3%, while the ratio of small firms (by legislation) in trade was 88.2%. In the overall economy in 2002, more than 7.7 million small firms (nearly 23% of all organizations) employed 8.8 million employees (11.8% of employment). Retail trade and catering represent 47.9% of small firms and account for 39.0% of small firms' employees. Industry and construction represent 20.0% and 18.6% of employees of small firms, respectively, while agriculture employs only 2.4% (Russia in Figures 2003, pp. 158-62).

Regarding the *gender dimension of employment*, in 2002, 31.1% of women and only 8.9% of men worked in health care, social security, education, culture, and research combined—i.e., so-called "public-sector" branches that are poorly paid and constitute the majority of the "working poor" (Labor and Employment in Russia 2003, p. 18). There are also more women than men in wholesale and retail trades and catering (20.9% for women compared to 11.4% for men). But more men than

FIGURE H Share of self-employment in total employment among men and women, 1996-2001

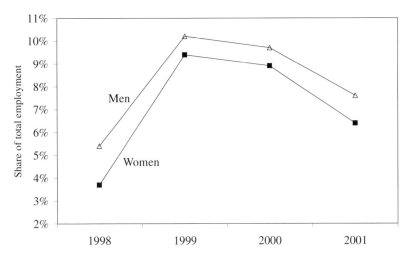

Source: Russian Bureau of Economic Analysis.

women work in industry (26.7% against 17.5%), agriculture and forestry (15.0% and 9.2%), construction (11.4% versus 3.7%), and transport and communication (10.1% compared to 5.1%) (Labor and Employment in Russia 2003, p. 18). In almost all branches, wages and salaries are lower for women than for men. There is no data on self-employment for a long period of time, but data available since 1998 prove that the share of self-employed men is higher than for women (**Figure H**).

Not surprisingly, employment is positively correlated with education. What is more important is that individual employers—i.e., unregistered business operators that employ other people—have higher education than other self-employed people and also higher educationi than paid employees (**Table 17**). Entrepreneurial activity correlates strongly with higher education: according to LFS data, 38.3% of individual employers have higher education, while the corresponding figure for the employed population as a whole is only 23.8%. At the same time, other forms of self-employment (own-account workers, non-paid family workers, etc.) absorb people with lower education, which speaks to the involuntary nature of such forms of self-employment.

TABLE 17   Distribution of employed population by education and employment status in 2001

| Education | Average | Employment | | |
		Paid employees	Self-employed	Including entrepreneurs
Higher education	23.8%	24.4%	15.8%	38.3%
Not finished higher education	2.5%	2.5%	2.5%	5.1%
Secondary special	31.1	31.5	25.3	29.1
Primary vocational	11.8	12.0	8.9	9.1
Secondary school	22.8	22.4	28.6	14.7
General (8-9 grades)	7.1	6.5	14.9	3.3
Without general	0.9	0.7	4.0	0.4
Total	100.0	100.0	100.0	100.0

Source: Authors' calculations from Goskomstat data.

Table 18 shows the dynamics of the average wage, which is marked by significant falls after liberalization of prices in 1992 and the August 1998 crisis. **Figure I** shows that, from 1991 to 1992 and from 1993 to 1996, real wages decreased faster than output, while employment declined only slightly. These data suggest that maintenance of relatively low unemployment was mostly possible by means of a sharp decrease of wages in the beginning of reforms. Wages as measured by current prices are still lower than they were in the beginning of the 1990s, although wages in dollar equivalents have grown since that time.

At the same time, processes of informalization should be taken into account. The hidden wage as a share of total wages rose throughout the period of reforms and reached 35% in 2000 (Figure I).[6] In fact, the actual wage could be higher than officially reported because, as a rule, people do not like talking about their secondary employment for tax reasons (Maleva 2002, p. 253).

There is high *wage differentiation* in Russia. **Table 19** shows the differentiation across branches, with the highest wages being paid out in the gas industry and the lowest in agriculture. Although wage differentiation within branches is even higher, the agriculture sector leads in this dimension: in 2001, the ratio of the lowest wage decile to the high-

TABLE 18 Average monthly wage of employees in Russia, 1980-2002

	Average monthly wage in curent prices			
	Rubles	USD (based on average annual official exchange rate)	Average monthly wage in constant USD	Real average monthly wage (2000=100)
1980	0.2	—	—	—
1985	0.2	—	—	—
1990	0.3	—	—	$290.3
1991	0.6	$7.50	$548.00	281.60
1992	6.0	22.00	369.00	185.00
1993	58.7	—	—	196.20
1994	220.4	—	—	179.40
1995	472.4	103.00	246.00	132.10
1995	790.2	—	—	117.10
1997	950.2	164.00	291.00	122.50
1998	1,051.0	108.00	253.00	106.00
1999	1,523.0	62.00	197.00	82.70
2000	2,223.0	79.00	238.00	100.00
2001	3,240.0	111.00	286.00	119.90
2002	4,414.0	141.00	320.00	—

Sources: *Russia in Figures, 2003* (Goskomstat 2003, p. 106); *Labor and Employment in Russia* (Goskomstat 2003, p. 358, 365); *Annual Review of Economic Policy in Russia in 2001*; Russian Bureau of Economic Analysis (2002, p. 359).

est wage decile reached 48.6 in the gas industry and 46.9 in banking. In agriculture, the ratio of the lowest wage to the average wage was the highest in 2001, and equaled 20.8.

Defining and measuring the informal sector and informal employment

Theoretical approaches to defining the informal sector and informal employment

All the processes described earlier belong to the "observable economy," i.e., the economy that can be measured statistically. At the same time,

FIGURE I   Hidden wage as a share of total wages, 1969-2000

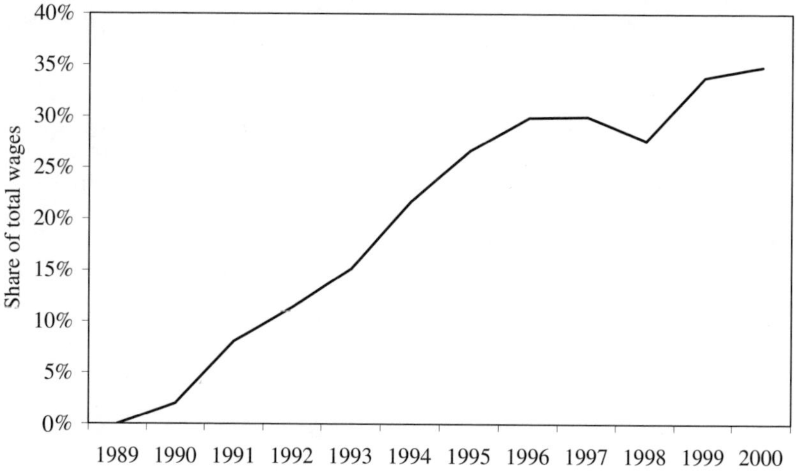

Source: Authors' calculations using Goskomstat data.

some economic processes and phenomenon cannot be captured by official statistics because of a lack of statistical instruments, data problems, or because business owners hide their activities so that they cannot be measured. The focus of this section is the issues surrounding informal employment assessment.

Studies of the informal sector—specifically, employment in the informal sector—are based on research and policy designed to provide support to developing countries in the 1970s. This approach is characterized by two main features. First, the formal and informal sectors were contrasted with each other. Second, the definition of the informal sector was based on the enterprise approach, according to which certain types of firms were labeled informal.

In compliance with the enterprise approach, the 15th International Conference on Labor Statisticians (held in January 1993) developed a conventional framework for defining and statistically measuring the informal sector. The ICLS conference reported that "the informal sector may be broadly characterized as consisting of units engaged in the production of goods or services with the primary objective of generating employment and incomes to the persons concerned. These units typi-

TABLE 19   Ratios of average wages in branches to average wage in economy, 1992-2002

Average wage=100	1992	1995	1997	1998	1999	2000	2001	2002
Industry	118.3	111.9	111.2	114.9	120.7	123.0	123.9	119.6
Oil production	336.7	301.9	315.8	275.0	339.0	407.7	440.4	376.5
Gas industry	428.3	410.8	405.6	421.9	462.6	495.1	491.5	444.6
Light industry	85.0	56.2	50.9	51.4	54.1	54.4	54.2	53.1
Food industry	126.7	117.8	114.6	115.5	118.8	107.6	104.5	100.8
Agriculture	66.7	50.1	46.2	44.5	41.3	40.1	40.3	39.4
Construction	135.0	126.0	128.5	126.5	118.3	125.7	128.3	116.8
Transport	146.7	155.9	140.8	143.7	150.7	150.4	136.9	135.9
Communication	91.7	124.1	142.8	139.8	138.5	129.5	127.5	127.6
Trade and catering	81.7	76.3	78.7	79.9	79.5	71.1	71.3	70.1
Data-processing services	81.7	86.6	122.5	125.0	126.7	146.8	121.7	125.4
Geology, hydre-meteorological service, etc.	166.7	145.0	161.9	172.3	170.9	196.6	208.4	180.6
Housing and communal services	81.7	102.4	107.0	104.9	91.5	88.1	86.3	85.2
Health care, physical training and social security	65.0	73.8	70.3	69.1	64.0	61.7	61.8	72.2
Education	61.7	65.5	64.8	62.8	58.1	55.5	56.2	66.6
Culture and art	51.7	60.6	61.6	62.2	56.1	55.3	59.1	66.6
Science	65.0	77.4	93.6	98.5	109.6	121.9	125.6	119.7
Finances, credit, and insurance	203.3	162.7	177.2	199.1	230.8	244.4	286.5	279.6
Administration	95.0	106.8	130.6	129.3	123.3	120.0	112.2	118.7

Source: Authors' analysis of Goskomstat data.

cally operate at a low level of organization, with little or no division between labor and capital as factors of production and on a small scale. Labor relations—where they exist—are based mostly on casual employment, kinship, or personal and social relations rather than contractual arrangements with formal guarantees."

For the purposes of statistics of national accounts, the informal sector is considered a part of the household sector or, equivalently, includes "unincorporated enterprises owned by households." Within the household sector, the informal sector comprises both "informal own-account enterprises" and the additional component consisting of "enterprises of informal employers."

It is important to note that the definition of the informal sector provided by the 15th ICLS conference allows significant flexibility in the operational definitions used for assessment of such sectors in different countries:

- Self-employed workers in the informal sector may cover either all self-employed workers or only those not registered in accordance with national legislation.

- In order to classify a firm as belonging to the informal sector, one or both of the following criteria may be used: (a) number of employees below a certain level, or (b) absence of registration either of a firm or of its employees.[7]

- Countries may also choose whether to include agricultural activities and domestic work in informal-sector estimations.

Following the method developed by the 15th ICLS conference, it is possible to estimate the approximate scope of employment in the informal sector using the published results of the LFS since 1999. Different (narrow and broad) approaches to such assessment are presented in **Table 20**. The main drawback to looking at informal-sector employment in such a way is that the reported LFS data do not include information on firms' registration or their size. Thus, figures obtained by this method are slightly overestimated.

It is evident that the number of entrepreneurs without registration as a "juridical person" has increased by more than 150% between 1999 and 2001.[8] A possible explanation for this increase is the change in the Russian tax system, especially the replacement of gradual individual income tax with a flat-rate tax. It can be assumed that some people from other components of employment in the informal sector became individual entrepreneurs, but there is no proof that this is the case.

Since 2001 the Russian state statistical agency (Goskomstat) has observed employment in the informal sector using criteria developed in the ICLS conference of 1993. The informal sector is regarded as a group of household enterprises or unincorporated enterprises owned by households that includes:

- informal own-account enterprises, which may employ contributing family workers and employees on an occasional basis; and

TABLE 20 Dynamics of main employment in informal sector based on different approaches to its definition (in thousands of people)

Main job	1999	2000	2001	2002	1999 q4	2000 q4	2001 q4	2002 q4
1. Entrepreneurs without registration as juridical person	2,664	2,628	4,278	4,315	2,655	2,504	3,644	3,967
2. People employed by natural persons (domestics)	2,364	2,508	2,738	2,950	2,349	2,534	2,746	2,730
3. Unpaid family workers	107	86	39	53	78	72	25	36
4. Self-employed farmers	263	161	145	124	109	163	140	83
5. Cooperatives' members	1,139	931	459	353	990	773	375	284
6. People producing something in household for future realization	2,792	2,747	869	1,964	2,430	2,379	1,215	1,545
7. People producing something in household for own consumption (working more than 30 hours per week)	1,595	1,242	1,533	1,264	683	333	334	373
Three definitions of informal employment								
Informal sector 1 = 1+2+3	5,135	5,222	7,055	7,318	5,082	5,110	6,415	6,733
Informal sector 2 = 1+2+3+6+7	9,522	9,211	9,457	10,546	8,195	7,822	7,964	8,651
Informal sector 3 = 1+2+3+4+5+6+7	10,924	10,303	10,061	11,023	9,294	8,758	8,479	9,018
Share of employment in informal sector in employment:								
Informal sector 1 = 1+2+3	8.2	8.1	11.0	11.1	8.1	7.9	9.9	10.2
Informal sector 2 = 1+2+3+6+7	15.2	14.3	14.7	16.0	13.0	12.1	12.3	13.2
Informal sector 3 = 1+2+3+4+5+6+7	17.5	16.0	15.6	16.7	14.7	13.6	13.1	13.7

Source: Authors' analysis of Goskomstat data.

- enterprises of informal employers, which employ one or more employees on a continuous basis.

In accordance with the approach of Russia's statistical agency (Goskomstat), the enterprise of informal employers must have no registration as an organization (a "juridical person," as stated in Russian legislation). There are no limits on the size of a unit, and agriculture is included.[9] People engaged in household production for realization (those who produce more than they personally need and sell the excess) are also considered to be employed in the informal sector.

As Goskomstat's data are the only numbers that can be extended to the universal state of Russia's population, they are included in this analysis. The other reason for including Goskomstat data in is that since 2001 the LFS questionnaire has contained questions on the registration of not only a firm but also a job. Therefore, if primary LFS data were available, one could estimate informal employment both inside and outside the informal sector in Russia. Unfortunately, at present Goskomstat does not report this information and does not open primary LFS data reporting. But it may be an issue in the future.

For the purposes of this report it is important to note that employment in the informal sector does not consider whether or not labor relations are registered. Therefore, this approach overlooks informal employment that exists within the formal sector.

At the same time, Russia inherited from the socialist era many large and medium-size enterprises at which more than two-thirds of all employed people in Russia are working. Strict labor regulation together with deep output declines led to accelerated informal labor among the formally registered employees at these enterprises. Formally registered small firms also used verbal agreements with employees who were entirely informal workers (i.e., unregistered employees) or partially contributed informal work to the enterprise. The most popular forms of partially informal work were gray remuneration (i.e., off-the-record payments) and different regulation of vacations and working hours.

In the past few years, the new approach to informality has triumphed over the former dualistic approach. The new approach to informal work emanates from the view of the informal economy as a continuum of relations existing in all sectors of the economy (Chen et al. 2002, p. 9). By this way of thinking, the informal economy is a sort of "fuzzy structure" that cannot be strictly contrasted with the formal economy. Therefore, the new, expanded definition of informal employment defines informal employment as employment without secure contracts (either commercial or self-employment) and without social security coverage. Informal employment can occur both inside and outside informal enterprises. This approach is called the *expanded conceptual framework* and was proposed by the International Labor Organization (ILO 2002, p. 12). For a transition economy like Russia, it is necessary to recognize the fruitfulness of this approach, which allows revealing real practices of labor relations inside both the formal and informal sectors.

At the same time, for the purposes of estimating the scope of informal employment in Russia as well as comparing the results obtained with the situation in other countries, it is necessary to develop some criteria that facilitate a distinction between purely informal labor relations, other transitory states, and purely formal relations.

For this purpose, we propose distinguishing between formal, informal, shadow, and fictitious employment (**Chart T1**).[10] These terms are defined in turn below.

- *Formal employment* refers to individuals whose actual working situation absolutely satisfies the contract terms.

- *Informal employment* is work carried out without a contract or registration.

- *Shadow employment* covers all cases in which actual labor relations differ from those described in the contract; for instance, if wages are partially paid "in envelope," or if actual wages are higher than declared in the contract.

- *Fictitious* employment reflects situations in which someone has a formal contract but does not work at all. For example, disabled people will sometimes agree to accept small remuneration in exchange for having their names listed as "employees"; the business owner is then able to reduce his tax burden by getting benefits for having a disabled employee.

To our minds, the absence of a contract enables infringements on formal labor regulations and the social security rights of the employee. The absence of a contract also means that that these informal employ-

CHART T1			
Fictitious employment	Real employment		
	With a contract		Informal
	Formal	Shadow	

Measured by statistics on employment

ees are not counted by any forms of reporting and statistics, whereas employees whose real working situation is contrary to their contracts (i.e., shadow employees) are more or less taken into account by statistics.

Hence, using the System of National Accounts (SNA) terminology, informal employment covers undeclared, unregistered employment in three sectors: formal, informal, and household (**Chart T2**). For this research we have narrowed the definition of informal employment, excluding household activities from the definition as much as possible.

There are two main groups of informally employed workers:

- *Informal self-employed*: Includes informal employers, individual entrepreneurs working without a license or a patent, unregistered farmers, members of producers' cooperatives, and unpaid workers of family enterprises.

- *Paid employees on informal jobs*: includes paid employees in informal firms, domestic workers, people involved in household production, those without permanent employers, and paid employees in formal enterprises.

Informal employment outside of informal enterprises largely consists of casual or day laborers, temporary or part-time workers, industrial outworkers (including home-workers), and unregistered or undeclared workers.

Data issues in measuring informal employment

The term "informal" describes a phenomenon or process that can hardly be measured by standard official statistics. Two approaches for measur-

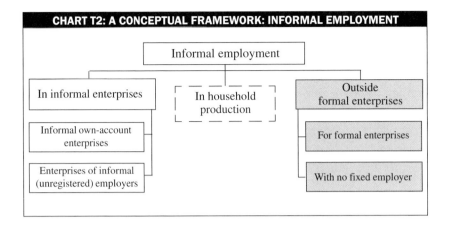

CHART T2: A CONCEPTUAL FRAMEWORK: INFORMAL EMPLOYMENT

Informal employment

In informal enterprises

In household production

Outside formal enterprises

Informal own-account enterprises

Enterprises of informal (unregistered) employers

For formal enterprises

With no fixed employer

ing informal sector and informal employment—indirect and direct measures—are usually considered.

Indirect measures include:

- the monetary approach, including analysis of demand on cash, of scope of monetary operations, and deals;

- analysis of the gap among different statistical data, particularly between incomes and expenditures of population;

- analysis of statistical data on employment;

- various methods of soft modeling and using dummy variables.

Direct measures of capturing informal employment are based on *special sociological methods,* either quantitative or qualitative, as well as on the analysis of firms' accounting systems and tax returns. Some believe that case studies are more effective for studying the essence and specific features of the informal economy and informal employment than sample-survey-based methods. At the same time, one certainly needs quantitative estimates comparable at the international level to understand the link between the informal sector and GDP growth, for example.

Compared to the censuses or the statistical reporting of enterprises, sociological surveys of the population may provide a better estimate of the scope of informal employment because employees usually have fewer reasons to hide unregistered employment than formal employment.

However, distortions of information given by people regarding income can be at least as high as those provided by employers.

As mentioned earlier, Russia's statistical agency (Goskomstat) currently reports data on employment in the informal sector exclusively and not informal employment as a whole. In the absence of special sociological data, secondary analysis of existing sociological surveys can be applied. Moreover, secondary sociological data provide a good basis for fruitful reflection over complex phenomena such as informal employment that are typically difficult to asses.

Data description and empirical definitions used in secondary data analysis

The rest of this report will be based on comparison of official LFS data with the following data sources:

- *Survey of Russia's population 18 years old and over on Social and Economic Situation of Russia's Population,* conducted by Carnegie Moscow Center (CMC) in November 2000 (N=5,028)

- *Fifth round of Russian Longitudinal Monitoring Survey (RLMS)* performed by the Institute of Sociology and Institute of Nutrition of Russian Academy of Sciences in partnership with Paragon Research International in October-December 2000 (N=approximately 4,500 households, more than 10,000 respondents). The Fourth, Fifth, and Seventh Rounds of the RLMS panel dataset were used for the analysis of dynamics of informal employment.

Estimations of the scope and dynamics of informal employment on the basis of the Russian Longitudinal Monitoring Survey (RLMS) are made for the population between the ages of 15 and 72 years old, i.e., the age limits used by Goskomstat for measuring economic activity. CMC data, on the other hand, are based on the population 18 to 72 years old. In both cases, levels of informal employment were calculated as percentages of the regularly employed and the percentage of regularly and casually employed. Panel estimations are provided for a censored sample with a lower age limit of 15 in 2002. The dynamics of informal employment from year to year are given for the population between 15 and 72 years old. Finally, for the purposes of comparing the two databases in 2000, we selected respondents age 18 and above. As there are

TABLE 21 Basic demographic characteristics of the samples

	Survey	
	RLMS	CMC
Sample size (respondents)	6,482	3,993
Rural population	25.7	25.8
Males	45.0	45.6
Younger than 30 years old	15.0	12.0
60 years old and older	21.8	29.7
With higher education	19.6	25.9
With main regular job	53.6	50.5
With second regular job	2.9	2.5
With occasional activity	9.3	7.2

Source: Russian Longitudinal Monitoring Survey (RLMS) and Carnegie Moscow Centre (CMC) data.

few working people older than age 72, variation due to changes of age limits is insignificant, but the exact interval is indicated in all the tables.

Special weights were also used for adjusting CMC data to conform with official statistics distribution by sex and rural/urban residence.[11] As a result, the data are quite comparable by main demographic indicators (**Table 21**).

A person is assumed to be employed if he or she has a paid job or is self-employed with or without employees. The main problem with the sociological data is that they are not aimed at studying employment, so standard and comprehensive questions of employment used in the LFS are omitted here. In the surveys, regular and occasional employment may be revealed. In the CMC survey regular employment is identified by positive answers to the question: "Do you currently have any regular gainful work?" Respondents are considered to be regularly employed if they report that they have gainful employment, are on maternity or parental leave for a child less than three years old, or on other paid or unpaid leave. Occasional employment was defined by positive answers to questions asking if respondents were working at an occasional job presently and during the past six months. In RLMS the following question was used for revealing occasional employment: "In the last 30 days did you engage in some additional kind of work for which you got paid? Maybe you sewed someone a dress, gave someone a ride in a car, assisted someone with apartment or car repairs, purchased and delivered food, looked after a sick person, sold purchased food or goods in a market or on the street, or did something else that you were paid for?"

If a respondent indicates that he or she has either regular gainful employment or occasional activities without any regular employment, he or she is assumed to have primary employment. In the case of primary regular employment, occasional employment activities are considered secondary. Additionally, in the CMC survey, secondary employment includes people with several regular employments (answers "more than one" to the question "How many places of employment do you have?"). In RLMS, people were asked only "Do you have some other kind of work?"

Unlike Goskomstat data, RLMS and CMC data sets collect no information on the registration of a firm at where a respondent is employed. Therefore, we cannot apply Goskomstat's empirical definition of the informal sector to our datasets. Hence, we propose the following methods to operationalize the definitions of the informal sector and informal employment for the purposes of the research:

- **Informal sector** covers self-employed workers, individual entrepreneurs without employees, individual entrepreneurs or paid employees working at firms with fewer than five employees (microfirms),[12] and domestics and family workers; this sector may include agricultural activities, but does not touch on the issues of registration of employment.

- **Informal employment** includes people employed both inside and outside informal enterprises and those working without any contract or license or patent (i.e., without any registration of their employment).

The average person is not very familiar with the characteristics of the firms or organizations where they work. Particularly, people from large enterprises can rarely name the total number of employees at the enterprise. Therefore, special attention was given to reducing the probability of including in the informal sector small units of corporations (when people are employed in small departments or offices of large firms but reported as though they work for a small firm). This was done by introducing special filters for the data. As was expected, there are some nonresponses on the question about the number of employees, but there is little reason to assume that nonresponses introduce systematic bias into our results.

In line with the CMC dataset, *employment inside informal-sector enterprises* covers respondents who described themselves as individual entrepreneurs (with fewer than five employees) or own-account workers, along with employees of micro-firms (with fewer than five employees). According to RLMS, this sector does not consist of employees of micro-organizations or firms and people who do not work at enterprises or organizations.

Neither the CMC survey nor the RLMS are specially designed for investigating employment—and especially informal employment—hence, it is not possible to apply the same definition of informal employment there. The CMC survey has direct questions: "How [are] your labor relations legalized?" and "How [are] your occasional activities legalized?" Possible answers include (1) "unlimited labor contract," (2) "fixed-term labor contract," (3) "contractor's or grant agreement," (4) "verbal agreements with the employer," (5) "not formalized because I'm an individual entrepreneur," (6) "not formalized because I'm self-employed (own account worker) with patent or license," and (7) "not formalized because I'm a self-employed without any patent or license." Options 4, 5, and 7 form the empirical definition of informal employment.

In the RLMS, if a respondent works at an enterprise or at an organization she or he is asked to tell "whether s/he is officially registered at this job, that is, on a work roster, work agreement, or contract." If someone works at neither an enterprise nor an organization, there is no need to question whether s/he has a contract, and if his/her entrepreneurial activity is registered. Thus, our judgments of informal employment based on RLMS data are overestimated compared to our original definition and the CMC survey.

Alternative estimations of employment in informal sector based on LFS

According to official estimates, employment in the informal sector reached 14.3% of total employment in 2001 and 14.4% in 2002 (**Table 22**). The data for the last quarter are presented here as well because sociological surveys are conducted at the end of each year. One can see

TABLE 22   Official estimations of employment inside informal sector, 15-72 years old (in thousands of people)

	2001	2002	2001 q4	2002 q4
All employment in informal sector	9,190	9,535	8,179	8,627
Including employment:				
Only in informal sector	7,126	7,407	6,504	6,789
Both inside and outside				
informal sector	2,064	2,128	1,675	1,838
Incl. main job in				
informal sector	10	8	11	4
Main job in informal sector	7,136	7,415	6,515	6,793
Employed in informal sector				
in the whole employment, %	14.3%	14.4%	12.6%	13.1%
Share of main employment in informal				
sector in the whole employment, %	11.1%	11.2%	10.1%	10.3%

Source: Authors' analysis using Goskomstat data.

that figures are lower in the fourth quarter compared to the year as a whole. Employment in the informal sector reached maximum values in summer, a phenomenon which can be explained by more involvement of population in agricultural household production aimed at selling surplus and some other seasonal jobs.

As the LFS data show, two-thirds of people working in the informal sector are self-employed, including employers, own-account workers, unpaid family members, farmers, members of cooperatives, and so on (**Table 23**). Not surprisingly, the informal sector covers mainly small enterprises (78% of them have fewer than five employees), and there are more self-employed people working in micro-firms than there are paid employees (**Table 24**).

It was said earlier that Goskomstat includes agricultural activities in its definition of the informal sector, which comprises 42% of total employment in this sector on an annual basis and slightly more than one-third on a quarterly bases (**Table 25**). According to our estimates based on LFS data, non-agricultural employment in the informal sector comprises 9.3% to 9.4% of employment outside agriculture and forestry for the given period of observations. As most agricultural activity is concentrated in rural areas, one can expect that the level of employment in the informal sector will be lower for rural citizens in the fourth quarter due to weather factors (**Table 26**).

TABLE 23   Official estimations of employment in informal sector by status, 15-72 years old (thousand people)

	2001	2002	2001 q4	2002 q4
All employment in informal sector	9,190	9,535	8,179	8,627
Employed as:				
Paid employees	2,920	3,163	2,836	2,914
Self-employed	6,270	6,372	5,243	5,713
Composition of employment in informal sector, %:				
Paid employees	31.8	33.2	34.7	33.8
Self-employed	68.2	66.8	64.1	66.2

Source: Authors' analysis using Goskomstat data.

TABLE 24   Distribution of employment in informal sector among people age 15-72, by status of employment and a firm's size, 2002

	Total (thousand people)	Fewer than 5 employees (thousand people)	Fewer than or equal to 5 employees (thousand people)	Fewer than 5 employees (%)	Fewer than or equal to 5 employees (%)
All employment in informal sector including:	7,415	5,798	1,617	78.2	21.8
Paid employees	2,950	1,654	1,296	56.1	43.9
Self-employed	4,465	4,144	321	92.8	7.2
Composition of employment in informal sector, %:					
Paid employees	39.8	28.5	80.1		
Self-employed	60.2	71.5	19.9		

Source: Authors' analysis using Goskomstat data.

Scope and basic features of employment inside informal sector and informal employment based on secondary sociological analysis

Table 27 presents estimates of total informal employment of people aged 15 to 72 (or 18 to 72) obtained from the sociological surveys described above, namely the RLMS and CMC surveys. These figures, which

TABLE 25   Employment inside informal enterprises in agricultural and non-agricultural sectors among 15- to 72-year-olds (in thousands of people)

	2001	2002	2001 q4	2002 q4
All employment in informal sector, including:	9,190	9,535	8,179	8,627
Agricultural activities	3,867	4,014	2,799	3,269
Non-agricultural activities	5,323	5,521	5,381	5,358
Composition of employment in informal sector, %:				
Agricultural activities	42.1	42.1	34.2	37.9
Non-agricultural activities	57.9	57.9	65.8	62.1

Source: Authors' analysis using Goskomstat data.

show that between 17.7% and 21.5% of respondents have either regular or occasional employment, reflect the *maximum estimate* of informal employment by given data and definition. It covers both regular and occasional informal employment as well as both primary and secondary. Primary informal employment—i.e., people who are not covered by official statistics based on the reporting of firms because their labor is "invisible"—encompasses more than two-thirds of total informal employment. At the same time from 6% to 7% of formal workers have some kind of secondary informal activity, or "moonlighting" (Table 27).

The most popular type of informal activity is occasional employment (**Table 28**). Most occasional employment and additional activities, called "perquisites," are carried out without any type of contract or registration, i.e., informally. Splitting the informal employment by the importance of activity (primary or secondary) and its regularity, results in three almost equal groups: full-time (regular) employees working in the informal sector as their primary work activity, part-time (occasional) employees working in the informal sector as their primary work activity, and full- or part-time workers employed in the informal sector as a secondary work activity (**Figure J**).

We were not able to determine the employment in the informal sector among those with occasional employment, but it is likely that almost all occasional activities are conducted in the informal sector. However, in

TABLE 26 Distribution of employment inside informal enterprises by type of activity and settlement, people age 15-72, 2002

	Total (thousand people)	Urban (thousand people)	Rural (thousand people)	Urban (%)	Rural (%)
All employment in informal sector, including:	9,535	4,989	4,546	52.3	47.7
Agricultural activities	4,014	604	3,410	15.1	84.9
Non-agricultural activities	5,521	4,384	1,136	79.4	20.6
Structure of employment in informal sector, %:					
Agricultural activities	42.1%	12.1%	75.0%		
Non-agricultural activities	57.9%	87.9%	25.0%		

Source: Authors' analysis using Goskomstat data.

TABLE 27 Share of informal employment among those with regular and occasional employment by years, 1998, 2000, and 2002

	RLMS 1998 (15-72)	RLMS 2000 (15-72)	CMC 2000 (18-72)	RLMS 2002 (15-72)
1. Number of regularly or occasionally employed (number of respondents)	4,033	3,973	2,252	4,081
Total informal employment (% of N)	17.5	21.5	17.7	19.2
Including informal employment that is combined with formal employment (% of N)	5.6	5.7	5.9	4.3
Informal employment as the only activity (% of N)	11.9	15.8	11.8	14.9
2. Number of formally employed (Number of respondents)	3,806	3,745	2,022	3,905
Percent of informally employed among those with formal work (%)	6.4%	6.8%	6.5%	6.3%

Source: RLMS (1998, 2000) and CMC (2000, 2002).

order to maintain correct and clear procedures and criteria for recognizing the informal sector, we limit this analysis to employment in the informal sector. According to our estimations, regular employment in the informal sector of people 18 years old and over was equal to 15.7% by RLMS data and 8.1% by CMC data in the fourth quarter of 2000.[13] The former corresponds to figures given by Goskomstat (**Tables 29, 30, 31,** and 22). Em-

TABLE 28   Structure of total informal employment by first, second, and additional (occasional) job, 1998, 2000, and 2002

| | RLMS (Respondents age 15-72) | | | | | | CMC survey (Respondents age 18-72) | |
| | 1998 | | 2000 | | 2002 | | 2000 | |
	N	Percent employed either regularly or occasionally	N	Percent employed either regularly or occasionally	N	Percent employed either regularly or occasionally	N	Percent employed either regularly or occasionally
All informal employment*	706	17.5%	853	21.5%	783	19.2%	398	17.7%
Informally employed at main regular job	213	5.3	290	7.3	274	6.7	141	6.3
Informally employed at second regular job	69	1.7	67	1.7	54	1.3	23	1.0
Informally employed at additional/the occasional job	449	11.1	540	13.6	477	11.7	250	11.1

* There are some intersections between the three selected groups, thus the total number of informal employment is smaller than the simple sum of three categories below.

Source: RLMS (1998, 2000, 2002) and CMC (2000).

FIGURE J   Structure of informal employment by the regularity of activity (respondents of 18 years of age and older), 2000

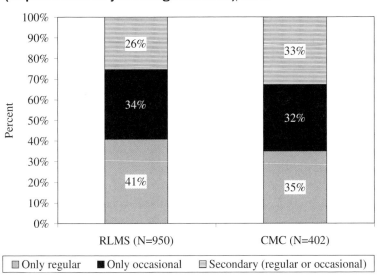

Source: Authors' calculations based on Russian Longitudinal Monitoring Survey (RLMS) and Carnegie Moscow Centre (CMC) data for 2000.

ployment in the informal sector as a main job comprises correspondingly 13.0% and 7.7% of total informal employment (Table 29). Informal employment on either a main or a second regular job reached 16.3% according to RLMS data and 7.5% according to CMC data for the same period. Informal employment measured exclusively by the main job was equal to 13.6% and 6.2%, respectively (Table 29).

As we mentioned earlier, there is no question in the RLMS questionnaire on the registration of self-employment status; i.e., we do not know whether those people have a license or a patent. Contrary, there is information on the licenses and patents in the CMC questionnaire, according to which slightly less than half of self-employed respondents had any sort of registration. If we correct RLMS data using the ratio of registered self-employed people to those not registered provided by CMC data, then the scope of informal employment on a person's main job decreases from 13.6% to 11.7% (**Table 32**). It is assumed that some paid employees not working at enterprises in the RLMS data have contracts as well and, thus, actual informal employment is even lower, but

TABLE 29   Matrices of informal employment and employment in informal sector on main job (respondents 18 years old and above), fourth quarter 2000

	Formal sector	Informal sector	Total
CMC survey (N=2,049)			
Formal job	89.2%	4.6%	93.8%
Informal job	3.2	3.0	6.2
Total	92.3	7.7	100.0
RLMS (N=2,693)			
Formal job	84.5%	1.9%	86.4%
Informal job	2.5	11.0	13.6
Total	87.0	13.0	100.0

Source: Authors' calculations based on Russian Longitudinal Monitoring Survey (RLMS) and Carnegie Moscow Centre (CMC) data.

TABLE 30   Matrices of informal employment and employment in informal sector on second job (respondents 18 years old and above), fourth quarter 2000

	Formal sector	Informal sector	Total
CMC Survey (N=99)			
Formal job	64.6%	10.1%	74.7%
Informal job	13.1	10.1	23.2
Total	79.8	20.2	100.0
RLMS (N=157)			
Formal job	39.5%	4.5%	43.9%
Informal job	14.0	42.0	56.1
Total	53.5	46.5	100.0

Source: Authors' calculations based on Russian Longitudinal Monitoring Survey (RLMS) and Carnegie Moscow Centre (CMC) data.

TABLE 31 Structure of employment in informal sector by employment status, 18 years old and over, November 2000

	RLMS			CMC		
	Main job	Second job	Total	Main job	Second job	Total
All employment in informal sector (respondents) including:	349	73	412	158	19	172
Paid employees (respondents)	228	34	255	93	13	105
Self-employed (respondents)	121	39	157	65	5	67
Structure of employment in informal sector:						
Paid employees (%)	65.3%	46.6%	61.9%	58.9%	68.4%	61.0%
Self-employed (%)	34.7	53.4	38.1	41.1	26.3	39.0

Source: Authors' calculations based on Russian Longitudinal Monitoring Survey (RLMS) and Carnegie Moscow Centre (CMC) data.

TABLE 32 Structure of informal employment by employment status, 18 years old and over, November 2000

	RLMS		RLMS (corrected*)		CMC	
	Main job	Second job	Main job	Second job	Main job	Second job
All informal employment (respondents) including:	365	88	314	75	128	23
Paid employees (respondents)	258	53	258	49	92	20
Self-employed (respondents)	107	35	56	26	36	3
Share of informal employment (%)	13.6%	56.1%	11.7%	47.8%	6.2%	23.2%
Structure of informal employment:						
Paid employees (%)	70.7%	60.2%	82.2%	65.3%	71.9%	87.0%
Self-employed (%)	29.3	39.8	17.8	34.7	28.1	13.0

* RLMS data adjusted to reflect ratios for self-employed from CMC sample.

Source: Authors' calculations based on Russian Longitudinal Monitoring Survey (RLMS) and Carnegie Moscow Centre (CMC) data.

there is no additional information for correcting the data further. Observed difference may also occur for slightly different facets of informal jobs and informal enterprises that fall into the RLMS and CMC samples.

Problems with the definition of informal employment

CMC data show that about half of the jobs in the informal sector are formal jobs, i.e., those with contracts (**Tables 29** and **30**). Thus, informal employment measured in compliance with the enterprise approach tends to overestimate the incidence of informality in the enterprises inside the informal sector, or even the scope of unobserved employment as a whole. The same may be true for Goskomstat data.

As expected, both total employment in the informal sector and the expanded definition of informal employment rose when including the second and additional jobs, especially at incidental ones (**Table 30, Figure K,** and **Figure L**). The main cause of informality is, of course, extra earnings, which usually take the form of individual economic activity. Almost nine out of 10 people with an additional job said that they did not have a contract at this job, as reported by RLMS data of 1998 and 2000. As Figure K shows, the number of people with additional jobs increased over time, although during the last few years this growth occurred mainly at the expense of people who did not have regular employment.

While describing the structure of employment as either informal or inside informal enterprises, we should note that our datasets gave us fewer self-employed people in the informal sector compared to Goskomstat data (**Table 31** and Table 23). Informal employment, according to our data, is even more typical for paid employees than for the self-employed (**Table 32**).

In addition, we were able to recognize fewer people involved in agricultural activities than Goskomstat (**Table 33**), which can be seen in **Table 34**, which presents the distribution across rural and urban residences. Such a difference is explained by the fact that the structure of the secondary data used prevents us from including involvement in household activities as employment. Only if a person described himself or herself as involved in individual economic activity, and that activity was subsistence farming, could we include this sort of activity into our analysis. Only in this situation could we take the significance of subsistence farming in household incomes into account (**Table 35**).

FIGURE K   Dynamics of informal employment and employment in informal sector according to RLMS data (workers age 15-72)

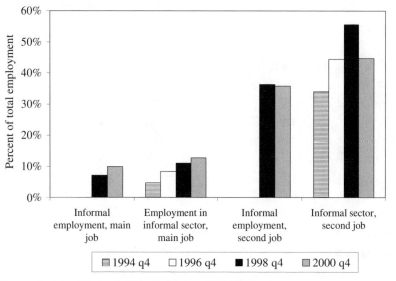

Source: *Review of Economic Policy in Russia in 2002* (2003).

FIGURE L   Dynamics of occasional employment (for last 30 days before the interview), RLMS data

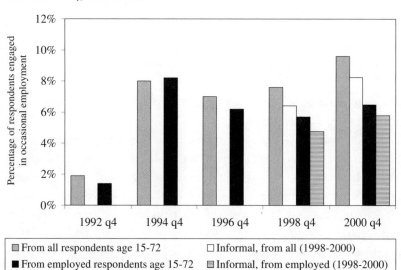

Source: Authors' calculations based on Russian Longitudinal Monitoring Survey (RLMS 1992, 1994, 1996, 1998, and 2000).

TABLE 33   Informal employment and employment in informal sector by type of activity (agricultural/non-agricultural) according to CMC survey, November 2000

	Main regular job		
	Informal sector	Informal employment	All informal employment
Total:	156	127	401
Agricultural activities	21	16	74
Non-agricultural activities	135	111	327
Composition of employment:			
Agricultural activities	13.5%	12.6%	32.8%
Non-agricultural activities	86.5%	87.4%	67.2%

Source: Authors' calculations based on Carnegie Moscow Centre (CMC) data.

TABLE 34   Employment in informal sector and informal employment by type of settlement (main job, 2000 q4)

	Informal sector			Informal employment		Employment	
	CMC N=157	RLMS N=349	Goskomstat (main job, 2001 q4)	CMC N=127	RLMS N=365	CMC N=2050	RLMS N=2693
Urban	79.6	84.0	64.0	76.4	86.3	77.9	79.6
Rural	20.4	16.0	36.0	23.6	13.7	22.1	20.4

Source: Authors' calculations based on Russian Longitudinal Monitoring Survey (RLMS) and Carnegie Moscow Centre (CMC) data.

Formal and informal employment: Some key characteristics over time

Trends

According to the LFS data the number of people involved in employment in the informal sector has been growing slowly (Tables 20 and 22). Meanwhile, within-group analysis of LFS data shows that from 1999 to 2001 the number of entrepreneurs and domestic workers has grown, while the number of other workers has decreased (Table 20). A significant rise in the number of individual entrepreneurs in 2002 may be the result of adoption of a new tax code, which reduced significantly the

TABLE 35 Composition of per capita aggregate receipts by income groups in rural areas, 1998, 2000, and 2001

| | Respondents with per capita aggregate receipts: | | | | | | | | |
| | Below SM* | | | 1x–2x SM | | | Above 2x SM | | |
	1998	2000	2001	1998	2000	X 2001	1998	2000	2001
Wages	17.6	18.5	18.4	14.4	18.3	21.4	11.3	20.7	18.0
State transfers	27.6	35.8	40.3	29.5	36.0	27.3	13.5	13.6	10.7
Receipts from household production, including:	42.0	34.9	26.5	43.2	35.1	37.7	55.1	37.9	49.9
Money income from household production	2.1	3.9	7.1	8.2	7.4	18.6	17.5	15.7	33.4
Money equivalent of consumed household production	39.9	31.0	19.4	35.0	27.7	19.1	37.6	22.2	16.5
Non-state transfers	11.3	9.4	7.7	9.8	7.6	7.9	10.7	11.4	6.3
Other money receipts (including rental of personal property, sale of personal things, securities, spending of savings)	1.6	1.1	7.0	3.0	3.0	5.6	9.4	6.8	
Total	100.0	100.0	100.0	100.0	100.0	100.0	100.0	100.0	100.0

* SM= subsistance minimum or poverty rate.

Source: Authors' calculations from Russian Longitudinal Monitoring Survey (RLMS) data.

rate of income tax on individuals. RLMS data for people between the ages of 15 and 72 show that employment in the informal sector has grown between 1994 and 2000, while the trend for informal employment is not so clear (**Figure K**). Because our figures are comparable to figures provided by Goskomstat, we can suggest that the number of jobs in the informal sector is increasing. But, taking into account the trend for second jobs, employment in the informal sector is often used as an addition to the primary formal job when times are hard (Figure K). Because of the limited number of observations, this is only a hypothesis and cannot be statistically proven.

The number of informally employed (**Table 27**) as well as the structure of informal employment by the first and second jobs and additional activities (**Table 28**) looks very stable, but again the limited number of observations does not permit us to draw a firm conclusion about trends. Does the data suggest that there is a certain stable core of informally employed people that prevent the scope of informal employment from decreasing? To answer that question, we address the panel data from the RLMS.

The data file covered respondents age 15 and older in 2002 who were captured in the surveys of 1998, 2000, 2001, and 2002. Results presented in **Figure M** and **Figure N** reflect the dynamics of primary informal employment. We concentrated on this group because income from informal employment was the main source of individual labor income for these people.

The panel shows the nature of informal work changes more dramatically over time than does the absolute number (Figure M). The growth of informal employment in primary work activities occurred largely due to an increase in the number of persons working without a contract. Their share of the population age 15 to 72 has increased for four years, from 0.6% in 1998 up to 1.4% in 2002.

Another important conclusion relates to the issue of stability of informal employment. We understand of course the serious limitations of our analysis based on the two-year span of the data. Within each interval, a person could change jobs several times. Nevertheless, involvement in informal employment at any period of observation (1998, 2000, and 2002) testifies to the permanence of that status and can be evidence of a certain strategy. On Figure N the intersection of circles shows that 6.7% of all informal employment for three points of observation forms

FIGURE M   Formal and informal employment, workers age 15-72, RLMS panel data for 1998, 2000, and 2002 (N=4,711)

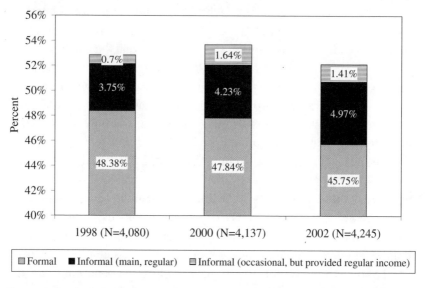

Source: Authors' calculations based on Russian Longitudinal Monitoring Survey (RLMS) data for 1998, 2000, and 2002.

FIGURE N   Informal employment over time

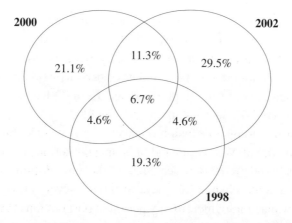

Source: Authors' calculations based on Russian Longitudinal Monitoring Survey (RLMS) and Carnegie Moscow Centre (CMC) data for 2000.

a core, which is made up of people who have been employed informally in 1998, 2000, and 2003. Crossings of pairs of circles correspond to shares of those who were informally employed at the moment that two of three surveys were conducted. As we can see, for a great bulk of respondents, participation in informal employment is limited to one year. Only 32% of the informally employed in 1998 kept the status in 2000, and only 39% of those employed in that way in 2000 have not changed the status in 2002. The most common destination for those leaving informal employment is formal employment, whereas the group of inactive people serves as the leader among "suppliers" of informal employment. It means that informal employment for a working person is, in general, unstable in modern Russia. While the labor supply of informal employment is unstable, with individual workers entering and exiting informal employment often, it may be the case that the demand for informal employment is rather stable, with formal-sector firms using informal workers as a way to smooth out their demand for workers during times of particularly slow or fast expansion.

There is evidence that the informally unemployed as measured by the International Labor Organization approach include many people who are officially inactive (like students or pensioners). However, the data used are not appropriate to ascertain the dynamic relation between unemployment and informal employment. Meanwhile, preliminary regression analysis of interactions between employment in the informal sector and unemployment provided by Gimpelson (2001, p. 23) on the LFS database revealed no significant impact of unemployment on employment in the informal sector.

Gender (Table 36 and Table 37): Russia differs from many developing countries in that there is no clear division between the involvement of men and women in employment inside the informal sector and informal employment. Moreover, our analysis shows that men usually slightly prevail over women both in informal employment and the informal sector. The same is true for the rates of employment between both sexes. According to CMC survey data, the rate of informal employment is slightly more than 14% for men and near 8% for women between 18 and 72 years old. This gap, although smaller, remains even if we take into account only the working age population, i.e., men between the ages of 18 and 59 and women from 18 to 54 years old. The

TABLE 36   Distribution of employment In Informal sector by sex, 2001 and 2002

	Informal employment			
	Both	Main/only job	Second job	Employment
November 2001				
Total	8,179	6,515	1,664	64,664
Men	4,327	3,405	921	33,435
Women	3,853	3,109	743	31,229
Total (percent)	100.0%	100.0%	100.0%	100.0%
Men	52.9	52.3	55.4	51.7
Women	47.1	47.7	44.6	48.3
2001				
Total	9,190	7,136	2,054	64,400
Men	4,784	3,679	1,105	33,319
Women	4,407	3,457	950	31,081
Total (percent)	100.0%	100.0%	100.0%	100.0%
Men	52.1	51.6	53.8	51.7
Women	47.9	48.4	46.2	48.3
2002				
Total	9,535	7,415	2,120	66,071
Men	4,913	3,778	1,135	33,902
Women	4,622	3,637	985	32,169
Total (percent)	100.0%	100.0%	100.0%	100.0%
Men	51.5	51.0	53.5	51.3
Women	48.5	49.0	46.5	48.7

Source: Authors' calculations based on Goskomstat data.

RLMS data show a similar picture—the informal employment rate is near 20% for men and 12% for women age 18 to 72. But bearing in mind that our data underestimate the number of people involved in household production, while the number of observations is rather small, we draw a softer conclusion: in Russia, women do not outnumber men in informal employment. This conclusion corresponds with Goskomstat data.

Age: The issue of the age distribution of those informally employed or working inside informal enterprises needs to be further clarified. Currently, we can say that in our samples middle age groups (between the ages of 24 and 45) seem to be slightly over-represented (**Figure O** and

TABLE 37   Distribution of employment in informal sector by sex, secondary sociological data, 2000 q4

| | CMC Survey | | | | RLMS | | | |
| | Informal sector | | Formal sector | | Informal sector | | Formal sector | |
	Main job	Second job	Main job	Second job	Main job	Second job	Main job	Second job
Total	158	18	1,893	77	349	73	2,344	83
Men	88	10	953	43	193	37	1,138	33
Women	70	8	940	34	156	36	1,206	50
Total (%)	100.0	100.0	100.0	100.0	100.0	100.0	100.0	100.0
Men	55.7	55.6	50.3	55.8	55.3	50.7	48.5	39.8
Women	44.3	44.4	49.7	44.2	44.7	49.3	51.5	60.2

Source: Authors' calculations based on Russian Longitudinal Monitoring Survey (RLMS) and Carnegie Moscow Centre (CMC) data.

FIGURE 0   Distribution of employment in informal sector by age, 2001 and 2002, according to Goskomstat

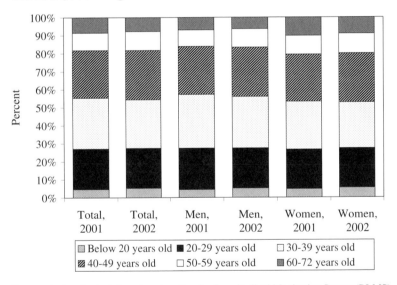

Source: Authors' calculations based on Russian Longitudinal Monitoring Survey (RLMS).

Figure P). Within-group analysis of the pool of informally employed workers shows that regular forms of such employment—and especially regular work among the self-employed, entrepreneurs, and individual employers—tends to be concentrated in the middle working ages.

FIGURE P   Distribution of informal employment by age, all jobs, 2000 q4

Source: Authors' calculations based on Russian Longitudinal Monitoring Survey (RLMS).

Education (Tables 38 and 39, Figure Q): The general trend reported by LFS and RLMS data testifies to the lower education level of people employed either in the informal sector or in informal jobs. This is because, while the general level of employment for less-educated people is decreasing and unemployment and inactivity rates are increasing, the level of informal employment, according to RLMS data, is growing. However, at the same time, the CMC dataset shows that informal employment among people with higher education is relatively high compared to those less educated (Table 39, Figure Q). Figure Q provides evidence that one source of the observed contradiction is the difference in educational structure in the given data sets. The discrepancies can be explained by the fact that the CMC dataset represents slightly different groups of informally employed than the RLMS. The CMC dataset includes more employers, a group of people that is generally more educated, more qualified, and presents significantly different labor market behavior than the other education groups in question. This is consistent with the distribution of education levels among different groups of the employed population (Table 16). The educational profile of different

TABLE 38   Distribution of people working in informal sector by education level, Goskomstat

	2001			2002		
	Total	Men	Women	Total	Men	Women
Total	100.0%	100.0%	100.0%	100.0%	100.0%	100.0%
Education level:						
Higher	11.3%	11.5%	11.1%	10.8%	10.8%	10.8%
Incomplete higher	2.5	2.6	2.4	2.1	1.8	2.3
Secondary vocational	27.3	24.2	30.7	27.1	23.3	31.3
Primary vocational	11.9	13.2	10.4	12.5	13.9	11.1
Secondary school	29.5	30.6	28.2	30.5	32.1	28.9
Basic	13.9	14.3	13.5	13.7	15.1	12.2
Primary and less	3.6	3.4	3.8	3.2	3.0	3.4

Source: Authors' calculations based on Goskomstat data.

sub-groups of the informally employed shows that, compared to the self-employed or part-time workers in general, the informally employed tend to be less educated. More generally speaking, informal employment is heterogeneous by education as well as by age.

Rural/urban residency (Table 34 and Table 26): The difference between the RLMS and CMC survey data and Goskomstat data was described earlier. It is difficult to definitively capture the scope of informal employment in rural areas because in most cases employment is not individual but collective (based on a household level), and the data are scarce. On the whole, according to Goskomstat data, most employment inside informal enterprises in rural areas is connected with agricultural activities (Table 25). In addition, there are far more people with secondary employment in the informal sector in rural areas than in urban (Unobservable Economy 2003, p. 44). According to our estimates, regular informal employment increases in large cities, whereas occasional informal employment is associated with rural areas.

According to the output index of production in agriculture, individual farming accelerated during periods of labor market stress. The RLMS data show that 36.7% of households have individual farms and 10.8% cultivate either individual or collective vegetable gardens. On average, 90% of Russian households in rural area have individual farms,

TABLE 39 Distribution of people working in informal sector or informally employed by education level, main job, 2000 q4

	Informal sector			Informal employment			Employment	
	CMC N=156	RLMS N=335	Goskomstat, 2001 q4	CMC N=126	RLMS N=351		CMC N=2047	RLMS N=2632
Total	100.0	100.0	100.0	100.0	100.0		100.0	100.0
Education level:								
Higher, including incomplete	32.7	16.7	13.5	38.1	16.0		32.8	26.0
Secondary and primary vocational	37.8	49.0	40.0	34.1	47.9		40.8	43.5
Secondary school	26.3	24.2	30.7	23.0	25.1		20.8	21.3
Basic, primary and less	3.2	10.2	15.8	4.8	11.1		5.7	9.2

Source: Authors' calculations based on Russian Longitudinal Monitoring Survey (RLMS), Carnegie Moscow Centre (CMC), and Goskomstat data.

FIGURE Q   Rate of employment in informal sector across different levels of education, 2000 q4 (main job of workers age 18 and older)

Source: Authors' calculations based on Russian Longitudinal Monitoring Survey (RLMS) and Carnegie Moscow Centre (CMC) data.

and 30% consider subsistence agriculture to be a successful income supplement (**Table 35**). In 2000, the RLMS data showed that 15.6% of households received some income from selling agricultural production of their subsidiary farms. In urban areas, 7.6% of households received such supplemental income, while in rural areas the number was 37.6%. In 2001, there were 16.0% of households receiving income from individual farms, with 7.8% and 40.5% in urban and rural areas, respectively.

Thus, we can state that barriers for increasing the number of income sources at the expense of informal employment inside the formal sector are higher in rural areas than in urban areas because:

- there are limited places of work in rural areas;

- employment in individual subsidiary farms (either one's own or someone else's) absorbs the most informal activity in the countryside; and

FIGURE R   Distribution of informal employment at main job by firm's size

Source: Authors' calculations based on Russian Longitudinal Monitoring Survey (RLMS) and
Carnegie Moscow Centre (CMC) data.

- informational limitations do not allow accurate estimates of the dynamics of informal employment in individual subsidiary farms and non-agrarian fields of economy like services in small and medium enterprises (SMEs).

Types of enterprises: It is logical to suggest that informality gives more flexibility in hiring and firing as well as in remuneration schemes; thus, informal relations might focus on certain types of firms, activities, and jobs.

Both official (Table 24) data and our data show that informal employment is concentrated in micro (fewer than 20 employees) private enterprises (**Figure R, Table 40**). On one hand, this proves the validity of using a criterion based on the number of employees when defining the informal sector, which was applied in our empirical definition. On the other hand, even among employees of firms with fewer than five workers, the majority of employees have contracts. Hence, we can hypothesize that informality on the Russian labor market might be shifted from the issue of contract registration to other sides of labor relations,

TABLE 40   Formal and informal employment by ownership of enterprise, main job, 2000 q4

Employment:	CMC			RLMS		
	Formal N=1,885	Informal N=96	Both N=1,981	Formal N=2,324	Informal N=88	Both N=2,411
Enterprise						
State	65.6	13.5	63.1	54.9	1.1	52.9
Private						
(non state)	34.4	86.5	36.9	45.1	98.9	47.1

Source: Authors' calculations based on Russian Longitudinal Monitoring Survey (RLMS) and Carnegie Moscow Centre (CMC) data.

usually placed inside the contract, such as wage level and regularity of payments, reimbursement of sick leave, working schedule, vacations, etc. This hypothesis is examined in more detail later in this chapter.

If we look at the age of a firm, we can see that informal employment is concentrated in relatively new firms founded during the last decade (by RLMS data, the average year a firm was founded is 1995 for informal jobs and 1965 for formal ones).

The fact that informal employment is concentrated mostly in small, new enterprises shows that the nature of such firms—specifically, their instability, rapid change, and limited access to credit—prevent them from following the strict rules of Russian labor legislation. When there is rapid turnover, employers must have flexibility in hiring new personnel when a firm grows and in firing excessive people when it retrenches. The other factor having an impact on the registration of labor relations is taxation. In Russia, employees pay no part of their incomes into the social security system (for pensions, unemployment insurance, etc.), while the rate of the single social tax (SST) for employers is more than 35%.[14]

Branches: When we turn to the issue of employment activities, both Goskomstat's and our data show that employment inside informal sector and informal employment are concentrated mainly in services, especially commerce (wholesale and retail) and catering (**Table 41**). There are also many people informally employed in agriculture and forestry, as well as in the construction and transport industries. Note that, informal employment in trade is usually primary, while in construction and

TABLE 41 Distribution of workers employed informally or inside informal sector for the main job, by branches

	CMC (November 2000)		Goskomstat (2002)	
	Informal sector N=100	Informal employment N=104	Employment N=1,334	Informal sector
Industry	5.1	5.5	21.2	10.2
Transport and communications and construction	17.3	15.7	16.7	12.4
Agriculture and forestry	13.5	12.6	10.0	29.7
Trade and catering	46.8	46.5	12.9	42.7
Health care, physical training, social security, education, and science	3.8	6.3	23.1	1.3
Finances, credit, insurance, housing, and communal services	2.6	4.7	7.7	2.0
Legal and other services (lawyers, etc.)	6.4	6.3	2.2	—
Other branches	4.5	2.4	6.2	1.7
Total	100.0	100.0	100.0	100.0

Source: Authors' calculations based on Carnegie Moscow Centre (CMC) and Goskomstat data.

agriculture informal employment is usually secondary. According to CMC survey data, almost every fourth person employed in commerce and food-delivering work is without a contract. Informal employment in those branches comprises 49% of total informal jobs in the sample, and employment in the informal sector represents 46% of all jobs inside informal enterprises, while in the whole sample, the ratio of jobs in commerce and food-delivering is only 14%. Five branches (retail trade and catering, wholesale trade, agriculture and forestry, and construction and transport) account for three-fourths of informal employment but only 38% of total employment.

Working hours: Our data testify to the greater number of actual working hours in the informal sector and informal employment (**Table 42**). In contrast, Goskomstat data shows that this is not the case (**Table 43**).

TABLE 42 Average working hours for different demographic groups employed either informally or inside informal-sector enterprises, RLMS, 2000 q4

	Main job			Second job		
	Informal sector N=337	Informal employment N=353	Employment, main job N=2650	Informal sector N=56	Informal employment N=73	Employment, second job N=134
Total						
Hours per day	9.6	9.6	9.2	5.4	5.6	5.9
Hours per week	52.3	51.4	44.6	22.3	21.9	21.7
Hours per month	199.0	193.6	174.0	76.1	76.7	76.9
Urban						
Hours per day	9.5	9.6	9.3	NA	NA	5.9
Hours per week	52.3	51.9	44.6	NA	NA	21.0
Hours per month	198.4	195.0	172.7	NA	NA	76.0
Rural						
Hours per day	10.3	10.1	8.9	NA	NA	6.2
Hours per week	52.0	48.5	44.8	NA	NA	28.6
Hours per month	202.7	184.4	179.5	NA	NA	87.1
Men						
Hours per day	9.9	9.7	9.8	NA	NA	6.5
Hours per week	55.0	53.7	47.9	NA	NA	22.7
Hours per month	204.9	200.3	185.8	NA	NA	83.6
Women						
Hours per day	9.3	9.5	8.7	NA	NA	5.6
Hours per week	49.2	48.3	41.5	NA	NA	21.0
Hours per month	192.0	184.2	162.5	NA	NA	71.8

NA = observations are too small to provide average values.

Source: Authors' calculations based on Russian Longitudinal Monitoring Survey (RLMS) data.

One explanation for the difference in findings is that, again, we underestimate agricultural activities, which usually take less time (**Table 44**). Another is that we consider working hours separately for the main and the second job, while Goskomstat reports working hours for both of them. Because second jobs normally take less time, they lead to fewer working hours in the informal sector reported by Goskomstat.

According to RLMS data, respondents working informally in their primary job outside the enterprise have the highest median of total working hours per month (from all jobs), at 192 hours. Primary unregistered employees, along with secondary informal employees, also work more than formal workers—180 and 185 hours compared to 168 hours per month, respectively. It is the occasional informally employed workers who work less than all others, logging an average of only 50 hours per

TABLE 43 Average working hours per week in general employment and inside the informal sector, Goskomstat

	Nov. 2001	Nov. 2002	2001	2002
Employment at main job	39.1	39.1	38.8	39.1
Men	39.7	39.7	39.5	39.7
Women	38.4	38.6	38.1	38.5
Employment at second job	15.3	14.5	16.5	15.7
Men	15.9	15.0	16.4	15.9
Women	14.6	14.0	16.5	15.6
Employment in informal sector	32.8	31.5	32.3	32.0
Men	34.0	32.4	33.5	33.0
Women	31.4	30.5	31.0	30.9

Source: Authors' calculations based on Goskomstat data.

month. According to the CMC survey, the median number of working days in a week is six days for all groups; average duration of a working day is nine hours for those with main regular or secondary informal employment, and six hours for occasional informal employment.

According to the CMC survey, informal workers are more likely to report that they work in the evenings and on their days off. Nearly one-third of all employed workers and more than one-half of those employed informally frequently work in the evenings and days off. There is a connection between the nature of the activity (e.g., in agriculture) and the hours worked: among the occasional informally employed, the share of those working outside the regular working days is two-thirds.

Holidays: As expected, RLMS data show that the right to annual vacation pay is reported by only 19% of those working on their main work without a contract, and by 93% of those employed with a contract. According to CMC data, 41% of the informally employed answered that they had a right to vacation pay, but only 29.3% have used this opportunity within the last 12 months. Within a year before the survey, 11.2% of all informally and 7.2 % of the formally employed took vacation leave at their own expense.

TABLE 44 Distribution of working hours and average working hours per week by branches in informal sector in 2002, Goskomstat

	Total	Less than 15	16-20	21-30	31-40	41-50	51 and over	Average hours per week
Total	100.0%	21.3%	9.5%	13.1%	34.2%	11.4%	9.2%	32.0%
Industry	100.0	14.7	6.7	7.4	47.1	12.2	10.2	35.7
Agriculture and forestry	100.0	40.5	17.5	22.8	10.4	4.5	4.1	21.8
Transport and communications	100.0	11.2	3.5	6.1	45.5	14.7	16.6	38.9
Construction	100.0	9.8	5.0	6.6	44.2	15.8	16.0	38.7
Trade and catering	100.0	3.5	2.7	5.9	54.8	18.1	13.0	40.8
Housing and communal services	100.0	20.7	8.2	10.0	39.1	12.5	6.1	30.7
Health care, physical training, social security	100.0	33.2	8.4	1.6	40.4	8.8	5.5	28.1
Education	100.0	43.5	11.2	9.9	27.0	4.4	3.2	22.8
Culture and art	100.0	21.4	3.7	8.2	49.1	10.4	2.8	31.1
Science and research	100.0	25.5	—	—	67.7	6.8	—	21.9
Finances, credit, insurance	100.0	11.0	—	—	88.9	—	—	19.5
Other branches	100.0	5.5	3.4	4.8	50.3	21.9	13.7	41.5

Source: Authors' calculations based on Goskomstat data.

Other social guarantees: In the sphere of formal employment, after vacation pay the most widespread labor guarantees are payment of sick leave and parental leave. RLMS data show that, of respondents working with a contract on the main job, 93% mentioned the right to use sick leave while 91% cited parental-leave guarantees. By the CMC survey, the right to payment of sick leave was reported by 89% of formal workers. Quite the opposite was true of informal workers: only 15% of primary informal workers by RLMS and 31% of them by the CMC survey indicated the presence of the right to sick leave pay. And only 3% of primary informal employees have the right to paid maternity leave, according to the RLMS. All other social guarantees (payment of health services, education, housing, transportation fees, and so forth) cover considerably smaller numbers of people employed either formally or informally.

Remuneration: One could expect that the reduced stability and lower rate of social guarantees among informal employees would be compensated by higher levels of remuneration. Among datasets we use, the only open source of information about wage levels in informal employment is the RLMS, which shows that the monthly wage paid to informal employees is slightly higher on these jobs than in formal employment (**Figure S**). When comparing wage rates (monthly wage paid per actual hours worked), one can see that there are some very well-paid employees in informal jobs. According to the RLMS, average wage rates are higher for workers in the informal sector than the formal sector, and higher for informal jobs than for formal. But the median wages of different groups are almost equal.

It is important to mention that the RLMS data show that wage arrears and involuntary administrative leaves are significantly more often used on formal jobs in formal sector enterprises. In reference to CMC data, 92% of respondents with primary informal employment answered that they received their wages on time, and only 12% acknowledged the existence of wage arrears, while the corresponding figures for respondents with formal employment were 73% and 30%, respectively. According to the RLMS, 17% of respondents with primary informal employment and 30% of those with formal employment had responded about wage arrears. In accordance with RLMS data, during the year before the survey, 3.4% of respondents with a contract and 1.2% of those without one had experienced involuntary administrative leave. The ratio of employees receiving

FIGURE S   Distribution of the informally and formally employed at first job by wage paid, RLMS, 2000 q4

Source: Authors' calculations based on Russian Longitudinal Monitoring Survey (RLMS).

remuneration in the form of their enterprises' production instead of cash totaled 9.0% for formal workers and 9.5% for informal ones. On the other hand, the reduction of working hours or wages by the employer covered 13% of informal employees against 7% of formal ones.

Thus, while not clearly offering higher wages, informal employment provides more stable current income, although without social guarantees. Taking this into account, one can suggest that informal employment is to some extent the rational choice of the employee. Results reported on the following pages prove that the high rates of informal employment are indeed a result of decisions made by the employees.

The initiation of informal employment relationships: RLMS data show that employees are sometimes just as interested in working without a contract as employers (**Table 45**), which is especially true for an employee's second job.

Additionally, CMC data provide another main finding. For the purposes of this research, we have defined informal employment as work

TABLE 45   Employer and employee interest in employment without a contract (RLMS)

	Informal employment	
	Main job N=97	Second job N=33
Employer	67.4	37.7
Employee	32.6	62.3

Source: Authors' calculations based on Russian Longitudinal Monitoring Survey (RLMS) data.

TABLE 46   Existence of informal agreements with employer on particular issues (CMC data, all jobs)

	Informal employment N=136	Exclusively formal employment N=1,874-1,882
	(% of positive answers)	
Working schedule	53.7%	36.5%
Time of vacations	30.1	37.4
Remuneration	52.2	28.2

Source: Authors' calculations based on Carnegie Moscow Centre (CMC) data.

without a contract. But CMC data prove that there is space for informality within a contract, including verbal agreements about working schedule, vacation time, remuneration, etc. (**Table 46**). It is important that, regardless of the type of employment (formal or informal), in most cases employees desire verbal agreements (**Table 47**).

It is clear that the main reason an employee would choose an informal employment arrangement is to receive regular and sometimes higher current incomes. There is a great distrust among the population of various state initiatives, including social security. Thus, state-sponsored benefits are not an incentive to formalize employment. In the case of shadow employment, another reason to hide actual incomes could be to avoid paying taxes, but it is unlikely an attraction to informal employment from an employee's perspective.

TABLE 47   Employer and employee interest in verbal agreements (CMC data, all jobs)

	Informal employment N=83	Exclusively formal employment N=638
Employer	18.1%	19.6%
Employee	20.5	17.6
Both employer and employee	61.4	62.9

Source: Authors' calculations based on Carnegie Moscow Centre (CMC) data.

TABLE 48   Special and general length of service by form of employment at main job, RLMS, 2000 q4

	Job		Sector		
	Formal	Informal	Formal	Informal	Employment
Average length of service at current main job (in years)	10.0	2.2	10.2	2.9	9.3
Average length of service at any job (in years)	20.7	14.6	20.6	15.1	19.9

Source: Authors' calculations based on Russian Longitudinal Monitoring Survey (RLMS) data.

Skills composition and mismatch

Informal employment and employment in the informal sector are unstable. The average length of service at a given job, sometimes thought of as a proxy for firm-specific human capital, is much less for informal employees than for formal (**Table 48**). Moreover, the RLMS panel data show that nearly one-third of informal workers leave these jobs within a two-year period. Thus, informal employment seems most likely to be a temporary refuge instead of permanent condition.

Although it is heterogeneous, there is some evidence that people with low human capital at extreme groups of age and well-educated middle-aged urban citizens from big cities have higher rates of informal employment. It is presumed that jobs in the informal sector and informal jobs require fewer qualifications than such people usually have (**Tables 38** and **49**). This is especially true for people who reported only the occasional informal job. Bearing in mind the sectoral structure of informal employment, it is not surprising that most informal employment is conducted by workers in services, followed by industrial workers (**Table 49**). The distribution of respondents across education levels shows that informal workers in services are more educated than their colleagues on formal jobs (**Table 50**). Nonetheless, two important things can be observed. First, there are more people with secondary and lower education on informal jobs compared to formal. Second, respondents with higher and secondary vocational education occupy jobs with lower qualifications when they are informal. This may indicate that an insufficient number of stable, secure, "good" jobs are available and informal jobs are used as a way of increasing current incomes.

At the same time, fast-changing economic situations result in shorter durations of informal employment. According to the RLMS data, nearly two-thirds of informal workers at enterprises, slightly more than a half of informal workers outside enterprises, and just over one-fourth of formal employees changed either their profession, their job, or both between 1998 and 2000. In the CMC data, about three-fourths of formal workers and only half of informal ones did not change a job at all. Thus, compared to the unemployed or the working poor from budgetary-sponsored jobs (school teachers, for example) informal workers seem to be coming out ahead.

Labor market policies and programs

Labor market policies are a set of instruments and actions aimed at improving the labor market situation, and consequently reducing the length of job searches and unemployment periods. Active labor market programs (ALMP), the main component of labor market policies, are a tool to lessen unemployment, which is especially important in transition economies such as Russia's.

As there was no officially recognized employment in the USSR, no agency responsible for passive or active labor market policies existed. A system of modern Russian labor market institutions was created by the Law on Employment (1991), which also established a State Employment

TABLE 49   Distribution of employment in informal sector and informal employment by occupations, main job, RLMS, 2000 q4

Occupation	Informal sector N=346	Informal employment N=363	Employment, main job N=2,688
Military personnel	0.0	0.0	0.4
CEOs, managers, administrators	16.2	14.0	7.8
High-level professionals	3.5	1.9	17.5
Specialists	6.6	7.2	15.1
Clerks	2.0	1.9	5.3
Employed in services	34.1	31.4	10.9
Skilled workers	14.7	17.4	15.6
Craftspeople	14.2	15.4	17.3
Unskilled labor	8.7	10.7	10.1
Total	100.0	100.0	100.0

Source: Authors' calculations based on Russian Longitudinal Monitoring Survey (RLMS) data.

Fund and a system of state employment services. There are two methods of financing of employment expenditures: contributions (set in the form of payroll taxes) and the federal budget (since 2001, this component has been funded by money from both federal and regional budgets). The employment tax rate was equal to 2% of payroll until 1996 and has been 1.5% since 1996. Up to 2001, these contributions were collected by regional branches of the State Employment Fund. In order to equalize the economic situation across regions, each regional branch was obligated to transfer a share of its employment tax income to the federal center, which then redistributed means to the most vulnerable regions. This share was established at a level of 10% in 1991 and then increased to 20% in 2001.

In 2001 the principles of financing employment policies in Russia changed. The State Employment Fund was abolished, along with dedicated taxes for the purposes of employment. The financing of employment policies was centralized and carried out through the budget rather than the off-budget fund. The current sources of financing for employment policies are federal, regional, and local budgets.

The main ALMP programs were developed and introduced into practice from 1992 to 1995. The list of such programs offered in Russia is

TABLE 50   Distribution of working respondents with different levels of education by professional groups, main job, RLMS, 2000 q4

	Secondary school and lower	Primary and secondary vocational	Higher	All
Formal employment				
N =	920	1,208	709	2,837
Professional group				
Managers, administrators	2.0	5.4	11.8	5.9
High-level professionals	1.5	10.0	52.5	17.9
Specialists	7.5	20.9	16.5	15.4
Employed in services	8.6	10.2	3.1	7.9
Skilled workers	19.5	18.1	4.9	15.3
Craftspeople	34.5	17.1	2.4	19.1
Unskilled labor	20.3	9.8	3.0	11.5
Other groups	6.2	8.5	5.8	7.1
Total	100.0	100.0	100.0	100.0
Informal employment				
N =	126	167	53	346
Professional group				
Managers, administrators	11.9	12.6	26.4	14.5
Specialists	4.8	5.4	20.8	7.5
Employed in services	30.2	33.5	26.4	31.2
Skilled workers	18.3	22.2	5.7	18.2
Craftspeople	19.0	15.0	3.8	14.7
Unskilled labor	14.3	9.0	3.8	10.1
Other groups	1.6	2.4	13.2	3.8
Total	100.0	100.0	100.0	100.0

Source: Authors' calculations based on Russian Longitudinal Monitoring Survey (RLMS) data.

quite standard and comprises the following programs: assistance (mediation) in getting employment; occupational guidance; vocational training and/or retraining; public works; programs of social adaptation (e.g., "Job Seekers' Club," "Fresh Start"); programs of subsidized employment and job quotas (including "Youth Practice" and quotas for hiring disabled employees); and support of client entrepreneurial activities. These activities are regulated by Federal Employment Law (1991) and various normative acts. According to Denisova (2003), the estimated expenditure on ALMP per one unemployed person is about 1,000 rubles per year (about $30).[15]

Active labor market programs in Russia can be divided into two main groups, depending upon their coverage. The first group was financed through payroll taxes and designed to be available for all population groups. This type of ALMP includes assistance (mediation) in getting employment (selecting decent work with regard to occupation, qualification, work experience, limitations in capacities to work, and other factors) and occupational consulting (including career guidance, psychological support, information about possibilities of vocational training, etc.). The other ALMP are financed though federal and regioinal budgets and address certain groups of the unemployed, non-active population and/or workers who have a high probability of being dismissed. Coverage of the programs of the second group depend heavily on the amount of funds transferred from budgets to employment policy.

- Occupational guidance services, aimed at improving the quality of occupational choice, are designed for all registered unemployed people and include informing, consulting, testing, and psychological support, which are described in more detail below. The program participation time typically does not exceed one week.

- Providing updates to the job seeker on the current and prospective occupational structure of demand in the local labor market, on the major characteristics of specific occupations, and on the terms of getting training or retraining for certain occupations.

- Consulting on occupational choice combined with examining possibilities of training and/or re-training.

- Evaluating a person's fitness for their chosen profession/occupation, and hence, their fit for a vacancy or training program.

- Psychological support aimed at developing the adaptive skills of the unemployed and improving an individual's self-esteem and motivation for the job search.

Vocational training is often considered to be the most effective way of returning the unemployed to the labor market. In Russia, this program is directed mainly at two target groups: the unemployed and the redundant employees of restructured enterprises. The following types of training are provided: vocational training for unemployed workers aimed at acquiring habits necessary to conduct a certain type of work; retraining of workers with the intention of placing them in new occupations; training for workers having certain occupations with the skills needed to pick up a second occupation; improving the qualifications of workers; vocational retraining of specialists; improving qualifications of specialists; and work on a probation period. Priorities are given to disabled, the long-term unemployed (those who have experienced at least a six-month period of unemployment), discharged workers, spouses of military personnel and those discharged, graduates, and new entrants to the labor market, including people without any occupation or profession. The standard duration of the program usually does not exceed six months.

Programs of social adaptation include the "Job Seekers' Club" and "Fresh Start," both aimed at improving the skills needed to search for a job, apply for a job position, and improve skills and motivation for the job search. Target groups include people with disabilities, youth, the long-term unemployed (more than six months), and other socially vulnerable groups. Collective and individual forms of support are provided together. The standard program duration is 36 hours (distributed across three weeks) for the "Job Seekers' Club" and 15 hours for "Fresh Start."

Public works are designed primarily for the long-term unemployed in order to support their labor motivation as well as to provide additional temporary earnings to unemployed workers. There is no special rule for who is assigned to the program, except that they generally come from the ranks of the unemployed. The participation time for the public works program varies across jobs.

Special programs and services aimed at creating and keeping jobs are meant for unemployed youth and the disabled. There are two especially popular programs for youth. The first, "Youth practice," is job placement in temporary positions for graduates registered as unemployed for more than three months. The second youth-specific program is temporary employment of teenagers (14 to 18 years old) in jobs subsidized by government funds, with employers getting subsides for hiring young workers, usually during school vacations. Employment programs for people with disabilities include measures for their professional rehabilitation, on one hand, and protected employment along with subsidizing of general employment, on the other. Jobs under quotas for the disabled are protected by the Law on Social Protection of Disabled. Currently the quotas are set at up to 3% of the number of workers on payroll in enterprises with more than 30 employees. But usually employers prefer either to hire the disabled as "straw persons" or to pay penalties, which are low.

There is no uniform set of criteria or rules for selecting a client to a specific program. The criteria used by regional employment offices are mostly social-demographic, educational, and/or skill-based, with the stress on pre-employment-period status in the labor market.

Since its founding and continuing through the mid-1990s, the State Employment Service became increasingly popular among the unemployed population and employers. The share of registered unemployed people in the total number of unemployed increased (Prokopov and Maleva 1999, p. 68). The number of people looking for a job turning to the state employment service rose as well (**Table 51** and **Table 52**). The State Employment Service dealt with between 30% and 50% of total vacancies by the mid-1990s (Prokopov and Maleva 1999, p. 68).

A sharp deterioration of the financial situation of the State Employment Fund has resulted in a decrease in financing even the obligatory employment programs in absolute and relative terms (Maleva 1998, p. 26). Some regions have in fact stopped financing ALMPs at all: In 1997, 42 regions spent only 0% to 5% of their total employment expenditures on ALMP (Maleva 1998, pp. 28-9). By 1998 the share of ALMP in total spending of the State Employment Fund was halved (**Table 53**).

The insufficient financing of state employment programs along with changes in the procedure for registering people as unemployed have resulted in declining interest on the part of the unemployed in taking part in services provided by state employment services. Since 1998, participation in programs sponsored by the State Employment Service has decreased (**Table 51**). The table shows that the most popular method of job seekers looking for work was through friends and relatives; social ties still play perhaps the most important role in job placement. Two other commonly used methods of job searching include job-seeking through advertisements and directly approaching employers.

There are only a few studies on the effectiveness of active employment programs in Russia. Moreover, the situation of permanent inad-

TABLE 51 Composition of the unemployed using different methods for job searching, 1992-2002*

Methods of searching	1992	1993	1994	1995	1996	1997	1998	1999	2000	2001	2002
Addressing to state employment service	28.1	28.3	34.4	36.4	39.0	39.9	37.2	29.4	25.9	30.3	33.4
Addressing to commercial employment service	1.0	3.1	3.8	3.8	4.2	2.4	2.4	1.5	2.3	3.5	4.2
Advertising in mass media and replying to the advertisements	8.7	13.6	15.6	16.9	17.6	16.3	18.6	18.0	24.0	24.7	20.2
Addressing to friends, relatives	29.9	36.7	37.8	38.5	37.0	55.0	57.8	54.5	58.4	59.1	54.8
Direct addressing to an employer	26.3	30.9	29.0	27.9	25.6	28.8	29.5	31.9	30.5	27.9	29.6
Looking for land, buildings, machines, etc.	1.8	1.9	1.4	1.4	0.9	1.1	1.0	0.7	0.9	—	—
Other methods	10.6	14.6	13.3	16.6	15.2	15.8	16.4	10.7	13.2	11.6	11.6
Average number of methods per one unemployed	1.0	1.3	1.3	1.4	1.4	1.6	1.6	1.5	1.6	—	—

*1992-95 and 1997-98 data provided for October; 1996 data are for March; 1999-2000 data are for November.

Sources: *Employment Outlook in Russia*, Issue 1 (2002, p. 127); *Labor and Employment in Russia* (Goskomstat 2003, p. 139).

TABLE 52 Job placement by state employment service, 1992-2002

	1992	1993	1994	1995	1996	1997	1998	1999	2000	2001	2002
Applied for job placement (thousands of people)	2,437.6	2,283.4	3,708.5	5,122.4	5,279.8	4,599.0	4,739.1	4,299.6	4,745.9	5,523.7	5,797.1
Including:											
Employed (in thousands)	95.9	74.0	125.1	169.9	150.2	102.9	119.0	113.3	177.7	206.6	196.9
Including those who wanted to work in their spare time	13.5	9.7	15.2	19.3	17.4	18.8	24.7	28.2	47.2	41.2	29.6
Students wanted to work in spare time	63.5	64.2	224.6	849.1	713.7	689.7	783.9	914.5	1,285.2	1,556.0	1,466.9
Not employed (in thousands)	2,225.1	2,062.5	3,193.8	3,937.3	4,415.9	3,806.4	3,836.2	3,271.7	3,283.0	3,761.0	4,133.3
Including those searching for a first job	—	427.5	619.2	619.2	1,351.2	1,300.9	1,467.6	1,608.0	2,049.1	2,449.1	2,396.0
Placed in a job (in thousands)	724.7	883.2	1,195.7	2,217.9	2,290.3	2,406.0	2,397.8	2,821.1	3,199.4	3,740.5	3,877.5
Share of people placed in a job of total number who applied (%):											
Placed in a job	29.7%	38.7%	32.2%	43.3%	43.4%	52.3%	0.5%	65.6%	67.4%	67.7%	66.9%
Including:											
Employed	15.2	18.4	10.0	10.5	16.3	29.1	33.2	43.4	54.4	58.5	62.4
Including those who wanted to work in their spare time	26.7	24.7	19.1	29.0	29.9	68.1	67.2	77.7	78.4	73.1	74.0
Students wanted to work in spare time	63.6	77.9	87.8	94.9	92.2	96.2	96.4	96.4	96.7	96.8	97.0
Not employed	29.7	39.0	30.2	34.6	35.8	45.0	41.8	57.8	56.7	56.2	56.4
Including those searching a first job	—	27.8	31.4	31.4	63.9	68.3	68.1	75.5	79.2	80.2	79.2
Pensioners	15.4	17.5	12.5	18.9	15.1	16.2	20.4	34.3	44.6	43.9	—

Sources: Labor Ministry data.

TABLE 53 Share of financing of ALMP in total spending of state employment services, 1992-2000*

	1992	1993	1994	1995	1996	1997	1998	1999	2000
Total expenditure of state employment fund	100.0%	100.0%	100.0%	100.0%	100.0%	100.0%	100.0%	100.0%	100.0%
Education and training	2.7	2.4	4.3	6.6	7.3	5.5	5.4	5.5	9.2
Public works	0.0	0.5	0.9	2.1	3.3	2.3	2.4	2.9	3.5
Supporting enterprises	18.2	24.9	16.7	17.8	8.7	4.1	5.6	7.0	20.7
Total ALMP	20.9	27.9	21.9	26.5	19.3	11.9	13.4	15.3	33.4

* The fund was cancelled on January 1, 2001.

Source: Maleva (1997).

TABLE 54 Comparative characteristics of costs and results of selected ALMPs, 1996-97

	In percentage to the total ALMP		Percentage to the number of unemployed		Costs per one participant, USD	
	1996	1997	1996	1997	1996	1997
Placed in a job, totally	100.0%	100.0%	23.2%	21.5%	$231.00	$238.00
Including:						
In organized jobs	2.8	1.7	0.7	0.4	1,100.00	1,422.00
By quotas	5.3	4.6	1.2	1.0	—	—
After training	11.9	9.4	2.7	2.0	543.00	621.00
Started own business	7.7	1.6	1.8	0.3	38.00	157.00
By programs for temporary employ- ment of teenagers	8.8	12.5	2.0	2.7	—	—
Mediation in job place- ment, including social adaptation programs	63.5	70.2	14.7	15.1	196.00	220.00

Source: Prokopov and Maleva (1999, p. 86).

equate financing of the State Employment Fund complicates any assessment of ALMP efficiency. Prokopov and Maleva (1999) estimated the impact of certain active labor market programs on individuals at the group and macro levels. In terms of participation and further job placement, the authors found that the training program to be relatively effective on individual and group levels for Russia on average, but the costs of this program were rather high. Prokopov and Maleva also compared costs and outcomes of these ALMPs. According to their evaluation, the mediation in job placement, including social adaptation programs, is the most cost-effective program (**Table 54**). The least cost-effective programs were the creation of new jobs by employment services.

Another way of evaluating ALMPs is by assessing efficiency in terms of duration of unemployment (see Denisova in Akhmedov et al. 2003) or by wages (see Nivorozhkina et al. 2003). Denisova has found that programs such as "Job Seekers' Club," "Fresh Start," public works, and occupational guidance

"seem to prolong the unemployment spells in one of the regions, and help to leave unemployment quicker in the other, with the size of the effects differing three to five times. The sizable difference in treatment effects prompt for substantial institutional differences: there seems to be high discretion in interpretation of employment service role in the local labor market revealed in procedures of program assignment....The decomposition of the aggregate result into components reflecting the treatment effect for the sub-groups of participants, in particular, for various age groups, education categories, localities and pre-history types, show that the treatment effect for certain subgroups, including those with redundancy pre-unemployment status and often those with secondary professional and secondary general education, are relatively 'positive' as compared with the average effect. The treatment effects turn to be better for females than for males for the majority of programs. (Akhmedor et al. 2003)

Nivorozhkina finds that vocational training positively affects the results of job placement of unemployed. If all other things are equal, wages of unemployed workers placed in a job after such programs substantially exceeded wages of non-participants. Women who participated in training programs increased their wages less substantially, but their occupational mobility after the training did not differ from that of men who received the training and was much better than the mobility of women who did not participate in the given ALMP.

The links between ALMP and informal employment are not clear. On the one hand, informal employment is already an active strategy in the labor market, while the aim of ALMPs is to return the unemployed to the labor market. Therefore, the sets of informal employment and unemployment can scarcely intersect. It is especially true that most ALMPs are aimed at the registered unemployed. And, in spite of some unemployed or inactive work informally from time to time, there is no evidence that correlates of trends of unemployment to informal employment. Alternatively, if one of the causes of informal employment is an insufficient number of "good" jobs, then employment services need sufficient financial resources to support the creation of good jobs by supporting entrepreneurs (as opposed to simply having enough money to cover individual worker training).

Conclusions and recommendations

Until 2001, Russia had no statistics on either informal employment or employment inside the informal sector. Since that time, statistics on employment in the informal sector—measured in accordance with ICLS 1993 recommendations—are published by Russia's state statistical agency, Goskomstat. Employment in the informal sector, according to Goskomstat, covers slightly more than 14% of the employed population in Russia.

Although presently the LFS questionnaire includes questions on registration of labor relations, no data on informal employment is published. Thus, the only source available for measuring informal employment is sociological surveys. As there was also no survey specifically targeted directly at the measuring of informal employment, we applied secondary sociological analysis here.

For the purposes of this chapter, informal employment covered all regularly employed respondents working without a contract, on verbal agreements with employers. This sort of employment absolutely prevents working people from earning legal incomes, paying taxes, and receiving social security. According to given sociological data, informal employment measured in this way covered from 17% to 22% of people with who reported informal employment as their regular or occasional work. Primary informal employment equals 12% to 16% of employment. Finally, the group of workers who work on their main job without a contract or another registration encompasses 6% to 13% of all regularly working people. These figures correspond to other estimates of informal employment in Russia based on sociological data when similar definitions are used (for example, Varshavskaya and Donova 2003, and Zaslavskaya 2002). Thus, overall informal employment (both regular and occasional) likely encompasses nearly 15-20% of all employed.

Even factoring in all people with any kind of labor activity, including occasional, our definition of informal employment gives minimum estimates of the informal employment phenomenon. It does not include other verbal agreements that may exist separately from the contract on, for instance, size of remuneration. This "shadow employment" is taken into account in this research, but if one includes people with informal wages in the overall definition of informal employment, its scope increases to more than a third of total employment according to CMC data. Our data also do not allow us to cover collective activities like subsistence farming, which also decreases our estimates of informal employment.

The limited number of survey respondents working either informally or in the informal sector prevents us from undertaking strict quantitative analysis, but comprehensive descriptive analysis was done and yielded the following main results:

Trends

- By both our analysis and Goskomstat data, employment in the informal sector and informal employment do not decrease in modern Russia. The number of observations is not, unfortunately, enough to provide grounded conclusions about the stability and causes of this trend. The RLMS panel data also indicate that not only is the number of informal workers growing, but more people are also staying in informal jobs more than a year.

- Component analysis of Goskomstat data shows that this growth is mainly due to an increase in the number of individual entrepreneurs and domestic workers. The former may be the result of changes in tax legislation that introduced a flat rate of income tax. Part of the observed growth can be illusory because there is evidence that some formal-sector employers register their employees as individual entrepreneurs in order to lower taxes. Employment within the household is also decreasing, a trend which corresponds with our observations on the role of subsistence farming in household incomes as measured by RLMS data. One can conclude that this trend relates to increases in well-being caused by economic growth.

- Whereas growth of the informal sector may in fact testify to increases in micro-firms and individual entrepreneurship, which is good for the economy, the growth of informal employment needs to be clarified further. If it really occurs, it may be a sign of inefficiency of the administrative and tax reforms. Further, one can assume that part of explanation lies in the sphere of labor regulation, which is strict enough in Russia.

Structure

- All data used include agricultural activities and THE rural population in the analysis. But our data underestimate these categories because of the understatement of involvement in subsistence farming. Under Goskomstat, the rural population comprises nearly one-half of all workers employed in the informal sector, and agricultural activities cover nearly 40% of all activities inside informal enterprises.

- The involvement of men in informal employment and employment in the informal sector is roughly equal in Russia, unlike in most of the developing world.

- In comparison with formally employed workers, fewer paid employees with higher education are working informally, while more workers with primary or secondary vocational or secondary school education are informally employed. Consequently, only a few of these less-educated workers are employed as professionals; most of them are service workers.

- At the same time, both employment in the informal sector and informal employment are heterogeneous. Regular and occasional informal employment consists of people with different socio-economic characteristics. Occasional informal employment is mainly rural, for "officially" inactive workers, or people with low education or skills. Regular employment is, for the most part, an urban phenomenon affecting mostly better educated people. Primary regular employment often occurs in trade and other commercial services, secondary regular employment is most often in industries such as in construction and transport, while occasional employment is common in agriculture. Further analysis should be conducted in order to reveal the strategies behind each form of informal employment.

- New private micro-enterprises prevail among firms that provide informal jobs, providing evidence that existing labor regulation is largely ineffective for many informal firms. It is not necessarily greed that is moving all these firms to informality. Many of them will be forced to close if they follow all the rules declared in the legislation. Ultimately, labor legislation needs to be carefully modified to lighten the hiring and firing costs of employers while maintaining some important employment and social guarantees afforded to employees.

Working conditions and security

- On average, the number of hours worked by people employed in the informal sector and on informal jobs exceeds the working hours of formal workers. At the same time, according to Goskomstat, the duration of working hours in the informal sector is varied, with the fewest hours worked in agriculture and education, and the most hours worked in trade.

- It is readily apparent from our definition that employees working under verbal agreements are not subject to social security protections at all. Preliminary descriptive analysis of two databases showed that informal workers receive social guarantees much more rarely than formal workers. Virtually no informal workers belong to a trade union. But it is said that in the absence of formal institutions, these workers develop informal instruments of dealing with an employer that are sometimes even more effective than those used by formal employees.

- The high level of remuneration compensates for the instability and insecurity of informal jobs. According to RLMS, on main regular jobs monthly wages paid are higher for informal jobs, but the hourly wage rate does not differ significantly. In contrast to formal jobs, remuneration in informal jobs is usually paid on time, and thus provides a source of regular current incomes. While full-time informal positions pay higher earnings than full-time formal jobs, they also demand longer working hours.

- At the same time, only a few workers consider this sort of informal employment as their stable strategy. Most of them leave informal employment after a short period of time. It is evident that there is higher labor turnover on informal jobs; average length of service in informal jobs is only 2.2 years, compared to 10.3 years in formal employment. Informal workers, as follows from RLMS, do not hold onto their jobs, but are ready to change at any time, and usually highly estimate their chances to find other "decent" work. It is not good of course in terms of human capital accumulation, but such a strategy provides more opportunities to survive in a transition economy.

Informal employment cannot be considered exclusively involuntary for a worker. Analysis of two sociological databases reveals that often employees are also interested in such form of employment. Taking into account that there was, historically, no period of high unemployment in Russia, it can be suggested that Russia's informal employment system has voluntary-rational character. For some age groups—for instance, for students—informal employment provides a good way of earning money and acquiring some labor skills and experience. For other inactive people, like pensioners or the unemployed, informal work provides (additional) regular monthly income.

In sum, informal employment is an important phenomenon in Russia's labor market. It closes down gaps that have existed within the formal labor market. One of the most important of these is wage arrears, which actually render even the most formally secured jobs insecure. Informal employment provides additional incomes to people on forced administrative leaves, i.e., the hidden unemployed population. It helps keep people economically active, raising the incomes of the unemployed and other "inactive" groups. At the same time, informal employment supplies the commercial services sector with a labor force that is cheap because of tax evasion.

Meanwhile, informal employment discriminates against people in terms of social security rights and their future incomes. In this sense, it is a factor in the future social exclusion of people currently working informally.

The fact that informal employment concentrates on micro-firms within the service sector casts doubt on the possibilities of decreasing informal employment via such steps as reducing the income tax or introducing a funded pension pillar.

It has been shown that there is no significant relationship between unemployment and employment in informal sector. Employment in the informal sector and informal employment are not coincident but overlapping subpopulations. All the facts taken together allow us draw conclusions about weak links between informal employment and unemployment, or even the absence of any connection at all. Informal employment is a widely used strategy on the labor market. Consequently, at present ALMPs can hardly have a serious impact on informal employment dynamics, especially because vacancies offered by the state employment service are mostly low paying. The effectiveness of certain

ALMPs needs to be further evaluated from a regional perspective. Profiling, which exists almost nowhere in Russia now, should also be introduced. While programs related to business start-up assistance and retraining could be effective, the most important issue is increasing the flexibility of the Russian labor market. This can be done through introducing changes in the Labor Code, specifically by introducing consistent liberalization of fixed-term labor contracts, reducing terms of preliminary notification about dismissal, and so on. In accordance with reducing the tax burden, such changes might lead to decreased labor costs for employers and, if enforced, could result in reducing informal employment.

Endnotes

1.   By official statistics, 38.7% of units among large and medium Russian enterprises were unprofitable in 2001 (Avdasheva, Astapovich, Batkibekov, et al. 2002, p.17).

2.   Note that the official estimates do not show this to be the case. Indeed, as noted earlier, the official estimates indicate a rise in poverty incidence from 24% in 1998 to 35% in 2000.

3.   Based on a comparison of household consumption to the household-specific poverty line and grossed up to population level by weighting by household size (World Bank 2000).

4.   The BLR is a method of accumulating data from all registered enterprises developed in socialist countries and kept in CIS countries.

5.   Author's calculation by: *Russia in Figures* (2003, p. 44); *Labor and Employment in Russia* (2003, p.181).

6.   Hidden wage is the wage paid to employees but not declared to official bodies. An employer pays no payroll taxes and an employee no income taxes on the hidden wage. It is measured by comparing wages obtained from LFS data with payrolls reported by firms in censuses, with further corrections based on expert estimates (Surinov 2003, pp. 214-35).

7.   In compliance with recommendations of the 2nd Delhi group (1997), published information on informal-sector counties should specifically select firms with below five employees. This criterion can be used as a strict definition of informal-sector enterprises for comparative purposes.

8.   This term relates to entrepreneurs that have a special license or patent allowing them to conduct their business as individuals instead of organizations. They do not need to conduct accounting or pay company income tax. Instead, they are obliged to pay individual income tax. We use the term "individual entrepreneur" to describe such individuals.

9.   See Methodological regulations on measuring employment in informal sector (Metodicheskie recomendatsii po izmereniyu saniatosti v neformalnom sektore ekonomiki) in *Methodological Regulation on Statistics* (Goskomstat 2003, pp. 226-34).

10.   The idea of selecting these four types of employment belongs to Dr. Svetlana Barsukova, from Higher School of Economics (Russia).

11.   For adjusting CMC survey sample to the Goskomstat population data, a proxy of universe, special weights reweighed. For calculation of these weights sex and settlement (rural versus urban) were taken into account. Let M11, M12, M21, M22 are the number of urban men, rural men, urban women and rural women in universe, while m11, m12, m21, m22—the same in the sample. Reweighed frequencies in the universe and the sample should be equal. For instance,

$$\frac{M11}{M11 + M12 + M21 + M22} = k_{11} \frac{m11}{m11 + m12 + m21 + m22}$$

From that formula a coefficient k_{11}, a weight for the given groups, is calculated:

$$k_{11} = \frac{M11(m11 + m12 + m21 + m22)}{(M11 + M12 + M21 + M22)m11}$$

Values of the coefficients are the following: $k_{11} = 1.3944$, $k_{12} = 1.1071$, $k_{21} = 0.9854$, $k_{22} = 0.8633$.

12. Delhi group 1997 criterion is applied.

13. By CMC data, if we add to that figure respondents with occasional work employed by persons instead of firms and/or self-employed, then the number of people working in the informal sector with regular or occasional employment increases by 26.3%.

14. Legislation fixes a regressive scale of SST if a worker's annual income is over 100 thousand rubles, by which a tax rate is gradually reducing even to 2% of payroll, but most small enterprises cannot afford paying wages at levels allowing such tax rate reductions.

15. The description of main ALMP in Russia in the following paragraphs is provided by using Denisova (Akhmetov et al. 2003, pp. 3-4), Nivorozhkina (Nivorozhkina et al. 2003, pp. 8-9), Prokopov (2001, pp. 67-81), Prokopov and Maleva (1999, pp. 77-85), and Yeltsova (2001, pp. 273-4).

Bibliography

Akhmedov A., I. Denisova, and M. Kartseva. 2003. *Active Labor Market Policies in Russia: Regional Interpretation Determines Effectiveness?* CEFIR Research Paper, June. Manuscript.

Avdasheva S., A. Astapovich, and A. Auzan, et al. 2001. *Survey on Economic Policy in Russia in 2000.* [Obsor ekonomicheskoi politiki v Rossii za 2000 god]. Bureau of Economic Analysis.

Avdasheva S., A. Astapovich, and S. Batkibekov, et al. 2002. *Survey on Economic Policy in Russia in 2001.* [Obsor ekonomicheskoi politiki v Rossii za 2001 god]. Bureau of Economic Analysis.

Avdasheva S., A. Astapovich, and D. Belyaev, et al. 1999. *Survey on Economic Policy in Russia in 1998.* [Obsor ekonomicheskoi politiki v Rossii za 1998 god]. Bureau of Economic Analysis.

Bangasser, P. 2000. "The ILO and the Informal Sector: An Institutional History." ILO Employment paper. ILO.

Bernabè, S. 2002. "Informal Employment in Countries in Transition: A Conceptual Framework." CASE Paper, April.

Carr, M., and M. A. Chen. 2002. "Globalization and the Informal Economy: How Global Trade and Investment Impact on the Working Poor?" ILO Working Paper on the Informal Economy, No. 2002/1. ILO.

Chen M., R. Jhabvala, and F. Lund. 2002. "Supporting Workers in The Informal Economy: A Policy Framework." ILO Working Paper on the Informal Economy, No. 2002/2. ILO.

Gaidar,Ye, et al., eds. 1998. *Economics of Transition Period* [Ekonomika perehodnogo perioda].

Gimpelson, V. 2002. "Employment in Informal Sector in Russia: Threat or Boon?" [Saniatost' v neformal'nom sektore Rossii: ugrosa ili blago?]. Preprint of Working Paper 4/2002/03.

ILO, 2002: *Women and Men in the Informal Economy: A Statistical Picture.*

Kabalina, V., and S. Clarke. 1999. *Employment and Household Behavior: Adaptation to Conditions of Transition to a Market Economy in Russia* [Zaniatost' I povedenie domokhosiaistv: adaptazia k usloviam perehoda k rynochnoi ekonomiki v Rossii].

Kapelyushnikov, R., and V. Gimpelson. 2004. "Labor Code: Has It Changed Firms' Behavior?" [Trudovoi kodeks: ismenil li on povedenie predpriatyi?]. Preprint of Working Paper 3/2004/03.

Maleva, T. 1998. T*he Russian Labor Market and Employment Policy: Paradigms and Paradoxes* [Rossiiskyi rynok truda: paradigmy i paradoksy] //

Maleva, T., ed. State and corporate employment policy [Gosudarstvennaia i korporativnaia politika saniatosti].

Maleva T., P. Kudiukin, S. Misikhina, and S. Sourkov. 2001. "How Much Does Labor Code Cost?" [Skol'ko stoit trudovoi kodeks?]. Carnegie Moscow Centre Working Paper No. 3. CMC.

Maleva T., N. Vishnevskaia, and V. Gimpelson, et al., eds. 2002. *Employment Outlook in Russia, Part 1 (1991-2000).* [Obzor zaniatosti v Rossii. Vyp. 1 (1991-2000 gg.)].

Methodological Regulations on Statistics. 2003. [Metodologicheskie polozhenia po statistike]. Vol. 4 / Goskomstat Rossii.

Nivorozhkina, L., A. Nivorozhkin, and O. Fedosova. 2003. *Modeling of Unemployed Behavior on Labor Market of a City* [Modelirovanie povedenia besrabotnyh na rynke truda krupnogo goroda]. Final report on the IISP grant No. SP-02-2-12. Manuscript.

Prokopov, F. 2001. "Policy Foundations on Labor Market in Transition" [Osnovy politiki na rynke truda v perehodnyi period] in L. Yeltsova, ed., *State Policy on Russia's Labor Market: Realities and Prospects* [Gosudarstvennaia politika na rossiiskom rynke truda: realii i perspektivy].

Prokopov, F., and T. Maleva. 1999. *The Policy of Counteraction to Unemployment* [Politika protivodeistvia berabotize].

Surinov, A., ed. 2003. *Unobservable Economy: An Attempt Of Quantitative Measuring* [Nenabliudaemaia ekonomika: popytka kolichestvennyh ismerenij].

United Nations Common Country Assessment for the Russian Federation. 2002. Office of the UN Resident Coordinator in the Russian Federation. Manuscript.

United Nations Development Program (UNDP) (2003), Human Development Report for 2003.

Varshavskaya, Ye, and I. Donova. 2003. *Informal Employment as the Main and Secondary Employment: Scopes, Composition of Employment, Specificity* [Neformal'naia saniatost' kak osnovnaia i dopolnitel'naia rabota: masshtaby, sostav saniatyh, spezifika]. IISP grant report.

Yassin, Ye, S. Alexashenko, Ye Gavrilenkov, and A. Dvorkovich. 2000. *Economic Strategy and Investment Climate in Investment Climate and Prospects of Economic Growth in Russia* [Ekonomicheskaya strategia i investizionnyi climat / Investizionnyi klimat i perspektivy ekonomicheskogo rosta v Rossii], Book 1.

Yeltsova, L. 2001. "Assistance to Employment of Citizens in Special Need of Social Protection" [Sodeistvie saniatosti grazhdan, osobo nuzhdaiushihsia v sozial'noi podderzhke] in L. Yeltsova, ed., *State Policy on Russia's Labor Market: Realities and Prospects* [Gosudarstvennaia politika na rossiiskom rynke truda: realii i perspektivy].

Zaslavskaya, T. 2002. *Societal Transformation of Russia's Society: Activity-Structural Concept* [Sozietal'naia tranformazia rossijskogo obshestva: deiatel'no-strukturnaia konzepzia].

CHAPTER 5

South Africa: bringing informal workers into the regulated sphere, overcoming Apartheid's legacy

by Wolfe Braude

Introduction

In South Africa, economic informalization can be viewed primarily through two lenses. First it is the actual growing informal (unregistered, unregulated) economy itself, spread across most sectors and intertwined with the formal economy in many ways. Second it is the process of informalization, whereby areas of full-time and permanent work are changed into "atypical" work, i.e., temporary, casual, or outsourced labor.

The informal sector in South Africa comprises between 7-12% of the overall economy, and it exists as a survival strategy for the unemployed. It has recently also become an area of policy focus, with the government noting the shockingly low salaries and poor working conditions faced by those who are employed in the informal economy. In a sense, the permanence of this area of economic life is being accepted by formal economy planners in a way that has hardly ever occurred in the past. This recognition gives hope for increased regulation and innovation.

In South Africa the Apartheid legacy still casts a long shadow over the labor market. It influences the way the labor market develops, its structure, its players, and its patterns. The legacy can be seen in the skills profile of the economy, in rapid urbanization, in the nation's poverty, and yet also in the determination of South Africans to make massive strides toward progressive legislation, innovative institutional responses, and the transformation of a previously highly dysfunctional labor market. The problems have led to possibilities, and whatever the setbacks or failures of the first 10 years of democracy, the changes have signaled a clear break with the oppression and intolerance of the past. The informalization of the economy occurs in the context of increasing poverty and unemployment and is linked to these two challenges. It is now the task of the new democracy to apply both policy formation and implementation to the challenges of the informal economy in order to increase the quality of life of those forced to work in this area, an area characterized by low levels of education, skill, income, opportunity, and access to state support.

Background

After assuming political power in 1994, the African National Congress proceeded to outline a macroeconomic strategy that sought to locate South Africa's developmental path within the broad economic consensus prevailing internationally. At first, the paradigm argued that redistribution, through the Reconstruction and Development Program, was vital to the growth of the South African economy and the development of all its citizens. After two years, however, the strategy markedly changed with the introduction of the Growth, Employment, and Redistribution Strategy (GEAR). Conservative in outlook, GEAR was implemented during the 1996-2000 phase as restrictive fiscal policy with a commitment to free-market principles through deregulation and privatization and a focus on improving the "global competitiveness" of South African corporations. GEAR was meant to restore fiscal discipline to a market and a state both cosseted by defensive economic planning and distorted by excessive state expenditure on Apartheid. This goal was allied with a reduction in government debt mainly to be achieved via a reduction in state spending. Together with a privatization strategy, a liberalization of trade policy, and regulation of industry, GEAR's focus on macroeconomic fundamentals was expected to produce growth and economic expansion sufficient to address South Africa's socioeconomic backlogs and absorb the unemployed. However, on the whole the developmental goals around employment and poverty relief have not been realized. After facing mounting criticism, the government after 2000 made a commitment to an expansionary phase, although many critics have noted that this expansion has been insufficient to address the challenges facing the country.

The reality from 1996 to 2003 has been that, while some of GEAR's technocratic targets were met, and a measure of economic stabilization was achieved, the end result remained stubbornly sluggish growth and only slight poverty reduction. Although government expenditure has been brought under control, debt levels decreased, inflation significantly reduced, the currency stabilized, and exports boosted, growth in gross domestic product has remained under about 3%, and as the 1996 GEAR strategy document itself noted, a growth trajectory of about 3% per annum would "fail to reverse the unemployment crisis in the labor market; or provide inadequate resources for the necessary expansion in social service delivery; or yield insufficient progress toward an equitable distribution of income and wealth" (GEAR 1996).

Although incomes and economic competitiveness have grown and development has occurred, it has been in the context of severe, ongoing job losses, as the economy has been restructured through increased liberalization and a focus on exports. This rising unemployment has led to increasing poverty and a further entrenchment of the "dualistic" society inherited from Apartheid. A larger, more multi-racial middle class has developed, but a significant part of the population remains in poverty. Increased unemployment has led to a growing informal sector, at the same time as unprecedented macroeconomic financial stability has been achieved. Campaigns by civil society, including unions, have been waged since GEAR's inception for a revision of the macroeconomic strategy in order to seek innovative solutions to the problem of serious unemployment and the attendant poverty levels. These efforts seem to have borne fruit.[1]

GEAR has been successful in the areas of fiscal restraint, tariff reductions, and inflation control—i.e., strategies implemented to correct the more obvious monetary and fiscal policy imbalances of the Apartheid era—and yet it has been weak in the real economy (growth and employment).

GDP growth overall and per capita

The South African economy was caught in a downward trend during the late 1980s and early 1990s, but this trend reversed with the peaceful transition to democracy. Economic growth, which had been declining since the early 1970s, dropped below population growth rates in the mid-1980s; real growth of GDP averaged 0.9% against population growth of 2.4% (Michie and Padayachee 1997). Indeed, by the end of the 1970s what analysts have described as an organic crisis had arisen. It stifled significant economic growth over the next 15 years, and formative reforms in the political dimension were deferred until the late 1980s (Marais 2001). Economic growth returned in the 1990s, but the rate of growth remained below 5%. The country's economy also experienced significant shocks, especially during the 1998 and 1999 cycle. In the main, these were externally driven vagaries, and the national currency, the rand, also took a heavy knock from global financial instabilities. In spite of such uncertainties the economy exhibited resilience. Real GDP grew at an average rate of 2.3% between 1994 and 2000. It then grew by 3.4% in 2000, 2.2% in 2001, 2.3% in 2002, and 2.8% in 2003. However, the GDP figures mask the fact that growth has been unequal both within industries and within categories of economic actors.

As can be seen from the data in **Table 1**, the government has succeeded in its stated goal of fiscal stabilization and consolidation within the GEAR macroeconomic framework. This is evidenced by the fact that the budget deficit has gradually been reduced from 4.6% of GDP in 1996-97 to 1.4% in 2002-03. The other indicator of this ongoing successful commitment to fiscal austerity is the drive to reduce the debt burden faced by the state. State debt costs as a percentage of GDP have shrunk from 5.5% in 1999-2000 to a projected 4.1% in 2003-04. This reduction was expected to release an additional R10 billion in potential spending. This spending restraint is an effort to move South Africa away from a reliance on borrowing and to reduce the legacy of excessive borrowing that characterized the latter years of the Apartheid state.

Excessive debt costs can reduce the spending capacity of the state, as can already be seen from the fact that servicing the debt absorbed 16-18% of the available budget in 2001 and 2002. However, the cost of a targeted debt reduction strategy under GEAR has been deferred poverty alleviation, with spending on services and delivery taking second place to fiscal austerity.

What is of interest is the "growth-oriented" nature of the annual budgets since 2000-01. This marked the start of a supposedly more expansionary budget process, although the expansion has been tightly controlled and focused. This stance has been carried through the 2001-02 and 2002-03 budgets and has been characterized by a commitment in

TABLE 1   Key indicators of the South Africa economy, 2000-01 to 2005-06 (in billion rands)

Indicator	2000-01	2001-02	2002-03	2003-04	2004-05	2005-06
GDP	3.40%	2.20%	3%	3.30%	3.70%	4.00%
Main budget revenue	213.4	248.4	275.7	304.5	331	361.2
Main budget expenditure	235	262.6	291.8	334	363.3	395.6
Main budget deficit	-18.3	-14.6	-16.1	-29.5	-32.4	-34.4
Deficit as % of GDP	2.00%	1.50%	1.40%	2.40%	2.40%	2.30%
State debt costs	46.3	47.5	47.3	51	53.1	55.1
State debt costs as percentage of expenditure	19.70%	18%	16.20%	15.30%	14.60%	13.90%
State debt costs as percentage of GDP	5.10%	4.70%	4.20%	4.10%	3.90%	3.80%
Inflation (CPI-X)	7.60%	6.60%	10%	7.70%	4.80%	5.20%

Source: National Department of Finance 2001, 2002, 2003.

principle to improved spending, increases in infrastructure allocations, and ongoing tax reform.

The fact that moves were made toward a growth orientation in the 2000-01 budget was perhaps an acknowledgment that the economy had not performed as well as expected under the first five years of GEAR, with the key indicators fiercely contested by society's various stakeholders. As noted in the introduction, the designers of GEAR had expected growth rates to climb steadily toward 6% by the year 2000. Yet growth reached just 3.4% in 2000-01, and it was accompanied by increasing rather than decreasing poverty and joblessness. It was within this context that increased spending may have been mooted. However, it is worth noting that the additional spending has not been a move away from the fiscal restraint policy platform of the previous five years, but has rather expanded within the space afforded the Finance Ministry through improved revenue collection by the South African Revenue Service. In other words, the state did not attempt to relax fiscal discipline, as can be seen by the ongoing efforts to cap the deficit at under 3%. The additional spending that did occur was made possible by increased revenue collection.

Critics of the decision to cap the deficit noted that South Africa's average annual budgetary deficit is no higher than that of several European Union members, and that South Africa has inadvertently fulfilled the necessary criteria for inclusion within the European Union Monetary Zone. In other words, critics questioned the wisdom or necessity of pursuing such spending restraints in the face of significant unemployment and poverty.

In short, although the budget has been labeled an expansionary one, it is only expansionary in the sense that the additional revenue created by increased tax collection has been earmarked for social spending rather than further debt reduction, and even allocation has not strictly been adhered to, since a sizable percentage of the increased revenue has been earmarked for tax relief, which, although expansionary for demand, does not strictly fall under poverty relief. The budget is not expansionary in the sense that the underlying premise of cost management and deficit reduction has been maintained. This approach has inherent limitations of sustainability (revenue may not maintain the same rate of increase) and flexibility (truly expansionary projects such as a universal poverty grant are disallowed). Furthermore, many of the increases are only just above inflation, meaning that spending in real terms is only slightly expansionary (Braude 2003, 10).

According to the latest preliminary indicators from Statistics South Africa (SSA), the country's official data collection agency, the seasonally adjusted estimate of real GDP at market prices for the third quarter of 2003 increased at an annualized rate of 1.1% compared with the second quarter of 2003. This followed real annualized growth rates of 0.9% (revised from 1.5%) and 0.5% (revised from 1.1%) in the first and second quarters of 2003 compared with the fourth quarter of 2002 and the first quarter of 2003, respectively. The revised real annualized growth rates for the four quarters of 2002 are 3.8%, 5.1%, 4.1%, and 2.6%, respectively, placing average annual growth at 3.9%. The quarterly figures were revised as part of SSA's annual independent compilation and revision of the GDP estimates for each quarter in the period 2001-03 (SSA 2003).

According to the revision policy of SSA regarding the compilation of national accounts for South Africa, annual and quarterly national accounts estimates are revised annually when independent annual national accounts estimates for the latest two years and the latest 10 quarters are compiled using more comprehensive economic and socioeconomic information, e.g., annual reports and financial statements of enterprises and results of household surveys, which tend to become available after the previous independent annual estimates are published. These sources

TABLE 2 Annual growth rates in real GDP at market prices from 1995

	1995	1996	1997	1998	1999	2000	2001	2002
Previous growth rate	3.1%	4.3%	2.6%	0.8%	2.0%	3.5%	2.8%	3.0%
Revised growth rate	3.1	4.3	2.6	0.8	2.0	3.5	2.7	3.6

Source: SARB 2003b.

are viewed as more reliable than the sources used for the quarterly estimates. Therefore, revisions are made to the annual value-added of an industry, the impact on the quarterly value-added of an industry of that year, as well as value-added estimates of the following quarters of that specific industry. Based on these revisions, **Table 2** shows the annual GDP growth since 1995.

Macroeconomic projections as of 2003 for the next period of the three-year Medium Term Expenditure Framework are shown in **Table 3**. Although household consumption is not seen as growing significantly, the successive tax cuts of recent years may still be working their way through the system, in which case domestic consumption may increase, providing some balance to the lack of domestic investment. **Table 4** shows tax cuts over the last four budget cycles. However, the tax cuts have not contributed to a rise in household saving, meaning that households used them to both decrease debt and increase spending. The decreased debt may start to underpin increased savings, however.

GDP sectoral composition over time

Tables 5 and **6** provide data on the breakdown of the economy's overall GDP into sectoral figures. Where possible, the figures include estimates of informal sector activity. Table 5 lists percentage changes in the sectoral GDP data, held at constant 1995 prices.

To demonstrate the current relative significance of the sectors to overall GDP, Table 6 gives the percentage contribution of each sector to GDP at current prices.

Liberalization and exchange rate policy

South Africa has undertaken a far-reaching trade liberalization program, agreed to under the General Agreement on Tariffs and Trade in 1994 and

TABLE 3 Macroeconomic projections, 2002 to 2005

Calendar year	Actual			Estimate	Forecast		
	1999	2000	2001	2002	2003	2004	2005
Percentage change unless otherwise indicated							
Final household consumption	1.4%	3.5%	3.1%	3.1%	2.9%	3.3%	3.7%
Final government consumption	0.1	3.1	3.3	3.5	3.1	3.7	4.2
Gross fixed capital formation	-8.1	0.8	3.6	6.3	5.8	6.4	6.9
Gross domestic expenditure	-0.1	3.0	2.4	4.3	3.8	3.7	4.0
Exports	1.4	8.4	2.5	-2.0	3.0	6.3	6.7
Imports	-7.4	7.1	0.4	2.5	5.2	6.5	7.2
Real GDP growth	2.0	3.5	2.8	3.0	3.3	3.7	4.0
GDP deflator	6.2	7.2	7.6	8.0	6.9	5.2	4.9
GDP at current prices (billion rand)	R800.7	R888.1	R982.9	R1,093.3	R1,207.1	R1,316.5	R1,435.3
CPIX (metropolitan & urban average for year)	6.9	7.7	6.6	10.0	7.7	4.8	5.2
Current account balance (% of GDP)	-0.5%	-0.4%	-0.2%	0.1%	-0.5%	-1.1%	-1.6%

Source: National Treasury Budget Review, Economic Policy and Outlook 2003.

TABLE 4 Personal income tax cuts, 2001-03

Budget year	2000-01	2001-02	2002-03	2003-04
Billions of Rands	R9,9	R 8,3	R15	R13,3

Source: South African Treasury, www.treasury.gov.za.

implemented under the World Trade Organization. This program built on trade reforms introduced by the previous government. In addition to lowering the average tariff level by approximately one-third over five years from 1995, more than 10,000 tariff lines have been rationalized to fewer than 6,000, and the differentiated tariff rates are being standardized to just six rates ranging between 0% and 30%. The steepest reductions have been in those sectors previously most heavily protected. Quantitative and formula duties have been converted to ad valorem tariffs, and other trade-related measures that contravene WTO rules, such as local content requirements and export incentives, have been abolished.

The tariff liberalization program, however, goes further than that required by the GATT agreement, and has been justified in the South African government's macroeconomic strategy as being essential for the generation of export-led growth. There has, however, been little evidence of export-led growth resulting from the altered incentives under liberalization (Roberts 2000b). The GEAR policy stated that "the central thrust of trade and industrial policy had to be the pursuit of employment creating international competitiveness" and identified the various trade liberalization measures as the policy "achievements" toward this end. While trade flows increased, the mean annual growth of manufacturing production over the 1990s was just 0.3%, and employment in manufacturing contracted over the decade to just 81% of its 1990 level by 1999.

Industrial policy measures instituted by the government since 1994 consisted of a range of support measures aimed at impacting the "supply-side" (Hirsch 1997). These included investment incentives and a tax holiday program, education and training measures, research support, and programs targeted at small and medium enterprises. Broadly, the basis of these measures reflected a belief in the need to improve produc-

TABLE 5 Percentage change in the annual GDP by industry (constant 1995 prices)

Industry	1995	1996	1997	1998	1999	2000	2001	2002
GDP	3.40%	2.20%	3%	3.30%	3.70%	4.00%		
Agriculture, forestry, and fishing	-19.9	24	0.9	-6.8	5.1	7.6	-3.3	6.5
Agriculture	-23.5	29	1.7	-7.4	5.8	8.7	-4	7.5
Forestry	2.4	1.3	-2.8	-3.6	0.7	0.7	0.5	0.3
Fishing	-3	-2.6	-10.9	3.5	1.7	2.3	2.7	0.9
Mining and quarrying	-3.1	-0.8	1.7	-0.8	-1.1	-2.3	-1.3	0.3
Coal mining	4.4	0.7	6.2	-0.3	0.4	0.7	-0.6	-2.2
Gold mining	-8.2	-3.7	-1.9	-6.6	-2.6	-4.6	-7.5	0.4
Mining of other metal ores	2.2	2.1	4.4	4.8	3.7	-6.5	4.1	3.3
Other mining and quarrying*	-4.7	0.5	0.8	3.6	-6.3	5.3	1.9	-1
Primary industries	-9.9	8	1.3	-3.2	1.3	1.7	-2.2	3
Manufacturing	6.5	1.4	2.7	-1.9	-0.3	5.1	3.6	5.3
Food, beverages, and tobacco	2.8	1.8	2.5	-1.5	-3.4	-1.9	7.9	-2.4
Textiles, clothing, and leather goods	5.6	-6.9	4	-8.1	1.6	-5	-2.7	6.9
Wood and paper; publishing and printing	3.5	-4	3.4	-3.4	1.8	3.3	0.1	2.6
Petroleum products, chemicals, rubber, and plastic	9.2	3	1.8	5.4	3.9	0.2	3	8.1
Other non-metal mineral products	8.2	-0.9	-1.3	-6.8	-7.9	13	3.5	0.4
Metals, metal products, machinery, and equipment	9	8.1	4.8	-4.7	-4.8	12.1	4.7	12.3
Electrical machinery and apparatus	11.6	-5.3	9.7	-3.6	-2.7	8.4	-1.2	7.8
Radio, TV, instruments, watches, and clocks	-10.7	-5.9	8.4	6.3	-1.5	-0.3	-16.4	-0.5
Transport equipment	16.7	-1.7	-3.1	-3.9	6.6	21.3	8.6	-0.1
Furniture; other manufacturing*	0	1.2	1.9	-1.7	2.2	3.4	2.1	4
Electricity and water	2	10.8	3.9	1.6	1.8	0.7	1.3	1.8
Electricity	1.8	10.4	4.1	1.1	1.2	1.3	0.7	1.6
Water	3.2	14.2	2.1	5.6	6.3	-4.1	6.1	2.8
Construction	3.6	2	3.4	2.6	-2.4	2.7	3.3	4.3

(cont.)

TABLE 5 (cont.) Percentage change in the annual GDP by industry (constant 1995 prices)

Industry	1995	1996	1997	1998	1999	2000	2001	2002
Secondary industries	5.6	2.6	2.9	-0.9	-0.3	4.2	3.2	4.7
Wholesale and retail trade; hotels and restaurants	5.9	3.7	0.4	-1.1	0.3	4.5	3.4	2.8
Wholesale trade	7.4	5.6	-0.1	-2.5	-1.1	5.5	1.8	1
Retail trade; repairs of household goods*	3	2.7	2.1	0.9	2.2	3.6	3.9	3.4
Motor trade; repair of motor vehicles	15.4	3.9	-3	-7.2	-3.2	12.6	8.3	5.3
Hotels and restaurants	4.6	2	-1.8	0.7	-0.8	-4.5	-0.5	2.9
Transport and communication	10.6	6.1	7.6	6.7	7.1	7	7.7	6.7
Transport*	4.7	2.6	3.7	2.4	1.2	2.4	2.9	1.8
Communication	29.1	15.2	16.5	15.4	17.9	14.1	14.2	12.8
Finance, real estate, and business services	3.5	6.8	4.7	5.3	7.7	4.8	4.2	3.8
Finance and insurance	5.1	12.3	6.8	6.5	13.7	7.4	6.6	5.3
Real estate	0.8	1.8	1.8	0.8	-0.5	0.3	-0.7	-0.2
Business services*	5	4.3	4.8	9.4	6.8	5	5	5.2
Community, social, and personal services*	10.2	3.8	-1.7	1	2.3	4.7	3.8	3.7
General government services	0.8	1.9	0.8	-0.4	-0.7	-0.7	-0.9	0.5
Other producers	1.2	1.5	1.6	2.3	2	1.9	1.6	1.4
Tertiary industries	4.5	4.3	2.7	2.3	3.5	3.7	3.4	3.3
All industries at basic prices	3	4.2	2.6	0.8	2.2	3.6	2.7	3.6
Taxes on products	4.8	4.9	2.9	0.5	0.1	2.3	2	2.8
Less: subsidies on products	8.3	4.5	3.8	1.8	1.1	1.5	1.3	4
GDP at market prices	3.1	4.3	2.6	0.8	2	3.5	2.7	3.6

* Includes estimates of the informal sector.

Note: Percentage change is the growth rate from one period to the next.

Source: SSA 2003d.

TABLE 6   Percentage contribution to annual GDP by industry at current prices

Industry	1995	1996	1997	1998	1999	2000	2001	2002
GDP	3.40%	2.20%	3%	3.30%	3.70%	4.00%		
Agriculture, forestry, and fishing	3.9	4.2	4	3.6	3.4	3.2	3.5	4.1
Agriculture	3.2	3.5	3.4	3	2.8	2.6	2.8	3.5
Forestry	0.6	0.6	0.5	0.5	0.5	0.5	0.6	0.6
Fishing	0.1	0.1	0.1	0.1	0.1	0.1	0.1	0.1
Mining and quarrying	7	6.9	6.5	6.4	6.3	6.8	7.5	7.7
Coal mining	1.4	1.4	1.4	1.4	1.3	1.3	1.5	1.5
Gold mining	2.8	3	2.6	2.4	2.1	2.1	2.1	2.6
Mining of other metal ores	1.6	1.6	1.7	1.9	2	2.7	3.1	2.9
Other mining and quarrying*	1.2	0.9	0.8	0.8	1	0.7	0.8	0.8
Primary industries	10.8	11.1	10.5	10.1	9.8	10	11	11.9
Manufacturing	21.2	20.2	19.9	19.1	18.7	18.6	18.6	19.4
Food, beverages, and tobacco	3.5	3.4	3.3	3.3	3.2	3	3	3.1
Textiles, clothing, and leather goods	1.4	1.3	1.2	1.1	1.1	1	0.9	1
Wood and paper; publishing and printing	2.2	2	2	1.9	2	1.9	1.9	1.9
Petroleum products, chemicals, rubber, and plastic	3.9	3.8	3.8	3.9	3.9	4	4.1	4.1
Other non-metal mineral products	0.9	0.8	0.8	0.7	0.6	0.7	0.7	0.8
Metals, metal products, machinery, and equipment	4.5	4.5	4.5	4.2	3.7	3.9	3.8	4.4
Electrical machinery and apparatus	0.7	0.6	0.6	0.6	0.5	0.5	0.5	0.5
Radio, TV, instruments, watches, and clocks	0.3	0.2	0.2	0.3	0.3	0.3	0.2	0.3
Transport equipment	1.7	1.6	1.5	1.3	1.4	1.4	1.6	1.6
Furniture; other manufacturing*	2.2	2	2	1.9	1.9	1.8	1.8	1.8
Electricity and water	3.5	3.3	3.2	3.3	3	2.8	2.6	2.4
Electricity	3.1	2.9	2.8	2.8	2.6	2.4	2.2	2
Water	0.4	0.4	0.4	0.5	0.4	0.4	0.4	0.4
Construction	3.2	3.1	3.2	3.2	3.1	2.9	2.8	2.6

(cont.)

TABLE 6 (cont.) Percentage contribution to annual GDP by industry at current prices

Industry	1995	1996	1997	1998	1999	2000	2001	2002
Secondary industries	27.9	26.6	26.2	25.7	24.7	24.3	24	24.4
Wholesale and retail trade; hotels and restaurants	14.3	14.1	13.7	13.3	13.1	13.3	13.3	13.1
Wholesale trade	4.6	4.6	4.4	4.2	4.1	4.3	4.4	4.5
Retail trade; repairs of household goods*	6.9	6.7	6.6	6.6	6.5	6.4	6.4	6
Motor trade; repair of motor vehicles	1.7	1.7	1.6	1.4	1.3	1.5	1.6	1.7
Hotels and restaurants	1.1	1.1	1.1	1.1	1.1	1	0.9	1
Transport and communication	8.9	9.2	9.2	9.4	9.7	10	10	9.8
Transport*	6.4	6.4	6.2	6.2	6.1	6.2	5.9	5.7
Communication	2.5	2.8	3	3.2	3.6	3.8	4.1	4.1
Finance, real estate, and business services	16.4	16.6	17.6	18.4	19.7	19.9	19.7	19.7
Finance and insurance	6.9	6.9	7.6	7.6	8.8	8.9	8.7	8.7
Real estate	5.8	6	6.3	6.7	6.8	6.9	6.8	6.8
Business services*	3.7	3.7	3.8	4.1	4.1	4.1	4.2	4.3
Community, social, and personal services*	2.7	2.7	2.8	2.9	3	3	3.1	3
General government services	16.2	17	17.2	17.3	16.9	16.4	15.9	15.1
Other producers	2.8	2.8	2.8	3	3.1	3.1	3.1	2.9
Tertiary industries	61.3	62.4	63.3	64.2	65.5	65.6	65	63.7
All industries at basic prices	100	100	100	100	100	100	100	100

* Includes estimates of the informal sector.

Source: SSA 2003d.

tivity and international competitiveness. These measures were influenced by the analyses of Joffe et al. (1995) and the World Bank (Fallon and Pereira da Silva 1994) and can be seen in the context of the World Bank's "market friendly" interpretation of measures taken by successful East Asian industrializers (World Bank 1993). Alongside the government's supply-side measures, the state-owned Industrial Development Corporation provides low-interest loans and equity finance mainly to large-scale minerals beneficiation projects (Roberts 2001, 3).

Adjustment

With a restrictive fiscal policy and a commitment to free market principles, GEAR is not very different from a standard IMF/World Bank structural adjustment program. In fact, the policy owes much to the "Washington consensus." The similarities between GEAR and the neoliberal model are in fact striking (Mather and Adelzadeh 1997, 2). GEAR's main tenets and its current approach to South Africa's problems reinforce such a description, namely:

- budget reform to strengthen the redistributive thrust of expenditure within deficit targets;

- fiscal deficit reduction across government to contain debt service obligations, counter inflation, and free resources for investment;

- an exchange rate policy of keeping the real effective rate stable at a competitive level;

- consistent restrictive monetary policy to prevent a resurgence of inflation;

- gradual relaxation of exchange controls with a view to their removal;

- tariff reduction to contain input prices and facilitate industrial restructuring, compensating partial exchange rate depreciations;

- tax incentives to stimulate new investment in competitive and labor-absorbing projects;

- restructuring of state assets to optimize investment resources;

- an expansionary infrastructure program to address service deficiencies and backlogs;

TABLE 7   GEAR projections and actual achievements, 1996-99

	Projected in GEAR	Actual
Fiscal and monetary variables		
Fiscal deficit (% GDP)	3.7	3.1
Real govt. consumption (% GDP)	19	19.6
Inflation (CPI)	8.2	6.6
Real bank rate	4.4	12.3
Real variables		
Real private sector investment growth	11.7	1.2
Real non-export growth	8.4	6.7
GDP growth	4.2	2.4
Average tariff as % of imports	7.6	4.4
Annual change in formal,		
non-agricultural employment	270,000	-125,200
Income distribution		
Gini coefficient	NA	0.68

Source: Seidman-Magketla 2001.

• structured flexibility within the collective bargaining system;

• a strengthened levy system to fund training on a scale commensurate with needs;

• an expansion of trade and investment flows in Southern Africa; and

• a commitment to the implementation of stable and coordinated policies.

As has already been noted, GEAR failed to achieve its own self-imposed targets, especially in terms of employment. It has been successful in the areas of fiscal restraint, tariff reductions, and inflation control, and yet weak in the real economy. These failures can be seen clearly by examining key indicators and their performance against the targets set by GEAR (**Table 7**).

Where the macroeconomic policy decisions of the last decade may have been of value is in reshaping the nature of the domestic business cycle. The domestic economic resilience and the surge in business confidence during 2001 and the first half of 2002 at the time of a synchronized world economic slowdown and major uncertainty in global financial markets seems to indicate that fundamental change in the domestic business cycle has occurred (Laubscher 2002). The business cycles over

TABLE 8　South African business cycles, September 1974 - August 2002

Downswing phases	Length (months)	Depth (peak-to-trough)*	Upswing phases	Length (months)	Height (trough-to-peak)*
Sept. 74 - Dec. 77	40	2.90%	Jan. 78 - Aug. 81	44	21.20%
Sept. 81 - Mar. 83	19	-4.70%	Apr. 83 - June 84	15	8.10%
July 84 - Mar. 86	21	-3.20%	Apr 86 - Feb. 89	35	9.50%
Mar. 89 - May 93	51	-3.70%	June 93 - Nov. 96	42	14.90%
Dec. 96 - Aug. 99	41	3.20%	Sept. 99 - present	36+	—
Average length % of period in recession	34.4 49.50%		Average length % of period in recession	34 50.50%	

* Percentage change in the level of GDP at constant 1995 prices.

Source:　SARB 2002c.

the 1990s, particularly since South Africa's reintegration with the world economy and the country's seminal political change, have not been consistent with South African business cycles in the previous decades (**Table 8**).

The 1989-96 (peak-to-peak) business cycle corresponds closely to those of the 1980s. The rapid transmission of external events to the South African economy and the resulting domestic economic fluctuations are overriding characteristics borne out by the close correlation between the domestic business cycle and the G7 countries' industrial production cycle over this period. The 1997-99 economic downswing phase of the business cycle presents the first evidence of meaningful structural change, being the first growth (as opposed to level) recession experienced since the second half of the 1970s. The steady real economic growth in the face of major financial volatility sparked by the East Asian economic crisis was surprising.

Likewise, the current economic upswing phase of the business cycle commencing in 1999 extends this positive change in business cycle behavior. Whereas the 1993-96 economic upturn and improvement in business confidence levels were cyclical in nature (and similar to the economic upturns during the 1980s), the current upturn provides a platform for a more fundamental lift in business confidence levels, signified by the Bureau of Economic Research (BER) business confidence index surpass-

FIGURE A   BER Business Confidence Index cycles, 1976 - 2004

Sources: BER, FNB press release 2003.

ing its 1996 peak despite major uncertainty on the world economic scene (**Figure A**). The index is constructed by interviewing business role players regarding how they feel about the business environment.

The Business Confidence Survey results are obtained from questionnaires completed by senior executives in the trade, manufacturing, and building sectors during the last month of every quarter. Questionnaires are sent to 1,400 business people in the building sectors, 1,400 in the trade sectors, and 1,000 in manufacturing. The response rate is about 50%. The sample of executives remains the same from one survey to the next. The business survey questionnaire contains questions on, among others, current and expected developments regarding sales, orders, employment, inventories, selling prices, and constraints (BER and Kershoff 2003, 2).

What is unusual in this cycle is that the domestic demand components of GDP are trending at weaker levels compared to previous cyclical upturns. Furthermore, South Africa's business cycles are mainly driven by household consumption, both in recession and recovery phases. This may be why the minister of finance has seen fit to implement three successive sets of budgetary tax cuts, with another expected in the 2004-05 budget. These cuts, although criticized as fruitless surrendered expenditure by civil society, may have served as counter-cyclical stimuli to reduce the impact of the downturn and boost the upturn in the current cycle (Laubscher 2002). The conservative economic policies introduced during the 1990s have exacted a steep price over the interim. There is clear evidence, however, of macroeconomic resilience in the 1997-99 economic downturn as well as in the economic upturn commencing in 1999, compared to the business cycles of the previous two-and-a-half decades. Low inflation, low budget deficits, openness to trade, and compensating exports allow South Africa to absorb external shocks. In terms of GDP, the business cycles since 1995 have been echoed by a volatile GDP, but since 2000 GDP growth has remained fairly steady (**Table 9**).

Unfortunately the financial volatility that South Africa attracted over this recent period increased the negative impact of GEAR's efforts to correct structural imbalances in the economy. The financial volatility of the 1990s meant that either economic upturns were delayed and/or downturns exacerbated. South African policy makers will need to introduce policies that will safeguard the country in this regard. A slower, more careful approach to the phasing out of exchange control, limited intervention in the currency market, and limited recourse to foreign finance are examples of such safeguards.

The increased domestic economic strength and resilience reveals that growth momentum in the South African economy is stronger, and the economy is becoming less dependent on the global economic cycle. This resilience comes on the back of improved productivity and profitability levels in the corporate sector, complemented by steady cumulative growth in real after-tax personal incomes, mildly stimulatory fiscal policy, and more competitive exports. South Africa may therefore be experiencing the maturation of the first phase of an "allocative shock" business cycle, i.e., the cost-cutting/downsizing/rationalization drive of the 1990s is bearing fruit and is likely to be followed by a cycle of growth and "upsizing." The real question in this regard is whether such growth will result in job creation.

As the export sector has been central in this process of cycle stabilization, it is imperative that jobs be created in this sector and its linked sectors. Exports as a share of GDP rose from 25.9% in 1999 to 28.2% in 2003. Beyond the export sector, policy options need to be considered

TABLE 9   GDP, 1995-2002

	1995	1996	1997	1998	1999	2000	2001	2002
Revised growth rate	3.1	4.3	2.6	0.8	2	3.5	2.7	3.6

Source: SARB 2003c.

that will augment job growth in the domestic economy (e.g., public works programs) and in industries with a domestic focus.

While there is evidence of a bottoming-out in the high rate of retrenchments in the formal sector of the economy during the second half of the 1990s (NALEDI 2003), it remains a question whether the export sector will deliver the required job creation, which can generate the multiplier effects to bolster the business cycle and economic growth. From the demand side of the economy, personal tax cuts, lower inflation, and more stable interest rates can go only so far in stimulating consumer spending; the critical missing variable remains formal sector job growth. In addition, where some growth in jobs has taken place, it is increasingly in non-permanent or insecure work. On the supply side improved profitability can only go so far in boosting business confidence — the more important factor is the relative buoyancy in demand conditions, which can boost fixed investment intentions.

As noted above, current business cycle prospects are promising, and it is possible that the South African economy has embarked on a higher growth path, but this will crucially depend on the future job growth performance and the structure that it takes. The trend experienced toward growth in informal sector employment will not serve to address this need, as the necessary stimulus is sustainable household wage expenditure, and, as will be seen later in this chapter, informal sector wages are mostly survivalist. The percentage of discretionary spending allowed by the low wages offered in the informal sector will provide at best a weak and pale imitation of the expenditure that increased formal sector employment would deliver.

Retrenchment in the public sector
The GEAR macroeconomic policy has as a central tenet the privatization of state assets, with the proceeds going toward stabilization of the

economy. The process is also meant to attract considerable long-term foreign investment interest. Privatization of state assets, although useful in reducing debt, has not had any significant effect on poverty or joblessness. The funds released by privatization have been used to meet debt obligations, and they may have allowed the treasury to commit funds to recent arms expenditure. The privatizations have promoted further retrenchments, which increase poverty. Those retrenched have often been unable to secure further formal sector employment and are forced to seek temporary employment within the informal sector. In addition, the process of privatization usually incurs large expenditure on improving efficiency in order to increase revenue streams and saleability of the asset. A question that must be asked is why such measures could not be implemented in order to retain the asset. Retention of state assets allows for some poverty reduction, in that nonprofit-based services are enjoyed by all. Obviously, if such inefficiencies are allowed to become significant, then the societal benefits, offered in the form of state-controlled prices, of retaining such services in the hands of the state is discounted. The services offered by the assets under privatization often cover general utilities and basic services such as water, electricity, and communication as well as inputs into manufacturing (such as forestry). These services and inputs are utilized not just by the taxpaying public, but by all South Africans. Even poor or unemployed citizens use electricity and water. To implement privatization or its cousin, cost recovery, is to restrict access to basic services and to pass a new burden of profit margins onto all citizens, rich and poor, employed and unemployed alike—as against unprivatized inefficiencies that are passed only onto taxpayers.

At best, partial privatization also allows an element of corporatization to creep in, alongside outsourced management support. This is evident in a change of focus toward market efficiencies rather than support for the developmental agenda of the state, and it is exemplified in the pricing policies of Iscor, the local steel producer, and the tariff policy of Eskom, the state energy supplier. Also, usually only the most profitable segments of state assets are sold, leaving the bulk of the inefficiencies to still be borne by the taxpayer and a reduced income stream for the state.[2] This is not to say that gross inefficiencies in the public assets should be tolerated, but that alternatives to knee-jerk privatization should be explored.

Thus, privatization is less an exercise in cost reduction than an exercise that passes benefits onto the asset-buying sector of society and reinforces the dualistic nature of the South African economy. Privatization or "restructuring," to use the current euphemistic term, has thus been fiercely contested as a viable economic strategy by organizations such as COSATU and the Anti-Privatization Forum. What is often not noted is that the sales price of such assets does not include the cost of building the asset but merely reflects the revenue-generating potential of the asset. Ironically, the increased fees and cost recovery that accompany the privatization of utilities may also directly undermine the competitiveness of South African industry, which has long enjoyed favorable cost ceilings in these areas.

Finally, privatization has failed to lead to ongoing levels of foreign direct investment outside of these specific offerings. Public sector restructuring has continued through 2002 and 2003, with Telkom's initial public offering now realized. A 20% stake in telecommunications company M-Cell was transferred in January 2002 from Transnet to an offshore passive holding company, and it has since been sold to local private operator MTN. For 2003-04, restructuring projects include the planned concessioning of the Durban port container terminal, sale of a 30% stake in Denel to British Aerospace, sale of 30% of Eskom's generation business, transformation of the electricity distribution industry under the management of the Electricity Distribution Holding Company, disposal of a 51% stake in the Western Cape Safcol forests, and completion of the sale of Aventura resorts.

Inflation

The rise in interest rates has been due largely to imported inflationary pressures following the sharp depreciation of the rand in the fourth quarter of 2001. The rand fell more than 37% for the year, making it the worst-performing currency after the Turkish lira, but it surged more than 34% in 2002 and became the world's best performing currency[3] (*The Star,* December 12, 2002). Figures from Statistics South Africa in February 2003 showed inflation as measured by the CPIX (consumer price inflation excluding bond rates) peaking in November 2002 at 11.3% and falling sharply to 4.0% in December 2003 on the strength of the recovery in the exchange rate, lower food prices, and moderate real demand trends in the economy (*Treasury Budget Overview* 2003, 6). The yearly average for the 2003 CPIX was 6.8%, down from 9.1% in 2002 and 6.9% in 2001. The producer price index also fell remarkably, from a 2002 average of 14.2% to an average of 1.7% in 2003.

In response to the 2002 inflation trend, the Reserve Bank raised its repurchase rate by four percentage points during 2002, which led to increases in bank interest rates and a steady moderation in private sector credit growth during the course of the year. Some analysts said that sustained high interest rates would cause more damage to growth than inflation, which would probably decrease naturally over time. The recovery in the exchange rate during 2002 resulted in less pressure on inflation, and by November 2003 the Reserve Bank had lowered the repurchase rate to 12.5%, its lowest level since 1986, and interest rates during 2003 were lowered five times.

The government's efforts at inflation targeting have been met with mixed responses. Some analysts have hailed what they see as a determined effort to bring stability and predictability to prices; the Reserve Bank says that inflation targeting provides long-term interest rate stability, cost continuity, wage stability, and certainty to the market. Critics note, though, that inflation targeting has meant the introduction and maintenance of high interest rates in order to curb inflationary pressures; they argue further that there is no proven link between forcing inflation rates below 10% and improved economic growth (World Bank 1994 cited in Marais 2001, 216). From this point of view, the ongoing passion for low inflation is more a function of purist economic theory and a desire for affirmation than it is a holistic strategy. An unintentional but negative side effect of the current fixation with low inflation is the increased repayment costs, brought about by high interest rates (among the highest in the world) of South Africa's domestic and foreign debt. Thus, although South Africa's debt levels are low enough that it need not fear falling into a "debt trap," the high interest rates make debt servicing a severe strain on the budget. The government has retained the high interest rates but has focused on cost cutting and debt reduction to compensate. The question that must be asked is whether low inflation through restrictive monetary policy is more desirable than the social spending on poverty and infrastructure that would necessarily be foregone through such policies. (Another interesting point is that high interest rates reduce the rate of return, and therefore attractiveness, of domestic investment but provide good returns for foreign portfolio investors.

Thus, the scenario favors marginal FDI over majority domestic investment.)

Food inflation also rose dramatically during 2002, peaking at 19.8% in October 2002 before slowly falling to 2.6% in December 2003. In 2002, food inflation on average accounted for 42.8% of the rise in the CPIX, compared with 20.5% in 2001. Given household expenditure patterns, food inflation reduces the real incomes of lower-income households more than others. The government has announced an inquiry into food prices, but was able to allocate only R400 million in additional funds over three years. The 2002 monies were used to subsidize cheap maize meal, but this supply ran out in a few weeks. Thus, although progress is being made in allocating funds to poverty reduction, events on the ground often outstrip the moderate increases allocated.

Poverty

Despite South Africa's status as an upper-middle-income country, its rate of poverty (a measure of the extent of absolute poverty) stood at 45% in 2000, a share translating into 3,126,000 households or more than 18 million citizens. South Africa's high poverty rate is primarily due to Apartheid's legacy, where the majority of the population was deprived access to income-generating assets. In 1995 the poorest 20% of households received a mere 1.9% of the total income in South Africa; by 2000 this share had dropped still further to 1.6% of total income. The poorest 50% of the country's households also slipped backward in these five years relative to the richer 50%. The poverty divide remained racial — in 1995 the average white household earned four times as much as its average African counterpart, and in 2000 the average white household was earning six times the average African household (UNDP 2002).

Poverty lowers the productivity of the labor force by making skills acquisition harder and increasing social fragmentation. Household incomes are thereby reduced, and in turn domestic markets are limited. South Africa has been described by the World Bank as among the world's most unequal economies. (The Gini coefficient, a measure of inequality, stands at 0.58; more recent analyses using 1996 Population Census data put it as high as 0.68, though the government disputes this figure.) Approximately 6% of South Africa's population captures over 40% of income earned.

As **Table 10** shows, the rate of unemployment is negatively correlated to the level of monthly household expenditure. High rates of un-

TABLE 10 Key indicators of household poverty and unemployment, September 2002

Monthly household expenditure category	Number of households	% with problems meeting food needs sometimes, often or always	% where children below 15 years collect water and/ or fuel	% with person(s) in permanent employment	% with member(s) of a trade union	% with person(s) in informal or domestic work	Expanded unemployment rate
R 0 – R 399	3,205,927	54%	13%	22%	6%	32%	55%
R 400 – R 799	2,890,267	42%	15%	34%	13%	26%	51%
R 800 – R 1,199	1,329,752	28%	9%	56%	28%	25%	41%
R 1,200 – R 1,799	831,533	19%	5%	63%	36%	17%	37%
R 1,800 – R 2,499	654,841	12%	2%	73%	46%	13%	24%
R 2,500 – R 4,999	826,267	8%	1%	74%	42%	10%	20%
R 5,000 – R 9,999	554,766	4%	0%	78%	34%	9%	10%
R 10,000 or more	224,252	3%	0%	78%	28%	6%	7%

Source: SSA 2002b.

employment in urban and rural areas also coincide with low-quality impermanent jobs and serious problems in accessing minimum basic needs like water, food, and energy.

As can be seen in the table, the quality of life of citizens appears to improve with an increase in income. Consider for example the figures for meeting food needs, permanent employment, and informal work. In families with a monthly expenditure of over R5,000, permanent employment is 78%; problems meeting food needs is 3-4%, and the share engaged in informal work is less than 10%. These families therefore have better access to resources such as higher incomes and quality formal sector jobs. In comparison, among families expending between R800 and R1,199, 28% sometimes, often, or always have problems meeting food needs, only 56% have permanent employment, and 25% are engaged in informal or domestic work.

While poverty has risen over the last few review periods, so has overall wealth via GDP growth, even if the growth rate driving that wealth has remained low. Although the policies of macroeconomic adjustment and stabilization epitomized in GEAR are aimed at providing a better life for all, they have reinforced the status quo by stabilizing and improving the workings of the *current* economic landscape and by opening up opportunities for individuals and groups who are *already* able to take independent advantage of opportunities. Thus, the largest share of new growth goes to those who are already economically, educationally, and logistically advantaged. Moves to alleviate poverty remain incremental in scope and impact because the problem is one of development as a whole, not fiscal efficiency.

A longstanding alternative to GEAR can be found in the People's Budget, which was drawn up by a coalition consisting of COSATU, the South African NGO Coalition (SANGOCO), and the South African Council of Churches (SACC). This initiative aims to stimulate debate, discussion, and critical comment on South Africa's development path in order to impact government thinking and actions (COSATU, SANGOCO, and SACC 2003, 1). It does more than simply look at differences with GEAR; instead, it is located within the context of a debate on South Africa's development path. The initiative offers a detailed proposal for a budget that will improve the lives of all South Africans in observable ways, with proposals designed to provide structured input around key budget events and demands for clear, coherent social, macroeconomic, labor, and trade and industrial policies (NALEDI 2002, 2003). To translate these proposals into reality, the People's Budget in 2001-02 called for increased social investment by means of the following:

- providing all people with a basic income grant —a small amount of money, between R100 and R200 per month, must be provided to all persons, with the potential to lift 80% of the poor out of poverty;

- implementing national health insurance—insurance paid as a levy would be pooled and distributed to service providers and institutions, substantially reducing the costs of medical care; the two-tiered health system (private and public) would be rationalized;

- extending the provision of free basic services;

- increasing spending on skills development;

- increasing spending on land redistribution;

- implementing an integrated treatment and prevention plan for HIV/ AIDS.

The People's Budget thus emphasizes the developmental role of the state. It believes that the state should drive a growth strategy, provide a social wage in the form of improved social security and public sector service delivery, and strengthen democracy and the public sector.

Human development indicators
As can be seen in **Table 11**, inequality and poverty remain ongoing 10 years after the democratic transition, as evidenced by the Gini coefficient of 59.3. Progress has been made, though, in literacy and access to water.

President Mbeki has referred to South Africa as two nations collapsed into one. The affluent sector, which is predominantly white, enjoys the privileges of a First World economy, while the other, with a significant proportion of black people, reflects a Third World existence. South African society still cannot escape the legacy of Apartheid social engineering that systematically disempowered and impoverished the African populace. Poverty and inequality are serious challenges confronting the country.

TABLE 11   Key social indicators for South Africa in 2002

Indicator	Rating
Human development index rating:	0.666 (119 out of 173)
Gini coefficient	59.3
Life expectancy at birth	47.7 years
Infant mortality of under fives	65 per thousand
Adult literacy	86%
Population with access to safe water	86%
Population growth rate	2%

Source: UNDP 2002.

A good example of the increase in poverty is the increase in malnutrition. Information collected by the Department of Health shows an increase between 1995 and 1999 in the number of malnourished children. Wasting among children (a measure of chronic malnutrition) has apparently increased dramatically in some provinces (Health Systems Trust 2002, cited in Watkinson 2003, 5). According to the 2001 Census (SSA 2003i), of South Africans age 20 and above in 2001, 20.4% had completed the full term of schooling, and 8.4% had attained some form of post-school higher qualification However, 18.0% had received no formal schooling at all. Housing categories were occupied by citizens in the following percentages: formal 64%, informal 16%, traditional 15%. Illustrating the ongoing challenges facing the government to electrify previously disadvantaged households, 20% of the population still used wood for cooking in 2001, 25% used wood for heating, and 23% used candles for lighting. As noted by the UNDP, 14% of the population does not have access to piped water, and 14% does not have sanitation facilities; of the 86% who do, only 52% have water-borne sewerage facilities. Regarding consumer goods ownership and telephone services, 73% of South Africans own radios, 54% own televisions, 9% own computers, 51% own refrigerators, 24% have telephones in their houses (however, only 6% do not have any access to a telephone), and 32% own cellular telephones. These figures exclude those living in hostels, hotels, and institutions.

TABLE 12   Unemployment rate (strict/official definition), Feb. 2000 – Sept. 2002

Category	Feb.-00	Sept.-02	Change +/-
Total employed	11,880,000	11,029,000	-851,000
Total unemployed	4,333,000	4,837,000	-504,000
Total economically active	16,213,000	15,866,000	-347,000
Total not economically active	10,242,000	12,118,000	1,876,000
Population, 15 – 65 years old	26,454,000	27,984,000	1,530,000
Participation rate (%)	61.30%	56.70%	-4.60%
Labor absorption rate (%)	44.90%	39.40%	-5.50%
Unemployment rate (%)	26.70%	30.50%	3.80%

Source: SSA 2002b.

Labor market trends

Unemployment and underemployment over time

Using the narrow definition of unemployment, the aggregate unemployment rate rose from 20% to 26% between 1994 and 1999.[4] However, according to the broad or expanded definition of unemployment, whereby a person is also unemployed if he or she has not actively sought work in the past four weeks, the increase between 1994 and 1999 was 33% to 36%. The expanded definition of unemployment is useful because it captures discouraged work-seekers, and it is therefore a more accurate reflection of long-term, structural unemployment. In 2000 the method of collection was amended,[5] and statistics for narrowly defined unemployment from that point onward are reflected in **Table 12**. The current official unemployment figures for 2003 are listed separately in **Table 13** because the 2003 population figures are based on the 2001 Population Census, whereas the 2000-02 figures are based on the 1996 Census. SSA is in the process of benchmarking the 2000-02 figures to the 2003 data to enable an exact comparison. A general trend can nevertheless be observed in the numbers, namely that unemployment is still rising, albeit at a seemingly slower rate. This conclusion corresponds to qualitative research by NALEDI among COSATU affiliated trade unions, which indicates that retrenchments are continuing, but at a slower rate than in the previous five years (NALEDI 2003b).

TABLE 13   Official labor market trends, March 2003

Category	March 2003
Total employed (a)	11,565
Total unemployed (b)	5,250,000
Total economically active (a+b)	16,815,000
Total not economically active	12,740,000
Population 15-65 years old (c+d)	29,555,000
Participation rate (%) (c*100/e)	56.90%
Labor absorption rate (%) (a*100/e)	39.10%
Unemployment rate (%) (b*100/c)	31.20%

Source: SSA 2003e.

Between September 2001 and September 2002 employment increased in the mining, manufacturing, and public sectors (formal sector) for the first time since 1996. Additional increases were noted overall across the informal sector. However, much of the increase results
from a methodology change introduced by SSA in 2000. SSA now counts
any income-earning activity, no matter how poverty-stricken or unstable,
as informal employment. Most of the jobs created will probably not
sustain longer-term development in the traditional sense, i.e., they will
not provide an income high enough to support a family, promote the
acquisition of skills, or increase productivity. From this standpoint, most
of the informal jobs created are a form of concealed unemployment, yet
are usually the only options available to millions of unemployed. A similar scenario applies to the biggest employment drive yet announced by
government, in November 2003. It comprises a massive public works
program that will provide up to 1 million mainly unskilled jobs over the
next five years in infrastructure repair and community service projects.
However, the longest of these jobs will be only of 18 months duration.
Most will have six-month contracts and will thus add only slightly to
the skills profile of these informal sector workers, who will return to the
informal sector once the initiative is complete.

The broad or expanded definition of employment (**Table 14**) reveals a far higher picture of joblessness. The expanded numbers essentially reveal that many workers are available but unable to find work,
and so have given up looking (potentially falling into underemployment).

TABLE 14   Unemployment rate (expanded definition), Feb. 2000 – Sept. 2002

Category	Feb. 2000	Sept. 2002	Change +/-
Total employed	11,880,000	11,029,000	-851,000
Total unemployed	6,553,000	7,925,000	1,372,000
Total economically active	18,432,000	18,954,000	522,000
Total not economically active	8,022,000	9,031,000	1,009,000
Population, 15-65 years old	26,454,000	27,984,000	1,530,000
Participation rate (%)	69.70%	67.70%	-2%
Labor absorption rate (%)	44.90%	39.40%	-5.50%
Unemployment rate (%)	35.50%	41.80%	6.30%

Source: SSA 2002b.

Under the broad definition, the unemployment rate increases to above 40% for the first time since the collection of standardized employment data. It is an unfortunate paradox that, although the African National Congress government has succeeded in bringing stability and competitiveness to the macroeconomy, this success has resulted in even lower levels of employment, thus concentrating the benefits of liberalization and stability in the hands of a small number of South Africans. The current broad or expanded unemployment figures for 2003 are listed separately in **Table 15**.

Within the official definition of unemployed, the 2002 statistics of those hunting for work are sobering (**Table 16**). Of the jobless total of 5.25 million, about 59% have never worked, 26% have been job hunting for one to three years, and 41% for more than three years. Among jobless people between the ages of 15 and 30, about 75% have never worked. This means that a large percentage of those available for work are still excluded from the formal economy simply by reason of lack of jobs, and it supports the assertion that in South Africa the primary driver for the growth of the informal economy is the lack of growth in the formal economy, rather than tax avoidance. It also means that this is a group of people for whom employment in the formal economy is not possible under the current economic circumstances. Even with future growth in the formal economy, the category of people who have never even been able to secure employment (the 41% of the unemployed who have been looking for over three years) are less likely to benefit, since ongoing

TABLE 15   Expanded labor market trends, March 2003

Category	March 2003
Total employed (a)	11,565,000
Total unemployed (b)	8,421,000
Total economically active (a+b)	19,986,000
Total not economically active	9,569,000
Population, 15-65 years old (c+d)	29,555,000
Participation rate (%) (c*100/e)	67.60%
Labor absorption rate (%) (a*100/e)	39.10%
Unemployment rate (%) (b*100/c)	42.10%

Source: SSA 2003e.

improvements to the Apartheid-era educational system produce better equipped school leavers who may tend to find employment first. This assertion is backed up by the belief of unions that, in the non-professional job categories, employers have been steadily retrenching older, less-educated workers over the last 10 years in favor of younger, better-educated school leavers, even though the older workers have more workplace experience.

In addition to the problem of absorbing underemployed workers, the social dimensions of long-term unemployment must be taken into account: potential job seekers are increasingly disconnected from the formal economy in terms of mindset and expectations. Long-term unemployment reduces loyalty to the state and the status quo, and renders people vulnerable to depression and the attractions of crime. Even where informal employment is found, it is unlikely that these workers will be able to migrate between the informal and formal sectors without significant economic growth in the formal economy, and even then workplace skills will be a potential constraint on employment. It is these concerns that will need to drive government policy in creating a more stable and regulated informal economy and ongoing re-skilling as interim measures until the entire economy picks up speed. Various analysts have estimated that GDP growth of above 6% will be needed to start reducing unemployment.

The gendered and racial nature of unemployment is still entrenched in the economy (**Table 17**), with present breakdowns still reflecting the

TABLE 16 The unemployed, by duration of job seeking, age, and whether they have worked before (official definition of unemployment)

Duration of job seeking**	15-30 years			31-46 years			47-65 years			Total		
	Total	Worked before	Never worked	Total	Worked before	Never worked	Total	Worked before	Never worked	Total	Worked before	Never worked
Total	3,135	791	2,342	1,703	1,034	569	412	325	87	5,250	2,149	3,099
Less than a month	168	62	106	79	57	22	20	17	*	268	136	132
1 month - < 2 months	155	58	97	68	51	17	13	11	*	237	120	117
2 months - < 3 months	164	50	114	64	46	17	13	12	*	240	108	132
3 months - < 4 months	132	36	96	39	33	*	*	*	*	179	76	103
4 months - < 6 months	138	33	105	56	42	13	11	*	*	205	85	119
6 months - < 1 year	341	88	253	118	84	33	30	26	*	488	198	291
1 year - < 3 years	958	243	715	326	223	103	56	46	*	1,340	513	827
3 years - > 3 years	1,002	203	799	922	475	447	249	189	60	2,173	867	1,305
Not applicable	31	*	20	22	*	*	*	*	*	44	19	24
Don't know/ unspecified	46	*	38	*	14	*	*	*	*	76	28	47

* For all values of 10,000 or lower the sample size is too small for reliable estimates.

** Information on this topic is not available for the expanded definition of unemployment.

Source: SSA 2003e.

TABLE 17 Official unemployment by race and gender, March 2003

Racial group	Unemployment totals by group	Percentage of overall total	Gender analysis of percentage	
			Male	Female
Black African	4,592,000	87.50%	47%	53%
Coloured	392,000	7.50	47	53
Indian/Asian	123,000	2.30	48	52
White	142,000	2.70	50	50
Total	5,250,000	100.00	48	52

Source: SSA 2003e.

economic patterns of the country's colonial and Apartheid forms of capitalism.

Unemployment rates are highest overall for rural African women (**Table 18**). The September 2000 and September 2002 Labor Force Surveys show that unemployment rose more for African women than for any other group (by 9% in just two years). Unemployment among African men rose by 6% between 2000 and 2002. These changes increased the number of unemployed by 757,122 among African women and by 528,474 among African men.

Sectoral shifts in GDP composition and employment
Only a handful of sectors have shown an increase in their demand for labor, including leather products, plastic products, wood and wood products, wholesale and retail trade, printing and publishing, medical services, basic chemicals and other chemicals, and television and communications equipment production (**Table 19**). In terms of labor demand, these industries are also relatively new on the scene, judging from the positions they held during the 1991-96 period. However, with the exception of wholesale and retail trade, none of these industries has a large weight in the total demand for labor, as can be seen in the second last column of the table.

Labor shedding has unfortunately been the trend in the relatively large sectors such as gold mining, agriculture, and general government, and these losses have cancelled whatever little gains in labor demand have been recorded anywhere (TIPS 2003). It seems that the ongoing

TABLE 18   Expanded definition of unemployment by race, gender, and location

	African	Coloured	Indian/Asian	White	Total
Urban men	41%	28%	19%	8%	32%
Urban women	53	34	33	11	43
Rural men	45	12	10	1	41
Rural women	58	34	4	13	56

Source: SSA 2002b.

employment crisis is not only the result of the poor performance of some industries; while a number have reported good growth, production processes have become less labor intensive, not only across the board but specifically in those industries that have performed well in terms of their contribution to GDP. Thus, although the GDP data have been fairly positive, the impact on employment has been fairly negative. The country is getting wealthier as a whole, but, as with employment, the wealth has become more concentrated within certain high-growth sectors.

Thus, the employment crisis will demand a nuanced policy solution, given that a number of industries have achieved relatively high growth in value-added while shedding labor at the same time, including financial services, business services, motor vehicles, parts and accessories, and communications services. Though the structure of the South African economy appears to have been successfully aligned and restructured to match global trends with a move in the direction of the "new economy," and though it has seen a shift in production toward tertiary industries, it is increasingly clear that this restructuring is not able to address the employment crisis and has, in fact, fueled it.

Average real wages over time
The average level of wage settlements rose over the last two years along with inflation. A recent survey placed wage settlements at 7.4% in 2001, 8.0% in 2002, and 8.9% in the first half of 2003. Statistics South Africa places the 2002 increase at closer to 10.2%. Most commentators expect that, with the rapid decline of inflation in 2003, wage demands will moderate accordingly in 2004. The pickup in nominal wage growth during 2002 is corroborated by information from the Automated Clearing

TABLE 19   Growth in labor demand in 46 industries, 1991-2001

	Sector	Annual change 1997-2001	Annual change 1991-96	1991-96 rank	Avg. share 1997-2001	1997-2001 rank	Avg. share 1991-96	1991-96 rank
1	Printing	5.0%	0.3%	16	0.7	27	0.7	29
2	Leather products	4.5	-6.4	43	0.1	43	0.1	44
3	Trade	4.3	-0.9	23	10.1	4	9.1	4
4	Plastic products	3.9	0.2	17	0.7	28	0.6	31
5	Wood & wood products	2.8	1.7	7	1.0	20	0.8	28
6	Other chemicals	2.3	-1.6	26	0.9	23	0.9	23
7	Other mining	1.3	6.8	1	1.9	12	1.7	13
8	Medical services	0.9	0.7	13	0.9	22	0.8	24
9	Business services	0.8	1.3	9	3.8	5	3.4	6
10	Other products	0.7	-0.3	18	14.7	2	14.0	2
11	Other services	0.6	2.6	5	1.6	15	1.4	16
12	Motor vehicles & parts	0.3	0.7	12	1.0	19	1.0	19
13	TV & communications equipment	-0.4	1.6	8	0.2	37	0.2	41
14	Furniture	-0.4	3.0	4	0.6	32	0.6	32
15	Clothing	-0.4	4.7	2	1.8	13	1.6	14
16	Electricity	-0.5	-3.2	33	0.9	24	0.8	25
17	Basic chemicals	-1.5	-2.7	31	0.4	33	0.4	34
18	Electrical machinary	-1.8	-1.1	24	1.1	18	1.2	18
19	Water supplies	-1.9	-5.1	41	0.1	44	0.1	42
20	Agriculture	-2.0	-0.9	22	10.6	3	11.0	3
21	Scientfic equipment	-2.0	1.2	10	0.1	45	0.1	45
22	Machinery	-2.4	0.9	11	0.9	21	0.9	21
23	Paper & paper products	-2.5	-0.7	21	0.6	31	0.6	30
24	General government	-2.5	4.0	3	20.1	1	18.2	1
25	Beverages	-3.1	-3.7	34	0.4	34	0.4	33

(cont.)

TABLE 19 (cont.) Growth in labor demand in 46 industries, 1991-2001

	Sector	Annual change 1997-2001	Annual change 1991-96	1991-96 rank	Avg. share 1997-2001	1997-2001 rank	Avg. share 1991-96	1991-96 rank
26	Financial services	-3.3%	2.5%	6	2.8	8	2.5	10
27	Food	-3.4	-2.2	30	2.3	10	2.5	11
28	Communications	-3.9	-1.6	27	1.1	17	1.3	17
29	Other industry	-4.3	-1.2	25	0.3	35	0.3	36
30	Metal products	-4.6	-0.5	20	1.5	16	1.6	15
31	Rubber products	-5.2	0.4	15	0.2	39	0.2	39
32	Other transportation equipment	-5.8	-8.4	46	0.2	41	0.2	40
33	Petrolium refining	-6.0	-3.9	37	0.2	38	0.3	37
34	Transportation & storage	-6.2	-5.0	40	2.9	7	3.4	7
35	Tobacco	-6.6	-6.6	45	0.0	46	0.0	46
36	Coal mining	-6.9	-4.1	38	0.8	26	0.8	27
37	Textiles	-7.0	-3.7	35	0.8	25	0.9	20
38	Glass & glass products	-7.3	0.4	14	0.1	42	0.1	43
39	Bas n-fer met	-8.1	-6.5	44	0.2	40	0.2	38
40	Cat & accomm	-8.1	-2.1	29	2.7	9	3.0	8
41	Civil engineering	-8.9	-0.4	19	1.6	14	1.9	12
42	Contruction	-8.9	-4.7	39	2.0	11	2.7	9
43	Bas iron & st	-8.9	-5.4	42	0.6	30	0.8	26
44	Gold mining	-11.0	-3.9	36	3.6	6	5.0	5
45	Non-met mins	-13.9	-2.9	32	0.7	29	0.9	22
46	Footwear	-15.0	-1.9	28	0.3	36	0.3	35

Source: TIPS 2003.

TABLE 20   Average monthly salaries and wages (including bonuses and overtlme payments), at current prices for industry, February 2003

Industry sector	Avg. monthly wage*
Total employed	11,565,000
Mining and quarrying	R5,604
Manufacturing	R5,488
Electricity, gas, and water supply	R16,277
Construction	R3,987
Wholesale, retail, motor trade, and hotels	R4,483
Transport, storage, and communication	R7,156
Governmental institutions	R8,729
Non-governmental institutions	R4,303
Financial institutions	R11,770
Community, social, and personal services	R7,681
National departments	R8,428
Provincial administrations	R7,697
Local governments	R5,933
Other government institutions	R10,136
Total government sector	R7,724
Laundries and dry-cleaning services	R2,010

* Figures in dollars for some of these tables are given in the accompanying dataset.
  The exchange rate as of November 25, 2003 was R6.65 to a U.S. dollar.

Source: SSA 2003g.

Bureau on the average salaries, wages, and pensions deposited into the bank accounts of almost five million salaried and retired workers. According to these statistics, the average payment rose by 10.1% in 2002 and by 10.3% on an annual basis through the first quarter of 2003. It moderated to 7.3% in the second quarter of 2003. According to the Survey of Average Monthly Earnings by SSA (see sector details in **Table 20**), nominal remuneration per worker increased by 10.6% in 2002 and by 10.0% through February 2003.

The average annual rate of productivity growth from 1995 to June 2002 was 4.8%. Over the same period, real wages grew at an average year-on-year rate of 2.5%, contributing to declining unit labor costs. These figures are a reflection of the form that restructuring has taken, with increasing capital intensivity and a concentration of job losses among lower-skilled (mostly black) employees. Economy-wide productivity growth fell during 2002 from a year-on-year rate of 3.7% in the

TABLE 21 Workers (employers, employees, and self-employed) by monthly income and sector (thousands)

Monthly income	Formal	Informal	Domestic	Unspecified	Total
Total number of workers*	8,223	2,265	1,005	73	11,565
None	33	317	*	0	351
R1 - R500	693	899	578	11	2,182
R501 - R1,000	1,187	486	308	*	1,991
R1,001 - R2,500	2,361	320	96	13	2,789
R2,501 - R8,000	2,526	131	*	14	2,674
R8,001+	726	32	0	*	764
Don't know/refused	679	76	16	*	780

* For all values of 10,000 or lower the sample size is too small for reliable estimates.
  Due to rounding, numbers do not necessarily add up to totals.

Source: SSA 2003e.

first quarter to 1.8% in the fourth quarter. Labor productivity increased in all the main sectors of the economy during 2002. In the transport, storage, and communication sector and in the financial intermediation and insurance industry, labor productivity growth remained robust. This growth was largely related to the capital-intensive nature of the expansion in production capacity in these sectors (South Africa Reserve Bank 2003).

However, the picture for monthly earnings by workers across a wider range of sectors, and analyzed by broad salary levels, shows that a large number of workers are earning very low salaries. **Table 21** shows that a significant percentage of workers still earn R2,500 or less a month across all the sectors. At a salary of R2,500 or less, it is unlikely that the worker will be able to access a bank loan to purchase a house or vehicle, and, in many sectors, these salaries would be largely those for unskilled work, thus providing another barrier to wage improvement through career advancement. In addition, slightly more than two million workers earn less than R500 a month ($71 at early 2003 exchange rates), which is far below the poverty line. Although the majority of these R500 workers fall in the informal sector, 31% class themselves as formal sector workers, revealing the disparities (often as a result of historical Apartheid

TABLE 22 Median monthly wage rates among working-class black households (Sept. 2002 rands)[1]

	Formal unionized		Formal non-unionized		Informal	
	Male	Female	Male	Female	Male	Female
Agriculture, etc.	R900	R652	R500	R448	R375	R326
Mining & quarrying	R2,000	R1,700	R1,640	R1,000	R350	R350
Manufacturing	R2,174	R1,652	R1,739	R1,225	R870	R400
Electricity, etc.	R3,000	R1,937	R1,937	R1,937	—	—
Construction	R2,000	R1,937	R1,225	R800	R800	R350
Wholesale & retail	R1,937	R1,600	R1,225	R1,000	R652	R350
Transport, etc.	R2,958	R2,958	R1,500	R1,937	R1,225	R500
Financial, etc.	R1,800	R2,000 [2]	R1,600	R1,800	R750	R500
Community, etc.	R3,500	R3,969	R1,937	R1,500	R707	R522
Private households*	R1,000	R665	R470	R250	R400**	R400**

Notes: Excludes missing values, extremes, and outliers. Includes African, Indian/Asian, and Coloured workers in households spending less than R5,000 per month

*   Refers to gardeners.
**   The same median values apply to domestic workers.

[1] Median values, as opposed to averages, give a better indication of the center of the dataset in skewed (non-normal) distributions.
[2] The wages given for female workers are higher in the financial and transport sectors in some cases. This may be due to a combined gendered and racial distribution of skilled job categories, with more female than male workers from traditionally higher paid and skilled groups (white, Indian, Coloured) often holding the majority of clerical or low to middle management jobs in these sectors. This ranges from 60–80% female.

Source: SSA 2002b (from Orr and Watkinson 2003).

wage policies) within this sector and the number of workers who earn informal sector wages within the formal sector.

Once again, black African workers (**Table 22**) make up the largest group of those earning low salaries. Out of a total of 7,818,000 black workers, 72% fell within the R12,500 bracket in September 2002. Table 22 shows that unionized workers earn consistently higher wages than non-unionized workers and that gender disparities still exist regarding wage levels, with female workers paid much less than male workers.

Migration (rural-urban and out-migration)
Out migration

Migration between South Africa and other countries after 2000 has been changing in nature as the economy and political situation have stabilized. Post-2000 emigration has been dropping and immigration has been climbing. The emigration data from 1970 to the present show three major peaks, in 1977, 1986, and 1994. During those years, the leading destination country for self-declared emigrants was the United Kingdom. In the post-1994 period, the trend in self-declared emigration from South Africa to other countries has been gradual. In 2002 the number of self-declared emigrants was 11.2% lower than that of 2001 (a drop from 12,260 in 2001 to 10,890 in 2002).

From 1990 on, the number of documented immigrants to South Africa trended downward. In 2002, however, the number of documented immigrants to South Africa was 6,545, an increase of 35.5% compared to the 2001 figure of 4,835 (SSA 2003c). However, the trend is still consistently negative since 1993.

Over the years official statistics on self-declared emigration from South Africa show that the five leading overseas destination countries to be the U.K., the United States, Canada, Australia, and New Zealand. For the U.S., Australia, and New Zealand, the estimated number of resident immigrants from South Africa far exceed the SSA estimate of total emigrants to those countries. The difference was a little over 40,000 for the U.S. by 1995 and close to 22,000 for Australia by 1998. The difference lies in the fact that emigrants from South Africa often do not declare their intention to South African authorities. The official statistics on emigration from South Africa to the five leading destination countries comes to 205,022 over the period 1970-2001. However, from the perspective of the receiving countries, the total number of South African citizens/residents who have immigrated to those countries was 322,499 by 2001. By this count the SSA figures represent a 57.3% undercount. SSA estimates the total emigration to all countries during the period 1970-2001 at 275,019; applying the above underestimate to this figure suggests that a total of 392,496 South African citizens/residents left the country between 1970 and 2001.

The skills breakdown of the emigrants and the percentage economically active shows that South Africa is losing skilled workers. Of those emigrating in 2000, 90% of those economically active were emigrating. This share dropped to 88% in 2001 and to 86% in 2002. It is not possible to pin down the exact reasons that such professionals emigrate, i.e., whether it is a normal matter of global labor migration or the reputed "brain drain" that the democratic South Africa has faced. Propo-

TABLE 23 Provincial GDP and population increase

Province	GDP growth in 2002 of 3.6% or over	Population growth in 2001 census over 1996 census
Gauteng	5.30%	20%
Western Cape	3.60%	14%

Source: SSA 2001a.

nents of the brain drain theory claim that affirmative action and increased crime and poverty have persuaded many professionals to emigrate. However, anecdotal evidence suggests that the rate of emigration is slowing as emigrants discover that South Africa offers a high standard of living for skilled workers. It is still, though, a matter of concern that a country with the potential and beauty of South Africa is not able to retain skilled citizens. It is worth noting that, of the economically active immigrants, 25% were from Africa, and if one adds Central and South America, the Middle East, and Asia, this number rises to 57% of total immigrants, which means that South Africa is attracting skilled workers from the developing and developed worlds in almost equal numbers.

Internal migration
The South African population grew by 10% between the 1996 and 2001 Census, but the growth rates of the provinces varied, with the most economically active provinces (those with 3.6% growth or more in 2002) largely showing an above average growth rate in population in 2001 (**Table 23**). The national average in 2002 was 3.6%. Although the Census does not distinguish between population increase as a result of birth versus that caused by migration, it is likely that the most economically active provinces attracted inter-provincial migrants.

It is predicted that 93% of urbanization in the next 25 years will take place in the developing world. As a result, it is expected that traditional big cities of the North will be exceeded in size by cities in developing nations. South Africa is ahead of the world average in terms of urbanization, at 65% versus 55%. It is estimated that by 2010 close to 70% of the South African population will be urbanized.

Legislation in the labor market and the rule of law

A range of legislation covers the working environment in South Africa. Many of these laws were passed in the 1990s and are among the most progressive in the world, providing for institutions to settle disputes and ensure fairness in the workplace. This has been a significant development for South African workers, as industrial relations in the Apartheid era were characterized by high levels of racial discrimination, conflict, union repression, cheap labor policies, and authoritarian management style. The post-1994 labor legislation has been the product of extensive consultation between government, labor, and employers and should be considered an essential piece of the democratization of South Africa. Alongside the various pieces of legislation have been the introduction of institutions to assist stakeholders in the implementation of the acts and interpretation of the laws in the workplace.

The legislation examined below deals specifically with the regulation of workplace safety and labor disputes. Legislation dealing with vocational training and skills development is covered in the later section, "Vocational training structure."

Occupational Health and Safety Act of 1993

The changes to the legal system commenced with the Occupational Health and Safety Act of 1993 (OHSA), which provides for the health and safety of persons at work and/or in connection with the use of plant and machinery, and provides protection against hazards to health and safety at work. It sets health and safety standards at work and attempts to prevent accidents from occurring. OHSA therefore places extensive duties on employers and users of machinery by, for example, obliging the employer to establish safety committees in various circumstances.

The act also established an Advisory Council for Occupational Health and Safety (Bowens 2002) to advise the minister of labor on policy matters relating to occupational health and safety. It is composed of 20 members who are nominated by trade union federations, employer bodies, and government departments. A major challenge facing the council has been to put mechanisms in place to reduce occupational accidents and fatalities, particularly in South Africa's mining industry, where the fatality rate is still unacceptably high (between 1991 and 2001, the gold mines claimed 3,496 lives in accidents).

National Economic, Development, and Labor Council, 1994

The National Economic, Development, and Labor Council (NEDLAC) is an institution of social dialogue that was launched in 1995 following the unanimous passage of the NEDLAC Act by Parliament in 1994. The basis of NEDLAC came from the anti-Apartheid movement's struggle against unilateral decision making and was driven by campaigns from all sectors of society for decisions to be taken in a more inclusive and transparent manner. NEDLAC is composed of representatives from government, organized labor, organized business, and community groups who debate and try to reach consensus on social and economic policy issues in what the body calls "social dialogue." This institution and its premise are almost unique in international labor structures. The consultative processes and ethos involved form a remarkable break with traditional approaches to industrial and labor relations. The consensus-based format has been remarkably effective in dealing with confrontation between labor, business, and government, thus saving the parties time, energy, and legal costs. It has also provided a vital bridge between what were previously two completely opposing camps under Apartheid—labor and business. Without such a structure, agreement on the shape of post-Apartheid labor relations and other societal issues would have been unlikely, putting the national reconciliation and development agendas at risk.

Funded by the Department of Labor, NEDLAC's work is conducted in four chambers: the labor market chamber, the trade and industry chamber, the development chamber, and the public finance and monetary chamber. The chambers report to a management committee that oversees the work program and administrative issues. Organized labor is represented in NEDLAC by the three main labor federations: the Congress of South African Trade Unions, the National Council of Trade Unions, and the Federation of Unions of South Africa. Organized business is represented by Business Unity South Africa, an umbrella body of 32 employer organizations established in 2003 by the merger of previously racially defined business organizations. The government delegation to NEDLAC includes ministers, directors-general, and senior officials from ministries and departments including labor, finance, trade and industry, and public works.

The act empowers NEDLAC to:

- strive to promote the goals of economic growth, participation in economic decision making, and social equity;

- seek to reach consensus and conclude agreements pertaining to social and economic policy;

- consider all proposed labor legislation relating to labor market policy before it is introduced in Parliament;

- consider all significant changes to social and economic policy before it is implemented or introduced in Parliament;

- encourage and promote the formulation of coordinated policy on social and economic matters.

NEDLAC's highest decision-making body is the executive council, which consists of senior government, business, and trade union officials as well as leaders of community organizations representing the women's, youth, disabled, and civic sectors. The executive council meets four times a year to discuss key strategic issues facing the economy. Once a year, NEDLAC holds an annual summit to review its work.

Labor Relations Act of 1995
The Labor Relations Act was passed in 1995 with the objective to promote economic development, social justice, labor peace, and the democratization of the workplace. The act seeks to:

- regulate the organizational rights of trade unions;

- promote and facilitate collective bargaining at the workplace and at the sectoral level;

- regulate the right to strike and the recourse to lockout in conformity with the Constitution;

- promote employee participation in decision making through the establishment of workplace forums;

- provide simple procedures for the resolution of labor disputes through statutory conciliation, mediation, and arbitration (for which purpose the Commission for Conciliation, Mediation, and Arbitration is established) and through independent alternative dispute resolution services accredited for that purpose;

- establish the Labor Court and Labor Appeal Court as superior courts, with exclusive jurisdiction to decide matters arising from the act;

- provide for a simplified procedure for the registration of trade unions and employers' organizations, and to provide for their regulation to ensure democratic practices and proper financial control;

- give effect to the public international law obligations of the republic relating to labor relations.

This act underpins the entire system of labor legislation and provides parties with legal recourse dedicated exclusively to labor issues with the establishment of the Labor Court and the Labor Appeal Court. However, the parties are also provided with another, innovative avenue to decrease the number of scenarios where legal remedies are pursued —the Commission for Conciliation, Mediation, and Arbitration.

Commission for Conciliation, Mediation, and Arbitration, 1995
The Commission for Conciliation, Mediation, and Arbitration (CCMA) was established under the Labor Relations Act of 1995 as a dispute prevention and resolution body.

Its policy-making structure is an 11-member governing body comprising three state representatives, three representatives of organized labor, three representatives of organized business, a chairperson, and the director of the CCMA. The governing body is nominated by NEDLAC, while the CCMA director is nominated by the governing body. The CCMA has offices in major towns in all of South Africa's nine provinces. The governing body appoints teams of full-time commissioners for each provincial office, supported by a complement of part-time commissioners (GCIS 2003). The commissioners are selected on the strength of their experience and expertise in labor matters, particularly relating to dispute prevention and resolution. Their main brief is to:

- mediate to prevent and settle industrial disputes;

- conciliate workplace disputes;

- arbitrate disputes that remain unresolved after conciliation.

In the five years since it started operating, about 460,000 disputes have been referred to the CCMA—an average of more than 92,000 cases per year. Between April 1, 2000 and March 31, 2001, 103,096 disputes were referred to the CCMA, representing a 16% increase over the corresponding period in 1999-2000. Nationally, the commission was achieving a settlement rate of 74% in the 2003-04 financial year as of this writing. The previous rate was 81% for the entire 2002-03 financial year, so the 2003-04 average settlement rate is consistent.

The Basic Conditions of Employment Act of 1997

The Basic Conditions of Employment Act (BCEA) establishes minimum standards of employment for virtually all employees in South Africa; the only exceptions are members of the National Defense Force, the National Intelligence Agency, the South African Secret Service, and unpaid volunteers working for charitable organizations. The BCEA requires an employer to regulate the working time of employees and enshrines certain employee rights as being "core rights"; such rights are incapable of being varied under any circumstances, even with the consent of the employees concerned. Core rights include ordinary hours of work (a maximum of 45 hours a week), the protection afforded to employees who perform night work, minimum annual leave, maternity leave, sick leave, and prohibition of employment of children under 15 years of age. Other rights in terms of the BCEA are capable of being varied within certain parameters.

The BCEA has introduced detailed provisions that impose administrative duties on employers. These include the employer being required to give each of its employees, on commencement of employment, detailed and written particulars of the conditions of employment that cover a host of information, including any period of continuous employment with any previous employer that counts toward the employee's period of continuous employment with it; the employee's ordinary hours and days of work; the employee's wage or the rate and method of calculating such wage; the rate of pay for overtime work; the place of work and, when the employee is required or permitted to work at various places, an indication of this; any other cash payments to which the employee is entitled; any payment in kind to which the employee is entitled and the value of such payment in kind; the frequency of remuneration; any deductions to be made from the employee's remuneration; and all periods of leave to which the employee is entitled.

The BCEA does not carry a direct legal sanction. Employers who breach its provisions are accordingly not subject to criminal sanction, but labor inspectors are given the power to enter premises in order to make investigations, to serve compliance orders on noncompliant employers, and eventually to enforce compliance by securing appropriate orders from the Labor Court.

Attached to the BCEA are also several Codes of Good Practice, which are meant to address some of the difficulties experienced by women in the labor market. The first is the Code of Good Practice for Pregnant and Breastfeeding Women. The second is the Code of Good Practice on Working Time and Night Work, which provides that affordable transportation must be made available for those who work night shifts (Devey et al. 2003).

Employment Conditions Commission
The Employment Conditions Commission was established under terms of the Basic Conditions of Employment Act to further the act's aims of advancing economic development and social justice by regulating the right to fair labor practices. The five-member commission's brief is to advise the labor minister on any matter concerning basic conditions of employment and trends in collective bargaining.

The Protected Disclosures Act of 2000
The "Whistleblowers Act" has as its purpose the protection of employees who, by exposing improprieties or illegalities in the workplace, fall victim to reprisals or occupational detriments. The purpose of the Whistleblowers Act is to create a culture in which employees will disclose information of criminal and other irregular conduct by employers or their co-employees in the workplace in a responsible manner, thereby promoting the eradication of crime and other irregular conduct in state and private bodies. The act ensures that such employees are not subjected to any occupational detriment by their employers on account of the protected disclosure being made. The Whistleblowers Act details which type of information may be disclosed, and to whom it may be disclosed, in order for the employee to quality for the protection afforded by the act. The intention behind the act is to co-opt employees to assist in eradicating corruption and maladministration in public service, and to highlight and expose general criminal activity and conduct in

both the public service and in private companies, without fear of reprisal.

The Unemployment Insurance Act of 2002

This act seeks to overcome shortcomings in the present system, including the scope of coverage, financial sustainability, enforcement, and compliance measures. In terms of the act, all employees will pay unemployment insurance and will be entitled to benefits on a sliding scale and subject to a cap. A recent amendment to the existing Unemployment Insurance Fund Act extended coverage of the 2002 act to domestic and seasonal workers so that a domestic worker who is employed by multiple employers can apply for proportional unemployment coverage from each one, and a domestic worker who is retrenched can claim partial unemployment insurance.

Amendments, additions, and sectoral determinations

Minimum wages vary across sectors according to the agreements reached with respective unions within respective bargaining councils. As noted previously, sectoral determinations, i.e., the setting of a minimum wage for an entire sector, are in place in a number of sectors where the national Department of Labor has deemed labor to be vulnerable. The most high profile of these has been the agriculture and domestic workers determinations. Available data indicate that a high percentage of employers of domestic workers are complying with both the sectoral determination and the unemployment insurance regulations for their employees. Amendments and additions to labor legislation and regulations in 2002, in addition to those described above, included:

- amendments to the Labor Relations Act and Basic Conditions of Employment Act, effective August 1, 2002;

- the Code of Good Practice on the Employment of People with Disabilities, effective August 19, 2002;

- a minimum wage for domestic workers effective November 1, 2002;

- the sectoral determination for the agricultural sector, promulgated on December 2, 2002;

- the sectoral determination for wholesale and retail trade, promulgated on December 19, 2002.

Defining and measuring the informal sector

Definitional limitations. Definitions around the formal and informal sectors in South Africa have been debated over the years, and the current official picture is drawn largely from the definitions employed by both Statistics South Africa and the South Africa Receiver of Revenue (SARS). With the lack of clarity over the size of the sector and what occurs within it, empirical studies have been limited. South Africa is not alone in this regard. The World Bank noted that the disparity of national results across countries shows the sensitivity of the measurement of the size and composition of the informal sector to the operational criterion chosen to define it (SSA 2002c).

In SSA's October Household Survey (the OHS, conducted annually from 1994 to 1999), the formal sector was defined as all businesses that are registered for tax purposes and that have a value-added tax number, i.e., those making more than R300,000 a year. The informal sector therefore is defined as consisting of those businesses that are unregistered and do not have VAT number, therefore making under R300,000 a year. A cautionary note is that the 1995 OHS did not ask respondents whether their employers were registered, thus undercounting the informal sector in that year.

After 1999, the survey gave self-definition predominance over VAT registration as the defining characteristic, i.e., respondents were specifically asked if they considered themselves part of the informal sector. The VAT definition reoccurs, however, in the Labor Force Surveys. For example, a focus of the 2002 Labor Force Survey is businesses that are not registered in any way, neither for tax purposes, VAT, the unemployment insurance fund, or the skills development levy or the regional services levy.

Alternatively, the 2002 SSA Analysis of Selected Time Based Social Comparisons within the labor market starts by defining the informal sector as including all employed people, whether self-employed or employees, who define themselves as working in the informal sector, irrespective of whether the business is registered for the purpose of value-added taxes.

Thus, the methods employed by statisticians in South Africa to define and measure the informal sector are inconsistent over time and, with the possible exception of broad trends, must be analyzed with caution. Overall, the definitions used have been too wide to allow a good estimation of how many people are employed in the informal sector and what contractual and benefit arrangements they operate under, if any. Within this broad category will be businesses that employ workers in the same fashion as those SARS recognizes as formal, i.e., they use contracts, set defined hours and pay benefits, but their turnover is small, or they may not be registered at all. A more nuanced description of a South African informal sector enterprises and employers/employees is therefore necessary. An element of uncertainty will always remain due to the preference of some businesses and employees to remain unregistered for tax or labor relations levies. In general, though, researchers believe that the size of the informal sector has been underestimated (Muller 2002).

Even with consistent measurement methods, there are a number of factors that make the task of quantifying the scope of informal work difficult. For example, respondents may not view survivalist or very limited activities as work. And those engaged in illegal activities, such as child labor, do not acknowledge it. A 1999 SSA survey on child activities found that approximately 26% of South Africa's 13.4 million children were involved in economic activities such as running a business, helping in a family business on a non-paid basis, and doing work for a wage, salary, or payment in kind (SSA 2001).

Furthermore, the surveys record only primary work activities and do not accurately capture secondary informal or formal work. Most employees in the informal sector are involved in more than one source of income. (This survey inaccuracy may have been resolved with a more detailed query in the 2000 LFS.) Another main source of underestimation is the growing incidence of part-time, casual, or outsourced work activities. Although many workers may record these activities as formal sector employment, there is disagreement as to whether these activities constitute formal or informal sector work because in most cases they do not offer benefits like medical aid, pension, or retrenchment. This is an important issue, since the use of outsourcing and part-time and casual labor is on the rise. The SSA OHS figures for 1999 found 15% part-time employment among workers, according to the standard ILO definition of fewer than 30 hours a week of work. The LFS figures for 2003 showed

TABLE 24   Status in employment based on self-perceptions

Percent	No paid leave	No medical aid	No employer pension	No written contract
Full-time	33	61	40	40
Part-time	86	95	91	76
Casual	91	96	94	83
Total	41	67	48	45

Source: SSA 2002c.

a temporary work incidence of 13.0% and a casual incidence of 6.6%. The figures for benefits from 1999 discussed in Muller (2002) are illustrative (**Table 24**). On average, 44% of all formal sector workers received none of the benefits usually ascribed to formal sector employment. Likewise, 9% of all casual workers reported receiving traditional formal sector benefits. Thus, it is problematic to accurately slot these part-time and casual workers into a formal or informal definition of employment.

Another source of misrepresentation is that the OHS surveys did not examine in sufficient detail the minimum number of hours worked. In some cases respondents worked for only a few hours a week—should this be regarded as informal employment? By the 2000 LFS respondents were asked to provide detail on work performed for more than an hour a week, thus capturing such workers, but whether this work could be considered viable for survival is a valid question.

SSA moved closer over the 1994-2000 period to encompassing the definition of informal sector enterprises that was agreed to at the 15th International Conference of Labor Statisticians, held in 1993. The conference resolution defines the informal sector in terms of the characteristics of the enterprises in which the activities take place, rather than the characteristics of the persons concerned or their jobs.

The resolution recommended that informal sector enterprises be identified in terms of one or more of the following criteria:

1. Non-registration of the enterprise under national legislation, e.g., factories or commercial acts, tax or social security laws, and professional group regulatory acts.

2. Non-registration of employees, i.e., the absence of an employee or apprenticeship contract that commits the employer to pay relevant taxes and social security contributions on the behalf of the employee or which makes the employment relationship subject to standard labor legislation.

3. Small size of the enterprise in terms of the number of people employed in the enterprise—preferably those employed on a continuous basis. It also specified that agricultural activities and household enterprises engaged exclusively in non-market production (i.e., the production of goods and services for own final consumption or own fixed capital formation) be excluded from the scope of the informal sector.

By the 2000 LFS, SSA had incorporated elements of all three criteria in its survey methodology, thus eliminating some areas of ambiguity.

Measurement variations. SSA has employed a number of data collection methodologies over the last 10 years to measure employment and unemployment in the formal and informal sectors. This affects the presentation of the information in this study and the longitudinal continuity of the employment statistics nationally. For the purposes of this study, two sets of figures will be used. The first is the 1993-99 October Household Survey, and the second is the Labor Force Surveys, which commenced in 2000 and which are carried out on a six-month basis. Limitations exist in both sets of data, the greatest of which is running a comparison over time both within and between the two sets.

The OHS surveys were inconsistent over the years, and in certain cases the resulting datasets are not comparable over time due to changes in the questionnaire, coverage of the population, and sample size. The previous "homeland" states of Transkei, Bophuthatswana, Ciskei, and Venda were included in the OHS only from 1994 onward, making the 1993 OHS unsuitable for comparison with subsequent ones. The sampling methodologies used in the 1993 and 1994 surveys also differ from those used in later years. Population weights based on the 1996 Census are not available prior to 1995, therefore only the 1995-99 OHSs are comparable. Of these, the 1996 OHS is based on a sample of just 16,000 households, while the 1998 OHS sampled 20,000. Researchers have therefore expressed concern about whether the results from these two surveys are consistent with those in other years. The information provided in these studies may therefore underestimate the size and nature of the informal sector (Muller 2002).

In February 2000, SSA introduced the new Labor Force Survey to replace the OHS. The pilot survey sampled 10,000 households, while successive LFSs, which take place biannually, survey a larger sample of approximately 30,000 households. These new surveys aim to improve measures of employment and unemployment and to provide more comprehensive information on the informal sector. The reliability of the third LFS is questionable, however, due to reports of interviewee fatigue experienced in the field. In considering a longitudinal picture, it must be noted that the sampling methodologies used in the LFS differ from those in the OHS. SSA has committed itself to the long-term reliability of its surveys, and thus it is hoped that the data will remain consistent from 2000 onward. The various shortcomings raised have in addition been increasingly addressed by SSA in the post-2000 surveys. In addition, OHSs after 1995 were based on the population weights of the 1996 Census, and LFSs after 2001 are based on the population weights of the 2001 Census. Longitudinal comparisons should therefore be treated with caution. Where possible in this study, the data from the surveys is represented in one table, and we believe that, all shortcomings notwithstanding, a fairly accurate picture has been drawn of the informal sector from these surveys.

Amendments that could still be made that could enhance the collection of data on employment, particularly informal sector employment, to include information on working children and whether workers hold more than one job, along with more comprehensive information on this work. Given the wide range of work covered, from full-time to survivalist jobs, it is also important that researchers are able to distinguish between workers who are employed in these different categories by capturing as much information as possible about the work that people do. Remaining areas of slight generalization would need to be refined further, e.g., hours worked and survivalist occupations. However, it is likely that measures of employment, and especially informal sector employment, will continue to be underestimated, in spite of carefully constructed surveys, because of the difficulties involved in capturing information on illegal work and illegal workers.

The size and nature of formal and informal sector work. As Devey et al. (2003) point out, the terms "formal" and "informal" create a perception that there is a strict division between the two, or that the formal sector is the norm against which the informal should be benchmarked. However, given the heterogeneous nature of the informal sector, the blurring of roles that has increasingly become apparent with outsourcing and subcontracting, and the difficulty of defining micro-enterprises, the term "informal economy" might be a better one for describing the range of activities that embody varying degrees of formality and informality. The informal economy would be defined as all those in informal employment without secure employment contracts, work-related benefits, and social protection. By understanding the informal sector as an economy, we are able to conceive of the numerous linkages that exist between it and the formal economy, with many workers and enterprises moving between formality and informality depending on circumstances.

Informal activity was a part of the South African economic landscape long before the present debates commenced around the "rise of the informal sector post-Apartheid." Research from the 1980s suggests that informal activity was widespread in the city of Durban, and many black Africans were forced to engage in informal activity to survive within a climate hostile to the regulation of small black enterprise under Apartheid. The flexible contracts and migrant labor systems were also informal in nature and existed for most of the last century (Devey et al. 2003). What is also interesting is that the nature of the South African informal sector is different than that in other African countries. Here, the sector displays less variety and, because regulations were designed to protect white manufacturers, a much smaller manufacturing base. Where informal manufacturing did occur, it was in low-value sectors.

As noted, it is difficult to accurately portray the growth of the informal sector in South Africa. While 1993-99 OHSs and the post-2000 LFSs reflect a picture of informal sector growth, SSA has noted repeatedly that it has been improving data collection and recording tools since the onset of the surveys. It is thus possible that any growth measured over the last nine years can be ascribed to better reporting and more detailed questioning. However, it is possible to draw overall estimates from the OHSs and the LFS from 2001 which show that, including subsistence agriculture and domestic work, around 30% of those working in South Africa are engaged in the informal economy (Devey et al. 2003).

For the purposes of this study, a static form of longitudinal comparison will be attempted where possible, by displaying various results

TABLE 25   Formal and informal economy, labor market trends, October Household Survey, 1997-99

Category	OHS 1997	OHS 1998	OHS 1999	% change 1997-99
Formal	6,405,953	6,527,120	6,812,647	6.3%
Commercial agriculture	495,530	726,249	804,034	62.3
Subsistence agriculture	163,422	202,290	286,856	75.5
Informal	965,669	1,077,017	1,573,986	63.0
Domestic work	992,341	749,303	798,524	-19.5
Unspecified	70,986	107,966	92,905	30.9
Total employed	9,093,901	9,389,946	10,368,951	14.0
Unemployed	2,450,738	3,162,662	3,157,605	28.8
Not econ. active	13,960,772	13,156,940	12,752,967	-8.7
Total not employed	16,411,510	16,319,602	15,910,572	-3.1
Total pop., age 15-65	25,505,411	25,709,548	26,279,523	3.0

Source: Muller 2002.

from the three sets of data. These datasets are all produced by SSA, and they constitute a comparison of elements of the 1995 and 1999 OHS, a comparison of elements of the 2000 and 2002 LFS, and data from the LFS release of March 2003 (the latest available at the time of this writing).

In any case, it is still not possible to ascertain whether the statistics given for overall informal sector growth are a result of real growth or improvements in sampling and assessment. As a result it is not possible to directly compare the various indicators over the entire 1995-2003 period. This report therefore seeks to illustrate the dimensions and key characteristics of the sector as contained in the October 1999 OHS, the September 2002 LFS, and March 2003 LFS.

A summary of the changing size of the formal and informal sectors is shown in **Tables 25** and **26**. Due to the limitations expressed above, this comparison should be treated with caution up to the September 2000 LFS data. The figures show that the formal sector grew by 6.3% over the period 1997 to 1999, the informal sector grew by 63.0%, and the subsistence agriculture sector grew by 75.5%. The number of unemployed grew by 28.8% over the period.

For 2000-03 (Table 26), the formal sector grew by 10.2%, the informal sector grew by 1.4%, and the subsistence sector decreased by 72.2%.

TABLE 26 Formal and informal economy, labor market trends, Labor Force Survey 2000-03

Category	LFS Feb. 2000	LFS Sept. 2000	LFS Feb. 2001	LFS Sept. 2001	LFS Feb. 2002	LFS Sept. 2002	LFS Mar. 2003
Formal	6,677,923	6,841,877	6,678,219	6,872,924	7,036,000	7,034,000	7,358,000
Commercial agriculture	756,984	666,940	698,879	665,941	734,000	811,000	865,000
Subsistence agriculture	1,508,264	964,837	653,428	358,983	792,000	520,000	420,000
Informal	1,820,350	1,933,675	2,665,227	1,873,136	1,767,000	1,703,000	1,845,000
Domestic work	1,001,108	999,438	914,478	915,831	972,000	875,000	1,005,000
Total employed	11,879,734	11,712,565	11,837,244	10,832,816	11,393,000	11,029,000	11,565,000
Unemployed (official def.)	4,333,104	4,082,248	4,240,034	4,525,309	4,738,000	4,837,000	5,250,000
Not econ. active (official def.)	10,241,611	11,100,135	11,043,527	12,006,413	11,543,000	12,118,000	12,740,000
Total Pop, age 15-65	26,454,449	26,894,948	27,120,805	27,364,538	27,673,000	27,984,000	29,555,000
Official unemployment rate	26.70%	25.80%	26.40%	29.50%	29.40%	30.50%	31.20%
Unofficial / expanded unemployment rate	35.50%	35.90%	37%	41.50%	40.90%	41.80%	42.10%
Labor absorption rate	44.90%	43.50%	43.60%	39.60%	41.20%	39.40%	39.10%

Source: SSA, various LFSs, 2000-03.

TABLE 27 Key to Statistics South Africa labor indicators

Key	Indicator formula	How calculated
a	Total employed	(a)
b	Total unemployed	(b)
c	Total economically active	(a+b)
d	Total not economically active	(d)
e	Population, 15-65 years old	(c+d)
	Participation rate (%)	(c*100/e)
	Labor absorption rate (%)	(a*100/e)
	Unemployment rate (%)	(b*100/c)

Source: SSA 2002c.

This subsistence decrease may be due to the recategorization of certain subsistence activities by SSA, to seasonal fluctuations, or to the decrease in rural farming due to urbanization. The total unemployed grew by 21.2% over the period.

It is useful in relation to the above tables to note the methods used to calculate various indicators by the statistical body (**Table 27**).

As can be seen in Tables 25 and 26, there is a significant variation between the end of the OHS series and the commencement of the LFS series. This is not a real variation, but an indication of the differences in sampling methodology employed. Within the LFS surveys, there is also a need to increase the frequency of measurement for the informal and subsistence categories, as these exhibit large fluctuations. In the subsistence agricultural sector and the informal sector, employment trends tend to vary as a result of seasonal and other factors. The informal and the agricultural sectors offer less secure, possibly short-term employment opportunities, and so people within these sectors may be leaving them and re-entering at different rates at various times of the year. People in these sectors who are perhaps having a downturn and are not working are likely to define themselves as not economically active, rather than as unemployed. In addition, unless carefully probed, respondents may not regard subsistence agriculture and informal economic activity as work. The picture on informal work is thus an unstable one (SSA 2002b).

A series of overall indicators of the formal and informal sectors in the figures below illustrate the size and nature of formal and informal sectors.

FIGURE B   Male and female workers by employment sector, March 2003

	Male	Female	Total
☐ Unspecified	0.7	0.6	0.6
▨ Domestic workers	0.8	18.6	8.7
☐ Informal sector	19.9	19.2	19.6
■ Formal sector	78.7	61.6	71.1

Sources: SSA 2003e.

Figure B shows employment in each sector by sex in March 2003. In this breakdown, the formal sector includes commercial agriculture, and the informal sector includes small-scale or subsistence agriculture but excludes domestic workers. The majority of workers were employed in the formal sector in March 2003, 78.7% of males and 61.6% of females. Roughly equal percentages of males (19.9%) and females (19.2%) were employed in the informal sector. The share of domestic workers among employed women was much larger (18.6%) than among employed men (0.8%). Overall, 8.7% of the working population were domestic workers (SSA 2003e).

Figure C shows that the informal and domestic sectors employ higher levels of black workers than other race groups.

An examination of the unemployment rate in terms of race and sex, as illustrated in **Figure D**, shows Africans having the highest unemployment rate in South Africa in March 2003, while whites had the lowest unemployment rate. The unemployment rate for women exceeded that of men in all population groups. While Indian/Asian women's unemployment rate was higher (28.8%) than that of Coloured women

FIGURE C Workers in each population group by employment sector, March 2003

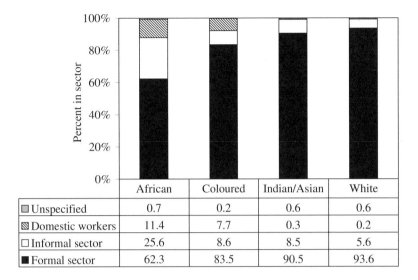

	African	Coloured	Indian/Asian	White
▨ Unspecified	0.7	0.2	0.6	0.6
▧ Domestic workers	11.4	7.7	0.3	0.2
□ Informal sector	25.6	8.6	8.5	5.6
■ Formal sector	62.3	83.5	90.5	93.6

Sources: SSA 2003e.

FIGURE D Unemployment rate (official definition) by population group and gender, March 2003

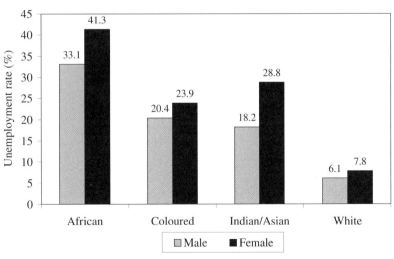

Sources: SSA 2003e.

TABLE 28   Summary of conditions of work of employees in non-VAT registered businesses, 2001

Total number of persons with at least one non-VAT-registered business with employees	338,000
Percentage of employers who provide:	
Regular paid leave	9.50%
Paid sick leave	9.20
Unpaid maternity leave	5.30
Paid maternity	3.00
Unpaid paternity leave	4.40
Paid paternity leave	2.10
Leave for other family responsibilities	10.40
Full medical expenses	3.30
Part of medical expenses	2.40
Contributions to medical aid	0.09

Source: SSA 2002d.

(23.9%), the unemployment rate for Indian/Asian men was lower (18.2%) than that of Coloured men (20.4%).

Benefits. The benefits available to informal sector employees—those employed by owners of non-VAT registered businesses—are summarized in **Table 28**.

As can be seen, conditions of work in the informal sector are poor, with many of the standard employment benefits found in the formal sector lacking.

Formal and informal employment: key characteristics over time

Age. An examination of unemployed South Africans reveals that the greater majority of unemployed black workers fall into the 15-34 age group (**Table 29**). This applies to both female and male workers.

Race. The official unemployment rate for Africans compared to the other population groups is sizably higher, as shown in **Figure E**. Unemployment rose sharply between February 2001 and September 2001 among the African population, probably related to seasonal agricultural factors. Unemployment in other population groups remained more or less stable from February 2000 to September 2002 (SSA 2002b).

TABLE 29 The unemployed, by age, population group, and sex, 2003 (thousands)

Age group	Black African			Coloured			Indian/Asian			White			Total		
	Total	Male	Female	Total	Male	Female	Total	Male	Female	Total	Male	Female	Total	Male	Female
Total	4,592	2,153	2,438	392	186	206	123	59	64	142	71	71	5,249	2,469	2,779
15-24	1,433	682	751	173	82	91	59	31	27	51	30	21	1,716	825	890
25-34	1,844	838	1,007	107	47	60	33	17	17	34	*	24	2,018	902	1,108
35-44	855	387	467	71	37	34	18	*	15	29	15	14	973	444	530
45-54	370	188	182	34	16	18	*	*	*	21	11	*	434	220	214
55+	89	58	31	*	*	*	*	*	*	*	*	*	107	69	38

* Too few observations to make an inference.

Source: SSA 2003e, 2003f.

FIGURE E   Official unemployment rate by population group, Feb. 2000 to Sept. 2002

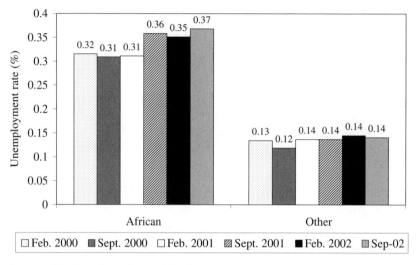

Sources: SSA Labor Force Surveys 2000-02.

Figure F shows the distribution of employment in the three broad industrial groupings of agriculture, industry (which comprises mining, manufacturing, utilities, and construction), and services (which comprises wholesale and retail trade, financial and business services, and personal and community services) between 1995 and 1999. Agriculture accounts for a larger percentage of total employment among African and Coloured workers than among either Indian or white. In both 1995 and 1999, more than one in every 10 employed African and Coloured people worked in the agricultural sector, compared with 5% or less among Indians and whites. Although services dominated the work opportunities available for all population groups, 70% of employed white people had jobs in the service sector in 1995, 73% in 1999. These shares are in line with other assessments which show that, although black workers have increased their skills levels over the last 10 years, white and Indian workers have increase their skill levels significantly as well, thus allowing the wage and skills gaps to continue.

Economic sectors. The bulk of informal economy employment—50% of workers in 2001—is found in the wholesale and retail sectors (**Table**

FIGURE F   Employment in broad industrial sectors by population group, 1995 and 1999

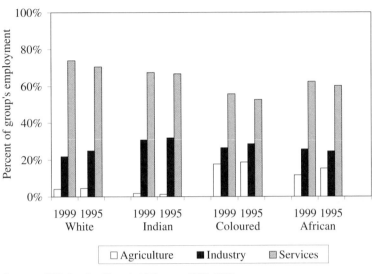

Sources: SSA October Household Surveys 1995, 1999.

30 and **Figure G**). Construction, manufacturing, and services accounted for 33% in 2001. What is interesting is that only 10% of informal sector workers were found in manufacturing, a much smaller share than the African average.

The data reveal that agriculture and construction are among the sectors with the highest percentage of informal activities. However, formal sector enterprises in these sectors do not employ an informal contingent, according to our definition. Both sectors do utilize a significant amount of what can be referred to as atypical labor (i.e., subcontracted, casual, or part-time workers), but these workers are employed under contract with fixed hours and are subject to the minimum standards of the BCEA and the LRA. They may not, in the case of subcontracted workers, be entitled to pension, medical aid, or retrenchment benefits, but they are employed as a flexible element of a formal sector workforce and are perceived as such by their employers.

What is of note about the construction and agricultural sectors is that they lend themselves to informal activities. They are also sectors that can be accessed by those with no formal skills and that are labor intensive.

TABLE 30 Employment in the formal and informal sectors by industry, March 2003 (thousands)

Industry	Formal	Informal	Domestic	Total
Agriculture	865	420		1 288
Mining	509	3		514
Manufacturing	1,462	196		1,668
Electricity	83	5		88
Construction	369	202		583
Trade	1,489	869		2,373
Transport	464	127		598
Business services	940	78		1,027
Community services	2,006	165		2,183
Private souseholds	1	196	1,005	1,202
Other/unspecified industry	34	3		42
Total	8,223	2,265	1,005	11,565

Source: SSA 2003e.

FIGURE G Workers by main industry, March 2003

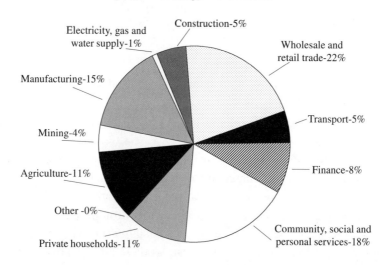

Sources: SSA 2003e.

The category of "private households" does not refer solely to domestic workers. With the amendments to the LRA in May 2003, these domestic workers could now be considered to be formal sector employees. SSA separates out the statistics for this group.

FIGURE H   Employment by industry, 1995 and 1999

*Miners are under-reported in 1995.

Source: SSA October Household Surveys 1995, 1999.

The data for employment by industry are shown in **Figures H** and **I**. The data for agriculture include subsistence (informal) or small-scale agriculture, and as such can fluctuate according to weather and season. In the post-2000 Labor Force Survey, these are listed separately in some tables (see **Table 31**), but in aggregated tables the subsistence or small-scale agriculture sector is included under the informal sector. Seasonal workers are classed as part of the formal agricultural sector.

Rural and urban. The official unemployment situation analyzed according to urban or non-urban areas is shown in **Figure J**.

Between February 2000 and September 2002 the official unemployment rate gradually increased in urban areas but increased steeply in non-urban areas. There may be a relationship between the unemployment rate in non-urban areas and employment in subsistence or small-scale agriculture. If the number of people employed in this agricultural sector increases, the unemployment rate decreases in non-urban areas. For example, a decrease in the unemployment rate in non-urban areas is

FIGURE I   Employment by industry, Feb. 2000-Sept. 2002

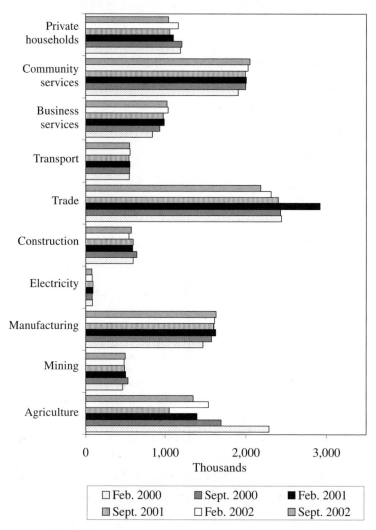

Source: SSA 2002b.

found between September 2001 and February 2002. This decrease could be due to the increasing employment in subsistence agriculture over this period (see Table 31). Similarly, a slight increase between February 2002 and September 2002 in the unemployment rate occurred in tandem with decreasing employment in subsistence agriculture (SSA 2002b).

TABLE 31 Labor Force Survey comparison, Mar. and Sept. 2003, sector in which employed people work

			Lower	Estimate	Upper	Precision of difference	Actual difference
Total employed	Mar.	2003	11,298	11,565	11,832	350	57
	Sept.	2003	11,395	11,622	11,849		
Employed in the formal sector (exlcuding agriculture)	Mar.	2003	7,147	7,358	7,568	284	103
	Sept.	2003	7,271	7,461	7,651		
Employed in commerical agriculture	Mar.	2003	768	865	945	110	-33
	Sept.	2003	767	832	897		
Employed in subsistence or small-scale agriculture	Mar.	2003	376	420	464	53	-70*
	Sept.	2003	321	350	379		
Employed in informal sector	Mar.	2003	1,772	1,845	1,918	100	54
	Sept.	2003	1,831	1,899	1,967		
Employed in domestic service	Mar.	2003	961	1,005	1,048	61	17
	Sept.	2003	980	1,022	1,065		
Employed sector unspecified	Mar.	2003		73			
	Sept.	2003		58			

* Statistically significant at the 95% level of confidence.

Source: SSA 2003f.

Formal and informal. The above characteristics can be applied to the difference between the informal and formal sectors, as shown in Tables 32-35.

The proportion of workers in the formal economy still outweighs those informally employed (**Table 32**), but the majority of informal sector workers are black or Coloured. Likewise, domestic workers are predominantly black or Coloured.

In terms of race (**Table 33**), the majority of workers in the informal sector are black (85% in 2001). However, although the other groups are in the minority in this sector, the majority of white and Indian workers in the informal sector occupy more senior and skilled positions. This has been largely a result of the access to capital and skills by these two groups.

FIGURE J   Official unemployment rate in urban and non-urban areas, Feb. 2000-Sept. 2002

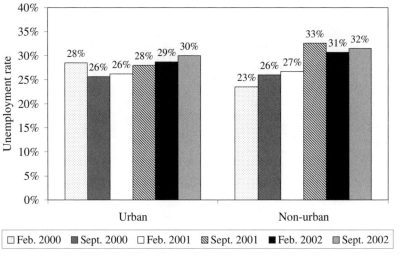

Source: SSA 2002b.

TABLE 32   Proportion of race group employed in each sector, 2001

Race	Formal employment percentage	Informal employment percentage	Domestic workers percentage	Total percentage
African	61.2	25.7	13.1	100
Coloured	79	11.6	9.4	100
Indian	91.1	8.3	0.6	100
White	93.2	6.5	0.3	100
Total	71.1	19.4	9.5	100

Note: Totals may not add to 100 due to rounding.

Source: SSA 2001.

The formal sector workforce contains a significantly larger number of male workers than female workers (**Table 34**), but in the informal sector the number of male versus female workers is closer. Although the table does not identify domestic workers as a separate category, the overwhelming number of domestic workers—98%—are female.

TABLE 33   Composition of workers in each sector by race group, 2001

Race	Formal sector percentage	Informal sector percentage	Domestic worker percentage
African	55.0%	84.5%	87.8%
Coloured	12.6	6.8	11.1
Indian	6.4	2.1	*
White	26.0	6.6	*
Total	100	100	100

* Figures too small, rounded off for total.

Source: SSA 2001.

TABLE 34   Proportion of workers in each sector by gender, 2001

Gender	Formal sector		Informal sector	
	Male/ female %	% of total* male/female labor force	Male/ female %	% of total male/female labor force
Male	62%	77%	56%	21%
Female	38	60	44	21

* "Total" here means formal plus informal labor force, by gender as per row.

Source: SSA 2001.

The informal sector has grown substantially between 1997 and 2001, as can be seen in **Table 35**. This is partly a result of new entrants coming onto the labor market faster than they can be accommodated, and partly a result of the improved data collection methodologies employed by SARS to assess informal sector employment.

Real wages over time by education

Incomes earned in the formal and informal economies are vastly different. It is useful to note the amounts as income, rather than wages, due to the wide variety of income streams evident in the informal sector. It is one indicator where informal work is shown to be unsustainable or often survivalist, which undermines assertions that the informal sector can still provide a necessary macroeconomic stimulus in the absence of for-

TABLE 35   Formal and informal economy labor market trends, 1997-2001

	OHS 97	OHS 98	OHS 99	LFS Feb. 2000	LFS Sep. 2000	LFS Feb. 2001	LFS Sep. 2001
Formal	6,405,953	6,527,120	6,812,647	6,677,923	6,841,877	6,678,219	6,872,924
Commercial agriculture	495,530	726,249	804,034	756,984	666,940	698,879	665,941
Subsistence agriculture	163,422	202,290	286,856	1,508,264	964,837	653,428	358,983
Informal	965,669	1,077,017	1,573,986	1,820,350	1,933,675	2,665,227	1,873,136
Domestic work	992,341	749,303	798,524	1,001,108	999,438	914,478	915,831
Unspecified	70,986	10,966	92,905	115,106	305,797	227,013	146,000
Total employed	9,093,901	9,389,945	10,368,952	11,879,735	11,714,564	11,837,244	10,832,815
Unemployed	2,450,738	3,162,662	3,157,605	433,104	4,082,248	4,240,034	4,525,309
Non economically active	13,960,772	13,156,940	12,752,967	10,241,611	11,100,135	11,043,527	12,006,413
Total not employed, total population, age 15-65	16,411,510	16,319,602	15,910,572	14,574,715	15,182,383	15,283,561	16,531,722
Total population, age 15-65	16,411,510	16,319,602	15,910,572	14,574,715	15,182,383	15,283,561	16,531,722

Source: SSA October Household Survey (OHS) and Labor Force Survey (LFS) as specified.

FIGURE K   Formal workers by personal earnings level, 2001

Source: SSA Labor Force Survey, Sept. 2001.

mal sector job creation. Whereas a majority of formal economy workers in 2001 reported incomes of over R1,000, in the informal sector a majority of incomes fell under R1,000. **Figures K** and **L**, drawn from the 2001 Labor Force Study, are illustrative (Devey et al. 2003).

As can be seen, most work in the informal sector could be described as survivalist, given that wages of below R1,500 are associated with high indicators of poverty. More recent figures for March 2003 show that by that time a significant number of workers in both formal and informal sectors were still earning wages of R1,000 or less, but the incidence of such wages in the informal sector is higher, i.e., a greater proportion of workers earn less than R1,000 in the informal sector. This low income illustrates the greatest weakness of informal work, namely that the incomes earned are at best equal to the lowest minimum wage in the formal sector (see the following section). Thus, the informal sector cannot provide an effective demand alternative to the formal sector. Jobs in the informal sector are created not through the expansion of economic opportunity, but the expansion of survivalist strategies. The macroeconomic argument laid out in above describing the limitations of GEAR noted that consistent domestic demand led by job creation is

FIGURE L   Informal workers by personal earnings level, 2001

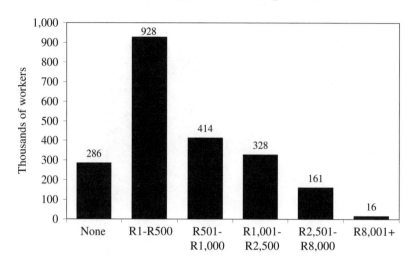

Source: SSA Labor Force Survey, Sept. 2001.

necessary to underpin a sustainable growth path. It is therefore not possible for the informal sector to provide even limited stimulus without
consistent efforts to strengthen income generation within the sector.

In terms of the interaction between education and income (**Table
36**), only at higher education levels is a higher level of income found.
What is of interest is that a limited level of education does not assist in
securing better pay in the lower-paying bands of the informal sector.
This lack of a payoff to education has implications for the effectiveness
of educational inputs to the sector (Devey et al. 2003). At the unskilled
level, large numbers of workers with secondary or college qualifications remain in this category of unskilled work.

Minimum wages

Minimum wages, although below actual wages, vary from sector to sector according to the agreements reached with unions within respective
bargaining councils. They also vary from job category to category within
each sector. The figures given in Table 36 are for the lowest possible
wage grade in that subsector. The wages are enforced by the Department of Labor, and its work is constrained by the number of inspectors

TABLE 36   Informal workers, proportion by income level and education level, 2001

Income Level	No education	Primary education	Secondary education	College	Post-college	Total
None	2.4	4.9	6.8	6.9	3.0	5.5
R1-200	32.0	22.7	16.7	12.1	7.1	19.2
R201-500	34.4	30.9	24.8	18.8	11.6	26.4
R501-1,000	21.0	23.7	22.5	20.7	8.6	21.8
R1,001-1,500	4.9	7.8	10.7	10.4	8.1	8.9
R1,501-2,500	3.4	7.1	10.0	12.1	10.1	8.6
R2,501-4,500	1.8	2.1	6.6	11.1	23.4	6.0
R4,501-11,000	0.1	0.8	1.6	7.8	21.3	3.1
R11,000+	—	—	0.3	0.1	6.8	0.5
Total	100	100	100	100	100	100

Percentage of informal economy workers with: (column span header)

Source: SSA 2001.

available. The labor movement, however, is quick to challenge employers when minimum wages are not adhered to, and this serves as an enabling factor for implementing and monitoring the legislation. Minimum wages are necessary in the South African context, due to the fact that the jobs paying these wages are usually occupied by black workers, and the Apartheid wage gap ensures that, left to self-regulation, sectoral employers would continue paying less than survivalist wages.

From a dataset of 43 (formal sector) bargaining councils, covering 1,557,132 workers, the Cape Town–based Labor Research Service analyzed minimum wages across these councils. The average weekly wage for the 43 councils was R371.75 for an average workweek of 42.47 hours, making an average monthly minimum wage of R1,609.69. Furthermore, 66% of the minimum wage agreements concluded at bargaining councils fell below R1,732 per month, less than the R1,871 per month that is needed for survival in 2003 by a family of five, according to research conducted by the Health and Development Research Unit of the University of Port Elizabeth.

Industry-specific minimum wages are similar to those for the councils, but range from R296.73 at their lowest to R559.52 at their highest. The Labor Research Service compiled the data presented in **Table 37** from 345 wage agreements entered into between trade unions and com-

TABLE 37   Average minimum weekly wages in various industries, 2003

Industry (SIC Major Divisions)	Average hours of work per week	2003 average wage (rands)	2002 average wage (rands)	Average nominal wage increase (%)	Average real wage increase (%)
Agriculture, hunting, forestry, and fishing	44.73	296.73	266.49	11.35%	4.55%
Community, social, and personal services	44.90	559.52	493.65	3.34	6.54
Financial intermediation, insurance, real estate	41.88	508.48	466.76	8.94	2.14
Manufacturing	43.25	532.25	484.75	9.80	3.00
Mining and quarrying	44.91	488.12	433.67	12.56	5.76
Transport, storage, and communication	43.50	526.85	512.33	2.83	-3.97
Wholesale and retail trade	43.88	355.95	328.47	8.37	1.57
Averages	43.86	466.84	426.59	9.60	2.80

Source: Labour Research Service 2003.

panies. The average minimum wage across all industries increased by 9.6% from 2002 to 2003. If the 6.8% consumer price index minus mortgage bonds (CPI-X) for the period is factored in, then the real average percentage increase in industries' average minimum wage came to 2.8% (Labor Research Service 2003, 28).

In addition to minimum wages, sectoral determinations—setting a minimum wage for an entire sector—are in place in a number of sectors where labor has been deemed vulnerable by the Department of Labor (**Table 38**). The most high profile of these have been the recent agriculture and domestic workers determinations of 2002-03. **Table 39** provides a sample of informal sector wages for black households.

Female workers in the informal sector are consistently paid less than their male counterparts, although this is partly explained by the fact that men occupy a greater percentage of the higher-paying occupations within the informal sector. That these wages for both men and women are survivalist at best is evidenced by the fact that the Minimum Living Level (MLL)[6] for 2003 for a family of five, a survival wage, was R1,871.95.[7] The Supplemented Living Level (SLL) for 2003 for a fam-

TABLE 38   Sectoral determinations, wages and occupations, 2003

Industry	Monthly minimum wages in rands	Occupation
Civil engineering sector	N/A	N/A
Clothing and knitting sector	R595.52	General employees not classified
Contract cleaning sector	R969.90	Cleaner
Domestic worker	R702.00	Domestic worker
Farm worker	R650.00	Farm worker
Learnership*	R480.00	Learner
Private security sector	N/A	N/A
Wholesale and retail sector	R1,234.77	Security guard

* Learnerships are described in more detail on p. 107.

Source: www.irnetwork.co.za.

TABLE 39   Median monthly wage rates among working-class black households (September 2002 Rands)[1]

	Formal unionized		Formal non-unionized		Informal	
	Male	Female	Male	Female	Male	Female
Agriculture, etc.	900	652	500	448	375	326
Mining and quarrying	2,000	1,700	1,640	1,000	350	350
Manufacturing	2,174	1,652	1,739	1,225	870	400
Electricity etc.	3,000	1,937	1,937	1,937		
Construction	2,000	1,937	1,225	800	800	350
Wholesale & retail	1,937	1,600	1,225	1,000	652	350
Transport, etc.	2,958	2,958	1,500	1,937	1,225	500
Financial, etc.	1,800	2,000	1,600	1,800	750	500
Community, etc.	3,500	3,969	1,937	1,500	707	522
Private households*	1,000	665	470	250	400**	400**

Notes: Excludes missing values, extremes and outliers. Includes African, Indian/Asian, and Coloured workers in households spending less than R5,000 per month
* Refers to gardeners.
** The same median values apply to domestic workers.
[1] Median values, as opposed to averages, give a better indication of the center of the dataset in skewed (non-normal) distributions.

Source: SSA, Labour Force Survey CD ROM, September 2002 (from a paper by E. Watkinson and L. Orr, Naledi, June 2003)

TABLE 40 COSATU union membership, 1997-2003

Category	1997	2002	2003
Total formal sector	1,247,600	1,128,700	1,033,000
Total public sector	543,400	739,900	734,100
Total affiliate membership	1,791,000	1,868,600	1,767,100

Note: Figures for union membership derived from reports to COSATU, and may vary due to poor membership systems.

Source: COSATU 2003a.

ily of five was R2,452.73.[8] This figure is not a wage, but is the estimated minimum income that a family of this size would need to survive on a monthly basis. Yet the sectoral determinations, minimum formal sector wages, and informal sector wages of such workers fall below these levels, and even the SLL itself has been criticized as being too low. This means that most of the workers in the informal sector barely survive on the incomes obtained there.

Unionization rates over time

Unionization rates overall have been dropping slowly since 1997, but with a faster drop in the last year due to ongoing layoffs. The Congress of South African Trade Unions is the largest federation in the country, constituting around 60% of unionized labor with almost two million members (Table 39). As with unionization rates, COSATU membership declined in 2003 (**Table 40**), a matter of debate at the group's meeting that year. Unions have pledged to stabilize and grow their membership base. Generally, where COSATU affiliates have low membership relative to their scope, the reasons are:

- their scope includes a lot of vulnerable workers, as in agriculture and retail.

- some unions have not managed to penetrate small employers and instead remain in historic strongholds in large companies. Meanwhile, some big employers, especially the parastatals, have seen huge job losses. In part, these losses reflect a shift to increased casual labor and outsourcing.

COSATU membership has also dropped as workers who are union members have been retrenched and as new jobs have tended to be casual, outsourced, or temporary. COSATU aims to recruit members from these employment subsectors, but at the same time each union is encouraged to grow its membership by 10% per year from 2003 to counteract declining membership. In most cases there is room for increased unionization in sectors. But while informal and casual workers are targeted by federation policies, in reality few serious attempts have been made to mobilize and organize them (exceptions exist, such as the SATAWU[9] efforts in the taxi industry.) The problem is perhaps that the formal sector remains fertile ground for recruitment, since in most cases (all federations and independents included) union density is below 50%. It is thus more viable and cost effective for the unions to recruit new members from existing sectors than to attempt to set up membership infrastructure within uncharted territory such as the casual and informal workforce. In addition, these groups of workers are harder to organize due to their dispersed and variable working conditions. As it is the largest federation and organizes large numbers of workers across the economy, COSATU membership figures are provided in detail in **Tables 41** and **42** to illustrate the pattern of union activity nationally.

Union membership numbers differ according to the institution reporting them. Nationally, across the federations and the largest independent union, the figure is close to three million. The figures from the Department of Labor (**Tables 43** and **44**), based on self-reporting by the federations, are higher than those collected by Statistics South Africa, which are based on household surveys. In addition, the Department of Labor estimates that there may be between 300,000 and 900,000 members belonging to small independent unions. These figures are in the process of verification by the department, which is now insisting that all unions submit audited financial and membership statistics in order to retain their mandatory registration. In May 2003 the minister of labor reported that South Africa had 362 trade registered trade unions; there were 282 trade unions registered in November 1996 when the Labor Relations Act came into force. A number of unions, almost 100, are now in danger of de-registration under the new regulations unless they provide audited figures. Analysts do not see this as political interference, and the move was welcomed by COSATU as necessary for weeding out "fly-by night" unions that collect union fees and then disappear.

TABLE 41   COSATU membership, 1997-2003

Affiliate	Membership		Change		% of COSATU members, 2003
	2000	2003	Number	Percent	
NUM	290,100	299,500	9,400	3%	17%
POPCRU	70,600	75,900	5,300	8	4
SACCAWU	102,200	107,600	5,400	5	6
SADNU	8,100	8,700	600	7	0
NEHAWU	234,600	234,600	0	0	13
Subtotal	705,700	726,300	20,600	3	41
FAWU	119,300	85,100	(34,200)	-29	5
NUMSA	200,000	174,200	(25,800)	-13	10
SATAWU	103,200	79,300	(23,900)	-23	4
SACTWU	119,900	110,200	(9,700)	-8	6
CEPPWAWU	73,700	6,200	(67,500)	-92	0
SAMWU	119,800	114,100	(5,700)	-5	6
CWU	35,000	29,300	(5,700)	-16	2
SASO	63,000	58,700	(4,300)	-7	3
SADTU	218,700	214,900	(3,800)	-2	12
SASAWU	18,000	14,600	(3,400)	-19	1
PAWE	2,600	400	(2,200)	-85	0
SAAPAWU	22,200	22,000	(200)	-1	1
SAFPU	400	200	(200)	-50	0
Subtotal	*1,095,900*	*970,100*	*(125,800)*	*-11*	*55*
Denosa	—	70,000	70,000	—	4
SAMA	—	4,200	4,200	—	0
MUSA	—	700	700	—	0
RAPWU	3,500	—	(3,500)	-100%	—
Subtotal	*3,500*	*74,900*	*71,400*	—	*4%*
Total	1,801,600	1,771,300	(30,300)	-2%	100

Note: As discussed at length in the Organisational Review Report, job losses in the formal sector explain most of the decline in membership in the past few years. Still, as the following table shows, there may have been a decline in COSATU membership compared to employment as well.

Source: COSATU 2003b.

Hours of work

Figure M provides an indication of the extent of casualization of the workforce based on the number of hours actually worked, relative to respondents' evaluation of their jobs as full time, part time, or casual. Casual work is grouped with part-time work in 1999. On the basis of the number of hours actually worked, it seems that people working less than a 40-hour week tend to regard their employment as part time. However, the percentage of "part-time" workers that have a longer working week has increased, since 26% worked more than 46 hours per week in

TABLE 42   COSATU membership by sector

Scope	Union	Density 1997	2000	2003
Private sector				
Agriculture	SAAPAWU	4%	3%	3%
Retail	SACCAWU	13	11	12
Chemical, wood, paper	CEPPWAWU	23%	18%	15%
Financial	SASBO	32	32	31
Metal industry	NUMSA	48	48	42
Mining/construction	NUM	38	45	45
Mining only	NUM	65	69	72
Food processing	FAWU	74	62	46
Clothing and textiles	SACTWU	70	53	52
Transport and communications	CWU and SATAWU	55%	63%	54%
Total private sector		30	28	26
Without agriculture		36	35	32
Public sector				
Police and corrections	POPCRU	29%	45%	0.46%
Local government	SAMWU	45	55	0.51
Education total	SADTU	32	52	0.52
Educators only	SADTU	37	63	0.57
Public service except police	NEHAWU, DENOSA,			0.77%
Corrections and education	SADNU, SAMA	60%	78%	0.6%
Toatl public sector		43	61	
Private and public health	DENOSA and SADNU	—	18%	—

Note: Figures for employment by sector do not include the informal sector. Figures for union membership derive from reports to COSATU.

Source: For the private sector, SSA, Survey of Employment and Earnings, long-term data series. Downloaded July 2003 from www.statssa.gov.za. For the public sector, departmental reports and budget notes. For health, the South African Health Review 2002.

1999, compared with 13% in 1995. The percentage of self-defined full-time workers who have a longer working week has also increased. In 1999, nearly three in every five full-time workers (58%) had a working week of 45 hours or fewer, compared to 1995 when 70% of those employed on a full-time basis worked 45 hours or fewer each week. These shares mean that the percentage of full-time people whose working week was above 45 hours in 1999 was 42%, compared with 30% in 1995.

TABLE 43   Membership shares for the four trade union federations and the largest independent trade union (Solidarity), 2002

Trade union federation	Paid-up membership	Percentage of total	Number of affiliated unions
Total formal sector	1,247,600		1,033,000
COSATU	1,844,211	58.50%	21
FEDUSA	515,658	16.36	22
NACTU	398,106	12.63	19
CONSAWU	264,745	8.40	26 (exact unknown)
Solidarity (independent union)	130,000	4.12%	0 (Solidarity is a single union)
Total	3,152,720	100%	88

Note: SSA gives the total number of unionized workers as 2,992,000. National statistics may differ because of survey methodologies and over-reporting by affiliates.

Source: Department of Labour 2003.

TABLE 44   Union membership by sector, 2003

	Trade union membership (thousands)				
Main industrys	Yes	Sector % yes	No	Unspecified	Total
Agriculture, hunting, forestry, & fishing	69	7.10%	795	0	872
Mining & quarrying	378	75.50	118	0	501
Manufacturing	551	38.40	852	32	1,434
Electricity, gas, & water supply	41	48.20	44	0	85
Construction	64	14.00	380	13	456
Wholesale & retail trade	297	20.00	1,123	40	1,480
Transport, storage, & communication	159	33.20	307	13	479
Financial intermediation, insurance, real estate, & business services	207	22.50	684	31	922
Community, social, & personal services	1,196	57.20	844	50	2,090
Private households & employed persons	21	1.80	1,145	15	1,182
Other	0	0.00	0	0	17
Total	2,998	31.50	6,308	208	9,509

Source: SSA Labor Force Survey, March 2004.

FIGURE M   Employment by hours worked, full-time and part-time workers, 1995 and 1999

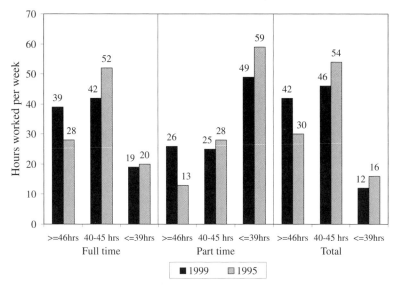

Note: Miners are under-reported in 1995.

Source: SSA October Household Surveys 1995, 1999.

Productivity per worker

The average annual rate of productivity growth from 1995 to June 2002 was 4.8%. Over the same period, real wages grew at an average year-on-year rate of 2.5%, contributing to declining unit labor costs. These figures are a reflection of the form that restructuring has taken, with increasing capital intensiveness and a concentration of job losses among lower-skilled (mostly black) employees. Economy-wide productivity growth fell during 2002, from a year-on-year rate of 3.7% in the first quarter to 1.8 % in the fourth quarter. Labor productivity increased in all the main sectors of the economy during 2002. In the transport, storage, and communication sector and in the financial intermediation and insurance industry, labor productivity growth remained robust, largely a result of the capital-intensive nature of the expansion in production capacity in these sectors (South Africa Reserve Bank 2003).

Productivity is still increasing ahead of wage costs, and the gap has been widening since 1999 (**Figure N**). This trend has led to calls by

FIGURE N   Real remuneration, productivity, and employment compared to real growth, 1994-2002 (1995=100)

Source: South Africa Reserve Bank, 2003b.

labor for higher wage increases, but business has maintained that productivity growth is enabling ongoing global competitiveness.

What is interesting is that traditionally, when business cycles in South Africa have swung upward, employment growth has usually accompanied manufacturing production. Yet the current business cycle upswing (since September 1999) has not been accompanied by the traditional upswing in employment growth. Although changes in manufacturing employment copied broadly the same pattern as manufacturing output growth in the past, they remain below zero in the current recovery, i.e., employment continued to decline. Thus, growth in manufacturing production during this phase of the business cycle was essentially underpinned by a rise in labor productivity growth—not employment—and a rise in the capital intensity of production processes. It is possible that declines in the user cost of capital relative to the unit cost of labor helped to intensify capital usage in the manufacturing sector; i.e., it is getting cheaper to use capital than labor in some instances (SARB 2003).

Skills composition and mismatch

The skills composition of the economy is still influenced heavily by the decades of Apartheid planning. A brief review of the history is necessary to illustrate the peculiar nature of South Africa's skills deficits. Apartheid planners were determined to retain skilled positions for whites, and so they consciously excluded black workers from skills training and even from holding skilled positions. This policy was referred to as the "color bar," and under legislation enacted for this purpose black workers were not allowed to hold positions higher than the category of "semi-skilled," thereby precluding them from becoming skilled artisans. Demand for skilled artisans, foremen, and production managers was met by immigration of skilled whites from other British colonies and Europe. This arrangement allowed the state and employers to pay less attention to the role of indigenous skills formation than would have been necessary otherwise (HSRC 2004, 12).

The private sector, especially the mines, tried to get around the growing racial categorization of skills in the 1920s as a result of the skills shortage experienced in World War I, but their efforts were stopped by the mobilization of white workers in defense of their jobs. The pressure led to the passing of legislation as early as 1922 reserving apprenticeships for whites. The white, skilled labor demands were met when the Afrikaner National Party came to power in 1948. An overlap of agendas between the ideology of the Nationalists and the demands for job security by white labor led to the passing of legislation formalizing the Apartheid division of labor. In the 1950s and 1960s white vocational and technical education was not actively developed. The immigration of skilled whites was accompanied by the growing shift of white labor into service and managerial occupations. The import substitution policies of the government, together with the dominance of the mineral-industrial complex in South African industrialization, meant that a diversified economy was not encouraged. As part of the failure to develop a mature, diversified, and inclusive economy, craft skills were neglected. This neglect was reinforced as industrial strategy contributed to the rapid growth of an Afrikaner middle class, which increasingly turned its back on craft and artisan skills as a route to social and economic betterment.

The result was an industrial strategy that produced an unusually bifurcated demand for labor, between a high-skill segment and a far larger low-skill segment (Altman and Meyer 2003, cited in HSRC 2004, 15). By the 1970s, when black workers began to demand increasing change in the workplace and society, white workers were unable to meet the need of employers for more skilled labor. Immigration had decreased due to the political unrest, and black workers were increasingly used in skilled positions.

However, as this change occurred the state was decreasing its support for skills development, as was the private sector. Thus, the absence of consensus and cooperation around skills development was not simply about issues of race. The state had abandoned much of its responsibility for building skills, and business seemed incapable of developing a strategic position. The possibility for tripartitism between business, government, and labor in the development of a coherent skills policy was almost non-existent given the Apartheid legacy of intensely conflict-ridden industrial relations.

South Africa's Apartheid-driven industrial development path had led to an intense polarization of skill between high-skill and low-skill elements and a serious underdevelopment of the intermediate-skill segment, which is seen as essential to successful industrialization and competitiveness internationally. All of these factors had, by 1994, resulted in a seriously dysfunctional skills development system (HSRC 2004, 16). It was in this context that a series of laws were designed and institutions created to transform the skills landscape in South Africa and return skills to center stage in the country's developmental plans. These laws and institutions are described later in this chapter in the section on vocational training.

Employment and level of education

Tables 45(a) and **45(b)** outline the educational levels of men and women in the economy in 2003. Among both men and women of working age, 30% (or 4.3 million) in 2003 had achieved grade 7/standard 5 educational level only. This is effectively a primary-level education, and people at this level are ill-equipped for the demands of the modern South African economy, and most of them may find it difficult to complete their studies. Out of the actual working population, 1.9 million workers, or 29% of the currently working population, has achieved standard 5.

Comparing the level of education by sector (**Table 46**) yields the following:

- formal sector workers with education up to standard five: 21% or 1.7 million workers;

TABLE 45(a) Population of working age (15-65) by education, sex, and labor market status (thousands)

Highest level of education	Male						Female					
	Total	Not economically active	Total N(1,000)	Economically active Workers	Economically active Unemployed	Rate %	Total	Not economically active	Total N(1,000)	Economically active Workers	Economically active Unemployed	Rate %
Total	14,026	5,112	8,914	6,445	2,469	27.7%	15,525	7,627	7,898	5,118	2,780	35.2%
None	801	318	482	388	94	19.6	1,238	773	465	360	105	22.6
Grade 0 to Grade 3/ Std 1	582	214	368	282	86	23.4	610	327	283	214	69	24.4
Grade 4/ Std 2	431	149	282	197	85	30.2	470	248	222	155	67	30.2
Grade 5/ Std 3	603	243	361	269	91	25.3	537	282	255	170	86	33.6
Grade 6/ Std 4	736	293	443	313	130	29.3	766	406	360	242	118	32.8
Grade 7/ Std 5	1,154	515	640	448	191	29.9	1,212	664	547	344	203	37.1
Grade 8/ Std 6	1,399	666	734	494	240	32.7	1,455	820	635	415	220	34.6
Grade 9/ Std 7	1,468	796	672	434	238	35.4	1,553	1,003	551	288	263	47.7
Grade 10/ Std 8	1,485	642	843	583	261	30.9	1,714	978	736	438	298	40.5
Grade 11/ Std 9	1,183	505	679	415	263	38.8	1,484	790	694	316	379	54.5
Grade 12/ Std 10	2,795	637	2,159	1,508	651	30.2	3,067	1,078	1,989	1,193	796	40.0
NTC I - NTC III	140	26	114	97	18	15.4	58	23	35	21	14	40.6
Dipl./cert. with Grade 11/ Std 9 or lower	94	11	83	70	13	15.2	126	32	93	72	21	22.5
Dipl./cert. with Grade 12/ Std 10	572	44	528	466	62	11.8	726	107	619	516	103	16.7
Degree and higher	486	32	454	422	31	6.9	426	66	360	331	29	8.1
Other	11	*	*	*	-	2.9	*	*	*	*	*	42.7
Unspecified	83	17	66	52	15	22.1	75	26	49	41	*	15.9

Due to rounding numbers do not necessarily add up to totals.
* For all values of 10,000 or lower the sample size is too small for reliable estimates.

Source: SSA 2003e and 2003f.

TABLE 45(b)   Population of working age (15-65) by education, sex, and labor market status (thousands)

Highest level of education	Total	Not economically active	Total N(1000)	Economically active Workers	Economically active Unemployed	Rate %
Total	29,555	12,740	16,815	11,565	5,250	31.2%
None	2,039	1,091	948	748	199	21.0
Grade 0 to Grade 3/ Std 1	1,192	541	652	497	155	23.8
Grade 4/ Std 2	901	397	504	352	152	30.2
Grade 5/ Std 3	1,141	525	616	439	177	28.7
Grade 6/ Std 4	1,503	699	803	555	248	30.9
Grade 7/ Std 5	2,366	1,179	1,187	793	394	33.2
Grade 8/ Std 6	2,855	1,486	1,369	909	460	33.6
Grade 9/ Std 7	3,021	1,799	1,223	722	500	40.9
Grade 10/ Std 8	3,200	1,620	1,579	1,020	559	35.4
Grade 11/ Std 9	2,668	1,295	1,373	731	642	46.8
Grade 12/ Std 10	5,862	1,714	4,148	2,701	1,447	34.9
NTC I - NTC III	198	49	149	118	32	21.3
Dipl./cert. with Grade 11/ Std 9 or lower	220	44	176	143	34	19.0
Dipl./cert. with Grade 12/ Std 10	1,298	151	1,147	982	165	14.4
Degree and higher	914	98	816	755	60	7.4
Other	19	*	*	*	*	13.5
Unspecified	158	43	115	93	22	19.4

Due to rounding numbers do not necessarily add up to totals.

* For all values of 10,000 or lower the sample size is too small for reliable estimates.

Source: SSA 2003e and 2003f.

- informal sector workers with education up to standard five: 45% or 1.0 million workers;

- domestic sector workers with education up to standard five : 59% or 0.6 million workers.

Figure O shows employment in each sector by level of education in September 2003. It indicates that the lower the level of education, the less likely it is for the individual to be employed in the formal sector. Conversely, the higher the level of education the more likely it is for the person to be employed in the formal sector. For example, among employed people with no education, 45.6% worked in the formal sector,

TABLE 46   Workers by highest level of education and sector (thousands)

Highest educational level	Formal	Informal	Domestic	Unspecified	Total
Total	8,223	2,265	1,005	73	11,565
None	330	276	137	0	748
Grade 0 to Grade 3/ Std 1	230	167	98	0	497
Grade 4/ Std 2	177	100	69	0	352
Grade 5/ Std 3	238	125	74	0	439
Grade 6/ Std 4	303	151	99	0	555
Grade 7/ Std 5	451	217	120	0	793
Grade 8/ Std 6	517	253	135	0	909
Grade 9/ Std 7	458	182	78	0	722
Grade 10/ Std 8	739	199	73	0	1,020
Grade 11/ Std 9	504	165	50	12	731
Grade 12/ Std 10	2,325	305	57	13	2,701
NTC I - NTC III	102	16	0	0	118
Dipl./cert. with Grade 11/ Std 9 or lower	132	0	0	0	143
Dipl./cert. with Grade 12/ Std 10	920	54	0	0	982
Degree and higher	728	26	0	0	755
Other	0	0	0	0	0
Unspecified	62	17	0	0	93

Due to rounding numbers do not necessarily add up to totals.

Source: SSA Labor Force Survey, September 2001.

35.0% in the informal sector, and 19.1% in domestic work. Among the employed with grade 12 as their highest level of education, 85.4% were employed in the formal sector, 11.1% in the informal sector, and 3.0% in domestic service.

This presents a real challenge to educational planners in South Africa, since without a higher education it is likely that these workers will battle to gain promotion in the workplace and higher standards of living. However, university qualification is no guarantor of employment; the September 2003 Labor Force Survey listed an unemployment rate of 9.3% among graduates, a possible result of the relatively high number of graduates with arts or humanities degrees, which are in low demand in the marketplace. South Africa suffers from a shortage of "technically" skilled graduates such as engineers, programmers, scientists, biologists, and technicians.

Further evidence of skills shortages and mismatching can be found in the same September 2003 labor force survey, which shows the num-

FIGURE O   Workers by employment sector and highest level of education, Sept. 2003

Source: SSA 2003f.

ber of those unemployed due to lack of skills or qualifications for available jobs at 922,000 (367,000 male, 555,000 female) and the number essentially having given up looking for work at 93,000.

The data for unemployment by qualification are interesting. In spite of the skills category shortages, which are usually highlighted by industry, out of a total of 302,000 unemployed workers with certificates, diplomas, or degrees, 41,000 possess a physical, mathematical, computer, or life sciences qualification, and 41,000 possess a manufacturing, engineering, or technology qualification (together 27% of the 302,000). The inability of these candidates to find work may therefore be an indicator that the qualifications being produced, even within these categories, are not suited to the marketplace. It may also be partly due to the sluggish rate of economic growth as well (less than 4% on average for the last decade).

Occupations

It is clear that the skills profile of the informal economy differs to that of the formal. The formal economy is dominated by skilled occupations such as management, professional, and technical positions, whereas the

TABLE 47   Occupations in the informal economy by education, 2001

	Percentage of informal economy workers with:				
Occupations	No education	Primary education	Secondary education	College	Post-college
Management	1.3%	17.8%	41.4%	26.8	14.8
Professionals	*	*	1.6	9.3	89.2
Technical	7.6	20.0	25.0	18.4	28.3
Clerks	2.1	12.0	31.2	42.8	11.9
Service and shop workers	8.1	29.3	40.7	17.6	4.3
Skilled agriculture	18.6	47.0	26.6	7.5	0.3
Craft-related occupations	10.3	41.0	34.7	10.2	9.8
Operators	4.8	27.8	46.2	20.2	1.0
Elementary occupations	12.0	24.6	38.8	12.5	2.1
Averages	10.0	33.7	36.5	14.2	5.5

* Too few observations to make an inference.

Source: SSA Labor Force Survey, September 2001.

informal is dominated by semi- or unskilled occupations. In addition, the educational level of those in the informal sector is low (**Table 47**), with 43% of informal sector workers possessing either no education or just primary-level education in 2001.

The link between education and income is detailed in **Table 48**. As noted above, without a further education, workers may be constrained to elementary work, with corresponding low wages and the potential for increased poverty.

The racial breakdown of workers in the informal economy partially mirrors that of the formal, namely that white workers are represented in larger numbers in the skilled managerial and technical occupations. What is different, however, is that the number of these positions is small in the informal sector.

Labor market policies and programs

Institutional and legal framework

An important concept, around which much of South Africa's labor relations system is developed, is that of voice regulation, or consensual labor relations (decisions based on consensus). This progressive system has attempted to regulate and facilitate labor relations by using a variety

TABLE 48 Workers by main occupation and monthly income (thousands)

Main occupation	None	R1 - R500	R501 - R1,000	R1,001 - R2,500	R2,501 - R8,000	R8,001 or more	Unspecified	Total
Total	351	2,182	1,991	2,789	2,674	764	815	11,565
Legislators, senior officials, and managers	—	12	16	50	243	244	110	677
Professionals	—	—	—	30	223	179	85	536
Technical and associate professionals	—	35	44	138	677	145	131	1,174
Clerks	—	36	85	292	534	58	125	1,137
Service workers and shop and market sales workers	23	209	260	415	278	32	94	1,312
Skilled agricultural and fishery workers	267	46	26	24	16	12	11	402
Craft and related trades workers	14	178	261	504	294	66	87	1,405
Plant and machine operators and assemblers	—	120	219	568	259	15	49	1,234
Elementary occupation	27	958	759	667	140	—	83	2,645
Domestic workers	—	578	308	96	—	0	18	1,005
Occupation not adequately defined	0	0	—	—	—	—	11	25
Unspecified	—	—	—	—	0	—	—	13

* For all values of 10,000 or lower the sample size is too small for reliable estimates.

Due to rounding numbers do not necessarily add up to totals.

Source: SSA Labor Force Survey, September 2001.

of innovative institutions and a range of progressive legislation. Voice regulation refers to the constructive role that collective bargaining between employees and employers plays in resolving disputes, and thereby promoting productivity and economic growth. In the labor market, it provides a mechanism to balance the often conflicting interests of employers and employees. Voice regulation also provides an alternative both to the bureaucratic regulation that some argue is inimical to governing the labor market, and to an over-reliance on market forces that is incompatible with labor market security. Voice regulation, by legitimizing and institutionalizing labor market conflict, provides the best means of charting labor market policies (Valodia 2000).

As noted earlier, an extensive system of labor legislation has been structured to regulate the labor market and protect both workers and employers. The legislative and institutional attempts to introduce equity and skills are covered in the later section on vocational training.

Compliance with labor laws

Compliance with labor legislation in South Africa varies from sector to sector. Although compliance is considered high within the formal manufacturing sector, abuses of labor are often reported in the agricultural sector, and health and safety standards are often disregarded in various sectors. Besides mining, the chemical and construction sectors are often associated with hazardous working conditions. The cooperative, consultative approach to settling labor disputes (through the Commission for Conciliation, Mediation, and Arbitration, or CCMA) combined with extensive space for the three major stakeholders—government, business, and labor—has, however, led to engagement of the stakeholder parties on compliance issues. This is not to say that disagreement and reluctance to abide by current arrangements does not exist, but it is channeled, and a forum exists in NEDLAC for all parties to request amendments if necessary.

Another reason why compliance with labor legislation is high is the existence of dedicated structures for the prosecution and sanctioning of labor law offenders. These structures include the CCMA rulings, plus the labor court and labor appeal court. The existence of these two layers means that parties have an immediate forum in the shape of the CCMA in which to begin addressing a particular labor dispute. This procedure restricts the number of cases that end up in litigation and allows the labor court and labor appeal court to process a smaller caseload. The system therefore allows for fairly rapid settlement of disputes. This expectation of swift justice acts as both a reassurance and a deterrent to all parties.

A third force ensuring compliance is the high degree of organization and political empowerment in the labor movement. These strengths enable the labor movement to insist on employer compliance with labor legislation. The existence of large, cohesive labor federations such as COSATU and FEDUSA provides a collective influence and impact on employers and employer federations. The labor movement is also vocal and politicized as a result of the struggle against Apartheid. This strong motivation gives it the confidence to tackle business and government on a range of labor issues and place pressure on the other two parties to enforce labor legislation.

A final reason for compliance is the existence of the National Department of Labor, which is authorized to inspect workplaces and enforce compliance. The department undertakes regular inspections of workplaces and makes regular interventions into particular sectors when required, e.g., to set minimum wage levels.

Examples of legislative implementation in two sectors
Implementation and compliance challenges still remain, as is evidenced by the ongoing struggle to implement various pieces of labor legislation in agriculture and construction.

Agriculture. Organizations within the democratic movement (including some government departments) continue to struggle for the protection of farm workers' livelihoods as well as for improvements in labor standards on farms. Over the last decade, a set of measures has been built to protect farm worker rights (**Table 49**). Implementing them has been a struggle, however. The Department of Labor received 4,336 complaints from farm workers between January and September 1999, and the South African Human Rights Commission initiated an inquiry into human rights in farming communities. More recently, tripartite agreements have aimed to protect and create quality jobs, in addition to increasing productivity.

Construction. The building and civil engineering industries, through BIFSA (the building federation) and SAFSEC (the civil engineers fed-

TABLE 49   Timeline progress toward improved labor standards and security of tenure in agriculture

1991	1993	1996	1999	2001	2003
					Minimum wage
			Protecting and creating quality jobs*		
		Ensuring security of tenure (LRLT and ESTA)			
	Farm worker trade unions				
Unemployment insurance (UIF)					
Transforming labor relations (LRA)					
Establishing basic conditions of employment (BCEA)					
Compensation for, and protection against, occupational injury (WCA, COIDA, OHSA)					

* 1999, Joint statement at the Agricultural Indaba; 2001, Vision for Labour Relations in Agriculture; 2001, Department of Labour Minimum Wage Investigation.

Source: Author's analysis.

eration) have run training schemes for many years, financed by compulsory levies on employers. These have been criticized recently for the small numbers trained in relation to the costs incurred, especially in BITS, the building industry scheme.

The Skills Development Act No.97 of 1998 and the Skills Development Levies Act No.9 of 1999 superseded these schemes. The levy grant scheme aims to expand the knowledge and competencies of the labor force so that employability and productivity are enhanced. The intention is to stimulate skills development by enabling employers to reclaim some expenditure on skills enhancement initiatives.

Employers pay levies into the National Skills Fund through the South African Revenue Services, from which Sectoral Education and Training Authorities (SETA) pay grants to qualifying employers. Through a process of consultation preceding the drafting of a skills plan, the Construction Education and Training Authority (CETA) was established as the SETA for the building and construction industry. One of the most serious concerns recorded in this process was that contractors no longer employ permanent staff; therefore, in-service training opportunities are limited. Another problem is that the large numbers of informal operatives are unlikely either to pay into the levy or to make use of the training facilities offered.

As its primary objectives, CETA has committed itself to supporting and developing skills for individuals through "learnerships" that focus on workplace learning. According to the CETA Web site, the aim of the learnerships is to provide "entrepreneurial and trade skills for 2,762 people in all provinces until March 2005," yet statistics on the extent to which they are achieving this goal are not available. Presently, data on any outputs relating to the CETA are inaccessible (if they exist). For example, information is available on the fairly extensive list of learnerships that have been registered, but number of trainees is not.

Collective bargaining system

When the new Labor Relations Act 66/95 came into operation, the names of the industrial councils changed to bargaining councils, and the act also provides for new councils to be established. Section 27(1) states that one or more registered trade unions and one or more registered employer organizations may establish a bargaining council for a sector and area by (1) adopting an institution that meets the requirement of Section 30, and (2) obtaining registration of the bargaining council in terms of Section 29. The functions and powers given to bargaining councils by the Labor Relations Act were provided so as to:

- conclude collective agreements;

- enforce those collective agreements;

- prevent and resolve labor disputes;

- perform the dispute resolution functions referred to in Section 51;

- establish and administer a fund to be used for resolving disputes;

- promote and establish training and education schemes;

- establish and administer pension, medical aid, sick pay, leave pay, and training schemes and funds and any similar schemes or funds for the benefit of one or more of the parties to the bargaining council or their members;

- develop proposals for submission to NEDLAC or any other appropriate forum policy and legislation that may affect the sector and area.

One of the most important functions of the bargaining councils is to conclude collective agreements and establish bargaining forums.

Employer organizations and trade unions can become a party to the bargaining council and negotiate minimum terms and conditions of employment on behalf of their members. In addition to providing collective bargaining forums for trade unions and employers' organizations, a bargaining council is entitled to make the terms of an agreement binding on all members of the council and in some circumstances on all who fall within the jurisdiction of the council. The effect of the provisions of the bargaining council agreement is that the minimum terms and conditions of employment negotiated by a bargaining council and contained in an agreement published in their *Government Gazette* will bind all the employers and employees in the industry.

Bargaining council agreements therefore reinforce and give expression to existing legislation. If a council agreement is declared binding on a trade union or employers organization, all members of that trade union will be bound by the agreement, including non-parties, on a date after the agreement has been declared binding. Members of the trade union or employers' organization will also remain bound by the provisions of the agreement even if they should subsequently cease to be members of the union or organization. A bargaining council agreement remains binding for the period specified in the notice in the *Government Gazette*.

An agreement can regulate a wide range of matters. For instance, it can regulate the relationship between a union and an employer by providing procedures for possible settlement of disputes. It can regulate the terms and conditions of employment. The intention is to apply these collectively agreed-upon terms and conditions of employment to the individual contracts of employment for all employees and employers in the industry. Employers not observing these standards may be fined. Although debate still occurs around whether collective bargaining provides a greater advantage to employers or unions, it nevertheless allows for a standardized framework for applying legislation across sectors. It also allows parties to spend less time and effort in labor negotiations than they might have to if each firm conducted its own negotiations.

Vocational training structure

The set of laws and institutions described below constitute policies that work on the demand side to stimulate employment growth by enhancing both the supply of skills and the regulation thereof. In most cases these policies and their associated laws and implementing agencies are examples of innovative collaborations between government and other stakeholders to dismantle the Apartheid workplace and enforce a new, progressive labor dispensation.

Through the application of active labor market policies comprising training certification and education, the government hopes to empower the workforce, which has emerged from Apartheid's social planning with fewer skills than are needed. As a result, unemployment has become structural in that the economy has shifted in process and requirements to a higher skills base, but most workers, and especially black workers, are not equipped for employment in this new economy. They are therefore unable to find employment, a situation borne out by the massive underemployment rate nationally. Within the official definition of "unemployed," the statistics of those hunting for work are sobering. Of the jobless total of 5.25 million, about 59% have never worked; among jobless people between the ages of 15 and 30, about 75% have never worked; and of the jobless total of 5.25 million, about 26% have been job hunting for one to three years and 41% for more than three years. The broad or expanded definition of employment reveals a far higher picture of joblessness. The expanded numbers essentially reveal that many workers are available but unable to find anything, and so have given up looking.

The need for training is widely acknowledged, but consensus is harder to find on the possible outcomes of the current vocational system and its impact on employment. In theory the skills training system would deliver two essential outcomes:

- A decrease in unemployment as the increasing skills profile of those who are employed and unemployed allows employers to diversify their activities, or an increase in production (by removing skills as a constraint on outputs), or an increase in the labor intensivity of the production processes. However, the last outcome is by no means assured, as employers in high-skill sectors such as automotive assembly have often supported skills enhancement in order to make effective use of increased capital intensivity in the production process. The skills development strategy is also aimed at re-skilling those older workers who were denied decent schooling, formal training, or qualifications under Apartheid. Re-skilling would allow these workers to compete on an equal basis with younger workers emerging from the improved educational system and would enable them to capitalize on their greater workplace experience.

- Increase economic growth through attracting foreign investment to South Africa. The investors would conceivably be attracted by the availability of skills and the comparatively cheap labor costs compared to developed countries. Such investment would then result in increased employment and economic growth, both reinforcing each other. Investment would probably be largely focused on exports, as the domestic consumption sector is widely believed to be well supplied by local and existing foreign investors. The weakness in this assumption is that India and China have a large pool of such labor already, often operating at a lower unit cost of production than in South Africa. This assumption is also challenged by the fact that, where growth has occurred in export sectors over the last five years, it has often resulted in only slightly increased employment, as borne out by NALEDI's research into the metal and engineering sector in 2003. This lack of an employment response owes to the fact that these sectors are often very price sensitive, facing massive competition for their products, and so resort to capital-intensive processes and strict restraint on labor costs in order to remain competitive. This practice is not limited to the export sector. The South African economy has been increasingly liberalized since the early 1990s, resulting in increased competition for domestic firms as well. Firms have responded by limiting labor costs in order to remain competitive, i.e., they have retrenched workers and reduced their hiring of new workers.

There are competing viewpoints as well on the linkages between skills and growth, with the relationship not seen as automatic (HSRC

2004). However, a consensus exists on the need to increase the skills distribution and profile of the South African economy, so that skills are removed as a possible constraint to economic or employment growth. Further research is needed to review the impact on production and employment of the rising skills profile of the domestic labor force to explore such linkages and outcomes. A review of the National Skills Development Strategy (NSDS) was launched in late 2003 by the Department of Labor to assess the progress of the NSDS and adjust the strategy accordingly. This is a precursor to the launch of the new phase of the NSDS for the next five years (2005-09).

Vocation skills legislation
Although skills development should play a dual role of satisfying industry as well as redressing past inequities, the problem is that few attempts have been made to create formal links between skills development, job creation, and industry development (NALEDI 2001). The links between development and equity are even weaker.

From the mid-1990s, a series of acts were passed that profoundly affected education and training in South Africa (THETA 2003):

* the South African Qualifications Authority (SAQA) Act, Number 58 of 1995, to make training effective;

* the Skills Development Act, Number 97 of 1998, to make training happen;

* the Employment Equity Act, Number 55 of 1998, to make training equitable;

* the Skills Development Levies Act, Number 9 of 1999, to make training affordable.

The South African Qualifications Authority Act of 1995. The SAQA Act set up a qualifications authority and outlined a new education and training system that is intended to help the country achieve further transformation by releasing the full potential of each learner through his or her participation in "outcomes-based education" that focuses on "competence." Central to this goal is the National Qualification Framework, which locates all education and training on a framework in a way that integrates formal education with vocational training. It also provides for the formalization of previously non-formal learning programs by requiring that they meet certain design and quality specifications. The modules are called "unit standards" and the whole program a "national qualification." The aim is to encourage the provision of all education and training in line with this framework, giving learners skills mobility and national recognition and employers a way of standardizing the quality of people they train and employ.

The other significant factor in this new system is the issue of competence, which focuses on the knowledge a person can demonstrate rather than how they acquired their skills/knowledge. This is the first time that learning achievements in both formal and non-formal learning environments have been recognized, thus including a wide range of learning achievements in the workplace. This practice in turn facilitates further learning, career-path development, and labor market mobility. It has also provided a solution to the Apartheid educational social engineering, whereby black workers were denied the opportunity to study or achieve promotion above a semi-skilled position. In that system, workers became skilled but were unable to formalize these skills through a qualification.

The SAQA Act stipulates that there be strong stakeholder involvement in determining standards of competence across all learning areas, and that new quality assurance measures improve learning provision. The SAQA's work also includes registering the National Standards Bodies (which are responsible for establishing education and training standards or qualifications) and accrediting Education and Training Quality Assurance Bodies (which are responsible for ensuring that the education and training provided is of the required standard).

The Skills Development Act of 1998. The Skills Development Act (SDA) introduced mechanisms to improve the relationship between the provision of education and the skills needs of workplaces (THETA 2003). These included new learning programs, new approaches to implementing workplace-based learning, and financial incentives. Like the SAQA Act, the SDA has changed workplace learning. The vision is of an integrated skills development system, which promotes economic growth, increased employment, and social development by focusing on education, training, and proper employment practices. The act seeks to address the reality of the global economy and the need to increase skills to improve productivity and the competitiveness of industry, business, commerce, and services. It also looks at ways of making society more inclusive.

A centerpiece of the act is the introduction of new forms of skills acquisition called learnerships and skills programs. It also creates a framework and structures to support the implementation of the National Skills Development Strategy, including Sector Education and Training Authorities (or SETAs, discussed earlier), a skills development levy-grant scheme, the National Skills Authority (NSA), the National Skills Fund (NSF), the Skills Development Planning Unit (SDPU), and labor centers.

The act aims to increase the amount of money spent on education and training in the workplace and to make sure the money is spent on activities that are in line with the national skills strategy. While the Skills Development Levy Act of 1999 sets up the rules for the collection of levies, the SDA specifies that the money should be spent on education and training that is registered on the National Qualifications Framework (NQF) and that meets real needs in the labor market. A new development for organized training is that the SETAs must promote and organize training within a sector, rather than within an industry, as the old Industry Training Boards had done. This means that people who are not formally employed in an industry but work or want to work within a sector (e.g., small business, the unemployed) can gain access to relevant training opportunities unavailable previously.

However, experience in industry appears to show that the SDA has focused more as an aid to employers and less as a tool for the redress of Apartheid legacies (NALEDI 2001, 5). Although this act and the levies act (below) have begun to address skill shortages in industry, leaving skills development largely to isolated companies does not provide for cooperative industrial strategies. It has become in essence reactive, not proactive.

The Skills Development Levies Act of 1999. The Skills Development Levies Act (SDLA) provides that employers paid a skills levy of 0.5% of their monthly payrolls for the year commencing April 1, 2000 to March 31, 2001. The levy was increased to 1.0% of payroll for the year commencing on April 1, 2001. Every employer in South Africa who is registered with the South African Revenue Services for PAYE or has an annual payroll in excess of R250,000 must pay the levy. An employer who is liable to pay the skills levy must register with SARS. The employer must choose one SETA that is most representative of its activities; the list includes accounting and other financial services sector, banking, chemical and allied industries, clothing textile and footwear, construction, defense, education training and development practices, energy, and so forth. A labor inspector appointed in terms of the BCEA is empowered to monitor and enforce compliance with the SDLA insofar as it relates to the collection of levies by a SETA or approved body. The inspector is granted powers to enter and search business premises.

Employers who are already training their workforce also qualify for a grant in terms of the SDLA. Training may be carried out in-house or by a registered trainer. Employers have to start the process by conducting a skills audit, which is then used to draw up and submit a Workplace Skills Plan to their relevant SETA. This plan should include a breakdown of all staff according to race and gender. The Workplace Skills Plan must detail what past training employees have had, and it has to link its training priorities with the strategic objectives of the organization. It must also show that employers have put in place some kind of quality assurance system so they can monitor the type of training that is done and link it to levels in the NQF. The next step is to actually implement the skills plan and to provide the SETA with a report detailing exactly how the firm has done so. For every step of the process completed, employers get back a percentage of the skills levy they have paid, up to a total of 70%. In addition, employers are entitled to a tax rebate of R25,000 for every person they place in a learnership. Eighteen percent of the remaining portion of each levy is sent to the National Skills Fund for national priorities like schemes for the unemployed, another 10% is for the SETA's running costs, and 2% is allocated to the receiver of revenue for the collection of the levies.

What has been observed, however, in research conducted by NALEDI and other bodies is that many companies (especially small- and medium-sized businesses) regard the detailed training process as a nuisance, and although they pay the levy, they write off the cost as a tax and do not submit the plans. Although failure to pay the levy is an offense, failure to conduct training is not. For example only 58% of companies in the Chemical Industries Education and Training Authority paying the levy have submitted skills development plans (NALEDI 2001, 5). A further complication is that equitable training is not mandatory under the act, i.e., many companies have been using the levy to train skilled white management and technical staff rather than their semi- or unskilled black staff.

In addition, although labor has identified the provision of Adult Basic Education and Training (ABET, often literacy, numeracy, basic mechanics, etc.) as one of the key goals for the SDA, only 7% of companies who have submitted Workplace Skills Plans have included ABET training in these. In short, without proper measures in place to enforce employment equity training, the disparities of the past will remain dominant in industry.

The Employment Equity Act of 1998. In line with the right to equality enshrined in the Bill of Rights, the Employment Equity Act (EEA) aims to promote equality in the workplace by eliminating unfair discrimination and ensuring employment equity as a form of redress. The act aims to create a workforce that is representative of all South Africans. The EEA affects almost every aspect of employment policy and practice, including:

- recruitment procedures, advertising, and selection criteria;

- appointments and the appointment processes;

- job classification and grading;

- remuneration and employment benefits;

- terms and conditions of service.

The chapter of the EEA that prohibits unfair discrimination applies to all employers. Every employer is obliged to take steps to promote equal opportunity in the workplace by eliminating unfair discrimination in any employment policy or practice, and no employer may unfairly discriminate, directly or indirectly, against an employee in any employment policy or practice on the grounds of race, gender, sex, pregnancy, marital status, family responsibility, ethnic or social origin, color, sexual orientation, age, disability, religion, HIV status, conscience, belief, political opinion, culture, language, or birth.

The EEA identifies "designated employers." An employer with 50 or more workers is deemed to be a designated employer, and if the employer employs fewer than 50 it will nevertheless be a designated employer if its total annual revenue turnover is in excess of designated thresholds, e.g., R10,000,000 per annum in the manufacturing sector or finance and business services sector, and R25,000,000 in wholesale trade, commercial agents, and allied services sector.

The act identifies a number of designated groups (or special groups) that require special attention in order for equitable workplaces to be created. These groups are black people (that is, African, Coloured, and Indian people), people with disabilities, and women. Employers are required to report on these categories of people in their Workplace Skills Plans and annual training reports. The Skills Development Act states that the Workplace Skills Plans must assist organizations to attain their employment equity targets.

The EEA specifically provides that it does not constitute unfair discrimination for an employer to take affirmative action measures in order to give employees from historically disadvantaged groups equal employment opportunities in the workplace or to distinguish, exclude, or prefer any person based on the inherent requirements of a job. However, the EEA makes it clear that employers are not required to adopt employment policies that adversely affect people who do not come from historically disadvantaged groups.

Designated employers must implement affirmative action measures for people from designated groups to achieve employment equity. To do so, they must appoint a senior manager in charge of employment equity; consult with employees; analyze employment policies, practices, and procedures to identify barriers to employment; prepare an Employment Equity Plan jointly with its employees; and report on progress to the Department of Labor. An employer who does not abide by these steps can be penalized; however, the failure of an employer to meet goals, achieve its self-imposed timetable, or achieve employment equity via affirmative action measures is not subject to penalties. The EEA does not penalize employers for failing to implement satisfactory affirmative action measures despite their intention, or stated intention, to do so.

The EEA seeks in a cooperative manner to intervene in the process of racial employment redress. The rationale is that, left to its own devices, the market will achieve equity only over a very long period, and the resulting social instability would be dangerous to society. In another innovative step, the act seeks to address the Apartheid wage gap that arose due to the artificial imbalance of power in the workplace that was fostered and maintained by Apartheid. This inequity allowed white management to significantly restrict the salaries of workers while awarding themselves large increases. Even in 2002-03 various media reports highlighted the incidence of managers receiving increases of up to 35% while trade unions had to fight for increases of 7-9% for their members.

As a result, the act requires designated employers to submit a statement, at the time that each skills and equity report is submitted, on the remuneration and benefits paid out to each occupational category and level of its workforce. This "income differential statement" is submitted to the Employment Conditions Commission. The EEA provides that where disproportionate income differentials are reflected, the designated employer must take measures to progressively reduce such differentials. The EEA does not attempt to define "disproportionate"; rather, the Employment Conditions Commission is obliged to research and investigate norms and benchmarks for proportionate income differentials and advise the minister of labor on appropriate measures for reducing disproportional differentials. The income differential statement submitted to the Employment Conditions Commission is to be kept confidential by the commission, although employees and their trade union engaged in collective bargaining with the employer (e.g., in annual wage negotiations) may request and receive the information contained in the statement, subject to certain safeguards contained in the LRA.

Vocational training institutions
Commission for Employment Equity. The Employment Equity Act also provided for the establishment of a Commission of Employment Equity, which is a stakeholder body responsible for establishing Codes of Good Practice. The act requires that these codes be monitored and enforced, and directs how this should happen. The nine-member commission monitors firms that employ 50 or more workers to ensure that they eliminate unfair employment discrimination by promoting equal opportunity and fair treatment and that they achieve a diverse workforce that is broadly representative of South Africa's people.

National Skills Authority. The 29-member National Skills Authority was established under the Skills Development Act and is made up of representatives from organized business, labor, government, and community organizations. Its main function is to advise the Labor Minister about a national skills development strategy and its implementation.

Sector Education and Skills Authority. A SETA is a body accredited in terms of the South African Qualifications Authorities Act to monitor and assess learning and training. As an accredited body, a SETA may establish learnerships if the learnerships consist of a structured learning component, practical work experience, and the possibility of leading to a qualification registered by the South African Qualifications Authority. The minister of labor may establish a SETA with a constitution for any national economic sector. The SETA will coordinate training and implement a skills plan for the industry in which it has jurisdiction. A SETA's management body consists of organized labor, organized employers, relevant government departments, and any interested professional bodies for each sector of an industry. The learnership involves an employer, training provider, and the learner. Skills development is funded by levies collected under the Skills Development Levies Act and monies appropriated by Parliament for the National Skills Fund.

Training needs within the informal sector

Informal sector traders are not ignorant of the need to receive training. Many seek to acquire technical, commercial, and managerial skills (Devey et al. 2003). However, this sector often falls between the cracks when it comes to training. For example, in a 2001 World Bank survey of informal enterprises in Johannesburg, 81% of the 500 traders interviewed had never received training.

Educational levels in the sector are low, with many workers poorly educated and 10% not literate in 2001, according to SSA. Table 48 above showed that 10.0% of workers have no education and 33.7% have only a primary level education.

As described above, the 1998 Skills Development Act set up sectoral education and training authorities. At the time of designing the skills development system there was debate as to whether a separate informal sector SETA was needed, or whether the sector should be incorporated into each SETA. The incorporation route was chosen, because the informal sector cuts across so many economic sectors. In theory, small- and medium-sized businesses are catered to in the SETAs with representatives and tailored training. However, this advantage seems to be bypassing micro and survivalist businesses. For example, in the 2000 LFS 50% of the clothing sector was estimated to be made up of informal enterprises (Devey et al. 2003), and yet in 2002 the clothing and textiles SETA noted that it had not trained any informal sector businesses, mainly because the businesses were not able to pay skills levies.

Twenty percent of the levies go to the National Skills Fund, which has tried to hire trainers to train informal sector employers and employees. However, the training has not been successful, with trainers complaining that it is not profitable to train in the informal sector, even with the government subsidy. Secondly, the low levels of education in the sector mean that training is difficult, and traditional training methods cannot be used. The recipients are also very mobile and work in unsafe areas where trainers do not want to go. Non-traditional methods will therefore have to be adopted if any successful training program is to be designed nationally. The training context, methods, timing, structure, and content will have to be tailored to each subsector and trainee group (Devey et al. 2003). This move will require a deeper level of government support than currently exists.

Union perspectives on labor legislation
The labor market was the centerpiece of Apartheid. The new, democratic government therefore sought to put in place a series of laws that would counter this history of labor suppression. As described earlier, these laws included:

- the Labor Relations Act, which regulates the relationship between trade unions and employers;

- the Basic Conditions of Employment Act, which sets minimum conditions for all workers, especially those who fall below a prescribed wage threshold;

- the Employment Equity Act, which tackles South Africa's history of racial job reservations and removes barriers to employment and advancement of historically disadvantaged groups (so-called "designated groups");

- the Skills Development Act, which addresses the Apartheid legacy of under-investment in skills development of black people and the growing tendency of companies to neglect training needs of their workforces and the broader economy;

- the Unemployment Insurance Fund (UIF) Act, which seeks to improve the functioning of the UIF, a contribution-based fund that provides short-term (maximum six month) benefits to five million formal sector workers. In the context of high and long-term unemployment, this fund is increasingly mismatched to the employment environment.

What do trade unionists feel about the impact of labor laws on workers in South Africa, especially low-income workers and vulnerable workers? In-depth interviews were conducted by NALEDI in 2001 with COSATU (federation), NUMSA (metal), NUM (mining), CEPPWAWU (chemical and paper), NEHAWU (public service), and SATAWU (transport) to get feedback on these issues.

In sum, unionists recognized the need to introduce these laws quickly. Further, unionists acknowledged that the new laws could all play a crucial role in bolstering the rights of workers (NALEDI 2001).

However, while the South African labor laws are progressive, innovative, and detailed, their implementation is often problematic. The current labor laws are seen as giving workers minimum protection, but this protection depends on how unions are using the space provided to pursue goals. Further, the largely simultaneous introduction of new laws has placed a massive capacity strain on both unions and the Department of Labor, which both need to understand the laws and put in place capacity to promote their effective implementation.

Finally, the progressive stance of the new labor laws is contradicted by neo-liberal economic policies. This contradiction reflects differences within the state and within components of the tripartite labor-government-business alliance.

Labor Relations Act. The LRA has resulted in many advances for workers in protecting their collective bargaining rights. However, the LRA excludes independent contractors from the definition of employees. This omission is a significant weakness, as many firms are employing so-called independent contractors in place of regular workers as a means of circumventing labor laws by turning a labor contract into an apparent commercial contract. In this sense, the LRA is seen as not protecting casual and contract workers, categories that are on the increase due to restructuring and globalization. In general there is a strong need to find ways, including amendments to the law, to organize vulnerable workers and allow them to have access to collective bargaining.

A further concern is that employers are allowed to retrench workers for "operational" requirements, widely defined. Thus, despite the perception that labor markets are inflexible, retrenchments are easy to implement and have recently resulted in massive jobs losses.

Dismissal of workers, however, does require employers to show "fair reason" and "fair procedure." This rule prohibits the past discriminatory practices inherent in easy dismissals and requires that employers change their approach to managing labor, something that they are generally reluctant or find difficult to do. Further, the law established the CCMA to be a mediation and arbitration body that workers and employers can call upon to resolve disputes. Though disputes are now being resolved more quickly, NALEDI research has revealed that some unionists do not have faith in the skills of some CCMA presiding officers, due to perceived inconsistency in the granting of awards or verdicts (NALEDI 2001).

Employment Equity Act. A NALEDI survey found much support among unionists for the EEA, which seeks to redress past inequalities in terms of employee recruitment and employment profiles with respect to blacks, the disabled, and women. Yet some respondents said that some employers emphasize the recruitment of white women or middle-class blacks for management or skilled posts, thus creating little benefit for those workers in the lower grades. The weakness of unions is evident in terms of driving or monitoring employment equity developments, with employers generally taking the lead in setting in place often inappropriate employment equity plans.

There appears to be non-compliance with the act, often with employers prepared to pay penalties instead of changing their employment profile. This level of non-compliance is exacerbated by the poor capacity of the Departmental of Labor to effectively monitor and evaluate compliance.

Basic Conditions of Employment Act. Most unionists saw the BCEA, intended to provide a basic floor of rights, as offering insufficient protection for vulnerable workers. A particular weakness is the absence of minimum wages and a requirement instead that workers negotiate to settle their own wages. However, the least organized and most vulnerable workers, particularly the millions of domestic, farm, and non-permanent workers, are at the mercy of employers and invariably earn wages far below the poverty line. These workers are extremely difficult to unionize, and repeated union attempts to do so have usually failed.

The new BCEA lowered maternity benefits to millions of women workers. The law imposed a universal minimum of four months unpaid leave on the Unemployment Insurance Fund that had until then allowed six months of paid benefits. Despite these weaknesses and setbacks, unionists saw the BCEA as a victory for most workers in South Africa.

Skills Development Act. This act levied employers to contribute to a fund that supports skills development in all sectors of the economy. Employers implementing a skills plan can recover their costs from the fund. The law thus forces all employers to share in the costs of skills development, and also creates incentives for them to establish workplace skills plans.

Given the shortage of skills in South Africa, most unionists regard the act as a good step. But unionists surveyed by NALEDI said that shop stewards and unionists are not active in participating in the newly established sector skills bodies. Further, the levy on companies, 1% of the wage bill, was seen as low compared to the much higher international norm of company expenditure on skills development.

The skills development area has been identified as one area where the lack of union capacity is most apparent, resulting in lower than average levels of union influence. The weakness of the Department of Labor also contributes to employers having most influence on the implementation of this law. A further concern among unionists was that the act benefited workers in big companies and gives short shrift to the interests of workers in small companies.

As a proposal for the future, unionists surveyed by NALEDI stressed the need to train shop stewards and union officials to understand the SDA.

Present labor laws and organizational rights. Most of the unionists surveyed by NALEDI agreed that the present labor laws promoted better organizational rights for workers. Some said that the LRA obliges employers to disclose relevant information for collective bargaining. However, respondents said employers often inundate them with volumes of useless information that they cannot work through. Where unions have developed their research or technical capacity, this is less likely to be a problem. However, companies are not required to disclose any information that they consider private and confidential, and the employer has the discretion to make that determination. On the other hand, the employer has access to all employee information.

Organizational rights, such as freedom of association and stop-order facilities, are regarded as being strengthened by the new laws. This helps unions to recruit and be financially independent and viable, thus limiting employer or state ability to disrupt them. Workers who go on a "procedural" strike (that is, follow the process as laid down by the act) cannot be dismissed. As the laid-down procedure is not particularly difficult, this is seen as a positive step. Yet some unionists are unhappy that the act excludes large categories of so-called "essential service" workers from the right to strike; these workers must settle disputes through arbitration.

To promote union democracy, the LRA stipulates clearly that unions are required to have audited statements and hold congresses and other open processes. Most of the unionists surveyed by NALEDI agree that unions are independent and are controlled by workers.

Conclusions and recommendations

Workers in South Africa today face key challenges. The struggles against Apartheid capitalism have given way to new forms of struggle that are not always as clear-cut as those of old. What are these key challenges that unions are addressing?

One of the important challenges is the struggle to transform the Apartheid workplace that, even after 10 years of democracy, dominates South Africa's economy. Key here is to ensure that the spaces opened up by legislation are taken advantage of. Workers need to have their skills developed, equity needs to be achieved in the workplace, and health and safety legislation should be enforced as it never was under a regime that saw black workers as second-class citizens.

However, unions grapple to ensure that the progressive outcomes of legislation are not subsumed and disempowered by better-resourced human resource machinery within companies. For example, how do unions ensure that skills legislation designed to benefit the historically disadvantaged isn't used to build the skills of elites and entrench their positions? This effort often requires combined strategies, such as input on redrafting of legislation at NEDLAC and in parliamentary committees, but it also requires strong organizers and shop stewards who understand the legislation and are able to fight for the rights of members.

South Africa has undergone a protracted shrinking of the economy, followed by what can only be termed jobless growth. Within this environment the restructuring of enterprises and the increasing shift toward engaging more casualized and temporary workers is further undermining quality jobs. Unions are addressing this issue both at the workplace and in forums at NEDLAC and processes such as Sector Job Summits. A major issue within this struggle centers on resources to fund research and develop alternatives. Another issue is the capacity of union officials to counter management proposals regarding restructuring, a key issue for capacity building.

Restructuring of the economy and labor market. The changes to the labor market, and the government's responses to them, are part of two parallel efforts at restructuring that have occurred in the South African economy since the advent of democracy in 1994. The first effort targeted the economy, which has been deliberately liberalized and restructured in order to meet GEAR's tenets of increased competitiveness and pursuit of export-led growth. Ironically, at the same time as these changes have occurred, democracy brought renewed efforts by the labor movement and government to restructure the workplace and the labor market in order to remove the legacy of Apartheid labor relations. However, these two approaches have not been able to balance one another. The labor market, although progressively restructured, has been facing increasing attempts by employers to reduce employment levels and increase efficiencies, as the restructured economy has exposed them to fierce international competition.

Structural legacy. The new competitive environment has not allowed employers or workers the opportunity to overcome Apartheid's legacy of planned labor surpluses or enforced skills poverty. South Africa has thus been faced with an enormous developmental challenge. Not only is it facing the challenges of being a small emerging market in the era of rapid globalization, it is also trying to ambitiously redress decades and even centuries of conscious neglect of capacity of the majority of its workforce. The skills sets inherited from Apartheid cannot be integrated easily into a formal sector that has rapidly responded to the liberalization of the GEAR macroeconomic program by shedding labor and focusing on competitiveness.

Obstacles to job creation through training. The government and civil society and labor itself have responded in a sophisticated manner to the skills challenge through a comprehensive range of vocational training legislation and the establishment of dedicated skills providers, the SETAs. These efforts have met with some success, but the employment rate has not expanded sufficiently to absorb the newly retrained workers as well as the newly graduated but untrained entrants to the labor force. As entrants finish school, they have to compete with an existing backlog of workers. Even re-skilling has not been able to create large numbers of jobs. Apartheid's social engineering not only artificially suppressed skill levels, it ensured that black businesspeople and workers could not grow the economy. The domestic market is therefore artificially small, with a small middle class. Although wealth was concentrated and multiplied in a white middle class, domestic demand suffered. With domestic demand constituting the engine of growth for economic development in most economies, South Africa's labor absorption capacity is constrained by the size of its domestic market. Without growing domestic sales, local industry cannot expand and absorb new entrants. Regional sales are also weaker than they could be due to the Apartheid regime's funding and support for regional wars. Export sales are constrained by the emergence of China and India as major exporters just as South Africa was fully re-entering the global economy. GDP growth needs to reach around 6% by Reserve Bank projections for labor absorption to impact the large pool of surplus labor. This means that the re-skilling of South Africa's workforce that is currently underway cannot significantly decrease unemployment, due to the structural factors outlined above. What re-skilling does do, however, is prepare the workforce for any possible economic growth prospects (remember that the economy has not stopped expanding on average since 1994, and has picked up speed with each post-2000 year) and at the same time potentially enables economic growth. Both are hard to quantify, but in theory a virtuous circle of capacity could be generated.

The analysis of South Africa's workforce development program could therefore be partly placed under the label "dualist,"[10] as it encompasses strong elements of a dualistic economy with a vibrant formal sector and a growing but poor and unskilled informal sector. Perhaps a label to describe the development and history of South Africa's workforce over the last 40 years could be "statist," which would denote the impact of the state in artificially affecting and shaping the labor market through massive negative social engineering in the decades prior to the 1990s. The new program of the democratic regime is also a social engineering intervention aimed at massive change in the workforce and labor market, and although it comprises significant elements of a structuralist[11] and legalist[12] paradigm, it is a state response to a previous statist intervention. The massive unemployment and skills shortage of the South African labor force is not the result of globalization, or employer action, or a pre-capitalist system, but a complex outworking of a process of social exclusion.

A resolution to the current crisis of unemployment will therefore require a new form of statist intervention, this time in collaboration with all stakeholders in society, to design a structural response to the challenges of workforce development in South Africa.

Such collaboration would entail the incorporation of efforts by the labor movement to recruit members from the informal sector. This could play an important role in the state's efforts because it could lead to increased reporting of labor standards abuses, as well as increased entry points for training agencies. As a starting point, unionized workers earn more than non-unionized workers in South Africa, so wage conditions would improve, although given the micro nature of most of the sector this would prove to be a highly contested undertaking. Likewise, state collaboration with the labor movement could see collective bargaining provisions being extended to cover informalized workers, i.e., those outsourced or made casual or temporary. Such inclusion in collective bargaining would allow the unions to demand better working conditions (benefits, wages, security of employment, health, and safety) for workers in these areas.[13]

Finally, any attempts to increase the standards of work for those working in the informal sectors would increase the costs for those employers who are using the informal sector to escape state regulation, since increased working standards would mean increased regulation and enforcement of existing labor regulations.

It is in the interests of all South Africans to analyze and plan around issues of informality and informalization in the labor market. Unless attention is paid to this "second economy" in policy formulation, legislation, and regulation, the developmental prospects of the nation will be undermined, as will ongoing efforts to coherently address the Apartheid legacies that influence labor market and broader socioeconomic dynamics in democratic South Africa.

Endnotes

1.   The People's Budget Campaign has successfully outlined alternative budgetary allocations focused on reducing poverty and stimulating domestic growth. These recommendations may have influenced the recent policy shift to a more expansionary spending focus by the National Department of Finance.

2.   The recent unsuccessful attempt by the national transport parastatal, Transnet, to sell off portions of state rail operator Spoornet is an example of such practices. The attempt was one of the few that was successfully resisted by organized labor.

3.   The rand depreciated dramatically by 33.3% against the dollar from June 30 to December 31, 2001 (South African Reserve Bank, *Quarterly Bulletin,* June 2002, p. 48) and apparently remains undervalued.

4.   The government introduced a revised system of official statistics following the advent of democracy in South Africa in 1994.

5.   Due to a change in statistical methods and survey implementation used in the national statistics after 1999, the figures for the 1990s are not strictly comparable to those commencing in 2000. Therefore, where necessary the post-2000 figures are reflected as a separate table. The two sets may be integrated in the future.

6.   The MLL and SLL are drawn up by the Bureau for Market Research at the University of Stellenbosch.

7. $241 at average 2003 exchange rates.

8. $307 at average 2003 exchange rates.

9.   South African Transport and Allied Workers Union, an affiliate on COSATU. See the interesting set of research papers produced for the ILO in 2003 on efforts within South Africa to organize within the informal and casual sectors of the workforce.

10.   *Dualist*: informal work seen as a feature of pre-capitalist societies, therefore requiring no policy response; it will merely go away.

11.   *Structuralist*: informalization is the outcome of a capitalist process that conspires to keep labor costs low. The policy response is on the bargaining-power side: enforcement, unions, minimum wages, regulation, labor rights, plus good macroeconomic policies.

12.   *Legalist*: informalization is not the degradation of work but a feature of entrepreneurs trying to escape burdensome regulation. The policy response may be on the product market side—enforcing property rights, changing the way taxes are levied and benefits conferred, and changing the structure of taxation.

13.   For example, workers who are fired and then rehired under labor brokers do not currently fall under the relevant bargaining council for their sector, as labor brokers are not counted as employers within the sectors concerned.

Bibliography

ABSA Bank. 2003a. "Long Term Prospects for the South African Economy 2003-2017." www.absa.co.za

ABSA Bank. 2003b. "South African Sectoral Outlook 2003-2008." www.absa.co.za

Adelzadeh, Asghar Cynthia Alvillar, and Charles Mather. 2000. "Poverty Alleviation, Employment Creation, and Sustainable Livelihoods in South Africa." In Khosa, ed. *Empowerment Through Economic Transformation.* Johannesburg: Human Sciences Research Council Press.

African National Congress. 1996. "Growth, Employment, and Redistribution: A Macroeconomic Strategy." Pretoria: ANC Policy Papers.

Alderman, H., et al. 2000. "Combining Census and Survey Data to Construct a Poverty Map of South Africa." Working Paper. Pretoria: Statistics South Africa.

Bhorat, H. 2002. "Employment Trends: Has the Economy Created Jobs Since Gear?" SA Labour Bulletin 26(1). www.commerce.uct.ac.za/DPRU/Employment_Trends_since_GEAR.pdf.

Bond, P., et al. 1997. "Resistance to Neo-liberalism: A View From South Africa." Paper prepared for the Second Intercontinental Encounter for Humanity and Against Neoliberalism, Madrid, Spain.

Bowens, Webber Wentzel. 2002. "Overview of South African Labor Legislation." http://www.wwb.co.za/invest_sa/18.htm

Braude, W. 2003. "Tinkering at the Margins of Gear." *Civil Society Review,* Interfund Development Update. Johannesburg.

Braude, W., M. Mbatha, and E. Watkinson. 2003. "Measures to Promote a Decent Work Agenda in South African Agriculture." Prepared for the ILO Decent Work in Agriculture Symposium.

Business Day. 2004. "Firms Feel Pinch as AIDS Hurts Profits." February 4. www.bday.co.za/bday/content/direct/1,3523,1535239- 6079-0,00.html.

Carter, M., J. May, and V. Padayachee. 2002. "Sweetening the Bitter Fruit of Liberty: Markets and the Persistence of Poverty in Post-Apartheid South Africa." Paper prepared for the South African National Human Development Report.

COSATU. 2003a. "Organisational Review Report to the 8th National Congress." Report for the COSATU Secretariat. www.cosatu.org.za, accessed December 2003.

COSATU. 2003b. "Secretariat Report 2003." www.cosatu.org.za, accessed January 2004.

COSATU, SANGOCO, and SACC. 2003. "People's Budget 2003-2004."

Creamer Media Research Unit. 2004. "South African Growth and Development 2003." Report for Research Channel Online. www.engineeringnews.co.za, accessed January 2004.

Denga, S., C. Horton, L. Modise, R. Naidoo, and T. Yanta. 2001. "The State of Unions in South Africa." Prepared for NALEDI.

Denga, S. 2003. "Building Effective Union Service Delivery." Prepared for NALEDI. www.naledi.org.za, accessed January 2004.

Department of Labour. 2003. "Labour Market Review." www.labour.gov.za, accessed November 2003.

Devey, R., C. Skinner, and I. Valodia. 2003. "The Informal Economy in South Africa: Who, Where, What, and How Much?" Paper presented at the DPRU Second Annual Conference on Labour Market and Poverty in South Africa, Glenburn Lodge, Johannesburg, October 22-24, 2002.

Fallon, P., and L. Pereira da Silva. 1994. *South Africa: Economic Performance and Policies.* Washington, D.C.: World Bank.

Government Communication and Information System (GCIS). 2003a. "Institutions Regulating Labour Relations." www.gcis.gov.za, accessed January 2004.

Government Communication and Information System (GCIS). 2003b. *South Africa Yearbook 2002.* http://www.gcis.gov.za/docs/publications/yearbook.htm.

Hassen, E-H. 2001. "Alternatives to GEAR." *NALEDI Policy Bulletin* 4(1)

Hassen, E-K. 2003. "Redistribution and Public Spending, An Assessment of the MTEF." http://www/naledi.org.za, accessed February 2004.

Hirsch, A. 1997. "Industrial Strategy in South Africa: A Review." Paper prepared for the 1997 Trade and Industrial Policy Secretariat Annual Forum.

Horton, C., and E. Watkinson 2001. "Characteristics of the South African Labour Force." Prepared for NALEDI.

Human Sciences Research Council (HSRC). 2004. Annual Report.

ICTSD Weekly Trade News Digest. 2000. "FDI to Top $1000bn, But Developing Countries' Share Remains Marginal." http://www.ictsd.org, accessed February 2004.

Interfund. 2003. "Development Update, Complexities, Lost Opportunities, and Prospects." *Interfund* 4(1).

Joffe, A., D. Kaplan, R. Kaplinsky, and D. Lewis, eds. 1995. *Improving Manufacturing Performance in South Africa: Report of the Industrial Strategy Project.* Cape Town: University of Cape Town Press.

Kershoff, G. 2003. "Business and Consumer Surveys in South Africa." Paper presented at the Joint European Commission-OECD Workshop on International Development of Business and Consumer Tendency Surveys, November 20-21.

Labour Research Service. 2002. "Annual Bargaining Indicators Report." Cape Town: LRS.

Labour Research Service. 2003. "The LRS Report." Cape Town: LRS.

Laubscher, P. 2002. "The South African Business Cycle Over the 1990s: What Can We Learn?" Paper presented at the 2002 Trade and Industrial Policy Secretariat Annual Forum.

Marais, H. 2001. *South Africa: Limits to Change.* Cape Town: Creda.

Mather, C., and A. Adelzadeh. 1997. "Macroeconomic Strategies, Agriculture, and Rural Poverty in Post-Apartheid South Africa." Johannesburg.

McGrath, S. 2004. "Introduction." In A. Badroodien, A. Kraak, and S. McGrath, eds., *The Shifting Understanding of Skills in South Africa.* Pretoria: HSRC Press.

Meth, C. 2001. *Social Exclusion, Social Protection, and South Africa's Unemployment Problem.* Durban: University of Natal.

Michie, Jonathon, and Vishnu Padayachee. 1997. *The Political Economy of South Africa's Transition.* London: Dryden Press.

Muller, C. 2002. "Measuring South Africa's Informal Sector: An Analysis of National Household Surveys." Paper presented at the DPRU Conference on Labour Markets and Poverty in South Africa, Glenburn Lodge, Johannesburg, October 22-24.

Naidoo, R. 1999. "COSATU Membership 1987-1999." NALEDI Internal Statistics. Johannesburg: NALEDI.

Naidoo, R. 2001. "Kick-Starting and Broadening the Growth Path." *NALEDI Policy Bulletin* 4(1).

NALEDI. 2001. September Policy Bulletin.

NALEDI. 2002. "People's Budget 2003-2004: Proposal From COSATU, SANGOCO, and SACC." Johannesburg: NALEDI.

NALEDI. 2003a. "People's Budget 2004-2005: Proposal From COSATU, SANGOCO, and SACC." Johannesburg: NALEDI

NALEDI. 2003b. "Employment Creation and Retention in the Metals and Engineering Sector." Johannesburg: NALEDI.

NALEDI and Bentley-West. 2003. "Growth and Employment in the South African Metals and Engineering Industry." Paper prepared for Industrial Development Corporation/Department of Trade and Industry FRIDGE Fund. www.nedlac.org.za.

National Department of Finance. 2000a. "Budget Review 2000." Pretoria: National Department of Finance.

National Department of Finance. 2000b. "National Expenditure Survey 2000." Pretoria: National Department of Finance.

National Department of Finance. 2001. "Budget Review 2001." Pretoria: National Department of Finance.

National Department of Finance. 2002. "Budget Review 2002." Pretoria: National Department of Finance.

National Department of Finance. 2003. "Budget Review 2003." Pretoria: National Department of Finance.

Orr, L., and E. Watkinson. 2003. "Extreme Poverty and Inequality Create Conditions for Highly Exploitative Jobs." Paper prepared for NALEDI.

Paton, C. 2004. "Government Looks for Key to Unlocking Poverty. http://www.sundaytimes.co.za, accessed February 2004.

Roberts, S. 2000. "A Preliminary Analysis of the Impact of Trade Liberalisation on Manufacturing in South Africa." *South African Journal of Economics.* 168: 607-38.

Roberts, S. 2001. "Globalisation, Industrial Development, and the Plastics Industry in South Africa." *Journal of International Development.* 13(6).

SARPN. 2003. "SA Poverty Indicators." www.sarpn.org.za, accessed November 2003.

Seidman-Magkelta, N. 2001. "Overview of the Economy." Unpublished paper cited in Padayachee and Valodia, 2001, *Changing Gear? The 2001 Budget and Economic Policy in South Africa,* Transformation No. 46.

South African Reserve Bank (SARB). 2002a. "Annual Economic Report 2002." Pretoria: SARB.

South African Reserve Bank. 2002b. *Quarterly Economic Review*, December. Pretoria: SARB.

South African Reserve Bank. 2002c. *Quarterly Economic Review*, June. Pretoria: SARB.

South African Reserve Bank. 2002d. *Quarterly Economic Review,* September. Pretoria: SARB.

South African Reserve Bank. 2003a. "Annual Economic Report 2003." Pretoria: SARB. www.resbank.gov.za, accessed December 2003.

South African Reserve Bank. 2003b. "Budget Overview." www.treasury.gov.za, accessed July 2003.

South African Reserve Bank. 2003c. "Quarterly Bulletin: December 2003." www.resbank.gov.za, accessed December 2003.

Statistics South Africa (SSA). 2001a. "National Census." www.statssa.gov.za, accessed September 2003.

Statistics South Africa. 2001b. "South Africa in Transition: Selected Findings From the October Household Survey of 1999 and Changes That Have Occurred Between 1995 and 1999." www.statssa.gov.za, accessed July 2003.

Statistics South Africa. 2002a. "Actual and Expected Capital Expenditure by the Public Sector 2001, 2002, 2003 and 2004." Pretoria: SSA.

Statistics South Africa. 2002b. "Labour Force Survey, September 2002." www.statssa.gov.za, accessed March 2003.

Statistics South Africa. 2002c. "The South African Labour Market, Selected Time-Based Social and International Comparisons." www.statssa.gov.za, accessed October 2003.

Statistics South Africa. 2002d. "Survey of Employment and Earnings, September 2002." www.statssa.gov.za, accessed July 2003.

Statistics South Africa. 2003a. Consolidated Expenditure by the General Government Sector 1999/2000." Pretoria: SSA.

Statistics South Africa. 2003b. "Consumer Price Index, December 2003." www.statssa.gov.za, accessed January 2004.

Statistics South Africa. 2003c. "Emigration and Immigration." Pretoria: SSA.

Statistics South Africa. 2003d. "Gross Domestic Product, Annual Estimates 1993-2002." www.statssa.gov.za, accessed November 2003.

Statistics South Africa. 2003e. "Labour Force Survey, March 2003." www.statssa.gov.za, accessed September 2003.

Statistics South Africa. 2003f. "Labour Force Survey, September 2003." www.statssa.gov.za, accessed September 2003.

Statistics South Africa. 2003g. "Survey of Average Monthly Earnings, February 2004." www.statssa.gov.za, accessed March 2004.

Statistics South Africa. 2003h. "Survey of Employment and Earnings, March 2003." www.statssa.gov.za, accessed September 2003.

Statistics South Africa. 2003i. "The 2001 Census in Brief." www.gov.za/reports/2003/census01_key.pdf, accessed January 2004.

Statistics South Africa. 2004a. "Labour Force Survey, March 2004." www.statssa.gov.za, accessed April 2004.

Statistics South Africa. 2004b. "Production Price Index (PPI) December 2003." www.statssa.gov.za, accessed January 2004.

Sunday Times Online. 2002. "Call for State to Review Skills Strategy." www.sundaytimes.co.za, accessed January 2004.

Terreblanche, S. 2002. "A History of Inequality in South Africa, 1652-2002." Durban: University of Natal.

Tourism, Hospitality, Education, and Training Authority (THETA). 2003. "Annual Report."

Tourism, Hospitality, and Sport Sector Education and Training Authority (THETA). 2004a. "An Overview of South African Legislation." www.theta.org.za, accessed January 2004.

Tourism, Hospitality, and Sport Sector Education and Training Authority (THETA). 2004b. "SAQA and the Skills Development Acts." www.theta.org.za, accessed January 2004.

Trade and Industrial Policy Strategies (TIPS). 2003. "Snapshot of Industry-Wide Trends in Employment, 1991-2001." TIPS Sectoral Focus Series. www.tips.org.za/research/papers, accessed January 2004.

United Nations Development Program. 2002. *Human Development Report.* New York, N.Y.: UNDP.

Valodia, I. 2000. "Economic Policy and Women's Work in South Africa: Overlooking Atypical Work?" Paper presented at the conference of the International Association for Feminist Economics (IAFFE), Bo_aziçi University, Istanbul, Turkey, August 15-17.

Van Holdt, K. 2003. "Saving Government From Itself: A Case Study on Engagement Around Restructuring." Paper prepared for SATAWU.

Watkinson, E. 2001. "Farm Workers and Labour Standards: Room for Improvement." Paper prepared for NALEDI.

Watkinson, E. 2003. "Wages, Benefits, and Union Membership." Paper prepared for NALEDI.

Watkinson, E., and N. Makgetla. 2002. "South Africa's Food Security Crisis." Johannesburg: NALEDI.

Wood, G. 2001. "South African Trade Unions in a Time of Adjustment." Paper presented on "Class and Crisis in South Africa" for the History Cooperative Online 47. www.historycooperative.org/journals/llt/47/06wood.html, accessed January 2004.

World Bank. 1993. *World Development Report.* Washington, D.C.: World Bank.

CONCLUSION

Informal employment: rethinking workforce development

By Martha Chen and Joann Vanek[1]

> We know only too well that it is precisely the world of work that
> holds the key for solid, progressive, and long-lasting eradication
> of poverty. It is through work that people can expand their choices
> to a better quality of life. It is through work that wealth is created,
> distributed, and accumulated. It is through work that people find a
> dignified way out of poverty....Poverty elimination is impossible
> unless the economy generates opportunities for investment, entre-
> preneurship, job creation, and sustainable livelihoods.
>
> — *Juan Somavia, Director General,*
> *International Labour Organization (ILO 2003)*

As the Director General of the International Labour Organization stated
in his report to the 2003 International Labour Conference, employment
and poverty are intrinsically linked. And, yet, sufficient attention is not
paid to employment issues in the debates on poverty or in poverty reduction strategies. In part, this is because the data to prove and illustrate
these linkages are not readily available. The five workforce development studies featured in this volume represent an important new source
of data and analysis on this relationship. Following a common framework of questions, each of the studies analyzed the links between macroeconomic processes and labor force development in their respective
countries. More importantly, they also disaggregated the labor force by
formal and informal employment, as well as by women and men.

In this conclusion, we begin by highlighting the contribution these
five country studies make to our understanding of labor markets and to

the field of labor statistics. We then summarize the common and distinct findings of the studies as well as their implications for future research and analysis. We conclude with a discussion of the policy and programmatic implications of the findings.

The importance of the five country studies to understanding labor markets

As noted in the introduction to this volume, the five country studies were designed to identify and document changes over time in the nature of work in informal and formal employment. Special attention was given to the skills and other characteristics of individuals engaged in informal and formal employment and to the terms and conditions of informal and formal employment.

In general, data that examine the numbers of workers in informal employment are not readily available, and there is even less information about the skills and other characteristics of different categories of informal workers or the terms and conditions of different types of informal employment. National statistical offices have only recently begun to give priority to the collection of data on informal employment and, in collecting these data, countries have often used different definitions. Over the past decade, the global research network Women in Informal Employment: Globalizing and Organizing (WIEGO) has worked to promote the collection of data on informal employment by national statistical offices and the analysis of these data by researchers and advocates. WIEGO has also worked closely with the International Labour Organization, the United Nations Statistical Division, and the International Expert Group on Informal Sector Statistics to broaden the definition of the informal economy to include informal employment both inside and outside informal (i.e., small, unregistered) enterprises. This expanded definition was endorsed by the 2002 International Labour Conference in the Conclusions to the General Discussion on the Informal Economy and by the 2003 International Conference of Labour Statisticians in a resolution on informal employment.

One of the major contributions of the country studies in this volume is that they have analyzed existing national data using this expanded concept of informal employment. Within the constraints of the available data sets, four of the country studies featured in this volume applied the expanded definition of informal employment described above. The exception is the India study, which did not analyze data on informal employment collected in the National Sample Survey of Employment and Unemployment but rather used estimates of employment in what are referred to in India as the "organized" and "unorganized" sectors based on administrative data of the Directorate General of Employment and Training.

For those who are interested in changing official labor force statistics to make these statistics more relevant to measurement of employment in developing countries, the use of these data by the research teams is of great importance. To justify the collection of new and improved data based on a broader definition of informal employment, the data already collected need to be tabulated and analyzed. Statisticians have made efforts in recent years to develop methods and statistics on the large share of the global workforce that remains outside the world of full-time, stable, and protected employment. Data sets are available now on informal employment that were not available 10 years ago.

But national surveys are expensive undertakings, and the resources that are required for new data collection efforts must be justified in terms of usage and the mobilization of advocates to plead the case for why the data are needed. At the same time, national statistical offices often do not make it easy for outside researchers to use their data. Whether or not they encountered such difficulties, the researchers who carried out the five country studies made the effort to use existing national data in their reports. By applying these data toward policy-relevant analysis, the five country studies in this volume make an effective case for the collection of more data on informal employment.

Moreover, these studies also made the case for *better* statistics on informal employment. They identified problems with the existing data— which often were not collected explicitly to look at issues of informal employment—as well as areas where additional data were needed. Thus, these studies suggest important directions for future data collection in the area of informal employment (the possible directions for future research are outlined in more detail at the end of this chapter).

Finally, the type of analysis undertaken by the researchers is considerably more complex than the standard tabulations that are released by national statistical services. In contrast to the more typical user, who is generally interested in published tabulations, four of the research teams who carried out the country studies did their *own* analysis of the data. The analyses they carried out were useful in suggesting linkages between informal employment, gender, and poverty, and further work based on these findings is proposed later in this chapter. Such analysis requires working with the actual data sets. This type of use relates to a long-term objective of the global research network WIEGO: namely, the creation of a comprehensive data archive of microdata from labor force and other related surveys on informal employment. Development of such a database is a complex undertaking that requires not only improvement in the available data but also widespread use of the data in analyses such as those undertaken here. Analysis of the data in multiple countries is essential to the creation of a harmonized classification system in which to store the data.

Major findings of the five country studies

While the introduction to this volume has summarized in some detail the main findings of the five workforce development studies, it is worth repeating here the common findings of these studies and the promising lines of future research and analysis that they suggest.

Common findings

The five studies found a number of commonalities in the size and makeup of the informal economy, including the following:

- The informal economy comprises a large share of total employment in all countries: ranging from about 15% in Russia to 25% in South Africa, 40% in Egypt, 70% in El Salvador, and over 90% in India.

- The informal economy as a share of total employment is growing in all countries except El Salvador (where out-migration may account for the lack of growth in the informal economy).

- The informal economy is visible in all sectors of the economy but tends to be concentrated in agriculture, light manufacturing, retail trade, construction, and transport.[2]

- Informal economy workers have, on average, less education and experience than those who work in the formal economy.

- Those who work in the informal economy work longer hours, on average, than those who work in the formal economy.

- A large share of informal workers are poor or earn below the minimum wage.

- Informal workers, especially women, earn less, on average, than their formal counterparts.

- Female informal workers also earn less, on average, than their male counterparts within the informal economy, leading to a gender gap in wages or earnings within the informal economy.

A related finding in four of the countries (Egypt, El Salvador, India, and Russia) is that economic reforms and restructuring have had a negative effect on the quality of employment in terms of earnings and benefits.

Promising lines of analysis
Considered as a whole, the five studies represent an important first step in understanding the impact of recent economic changes on workers, especially those who are engaged in the informal economy. They also suggest some promising areas of analysis for future research, such as:

- The links between race/ethnicity and informal employment (South Africa); age and informal employment (Egypt); and education and informal employment (Egypt, El Salvador, and South Africa).

- The share of the informal and formal workforce that earns above or below a certain level, e.g., the minimum wage or living wage (El Salvador and South Africa).

- The relationship between unemployment and underemployment in the informal economy (El Salvador).

- Worker benefits and informal employment (Egypt, El Salvador, and South Africa).

- The rate of unionization and informal employment (South Africa).

The studies also point to the need for further analysis that would look more deeply into the heterogeneity and composition of informal employment, such as:

- sectoral composition of informal employment, including dynamics of change within different economic sectors;

- segmentation of the informal economy by employment status, gender, and race/ethnicity; and

- categories of the informal workforce that earn above or below the stipulate level (e.g., the minimum wage or living wage).

We acknowledge that the existing national data in the five countries may simply not lend itself to this kind of disaggregation. But we would like to highlight the need for official data on informal employment that can be disaggregated by branch of economic activity or industry and by employment status, place of work, gender, and race/ethnicity. Findings from the country studies collected here as well as from sub-national and local surveys in other countries suggest that the informal economy is segmented by employment status, gender, and race/ethnicity. An informed policy approach to the informal workforce would require an understanding of its heterogeneity as well as its segmentation.

Comparing average wages or earnings *between* the formal and informal economy is an important first step in analyzing the linkages between employment and poverty. The next important step is to compare average wages or earnings *within* both the formal and informal economies. While it is true that informal workers are more likely to be poor than formal workers, not all informal workers are poor and not all formal workers are non-poor. While the five country studies compare earnings in formal and informal employment, they do not provide findings on relative earnings *within* the informal economy. In a recent publication, we featured data from 15 countries (compiled by our colleague Jacques Charmes) on earning differentials within the informal economy that suggest that the average monthly earnings of micro-entrepreneurs who hire others is higher than their employees (as might be expected) but also higher than the earnings of own-account operators who do not hire others. In fact, in most of these countries, own-account operators earned only slightly more, on average, than the employees of micro-entrepreneurs (Chen, Vanek, and Carr 2004).

Informal employment and poverty reduction
Perhaps most important in future research is to link research findings on employment and poverty to the wider debates on poverty reduction (e.g., the Poverty Reduction Strategy Papers or the Millennium Development Goals). It is our contention, and that of the global research network WIEGO which we represent, that addressing employment issues—or, more precisely, informal employment issues—is an essential pathway to poverty reduction. These studies provide important new comparisons of the average relative earnings in the formal and informal economies. But more analysis is needed to highlight the linkages between informal employment and poverty, especially analysis that looks at relative poverty levels *within* the informal economy and at the insecurity of work and income within the informal economy.

Informal employment and macroeconomic policies
In analyzing recent trends in workforce development in their respective countries, each of the studies have focused on macroeconomic processes. But, in teasing out the policy implications of their findings, the studies (and the overall workforce development initiative) have tended to focus more on the supply side—rather than the demand side—of labor markets. As a result, none of the studies has proposed an employment framework for macro-economic policies.

    In the concluding sections of this paper, we make some recommendations regarding what can be done in the future to improve workforce statistics and research and promote appropriate workforce development policies and programs that take into account the reality of informal employment, particularly in developing countries.

Implications for workforce statistics and research
The implications for further workforce statistics and research fall into two main categories, data collection and data analysis.

Data collection
By using existing national statistics, this volume's five country studies have taken an essential first step in influencing the collection of more and better national labor statistics that include both formal and informal employment. It is hoped that the publication of findings from the set of pioneering studies in this policy-oriented volume will help influence

the collection of more and better labor statistics not only in the five countries that were studied, but also in other countries.

It is important, therefore, to use the expertise gained through this research to advocate with statistical authorities and other government officials for technical improvements in and the further development of statistics in this area. In working with national governments and United Nations agencies, WIEGO has found that active collaboration between the producers and users of statistics is essential to improving the statistics on informal employment by showing the usefulness of doing so and, more specifically, to getting countries to make special efforts to collect data on informal employment.

The overall objective of future work on statistics on the informal economy should be to ensure that estimates on the size, composition, and economic value of the informal economy, disaggregated by sex and by employment status, are incorporated into official statistics at national, regional, and international levels in a systematic and ongoing basis. The specific goals should be to improve statistical methods and measures to strengthen data collection systems; to develop and manage a pooled data base; to promote on-going compilation and analysis of existing statistics; to generate national, regional, and global estimates; and to disseminate improved concepts, methods, findings, and estimates. To pursue these objectives, the joint action of national, regional, and international statistical services, relevant governmental agencies, and activists and researchers working on the informal economy will be required.

Data analysis

As we noted at the beginning of this chapter, more efforts need to be made to analyze the links between working in the informal economy, gender, and poverty. A major problem is that standard poverty measures are based on income or expenditure data for households, while labor force data are collected at the individual level. There are technical problems in linking these two types of data, but these are not insurmountable. For example, as a follow-up to this project, the research teams in Egypt and El Salvador are carrying out additional analyses of national data from their respective country data at two different levels: average wages or earnings and benefits at the *individual* level, and sources of income (all formal, all informal, or both) at the *household* level.[3]

As part of this line of analysis, more efforts need to be made to disaggregate the informal economy by employment status, gender, and race/ethnicity, and to then compare average wages or earnings and benefits—plus the terms and conditions of employment—of workers across these various categories.

Implications for workforce development

The overall goals of this research initiative were to analyze formal and informal labor markets and to explore whether policies can be developed that would 1) raise worker productivity, employability, and competitiveness and 2) improve the terms and conditions of employment, particularly informal employment. Explicit attention was paid to *active labor market policies* and their relevance for particular groups that may be disproportionately vulnerable to—or confined to—informal employment, including, youth, women, displaced rural workers, and migrants.

In developed countries, active labor market policies (ALMPs) generally fall into three main categories: skills training, direct job creation or subsidies, and improved job matching. The researchers who carried out the five country studies featured in this volume attempted to review which active labor market policies would prove most relevant and effective to workforce conditions in their respective countries. In their introduction to this volume, Bivens and Gammage have raised questions regarding the relevance of the standard set of ALMPs for developing countries, specifically, "to what extent do such programs offer relevant or useful guidelines for labor markets where informal employment exceeds formal employment and where worker skills might be limited by a poorly functioning and degraded education system?" The underlying issue is whether and in what ways active labor market policies need to be refined to address the existence of highly segmented formal and informal labor markets in developing countries.

In concluding this volume, we would like to offer our own analysis of what kinds of labor market policies and programs are required in countries where informal employment constitutes a large or major share of total employment. To begin with, it is important to recognize that there is an ongoing process of informalization in both developed and developing countries, and that relatively few formal jobs are being created. The dearth of formal employment opportunities has brought up a key workforce issue: how to protect workers from the "downside" effects of informalization. In other words, active labor market policies need to encompass both workforce *protection* measures as well as workforce *development* schemes. Second, it is important to recognize that in most developing countries the share of self-employment in total employment is quite high. As a result, active labor market policies in developing countries need to address self-employment as well as wage employment, both formal and informal.

More fundamentally, we would argue, active labor market policies in developing countries need to address demand-side structural constraints that discourage the creation of formal jobs, encourage informalization of employment relations, and undermine the competitiveness of micro-entrepreneurs and own-account producers. That is, the challenge of workforce development initiatives in developing countries is not just to address supply-side constraints such as low worker skills and education or to overcome the mismatch between skills and jobs. There are larger structural issues at play that help shape who has access to what resources (including bargaining power) and how goods and services are produced and distributed. It is important to gain a political-economy and institutional understanding of who wins and loses—including why and how—in the process of economic reforms and trade liberalization.

In addition to generating higher rates of economic growth, all economic policies—not just labor market policies—need to increase the market access and productive capacity of a broad cross-section of economic actors. The appropriate policy framework to ensure that growth is broad-based and reduces poverty should include the following interrelated components:[4]

- *Employment intensity*: policies to increase the quantity of employment opportunities, notably, labor-intensive production.

- *Employment quality*: policies to improve the quality of employment opportunities, including appropriate skills and technologies, labor standards, social protection, organization and representation, and a conducive regulatory environment.

- *Employment opportunities:* policies that target employment opportunities to—and build the skills and capacity of—the working poor (especially women) in the informal economy, as well as policies targeted toward improving terms of trade and/or employment of the working poor (especially women) in the informal economy. These include skills training and capability building, expanded assets and resources, improved access and competitiveness of the working poor, and increased bargaining power and negotiating opportunities.

These components of effective policy should be promoted through three basic types of interventions:

- *Employment-oriented economic policies*: macro-economic, trade, financial sector, revenue and expenditure, infrastructure and services, labor, social services and social protection, and labor statistics and other labor force information.

- *A combination of employment-oriented programs and policies:* credit, basic infrastructure, skills and training, market access and competitiveness, and organizing and collective bargaining.

- *Employment-oriented institutional reforms*: negotiating, conflict resolution, and demand-making institutions, and institutional representation of the working poor in such institutions.

Clearly, what we have outlined in this chapter represents an ideal and comprehensive response to workforce development, especially targeted at the working poor in the informal economy. We do not expect that many countries or institutions will attempt—much less successfully develop—a comprehensive policy or programmatic response to this type of workforce development. But we hope that those who seek to promote workforce development for the working poor, especially in the informal economy, will use this framework to identify their points of intervention—their points of comparative advantage—as well as those of other stakeholders. And, in doing so, develop collaborative ties with other stakeholders to build incrementally toward a comprehensive policy and programmatic response to informal employment, with the ultimate goal of helping to reduce poverty and increase equity, including gender equity.

Endnotes

1.   Martha Chen, a lecturer in public policy at the Kennedy School of Government, Harvard University, is the Coordinator of WIEGO. Joann Vanek, a specialist in social and gender statistics, is the Director of WIEGO's Statistics Program. Women in Informal Employment: Globalizing and Organizing (WIEGO) is a global research policy network that seeks to promote better statistics, research, and policies in support of the working poor, especially women, in the informal economy.

2.   Historically, the informal sector was thought to be a non-agricultural phenomenon or, more narrowly still, an urban phenomenon. The official international definition of the informal sector, adopted by the International Conference of Labour Statisticians, gave individual countries the flexibility to decide whether or not to include agriculture in their measures of the informal sector. The new expanded definition of informal employment includes informal employment in agriculture.

3.   WIEGO has been asked by the United Nations Development Fund for Women (UNIFEM) to write the 2005 Progress of the World's Women—UNIFEM's flagship publication—on the relationship of informal employment, gender, and poverty. To do so, WIEGO requested that funds be made available to commission additional analysis of national data in a number of countries, including Egypt and El Salvador.

4.   This framework builds on the "Employment Framework for Poverty Reduction in Ghana" developed by James Heintz of Political Economy Research Institute at the University of Massachusetts/Amherst in his report of a joint ILO-UNDP mission to Ghana.

References

Chen, Martha, Joann Vanek, and Marilyn Carr. 2004. *Mainstreaming Informal Employment and Gender in Poverty Reduction: A handbook for policy-makers and other stakeholders.* London: Commonwealth Secretariat.

Heintz, James. 2004. *Elements of an Employment Framework for Poverty Reduction in Ghana.* Report of a Joint ILO/UNDP Mission.

International Labour Office. 2003. "Scope of the employment relationship." *Report IV, International Labour Conference, 91st Session.* Geneva: International Labor Office.